Studying the Synoptic Gospels

Studying the Synoptic Gospels

E. P. Sanders and Margaret Davies

SCM Press · London

Trinity Press International · Philadelphia

First published 1989
Second impression 1991

SCM Press   Trinity Press International
26–30 Tottenham Road   3725 Chestnut Street
London N1 4BZ   Philadelphia, Pa. 19104

British Library Cataloguing in Publication Data

Sanders, E. P. (Ed Parish, *1937–*)
    Studying the synoptic gospels.
    1. Bible. N. T. Synoptic Gospels – critical studies
    I. Title   II. Davies, Margaret
    226'.06

    ISBN 0–334–02342–4

Library of Congress Cataloging-in-Publication Data

Sanders, E. P.
    Studying the synoptic gospels / E. P. Sanders and Margaret Davies.
       p. cm.
    Bibliography: p.
    Includes index.
    ISBN 0–334–02342–4
    1. Bible. N.T. Gospels—Criticism, interpretation, etc
2. Synoptic problem. I. Davies, Margaret. 1941– . II. Title.
BS2555.2.S23   1989
226'.061—dc20   8935754
                                     CIP

334 023416 (cased)
334 023424 (paper)

Typeset at The Spartan Press Ltd, Lymington, Hants
and printed in Great Britain by
Dotesios Ltd, Trowbridge

Contents

v

Contents

Preface

The first three books of the New Testament, the gospels according to Matthew, Mark and Luke, present three different versions of the life, death and resurrection of Jesus of Nazareth. Matthew and Luke begin with birth narratives and end with explicit descriptions of Jesus' resurrection, although with considerable variations in content, while Mark begins with the ministry of John the Baptist and ends with an empty tomb. Nevertheless there are many episodes and sayings which two or three of the gospels have in common, and these often share the same Greek vocabulary, suggesting literary dependence. The similarities and differences among these three gospels prompt a series of questions about the sources used, the historical developments of traditions about Jesus, the interests served by each of the gospels, their genres, and the historical realities of Jesus of Nazareth's life to which they refer. Scholars have asked all these questions and have studied the gospels in detail to find satisfactory answers.

Each of the synoptic gospels tells a simple story in a simple way, and therein lies much of the appeal which they have exercised for almost two thousand years. Yet the fact that they are in many ways so similar, and in others so different, makes their analysis quite difficult. Students also soon discover that each one is more complicated than at first appears. Those who wish to understand fully their origins, the history of the traditions which they contain, their interrelationships, and the message of each soon find that they are embarked on one of the most difficult subjects in the humanities. The problems which the synoptics pose are not impossibly difficult, but difficult they are.

The present volume is a fresh discussion of the principal issues, and initially it was written to provide an introduction for the undergraduate students taught by the authors. It has, however, developed beyond this. It begins at an elementary level, and in each section we have tried to explain the problems and present the material in a way that will be useful to readers who have no previous knowledge of the subjects. But we proceed to a level of detail which is appropriate to advanced study and research. The ideal reader of the gospels and of this volume is someone who can read the texts in Greek, but we have tried to present the material and arguments in a manner which makes sense to those who rely on English translations.

Too many introductions, in our opinion, give many conclusions and very little evidence, and they hide uncertainties or pass over them too quickly. Whatever the other faults of the book, we hope that we have avoided these.

Acknowledgments

Margaret Davies has pleasure in recording her gratitude to Professor Kenneth Grayston and Dr John Ziesler for reading and making thoughtful comments on chapters 14 to 19, and to Blackwells for allowing the quotation from Terry Eagleton's *Literary Theory*. Ed Sanders joins her in expressing appreciation of the assistance of SCM Press and the patient care of Miss Linda Foster.

Abbreviations

Books of the Bible and the Apocrypha are abbreviated in a way which will be familiar to many readers. Full titles and their abbreviations are given in the index.

BCE, CE	Before the Common Era, Common Era (= BC, AD).
c.	Approximately.
CD	Covenant of Damascus *or* Damascus Document *or* Zadokite Document. See Bibliography of Ancient Literature, Rabin and Vermes.
Cf.	Compare.
Eccl. Hist.	Eusebius, *Ecclesiastical History*, LCL.
ET	English translation.
et al.	And others.
Ibid.	The same.
JSNTSS	*Journal for the Study of the New Testament* Supplement Series, The University of Sheffield.
LCL	Loeb Classical Library, London and Cambridge, Massachusetts.
LXX	The Septuagint, Greek Translation of the Hebrew Scriptures.
OTP I, II	James H. Charlesworth, ed., *The Old Testament Pseudepigrapha*, vol. I, *Apocalyptic Literature and Testaments*, Garden City, New York 1983; vol. II, *Expansions of the 'Old Testament' and Legends, Wisdom and Philosophical Literature, Prayers, Psalms and Odes, Fragments of Lost Judeo-Hellenistic Works*, 1985.
Par., parr.	Parallel, parallels.
SBLDS	Society of Biblical Literature Dissertation Series, Scholars Press.
SBT	Studies in Biblical Theology, SCM Press.
SNTSMS	Society of New Testament Studies Monograph Series, Cambridge University Press.

Part One
Introduction

1 Definitions, Authorship and Dates

Matthew, Mark and Luke, the first three books in the New Testament, are called 'the synoptic gospels'. Studying them is important if one wishes to understand (1) the historical Jesus; (2) substantial aspects of the development of the early Christian movement; (3) the theologies of three works which have had great influence on subsequent religious developments in the West.

- Why are they 'gospels', and why are they 'synoptic'?

The modern English word 'gospel' is derived from the Old English 'godspel', which means 'good message' or 'good news'. 'Godspel' was simply the direct translation of the Greek word *euangelion*, which means 'good announcement'. This, in turn, is what the gospels were called in the Greek-speaking world of antiquity, and it is also the key word in Mark's opening sentence: 'the beginning of the good news of Jesus Christ'. The 'good news' or 'gospel', then, is the story of Jesus of Nazareth in Galilee, who lived from approximately 4 BCE to CE 30.[1]

Matthew, Mark and Luke are called 'synoptic' because they tell basically the same story in the same sequence, and often in the same precise wording. They can be studied side by side, in a book called 'a synopsis' – 'seeing together' – and from this type of aid for study they get their collective title. We shall spend quite a bit of time on the knotty question of why the accounts are so closely parallel; that is, why they agree with one another the way they do; and so for the moment we only record the fact that they do offer parallel accounts.

- The synoptics and John

The synoptics differ quite substantially from the gospel of John. Since John will be excluded from the remainder of this book, we shall say something about it here. First of all, the outline of John is different from that of the synoptics. In the synoptics Jesus' career seems to last only a few months. In John it covers somewhat over two years, since three Passovers are mentioned during his ministry. More substantially, the synoptics sayings material is very different from the Johannine discourse material. We may compare the synoptics and John on 'sheep' used as a figure for people. In Matthew and Luke we find this:

> What man of you, having a hundred sheep, if he has lost one of them, does not leave the ninety-nine in the wilderness, and go after the one which is lost, until he finds it? And when he has found it, he lays it on his shoulders, rejoicing. And when he comes home, he calls together his friends and his neighbours, saying to them, 'Rejoice with me, for I have found my sheep which was lost' (Luke 15.3–6; cf. Matt. 18.12–13).

This is a **parable**. It is short, the similitude or metaphor is simple, and it makes one point. That is not to say that it is only a commonplace. It is quite surprising that the shepherd leaves the ninety-nine without protection, and the surprise lends emphasis to the point that God seeks the lost. We note that the primary point of the similitude is that of a situation: as it is with this shepherd and the sheep, so it is with God and people. To the degree that the 'characters' in the parable have counterparts, the shepherd represents God himself: it is God who goes in search of the 'sheep' (the lost person), God who rejoices when it is found. There is no explicit self-assertion on the part of Jesus, though he presumably sees himself as doing God's will and seeking the lost.

John's passage which uses 'sheep' as a figure is a long monologue, covering eighteen verses, which focuses precisely on the person of Jesus. First, we read that it is the shepherd, not a thief, who enters by the door of the sheepfold. 'To him the gatekeeper opens: the sheep hear his voice, and he calls his own sheep by name and leads them out'. These sheep will follow only their own shepherd (10.1–6). Next, Jesus states that he himself is 'the door of the sheep' and that only those who enter by him can be saved (10.7–10). Third, he says that he is the good shepherd and that 'the good shepherd lays down his life for the sheep', and then he reiterates and explains:

> I am the good shepherd; I know my own and my own know me, as the Father knows me and I know the Father; and I lay down my life for the sheep (10.11–15).

Fourth, he adds that he has other sheep 'that are not of this fold'. He will bring these as well, 'so there shall be one flock, one shepherd' (10.16). The monologue concludes with the reassurance that the Father loves him, Jesus, because he lays down his life, and that he lays it down of his own accord and has the power to take it up again (10.17–18).

Very little of this long passage could possibly make parabolic sense. In a parable a person could not be both 'door' and 'shepherd'. Further, in real life sheep can be driven by anyone and do not respond only to their own shepherd. Finally, if one wanted to define a 'good shepherd' in the Galilean hill country, it would be one who successfully kills the wolf, not one who voluntarily dies and who can take his life back up again. This is not a parable, but an involved series of metaphors which can be understood only if we see that the different parts apply to Jesus in different ways. He is both the way in – the door, the means of access to salvation – and the leader of his followers – the shepherd. The passage also depends on knowing important points of

Christian doctrine: that Jesus willingly gave his life, that he had the power of resurrection, and that he was the intermediary in all ways between the Father and the believers. We even learn that the importance of Jesus as mediator extends beyond Palestine: there are sheep 'who are not of this fold'. Here the worldwide mission of the church is indicated. We have, in short, a complicated theological meditation on the figure 'sheep', one which shows how many ways it can be turned. It makes sense only when one knows the view that those who believe in Jesus are saved by his death. A parable may be surprising, but it must make sense in everyday life. The discourse on sheep in John 10 does not do so.

The entirety of the sayings material in the synoptics and in John differs in just these ways. In the synoptics there are short, pithy statements, aphorisms and parables which focus not on Jesus' person but on the kingdom of God. The synoptics' Jesus must ask his disciples who they think he is (Mark 8.27 and parr.*), and it is clear that he has not identified himself explicitly. He refuses to give a sign to those who ask (Mark 8.11–13). When he is on trial, according to Matthew and Luke, he will not even give a straightforward answer about who he is when asked by the high priest. The Jesus of the Gospel of John, however, talks in long monologues, and the subject is usually himself: his relationship to God on the one hand and to the disciples on the other. He offers 'signs' in abundance (see, for example, John 2.11), and he says explicitly that 'I and the Father are one' (John 10.30).

If one looks at other features of the Gospel of John, one sees various differences. We have seen that the timespan of Jesus' career is different, and there are other substantial disagreements with regard to the historical outline. In John the 'cleansing of the temple' comes at the beginning (2.13–22), in the synoptics at the end (Mark 11.15–19 and parr.). In the synoptics there is a last supper at which Jesus uses bread and wine as symbols (Mark 14.22–25 and parr.), in John at the last supper Jesus washes the disciples' feet, but says nothing about the bread and wine (ch. 13); John has, instead, a discourse on Jesus as the bread of life, which is placed early in Jesus' career (ch. 6). John's account of the arrest and trial of Jesus is quite different from that of the synoptics. For example, Jesus is tried by the high priest and his father-in-law (John 18.13–24) rather than by the Sanhedrin (Mark 14.53–64 and parr.). The miracles are appreciably different. Exorcisms are frequent in the synoptics, but none are mentioned in John. There are only seven miracles in John, and of these only three (the centurion's son, 4.46–54; the feeding of the 5,000 and walking on water, 6.1–21) are similar to those of the synoptics.

The distinctiveness of John requires that it be accorded separate treatment. A few Johannine passages will be mentioned in passing, but we shall concentrate exclusively on the synoptics.

• Dates and authorship

Scholars disagree a bit about when each gospel was written, but most would propose no earlier than CE 65 for the earliest – usually thought to be the Gospel of Mark – and

---

*'And parr.' means 'and the parallels, which will be seen in a synopsis'; 'and par.' means 'and the one parallel'.

no later than CE 100 for the latest – probably Luke. The other synoptic, Matthew, is from approximately 80–85. Thus the synoptics were written one or two generations after the death of Jesus. The dates of the synoptics, however, are very difficult to determine with confidence, and those just given may be considered as the outside possibilities. The question of who wrote the gospels is, as we shall see, even more vexed.

Questions of the date and authorship of works written in Greek, as were the gospels, are ordinarily quite simple. Usually they were published[2] in the author's name, and usually there is enough biographical information about the author to allow the reader to date the work, at least approximately. At first glance this appears to be the case with the synoptic gospels. As we now have them they are attributed to known authors: Matthew to one of Jesus' disciples (Mark 3.18 and parr.), Mark to an early Christian in Jerusalem (Acts 12.12,25; 15.37), Luke to a companion of Paul (Col. 4.14). These titles, however, were not originally attached to the gospels: the author of Mark did not write, 'The Gospel according to Mark', but simply 'the beginning of the gospel of Jesus Christ, the Son of God' (Mark 1.1). The gospel writers, it will turn out, did not follow the usual Greek (and Roman) practice of naming themselves, but rather the tradition of anonymous publication, a practice frequently followed in Jewish literature. Below we shall consider more fully the significance of anonymity. Here, however, we explore the possibility of penetrating the original anonymity and discovering the authorship and dates of the gospels.

There are two types of evidence which bear on these questions: evidence external to the documents and that provided by the texts themselves. We shall now conduct a short search of some of this evidence in order to answer three questions:

1. What is the earliest proof that each of our gospels existed as a document? This question is answered by discovering the earliest source which quotes one of the gospels, and quotes it in a way that allows us to say, 'that author quotes Matthew as we now have it, not just a tradition about Jesus'. Once we have answered this question we know the latest possible date at which the gospel in question was written: it must have been written before it was quoted. This question requires us to search external evidence – other works which show dependence on one or more of our gospels.

2. When were the present names of the authors attached to our gospels? This is a separate question from 'when were they first used?', and it will turn out that they were quoted before they were named. There may be clues within the gospels to the identities of their authors, but again we must look mostly to external sources, asking when was it first said that Matthew, Mark and Luke wrote the gospels which now bear their names.

3. What is the latest fact or event of which each shows knowledge? In answering this question we explore internal evidence to see if passages in our gospels definitely reflect events which took place after the death and resurrection of Jesus. If we find such evidence, we have fixed the earliest possible date of the gospel: it was written after the last event to which it refers.[3]

The evidence which bears on one of these questions frequently bears on another, and to save repetition our discussion will be divided into two parts: external and internal evidence.

• External evidence

It may be helpful if we begin at a point at which everything is clear: a Christian author who knew all of our gospels as we now have them and who knew them by the names which we now use. Irenaeus, Bishop of Lyons, around the year 180 wrote a work called *Against Heresies*. He named all four gospels (the synoptics plus John) in book 3 of his work (III.11.7), and he quoted passages which show that he knew the gospels as we have them. Thus he quoted from the preface to Luke, which was certainly written by the author of the gospel (Luke 1.2, quoted in III.14.2), and he also quoted the first sentences of our Matthew (quoted in III.16.2) and of our Mark (III.16.3).

With regard to dates, Irenaeus stated that Matthew was written in Hebrew 'while Peter and Paul were preaching at Rome'. Mark was written 'after their departure' (presumably meaning their deaths) and was based on Peter's preaching. Luke, according to Irenaeus, was written by a companion of Paul, though the precise time is not specified (Irenaeus III.1.1). Paul and Peter are usually thought to have been martyred at the time of Nero's persecution (CE 64) or a little before. This would mean that Matthew was written before 64, Mark a little later, and Luke presumably later as well. This evidence is entirely straightforward. The only question is whether or not Irenaeus himself possessed good information.

If we move back just thirty years we meet a much more uncertain use of the gospels. Justin Martyr, who wrote in approximately 150, quoted sayings attributed to Jesus from what he called 'the Memoirs of the Apostles'. He did not, however, quote the sayings precisely as we have them, and diverse readings among our gospels not infrequently appear together in Justin. In the following quotation from Justin, we underline the words which agree with Matthew, capitalize the words which agree with Luke and print in bold the words which agree with neither. The differences and similarities may not always be seen if one compares English translations of the passages. We shall show disagreements and agreements which are seen clearly only in the original Greek:

Do NOT FEAR THOSE [who] **kill you** and AFTER THESE THINGS are not able TO DO ANYTHING, but FEAR THE ONE [who] AFTER KILLING [you] is able TO CAST both soul and body INTO GEHENNA (Justin, Apology I.19.7; Matt. 10.28; Luke 12.4–5).

To help the reader follow this way of marking agreements and disagreements, we list them separately:

Justin	Agrees with
not fear those	Matthew and Luke
kill you	neither
after these things	Luke
are not able	Matthew
to do anything	Luke
but	Matthew

7

fear	Matthew and Luke
the one after killing	Luke
is able	Matthew
to cast	Luke
both soul and body	Matthew
into	Luke
Gehenna	Matthew and Luke

If Justin had our gospels before him he was very careful to alternate words in copying from Matthew and Luke, taking 'after these things' from Luke, 'are not able' from Matthew, and so on. There are two more likely explanations. One is that he quoted from memory and naturally conflated two similar passages. The other is that he had not our gospels but a collection of sayings which itself depended on them: that he used a prepared harmony.

In any case we note: (1) that Justin did not name the authors of the gospels; (2) that he was not concerned to keep them distinct, quoting precisely from one or the other. He seems not to have attached importance to 'the Gospel according to Matthew' and 'the Gospel according to Luke' as written documents, but rather simply to the sayings of Jesus which he received from Christian tradition. Christian tradition by then included our gospels (as we shall see), but Justin seems not to have cared for each document as a canonical text. It is noteworthy that when quoting the sayings of Jesus Justin spoke of the 'Memoirs', not of 'the Scripture', which was his name for the Old Testament.

Justin, who was active in Rome, was not far distant from Irenaeus in either time or space. Irenaeus represents Roman Christianity as well, rather than that of Alexandria or Antioch. It seems that, in Rome, the gospels grew in importance between Justin and Irenaeus. This is usually explained as being partly due to the influence of Marcion, who was a contemporary of Justin. Marcion was a dualist who rejected the Old Testament and denied the goodness of the created order. He was eventually condemned as a heretic. Marcion accepted only one gospel, that of Luke, and then only a truncated form of it. In response to Marcion, mainline Christians seem to have begun to emphasize that four gospels should be accepted and should be given equal status to that of the Old Testament. This development is reflected in Irenaeus.

If we move back just a few years earlier than Justin, we come to Papias, the Bishop of Hierapolis in approximately 125–150. Writing about 140, but referring in part to an earlier elder, he attributed some material about Jesus to Mark and some to Matthew. It is worth quoting as much of what he said as is possible (from the selected portions quoted by Eusebius, the fourth-century church historian):

And the Presbyter [or Elder] used to say this, 'Mark became Peter's interpreter and wrote accurately all that he remembered, not, indeed, in order, of the things said or done by the Lord. For he had not heard the Lord, nor had he followed him, but later on, as I said, followed Peter, who used to give teaching as necessity demanded, but who did not make, as it were, an arrangement of the Lord's oracles, so that Mark did nothing wrong in thus writing down single points as he remembered them. For to one thing he gave attention, to leave out nothing of what he had heard and to make no false statements in them.'[4]

With regard to Matthew, Papias wrote, 'Matthew collected the oracles in the Hebrew language, and each interpreted them as best he could' (Eusebius, *Eccl. Hist.* III.39.16).

This answers one of our questions. Papias was the first person to assign written material about Jesus to one of the men whose names are attached to our gospels, and he offers both 'Matthew' and 'Mark'. Papias' statements, however, raise further questions, of which these are two of the most important: Did he have in mind our Mark and our Matthew? How far does the Elder's statement go? To take the second first: the translation given above attributes the entire statement about Mark to 'the Elder', which would push the attribution back from around 140 to 125. Many scholars, however, think that the Elder supplied only the first sentence (Mark wrote accurately but not in order), while the rest is Papias' own commentary (the explanation that Mark had not heard the Lord, and especially the statement that he left out nothing that he had heard). We think that the second is the stronger position. Ancient documents do not have quotation marks or inverted commas, but it was natural to begin one's own interpretation with 'for', and thus we would assign to the Elder only the first sentence.

Before trying to answer the first question (did he have in mind our Mark and our Matthew?), it will be useful to put Papias' statement in the context of earlier quotations from the gospels, or from material which is now in them. Prior to Papias, Christian quotations of the sayings of Jesus are like those of Justin: anonymous and often conflated (combining two of the gospels). The most quoted gospel was Matthew,[5] though it was quoted without being named. Ignatius of Antioch, writing to the church at Smyrna about 110, used the phrase 'fulfil all righteousness' in discussing Jesus' baptism (Smyrnaeans ch. 1). This phrase comes from Matthew's account (Matt. 3.15), but the source is not named. Similarly the Didache (also *c.* 110) quotes the Lord's prayer according to Matthew's version rather than Luke's, but the prayer is attributed to 'the Lord in the Gospel', and the author does not say, 'as it is written in the gospel according to Matthew' (Didache 8.1–3).

The most typical way of quoting the gospel material, however, is seen in this example from Clement of Rome (*c.* 90):

Above all, remember the words of the Lord Jesus which he uttered while teaching forbearance and patience, 'Be merciful, that you may receive mercy. Forgive, that forgiveness may be given you; as you do, so it shall be done to you; as you give, so shall it be given you; as you judge, so shall you be judged; as you show kindness, so will kindness be shown to you; the measure you give will be the measure you get' (I Clement 13.1–2).

This combines material now found in Matt. 5.7; 6.14 [//Mark 11.25]; 6.15; 7.1,2,12; Luke 6.31,36–38, and it is assigned simply to the Lord Jesus.

Since in the late first century and for more than half of the second century the gospel material was used without naming the author, several scholars have doubted that these early Christian writers had the gospels as we know them, proposing that they had instead 'free traditions', oral tradition, sayings collections, or even the sources of our gospels. It is our own view that the Didache (though probably not I Clement) used the Gospel of Matthew directly, though we shall not argue the case here.[6] What is noteworthy is that the material was not assigned to an author, but was used as if it were anonymous – or, put another way, as if it went directly back to Jesus without the intervention of an author or editor with a distinct point of view. The compiler of the Didache thought only of 'the gospel', not 'the gospel according to x' in contradistinction to 'the gospel according to y and z'. Later Christians would study and compare the gospels and remark on their distinctive traits and material. Early writers, however, did not do this.

In the period 90–150, though our gospels probably had been written, the authors' names were either not known or were regarded as irrelevant. In this period Papias stands alone. Before him (Didache, Ignatius and Clement, among others), and immediately after him (Justin Martyr), the gospels were quoted without naming the authors. There is no sign of a continuing tradition assigning the gospels to Matthew, Mark and Luke. It is at least slightly dubious that Papias got it right when other Christians seem not even to have been interested in the question.

If, slightly suspicious, we examine Papias' statements, we first note that the description of the material collected by the disciple Matthew cannot refer to the Gospel of Matthew as we have it. Papias mentioned 'sayings' written 'in Hebrew' (that is, Hebrew or Aramaic, which were not always distinguished). Our Gospel of Matthew is not just sayings, but includes also narrative; and it does not show signs of having been directly translated from Hebrew or Aramaic. The study of 'Semitisms' in early Christian literature – traces of Semitic grammar, syntax or idiom in Greek documents – is a complicated and difficult task, and we cannot here delve into it. We shall, unfortunately, have to appeal to academic authority. Most scholars who have studied Semitisms have found Mark to be the most Semitic gospel, though one scholar awards the prize to Luke. The Gospel of Matthew does show very good knowledge of contemporary Judaism, and the author may have been able to read the Bible in Hebrew. The gospel, however, is not a direct translation from a Semitic language.

Papias' description of the 'sayings' recorded by Matthew fails to correspond to the Gospel of Matthew in a third respect: a great deal of Matthew is identical with Mark, and most of it is in the same order. Since Papias commented on Mark's order as being incorrect, one would expect him to say something about Matthew's agreement with Mark – if it were our Matthew which he had in mind.

Thus we have this: the Gospel of Matthew was used anonymously in the late first and early second centuries; about 140 one Christian said that the disciple Matthew collected sayings; this statement seems not to refer to our Gospel of Matthew. The soundest conclusion to draw from this is that the gospel which we now call 'Matthew' (or, more fully, 'the Gospel according to Matthew') was in fact anonymous. Its existence is shown by the use made of it, and it must be dated before 110, when Ignatius and the Didache quoted it. That it went by its present name, however, is not certain.

It seems quite possible that the gospel now called Matthew circulated, and that the tradition that Matthew had collected sayings also circulated, but that these two traditions were not combined until sometime after 150, when Papias' testimony was interpreted as applying to our gospel. This would account for the fact that Irenaeus was, to the best of our knowledge, the first to call the Gospel according to Matthew by that title.

Papias' statement, we add parenthetically, is sometimes taken to refer to a collection of sayings which ended up in the hypothetical source Q, to which we shall turn in Part II.

With regard to Papias' statement about Mark we can be less certain. The Elder whom Papias quotes is apparently responsible only for the first sentence, 'Mark . . . wrote down accurately all that he remembered . . . but not . . . in order'. Papias then elaborates: in effect he grants that Mark was bound to make mistakes, since he used the preaching of Peter, who did not give an orderly account but who adapted his preaching to the circumstances. Papias, to be sure, *said* that Mark 'made no mistake' and neither omitted anything nor inserted incorrect material. We shall see below what ancient claims to 'accuracy' meant. Just now we note that Papias felt the need to defend Mark. Behind the defence one perceives criticisms of the gospel's order and completeness.

Since Papias' statement about Matthew does not refer to our gospel, does his statement about Mark refer to Mark as we now have it? Probably it does. Luke, who seems to have used Mark, stated that he had followed all things 'accurately' and that he would write an 'orderly account' (Luke 1.3), thus implicitly criticizing his sources. Conceivably Papias knew this criticism and wished to defend Mark against it. In any case it is probable that his statement intends to establish the authorship of the Second Gospel. If 'the Elder' whom Papias quotes also meant our Gospel of Mark, the attribution is pushed back to about 125.

The Mark to whom Papias referred is presumably the 'John called Mark' who is mentioned in Acts 12.12,25; 15.37,39 as a Christian in Jerusalem who subsequently travelled with Paul and Barnabas. A Mark is also referred to in the Pauline corpus (Philemon 24; Col. 4.10; II Tim. 4.11). Most important for the present point is that the author of I Peter refers to 'my son Mark' as sending greetings to the churches (I Peter 5.13). This is the passage which identifies Mark as a companion of Peter, and it is possible that here we have the origin of Papias' connection of Peter with a gospel by Mark.

There is the possibility that Justin (150) identified the gospel Mark as coming from Peter. The key sentence is this:

It is said that he [Jesus] changed the name of one of the apostles to Peter; and it is written in his Memoirs that he changed the names of others, two brothers, the sons of Zebedee, to Boanerges, which means 'sons of thunder' . . . (*Dialogue with Trypho* 106.3).

11

The joint name 'Boanerges, sons of thunder' is in Mark 3.17, and there alone. Thus Justin may attribute a passage in Mark to Peter's Memoirs. What is not certain, however, is the referent of 'his' in the phrase 'his Memoirs': does it mean Peter's Memoirs or the Memoirs about Jesus? There is no certain answer, but it is at least possible that Justin has connected the Gospel of Mark with Papias' statement about Mark, writing a gospel on the basis of Peter's preaching.

The first unambiguous evidence that Papias' statement about Mark was understood as referring to the Second Gospel comes again from Irenaeus, *c.* 180, who (we recall) stated that Mark, the interpreter of Peter, wrote the gospel which begins 'the beginning of the gospel of Jesus Christ, the son of God' (Irenaeus, *Against Heresies* III.10.6).[7] Again we see that the definite attribution of one of our gospels to a named author comes from the period 150–180, the time of Justin Martyr and Irenaeus. Justin Martyr had a copy of our Mark, or a source which depended on it, and thus Mark must have existed before the year 150, though it may not yet have been known by that name.

The connection of the name Mark with the Second Gospel, then, depends on Papias and on the view that when he referred to a gospel written by Mark he meant Mark as we have it. If, as seems probable, that is the case, it may still be questioned whether Papias' information or guess was correct. This cannot be decisively proved one way or the other. The key fact to recall is that the tradition about Mark does not surface until approximately 140, which on balance must make us doubt that Papias had an old and reliable tradition.

The gospel of Luke was also used widely in the second century, though it was not as popular as Matthew. We have seen that Justin knew some of the sayings of Jesus as they now appear in Luke, that Marcion used a version of our Luke, and that Irenaeus called the Third Gospel the Gospel according to Luke. From external sources we gain no more light on the author or on the date of composition, and so we should accept in this case too the probability that the identification of the third gospel as being 'according to Luke' may have been made as late as the year 150.

We have thus far learned nothing decisive about *dates*. We have seen that Matthew was written by 100 at the latest, since some of the material characteristic of that gospel, and that gospel alone, was used *c.* 110. If Papias meant our Mark, it must have been written before 140. If the Elder meant our Mark, it is to be dated before 125. About the date of Luke we can say even less. The gospel was used by Marcion *c.* 150, and some of its sayings material was known by Justin at about the same date, but there is no earlier completely firm evidence of its existence. One scholar, in fact, dated it in the fourth decade of the second century.[8] The external evidence allows any date before 150.

Thus we see that the significance of external evidence for conclusions about the dates of the gospels is less than we might have hoped for. Only Matthew can be shown by external evidence to be as early as 100. Few contemporary scholars place any of the gospels that late, and thus external evidence often does not figure very large in attempts to date the gospels. For what it is worth, though, it shows that Matthew was written by about 100 and that Mark and Luke were written by 150 at the latest. Possibly Papias' statement shows that our Mark existed by 125.

When it comes to the attribution of names to the gospels, however, external evidence is of more help. In assessing it we should note two general considerations at the outset.

1. The attributions are surprisingly late. If most scholars are right in thinking that the gospels were written between about 65 and 85, it appears that each gospel was used for at least 50 years before an author was assigned to it. In order to consider the attributions to be based on certain knowledge, we would have to suppose that early Christians transmitted the authors' names but that for 50 to 80 years no one who wrote literature which has survived mentioned them. When one considers how widely they were used (especially Matthew), this silence seems inexplicable, if accurate information about the authors was available. The early Christians seem genuinely not to have cared who wrote the gospels, and it is difficult to combine a theory of carefully maintained tradition with the fact of literary silence. This consideration counts in favour of the view that the names which were attached to the gospels were not based on an unbroken tradition.

2. The second consideration is usually thought to support the reliability of the attributions to Mark and Luke. B. H. Streeter put it this way: 'the burden of proof is on those who would assert the traditional authorship of Matthew and John and on those who would deny it in the case of Mark and Luke.'[9] The argument which leads to this view is straightforward: the Christians of the time of Irenaeus (*c.* 180) would have been tempted to favour a view 'which gave the maximum of Apostolic authority to those Four Gospels which were regarded as the pillars of the Church' (p. 560). Mark could have been assigned directly to Peter; Luke could have been attributed to Paul himself. They were not, and thus the attributions to Mark and Luke may be viewed as credible. Streeter very effectively presented the church's increasing tendency to attribute material to Peter:

> The Gospel of Mark was written, according to Irenaeus (185) after the demise of Peter, according to Clement (200) during Peter's lifetime, but without his approbation, according to Eusebius (324) with his authentication, according to Jerome (397) at his dictation (p. 561).

The argument, then, is that Irenaeus and others would have assigned Mark directly to Peter, except that they knew better. The tradition overcame their inclination.

This is plausible enough, but it is not entirely persuasive. One can readily offer an alternative explanation. Irenaeus (and others) did not have a clue where the Gospel of Mark came from or who wrote it. They loved the gospel and found in its rough and plain prose an echo of an earlier day and a place where Greek was not fluent. They wished to assign a gospel to Peter, and the apparently simple gospel now called Mark was the likeliest candidate. They could not, however, attribute it to Peter himself, since it had been around for almost a hundred years without having been ascribed to him. They put together Acts 12.12 (Peter went to Mark's mother's house in Jerusalem) and I Peter 5.13 ('my son Mark') and concluded that the historical person Mark could have written the gospel.

To this alternative explanation there is a counter argument: if the second-century

13

fathers were just guessing, why did they not pick Silas (or Silvanus) as the author of the Second Gospel? He seems actually to have written I Peter (see 5.12), and he was also active in Jerusalem (Acts 15.22).

This shows the real problem. We are forced to guess how the second-century Christians thought. Streeter's argument, the alternative to it, and the counter argument are all guesses about what people 'would have done'. We shall find throughout our study of the gospels that we must often guess what someone would have done, based on our reading of general tendencies. We might as well start now emphasizing that such guesses, though 'informed' to some degree or other, are never certain. Our own judgment is that the 'alternative explanation' of two paragraphs above is more likely than Streeter's argument, but 'more likely' is the strongest term to use for arguments of this sort. We shall present the alternatives again: Streeter: the second-century Christians would have assigned Mark to Peter if they could, but their inclination was overcome by their knowledge that actually Mark wrote it. We have proposed instead: the second-century Christians assigned Mark as close to Peter as they could, since it was well known that he did not write a gospel himself.

If we follow the suggestion offered here and suppose that, in the second century, Christians started guessing about the authorship of the gospels, choosing Mark for the second, we must ask how they hit upon Matthew and Luke. It appears that the name 'Luke' was picked for the Third Gospel because of Acts, which was written by the same author. In Acts there are 'we' sections, places where the first person plural instead of the third person plural is used. This happens for the first time shortly after Paul and his companions had passed through Phrygia: the author first writes '*they* went through the region of Phrygia and Galatia' and '*they* went down to Troas'. Two verses later he writes, '*we* sought to go on into Macedonia' (Acts 16.6–10). Thus there is the possibility that Paul and his companions acquired another member of the party in Troas. Casting around through the New Testament, subsequent Christians found no one named whom Paul might have picked up in Troas, and so they backtracked along his trail. They soon came to Phrygia, and here there was a likely candidate: the physician Luke is placed in Colossae, one of the towns of Phrygia, by both Philemon 24 and Col. 4.14. Thus the detectives of the second century, just like some of those of modern times, thought that Acts was written by someone who was picked up as Paul passed through Phrygia, and they concluded that Luke, the physician of Colossae – surely a learned man – was the author. They then naturally assigned him the gospel as well. The attribution to Luke had the advantage of connecting it with Paul, who dominates so much of the New Testament.

Matthew may well have been chosen for the First Gospel because only there is the tax collector who followed Jesus named 'Matthew'. Mark and Luke list a Matthew as a disciple of Jesus (Mark 3.18 and par.), but only Matthew connects this name with an individual mentioned elsewhere: the tax collector whom Jesus called to follow him (Matt. 9.9–13 and parr.; he is named Levi in Mark and Luke). Who better to know the 'real' name of the tax collector than the man himself? This bit of detection was probably added to Papias' tradition about Matthew as the collector of sayings. The sayings material in the First Gospel is extremely well organized and prominent, and the conclusion that the author of the gospel was Matthew doubtless seemed evident.

In favour of the theory of detection as the source of the assignment of names is the evidence of the Fourth Gospel. John 21.24 states that the gospel is based on the testimony of the disciple 'whom Jesus loved' (see 21.20) This nameless disciple, who figures prominently in the Fourth Gospel, was probably considered to be 'John' because the name itself does not appear. Peter, Andrew and others are named, but not John. Thus detective work led to the conclusion that the beloved disciple was John, and then that he wrote the gospel.

We should repeat that our attribution of 'detective work' to the Christians of the second century is a hypothesis which attempts to make sense of the evidence, but which in the nature of the case can be no more than a hypothesis. When we review the arguments about authorship which are based on external evidence (second-century opinions), we find that the fact of anonymous authorship and circulation is the most telling. Our judgment is that the gospels were truly anonymous and that the authors were not known outside their own immediate circle.

• Evaluating external evidence

Our discussion of the church fathers leads us to make a general observation about the assessment of ancient evidence. 'Conservative' critics, who wish to believe as many statements made by ancients as they can, nevertheless have a breaking point, a point at which they stop believing them. One scholar may say about a passage in Mark that 'it must be true because Mark (i.e. the gospel, not necessarily the man) said so', but doubt that Papias knew what he was talking about. Another may swallow Papias whole and further believe that Irenaeus knew who wrote which gospel, but doubt Epiphanius. Epiphanius (mid-fourth century) wrote, for example, that Mark was present when Jesus said 'unless you eat my flesh . . .' (John 6.66). H. B. Swete, who accepted Papias without question, wrote of the statement in Epiphanius that it 'is probably as baseless as many others which are due to that writer'.[10] In some instances Swete cited the church fathers as 'authorities' who prove a certain case (e.g. p. xxiii), while at other points he denied 'any authority' to a statement by an ancient. A major instance is the sequence of the gospels. According to numerous church fathers Matthew was written first. Swete comments about this that 'the Alexandrian elders were . . . imperfectly informed as to the relative age of the Gospels' (p. xxv). This must also apply to Irenaeus, the great 'authority', who did so much to fix opinions about the gospels. He explicitly stated that Mark wrote the Second Gospel and that he wrote it after Peter's death, and many commentators take his word on both points. But he just as explicitly said that Matthew wrote his gospel while Peter and Paul were alive and preaching in Rome – thus before Mark – and on this point the same commentators must believe him to be wrong (Irenaeus III.1.1; Swete, p. xxxv). The statement about Matthew's date is dismissed as impossible because of the modern academic theory that Matthew used Mark, which is held by most scholars, including the most conservative. They believe that this theory is sound, and therefore they dismiss ancient evidence which runs contrary to it. This does not show that they are

15

wrong, but rather that they are prepared to reject ancient 'testimony' when it conflicts with their own scholarly stance. In this discussion we have used as an example the old commentary by Swete because he dealt with the evidence of the church fathers extensively, but the very same observations can be made about much more recent conservative commentators, such as Vincent Taylor and Martin Hengel. Thus in Hengel one finds both the acceptance of Irenaeus with regard to the date of the gospel and also the abrupt dismissal of his view of the sequence of Matthew and Mark.[11]

The authors of this book fault others only for not following the spirit of critical scholarship consistently enough. In the study of the New Testament in particular, piety and wishful thinking intervene sporadically and create blind spots. In general the same view is shared by all scholars, and we shall attempt to pursue it rigorously: the gospels are texts which are to be studied on the basis of information which they themselves provide, or which is provided by closely related sources, and we do not know in advance what conclusions we shall come to. The genius of 'critical study', a method sometimes employed in the ancient world, but which we have inherited from the renaissance, is the willingness to examine and assess all the available evidence and to comprehend the range of possible conclusions. Conforming the evidence to fit prior conclusions is a temptation which we shall try to avoid.

Students should not be misled by scholars who claim to 'trust the evidence' and 'believe the sources' in order to justify conservative conclusions. The truth is that all scholars make critical judgments at point after point and, when dealing with ancient authors, will find them convincing in some cases and not in others. At some point or other a modern reader will become convinced that an ancient author simply did not know but wished to say something concrete, and so wrote something that was not factually accurate. We are inclined to put the ascriptions of the gospels to Matthew, Mark and Luke in this category. The principal reason, we repeat, is the lateness of the attributions.

• Dates: internal evidence

Numerous scholars have recognized that the most worthwhile evidence for dating the gospels is that which they themselves contain. If they clearly refer to an event which we can date, we have fixed the earliest possible time of composition. The general inclination now is to date the gospels as early as possible. We are here going to accept this convention. As we noted, there is no firm literary evidence which dates Luke before about 140. Rather than assume, however, that it was written very close to that date, we shall assume that it was written closer to the dates of its sources – which can be shown to have been appreciably earlier. We shall apply this assumption to all three gospels, and assume them to be fairly early until evidence pushes them later.

The rationale for fixing the date of each gospel close to the earliest possible time, rather than close to the latest, is that it is difficult to suppose that the authors concealed knowledge of recent events. A proposal that Luke was written about 130 (close to the latest possible date) would have to concede that the author shut out of his mind, or at least kept out of his work, at least 50 years' worth of events. There is, for example, no reference, even in coded language, to the persecution of parts of the church under Domitian (in the mid-90s). The author of Luke–Acts held the view that God punished the Jews for rejecting Jesus, and he seems to have seen the destruction of the temple (CE 70) in this light (see below). But in 115–117 there were major revolts of Jews against Rome in Egypt, Cyrene and Cyprus, revolts which destroyed cities and led to much bloodshed. There is no hint of this further 'punishment' of the Jews in Luke–Acts, and this counts as evidence for dating his work before 115–117, and possibly before the mid-90s. A theory that Luke wrote very late must be based on the supposition that he successfully maintained his focus on an earlier period. Few authors can be entirely successful in such an effort.

This rationale for looking for early dates, to be sure, does not provide conclusive proof – far from it. By itself, for example, it would lead to dating Acts before CE 64. When Acts closes, Paul is in prison in Rome. A lot of evidence indicates that Paul was martyred in Rome *c.* 62–64. If that is so, and if Acts was written later, would not the event have been included? Not necessarily. The author might have written for an audience which did not need or want to be reminded of the grim details of the deaths of some of the Christians in Rome; or he might have wanted to finish on an upbeat note, with Paul still proclaiming the gospel and promising salvation to the Gentiles. Perhaps he thought it dramatically effective to stop the story where he did. In short, he may have had his own reasons for not continuing the story, and the supposition that an author would not or could not conceal subsequent events cannot be given much weight in any individual case, such as Paul's death. Cumulatively, though, such points amount to an argument. Neither Matthew, Mark nor Luke reveals definite knowledge of any event which happened after 90; it is unlikely that this would be the case if all three of them had been written after 90.

There is, then, good reason not to date all the synoptics very late, and some reason – by no means conclusive – to fix them close to the earliest possible date. Thus we turn to internal evidence to seek that date: what is the last event of which they show knowledge?

We may first ask whether the gospels reflect knowledge of the destruction of Jerusalem in CE 70. That event must have been of great moment throughout the Christian movement. The clearest reference is Luke 21.20: 'When you see Jerusalem surrounded by armies, then know that its desolation has come near.' At this point Matthew and Mark write of 'the desolating sacrilege . . . standing in the Holy Place' (Matt. 24.15//Mark 13.14). This seems to refer to the threat of Caligula in CE 40–41 to have his statue set up in the temple. Luke's alteration to 'Jerusalem surrounded by armies' probably reflects the actual siege of Jerusalem, and thus the dramatic event which would precede the end is shifted from 40 to 70. The prophecy has been updated in light of recent events, and this clearly puts Luke after 70. (We note here how useful a synopsis is: it allows one immediately to compare the statements in the three gospels.)

There is a similar tell-tale sentence in Matthew. In the middle of the parable of the marriage feast Matthew has this sentence: 'The king was angry, and he sent his troops and destroyed those murderers and burned their city' (22.7). The parable, but not the verse, is in Luke; and the readiest explanation is that Matthew has inserted a sentence to make the parable more relevant.

These apparent references to the destruction of Jerusalem have been challenged, but not effectively.[12] The general scholarly explanation remains the simplest and most persuasive: Matthew and Luke in their present forms were written after 70.

It is possible that the two-volume work, Luke–Acts, can be dated more precisely yet. In Acts 5.36–37 the author attributes to the Pharisee Gamaliel this speech in the Sanhedrin:

> . . . take care what you do with these men. For before these days Theudas arose, giving himself out to be somebody, and a number of men, about four hundred, joined him. . . . After him Judas the Galilean arose in the days of the census. . . .

There are here two historical errors. First, Judas in fact preceded Theudas by about 40 years: Judas' uprising was at the time of Quirinius's census in CE 6, while Theudas's activity fell during the time of the procurator Fadus, between CE 43 and 47. Secondly, Gamaliel's speech must be dated before CE 35, approximately ten years before Theudas and many of his followers were killed. Here Luke has committed an anachronism: having one of his characters refer to an event which in fact took place subsequently. Many scholars have thought that Luke's errors came from reading too hastily the account by the Jewish historian, Josephus, in his work *Jewish Antiquities* 20.97–103.[13] Josephus discusses Theudas before Judas, and this may have misled the author of Acts, who then put him chronologically out of place. An apparent error with regard to Lysanias (Luke 3.1) may also be explained as arising from a misreading of *Antiquities* 18.[14] Josephus dates the *Antiquities* in the thirteenth year of the reign of Domitian, CE 93–94. If the author of Luke–Acts read it, his work obviously must be dated a bit later. It is this which has made many scholars propose *c.* 100 (that is, as early as possible after the publication of Josephus's Antiquities). The evidence from Josephus, however, is not entirely compelling. We noted above that there is no obvious reference in Luke–Acts to the persecutions under Domitian, and most modern scholars push the date back closer to 70. Joseph Fitzmyer, for example, proposes *c.* 80–85.[15] This general period is widely accepted for both Matthew and Luke.

What about Mark? The verse in Mark which may refer to the destruction of Jerusalem by the Roman army under Titus is 13.2: 'And Jesus said to him, "Do you see these great buildings? There will not be left here one stone upon another, that will not be thrown down" (//Matt. 24.2; Luke 21.6). Instead of proving that all three gospels were written after 70, however, this saying seems rather to show that they did not always 'update' their material. The temple was destroyed by fire, and many of the stones remained standing – some can be seen to this day. Here we probably have a genuine prediction, not a fake one written after the fact, since it did not come true in a precise sense. There is no material in Mark which must be dated after 70.

Martin Hengel has argued that Mark 13 reflects not the destruction of Jerusalem, but rather the 'year of the four emperors', CE 69. He thinks that this year is reflected especially in Mark 13.8: 'For nation will rise against nation, and kingdom against kingdom.' In 69 the Empire seemed to be coming apart. Nero had been forced to commit suicide, and there was a massive struggle among competitors to succeed him. Further, Judaea was already in revolt, there was revolt in Germany and Gaul, and 'further unrest in Britain, Africa, on the lower Danube and in Pontus' (p. 22). Vespasian finally seized control, and order was restored in 70 – the same year that Jerusalem fell. Hengel proposes that Mark was written during the wide unrest and before the restoration of order. This seems to us to be a plausible explanation, but wars and unrest were (and are) common enough, and hence the material in Mark 13 need not be associated exclusively with the year 69.

In dealing with Mark 13, it is important to note that it takes account of the problem of 'the delay of the parousia'. The first Christians had expected the Lord's return or appearance (parousia) imminently, and the Thessalonians were surprised when some of them started dying before that event (I Thess. 4.13–18). Mark 13 reckons with the delay more fully:

> Take heed that no one leads you astray. Many will come in my name, saying 'I am he!' and they will lead many astray. And when you hear of wars and rumours of wars, do not be alarmed; this must take place, but the end is not yet (Mark 13.6–7).

Here we see the indication that some time has passed: people keep saying that the Lord is about to return, but his return continues to be delayed. Another clue to the date of Mark is found in 9.1:

> And he said to them: 'Truly, I say to you, there are some standing here who will not taste death before they see that the kingdom of God has come with power' (// Matt. 16.28; Luke 9.27).

Chronologically this prophecy seems to come between statements about the end by two other authors. According to Paul *most* of those who had seen the risen Lord were still alive, though some had died (I Cor. 15.6). According to John 21.21–23 it seems that only one person – the beloved disciple – had been expected to be alive at the time of Jesus' return. I Corinthians was written in the mid-50s, John 21 perhaps as late as 100. Mark 9.1 and parr. supposes that some – neither most (Paul) nor one (John 21) – would be alive at the climax of the age. The passage in the synoptics seems to come from some intermediate period, which puts it between 55 and 100, more probably earlier than later, since it is unlikely that many of Jesus' disciples survived the year 70. Similarly Jesus' prediction to James and John, 'you will drink the cup that I drink; and with the baptism with which I am baptized, you will be baptized' (Mark 10.39// Matt. 20.23) seems to presuppose that both men are dead. James the son of Zebedee was executed in the early 40s (Acts 12.2), while John was still alive in the mid-50s (Gal. 2.9). These passages do not give us decisive dates, but they point to the period after 55 and around 70.

There is another type of internal evidence which may be considered in discussing Mark, the hardest of the gospels to date. We must consider the state of the material, applying to it an educated guess about how long it took to get that way. Most now think that there are not many signs of eyewitness material in any of the synoptics, and the minor and colourful details in Mark which were once regarded as stemming from Peter are now regarded as indications not of eyewitness testimony but of stylistic preference. Details give life to the narrative, but they need not come directly from observation. They can be employed by a later author to imitate life. We should note, however, that Mark contains relatively little of either the reflection or the imitation of life. Most of the details of daily life are missing. We do not learn, for example, where Jesus and the disciples ate and slept, how they obtained money and food, whether or not they travelled around Galilee more or less constantly or assembled together only for short periods of time. The material consists of a series of episodes which concentrate on teaching, disputes and miracles. Only the last week of Jesus' life appears in anything like a connected narrative, and even there the details serve an evangelistic purpose, not that of historical curiosity. From the story of the colt one may infer that Jesus and his disciples usually walked, but the story appears in Mark because it depicts Jesus prophetically commandeering a mount and messianically riding the colt of an ass into Jerusalem (Mark 11.1–10). It is not the sort of incidental detail that an eyewitness might put in here or there.

We shall return to these details in considering the relationship between Matthew and Mark, and also in evaluating form criticism (below, pp. 127f.). Thus here we give no further examples. Those who cannot now restrain their curiosity may spend a few minutes comparing The Healing of the Paralytic in Mark and Matthew (Mark 2.1–12).

Whether one regards the details as remnants of eyewitness material or novelistic colouration, one must still note that the episodic and thematic arrangement of the material is artificial rather than natural; it responds to the needs of the churches, and it has been shaped by the concern to show the prophetic and messianic character of Jesus' life and work. It is striking that Papias said this of Mark's account of Peter's preaching: 'Peter used to adapt his teaching to the occasion', and therefore Mark's account was not in the correct order. We now note that it does not read like a first-hand account. Study of the first chapters of Mark reveals that they consist simply of a string of individual passages (pericopes), either with no connection between them or with a minimal one, such as the word 'immediately'. The individual pericopes seem to have pre-existed Mark, probably being used as sermon illustrations and the like. Some may have been put together before Mark (see below, pp. 148–51.), but the only connected account is the Passion Narrative.

Mark, as we said, is usually considered to be the earliest gospel. We have just seen that even it is second-hand and therefore probably second generation. 'Second-hand' does not, to be sure, necessarily mean 'second generation'. Scholars customarily allow a few years for the material to be cut up into pericopes, to develop in certain ways, to circulate, to be translated into Greek, to be used by churches, and to be put together in larger collections. The truth is that all this could have happened within twenty years of Jesus' death.

When, however, we combine these facts about the nature of the material with the indications that only some of the disciples were still alive, and that John in particular was already dead, and add in Hengel's argument that Mark 13 reflects the years 68–69, we must conclude that Mark is no earlier than that. It could be later: it is possible, for example, that the temple had already been burned, but that Mark had heard only that it had been destroyed, not details of how; or possibly he knew how but chose not to change the prediction that 'not one stone would be left on another'. We must assume that Matthew and Luke did not alter the saying, though they were certainly written later, and the same may have been true of Mark. Cumulatively, however, the absence of decisive references in Mark to events which were post-70 add up, and they make it likely that Mark was written near the end of the first generation of Jesus' followers: approximately 65–70.

The evidence for dating, then, is not entirely rock hard. The reader will learn that we do not share many of the consensus judgments about the synoptics. This one, however, seems correct: on the basis of the most likely assessment of each bit of evidence, the gospels are seen to be from the first or second generation after Jesus' death, i.e. *c*. 65–90 – neither earlier nor later. The most salient facts are these: (1) Mark, probably the earliest of our gospels, stands at an appreciable remove from the lifetime of Jesus. The material has been refined into separate units and subsequently collected; most of the disciples (or possibly all) were dead; the return of the Lord had been delayed, and there had been time for various 'wars and rumours of wars' which triggered the expectation of the end. (2) Matthew, the most widely-used gospel, must have been written by 90–100 at the latest, since it was used *c*. 100–110. (3) The gospels do not reveal knowledge of what happened in the nineties and later, and thus it is probable that each was written close in time to its sources. On our view of their sequence of composition (Part II), this means that Mark was followed fairly closely by Matthew, and Matthew fairly closely by Luke. If Mark is second generation (one generation after Jesus' death), Matthew and Luke are late second or early third generation. These are the facts and considerations which persuade most scholars to date the gospels *c*. 65–100.

• Anonymity

Since the attributions of the gospels to named authors come so late, it is very likely that they were written anonymously. The local churches in which they were written, of course, knew who the authors were, but that was not regarded as a vital fact, and each gospel was considered important because it was *the* gospel, not because it was the gospel *according to* a named individual. Writing anonymously is quite distinct both from writing under one's own name and also from writing under someone else's name (pseudonymity). Paul, whose letters bear his own name, was highly conscious of a distinctive individual call (to be apostle to the Gentiles) and a distinctive message (salvation for Gentiles apart from the law). He argued ferociously against opponents (usually without naming them), and he sometimes distinguished a view as his own personal opinion (I Cor. 7.40), though he could also appeal to agreement with other churches (I Cor. 11.16). Paul functioned as do most of us when we write letters, essays or books. The reader of this book will note instances in which we agree with the majority of scholars and some in which we do not, and we self-consciously want to make these distinctions and in numerous ways to single out our opinions as individuals.

Pseudepigrapha – works written under a 'false' name – are quite different. In many instances they are based on visions, dreams or other forms of direct revelation; and whether such devices are used or not pseudonymous works take the authority of an earlier famous person (e.g. I Enoch; 4 Ezra; Daniel). Several of the letters of the New Testament are now considered to be pseudepigrapha (e.g. I and II Timothy; Titus). Pseudepigrapha are intentionally individualist, just as are works written under one's own name; the difference is the appeal to the authority of another person.

Anonymous works, however, in many ways claim much more: by implication they claim to be 'the truth about x, y or z'. The modern equivalent is an article in a dictionary or an encyclopaedia. In many modern encyclopaedias the author of each article is identified by initials, and the knowledgeable reader can see what in fact is distinctive about the article, when it reveals a pet theory of an individual, and when it reflects a consensus. The average reader, however, takes the article to be 'the truth about the topic'. In a similar way textbooks, which usually do not discuss disagreements and difficulties, are written as if they state the simple truth, rather than the views of individuals. In this case the authors are named, but the style of writing is 'anonymous'.

It is very likely that our gospels were written anonymously because their authors wished to present them as 'the simple truth about what Jesus did and said'. We noted above that the Didache treats the Gospel of Matthew in just this way: the Lord's prayer is from 'the Lord in the gospel'. This is quite different from saying 'the Lord, at least according to one report'.

The authors of our gospels were all students of Jewish Scripture, which came to be called 'the Old Testament' by Christians, and they would have noted that many of the biblical books are anonymous. The Hebrew prophets were self-conscious about their distinctive messages, as was Paul later, but most of the books are anonymous and are named by their subject rather than by the author; and this is true of later Jewish works as well, such as I and II Maccabees. We are not proposing that the authors of our gospels were conscious of writing what would be considered Scripture in days to come, but they were influenced by the biblical style, which helps to explain their being anonymous.

The Third Gospel constitutes a partial exception to this understanding of the work of the evangelists. Luke (as we shall continue to call the author) knew the style of Hellenistic histories, and his preface shows self-consciousness about his own view and the way in which it was different from that of others. He claimed to have used other accounts, and he acknowledged that 'many' had written narratives about Jesus before. Of his own work, he stated that he had 'followed all things closely' (or, better, 'precisely') and that he would write 'an orderly account' (Luke 1.1–4). He implied, then, that his version was an improvement. After the preface, however, he dropped the individual style and did not subsequently point out when he was rearranging or supplementing his sources (as the Jewish historian Josephus, for example, sometimes did). Apart from the preface the Gospel of Luke is an anonymous statement of 'the truth'.

In Mark and Matthew the anonymous claim to truth is consistently maintained throughout. Mark, as we saw, began by simply saying 'the beginning of the gospel of Jesus Christ', and Matthew called his work 'the book of the genealogy of Jesus Christ'. Matthew probably had in mind I Chronicles, which opens with a genealogy and then proceeds to a history. I Chronicles, like the other historical books of the Hebrew Bible, is anonymous. We proposed just above that Jewish Scripture influenced the evangelists. This is seen most markedly in the opening verses of Matthew, but only the preface of Luke reveals the influence of the alternative model, Hellenistic historiography.

Matthew and Mark, then, were each very likely written as 'the gospel' for a local church. We cannot know what other traditions their churches had. Luke was written with the intention of improving upon other accounts, and possibly in the hope of replacing them entirely. It is likely that the material which the evangelists used was also anonymous – stories about and sayings of 'Jesus', not 'Jesus as recollected by . . .' Scholars think that they can now identify numerous additions to the material about Jesus, but at no point does the text itself identify 'the author'; rather, Jesus says the words, while an anonymous and omniscient narrator provides the setting. We may take a few examples.

1. 'Interpretations' are attached to some parables. A major case is the Parable of the Sower, to which all the synoptics attach an explanation (Mark 4.1–12 and parr.). Scholars commonly believe that the explanation is secondary to the parable itself and serves to relate it to an issue different from the one originally addressed by Jesus. In the text of the gospels, however, there is no indication that some early Christian wanted to step forward and claim for himself the ingenious interpretation: it, like the parable itself, is attributed to Jesus. In fact it may well be from an intermediate layer between Jesus and the synoptics.

2. In Mark there are a few editorial asides – instances in which the narrator turns to the reader and comments in his own voice. The narrator explains to the Gentile readers that the Jews 'do not eat unless they wash their hands' (Mark 7.3), and he carefully interprets the meaning of Aramaic words: Jesus said to a girl believed to be dead, 'Talitha cumi', and the narrator explains that this means 'Little girl, I say to you, arise' (Mark 5.41). These and a few other similar cases, however, stand out from the rest of the synoptic gospels, in which for the most part the narrator is not only omniscient and anonymous but also unobtrusive. The synoptic material, as far as we can tell, was always transmitted without appeal to individual testimony. The result is that the reader is not encouraged to ask the narrator, How do you know? Use of an omniscient, anonymous and unobtrusive narrator constitutes a stronger claim to truthfulness than would employment of a named author. A named individual would have to say, 'Jesus managed to whisper to me, just as the guards marched him off, what his final prayer had been'. The anonymous narrator can simply report what Jesus prayed when entirely alone (Mark 14.36–42 and parr.).

Just as Matthew and Mark themselves did not wish to present their accounts as 'my individual version of the story of Jesus', but rather simply as 'the story of Jesus', so also the editors and organizers of the material at earlier levels. The final documents are in fact distinctive, and we can also sometimes suspect that we can identify a distinctive layer underlying what are now diverse passages, but the authors and editors did not wish to call attention to the exercise of individual judgment and the production of reconstructed accounts. The synoptics were copied and circulated, and they went forth from their original settings anonymously.

For a long time the users of the gospels seem to have shared the authors' view that what they narrated was important, not who the narrator was. Papias is the first person whom we know to have been conscious of the individual characteristics of the gospels or collections which he knew: Mark wrote an account, though not necessarily in the right order. Matthew collected sayings, but different people interpreted them differently. Irenaeus was highly conscious of the distinctive characteristics of the various gospels and thought that in order to have a full and accurate picture all four accounts should be used. Early in the second century, however, the Christians seem to have used the gospels as they were intended: not as expressions of individual judgment, but as simple statements of the truth about Jesus.

2 Genre and Purposes

• Genre: preliminary

When we read the gospels, what kind or kinds of literature are we reading? One answer which will readily come to mind is that they are biographies or histories, but in the previous chapter we began to see that neither term will quite do. We noted that Luke exhibits some of the traits of a Hellenistic history, but only some. We further remarked on the artificial arrangement of material: artificial in the sense of 'not arising naturally from observation'. The material has been shaped into individual episodes which are either loosely linked together or arranged according to theme. It is not entirely inaccurate to speak of Matthew and Luke as ancient 'lives'. One must, however, accent the word 'ancient' quite strongly and distinguish an ancient life from a modern biography. In this preliminary section on genre we shall not go into the similarities between, say, Matthew and Plutarch's Life of Alexander, but shall rather focus on the degree to which the gospels are *not* biographies or histories of Jesus as most of us understand those terms. We shall get some feel for the difficulties if we consider two reconstructions of the life of Jesus which were based on the assumption that the synoptics are biographies in more-or-less the modern sense of the word.

The first is a short sketch by H. J. Holtzmann, published in 1863. Albert Schweitzer said of it this: 'Scarcely ever has a description of the life of Jesus exercised so irresistible an influence as that short outline'.[1] Holtzmann's view was that Jesus had desired to found an ideal kingdom, one which was based on inner conversion to a life of love, that he sensed that it was not working, and that over time he developed the view that he must put his cause to the test in Jerusalem, being prepared to suffer and die.

If we simply thumb through Mark we shall see the building blocks of Holtzmann's view. Jesus began with preaching and miracles and attracted a large following (Mark 1.21–27, 32–34). He began to think over whether or not he was doing the right thing (1.35), but his popularity continued for some time (1.45; 3.7–10; 3.20; 4.1). Mark 3.7–8 is an especially good example: people came to him from Judaea, Jerusalem, Idumea (south and east of Jerusalem), from the other side of the Jordan, and from Tyre and Sidon in Syria. Jesus found, however, that even his disciples did not gain the inner enlightenment which he sought to impart (e.g. 6.52). He withdrew to Syria in order to think it over (Mark 7.24–30). He had made up his mind that he must go to Jerusalem and be prepared to suffer, he announced this to the disciples (8.31–33), and he preached the gospel of 'taking up the cross' to many of his followers (8.34–38). Yet there was opposition, and he then began to hide from the crowd and to teach his disciples privately, still emphasizing the need to suffer (9.30–32). The message was repeated (10.32–34), but still the disciples did not grasp it: they discussed who would be first in the kingdom (10.35–45). Finally Jesus went to Jerusalem and tried to cleanse the temple of everything external, so that the pure spiritual kingdom might enter people's hearts (11.15–19). He finally died for the cause, and dying won.

We note these elements: (1) a theory of psychological development, one of the chief characteristics of nineteenth-century biography; (2) the desire to make religion interior and to exclude externals, a major characteristic of liberal Protestantism; (3) the view that Jesus expected nothing to happen in the future, except inner enlightenment.

Albert Schweitzer read the gospels and found a completely different Jesus – the one seen especially in Mark 13 and Matthew 10. He published a short sketch of the life of Jesus in 1901 and his great work, called in English *The Quest of the Historical Jesus*, in 1906. His view can be summarized in nine points:[2]

1. Jesus expected the end of the present order to come at the time of the next spring's harvest: this is shown by the parables about sowing and harvesting, which indicate when the end will come. John the Baptist was the one who sowed the seed which grows of itself (Schweitzer, pp. 355–377).

2. Jesus thought that suffering must precede the kingdom, and he sent out the twelve expecting them to suffer. He thought that the Son of man would come before the disciples completed going to all the cities of Israel: this is shown by Matt. 10, which is authentic and chronologically accurate.

3. Jesus' expectation of suffering was not fulfilled, and he withdrew, apparently to consider his next move: shown by Mark 6.30–31,45, which must be placed chronologically after Matt. 10 (p. 364).

4. Jesus finally decided to suffer himself and thus force God to bring in the kingdom: based on the Predictions of the Passion in Mark 8.31–33 and subsequent chapters.

5. Jesus' own identity as Son of man and Messiah was revealed to Peter, James and John: the Transfiguration (Mark 9.2–8).

6. The secret that Jesus was Messiah was revealed to the other disciples: Mark 8.27–30, which must be put after the Transfiguration (pp. 386f.).

7. Judas revealed the secret to the chief priests: Mark 14.10–11, supplying what it was that Judas betrayed (pp. 393, 396).

8. The high priest then had possession of the secret, which he used in order to condemn Jesus: Mark 14.61 (p. 397).

9. The kingdom did not come, and Jesus died disillusioned. Schweitzer put it this way:

There is silence all around. The Baptist appears, and cries: 'Repent, for the Kingdom of Heaven is at hand.' Soon after that comes Jesus, and in the knowledge that He is the coming Son of Man lays hold of the wheel of the world to set it moving on that last revolution which is to bring all ordinary history to a close. It refuses to turn, and he throws Himself upon it. Then it does turn; and crushes Him. Instead of bringing in the eschatological conditions, He has destroyed them. The wheel rolls onward, and the mangled body of the one immeasurably great Man, who was strong enough to think of Himself as the spiritual ruler of mankind and to bend history to His purpose, is hanging upon it still. That is His victory and His reign (pp. 370f.).

He comes to us as One unknown, without a name, as of old, by the lake-side, He came to those men who knew Him not. He speaks to us the same word: 'Follow thou me!' and sets us to the tasks which He has to fulfil for our time. He commands. And to those who obey Him, whether they be wise or simple, He will reveal Himself in the toils, the conflicts, the sufferings which they shall pass through in His fellowship, and, as an ineffable mystery, they shall learn in their own experience Who He is (p. 403).

Schweitzer's negative portrait of Jesus – a deluded visionary – did not lead him to renounce following him: Heeding the command, 'Follow thou me', Schweitzer went to Africa as a medical missionary.

There are very few agreements between Schweitzer's Jesus, produced by considering the gospels as biography and history, and Holtzmann's, produced in the same way. They have in common that Jesus withdrew to re-think his mission. But Holtzmann thought that the mission was to spiritualize and interiorize Judaism; Schweitzer thought that it was to bring in the close of the age.

How can careful scholars come up with such diverse views? There are two obvious explanations. One is that Holtzmann, like many others before and after him, created Jesus in his own image – or, better, found in the story of Jesus the values of his own age. Tyrrell described nineteenth-century scholars as looking into the well of history for Jesus but seeing their own reflections,[3] and this description fits Holtzmann quite well. Schweitzer very self-consciously wanted not to do this, and he sought a Jesus who did not correspond to his own values or those of his time. He found material in the gospels which is antithetical to the main line of pre-World War I European thought, a radical eschatology which sets at nought hope for spiritual progress over generations and centuries, but which rather expects a sudden cataclysm which will change the world order.

Thus far Schweitzer's reconstruction of the historical Jesus is seen clearly to be superior. He intended to settle the question of the Jesus of history by giving a definitive answer, and simultaneously he argued that the meaning of Jesus for the modern individual does not depend on what he said and did in ancient Palestine. Thus he was psychologically free to describe Jesus as he found him, not as he wanted him to be. Schweitzer's work produced a Jesus whom many find hard to accept, and he is often cited as having proved that the search for the historical Jesus is futile.

Those who still wish, however, to talk about the Jesus of history almost universally grant the force of Schweitzer's main point: Jesus expected something dramatic to happen in the not-too-distant future. Holtzmann's depiction of Jesus, on the other hand, has ceased to be even partially persuasive.

One explanation of the difference between Schweitzer and Holtzmann, then, is that Holtzmann projected his own view of religion on to Jesus. The second explanation, however, is that both worked on a false premise.

They both regarded the material as being essentially biographical in the modern sense: it presents information about Jesus in chronological order, and from that order can be derived information about what he thought when, and when he changed his mind about what. They disagreed with each other because they applied this assumption to the material in different ways. Holtzmann worked exclusively with the gospel of Mark. His work depended on the view that Mark was the earliest gospel, and the attractiveness of his Jesus helped to establish that view. Schweitzer was sceptical about the absolute priority of Mark, and he depended in part on Matthew. The chronology of events, however, was as important to him as to Holtzmann. The difference was that he was prepared to reconstruct a 'critical' chronology by switching between Matthew and Mark and also by transposing events. Thus, returning to the list of nine points above, we note that Mark 6.30–31,45 must (in Schweitzer's view) be placed after Matt. 10, while Mark 8.27–30 must follow Mark 9.2–8.

When Schweitzer wrote, it had already been shown that the gospels are not chronicles and that the arrangement of material need not reflect the original chronology of the life of Jesus. William Wrede argued successfully that the arrangement of Mark is, at least in part, theological (*The Messianic Secret*, first published 1901), and the same must be said of Matthew and Luke. Schweitzer no less than Holtzmann erred in thinking that the gospels are biographies in the modern sense, and that a life of Jesus could be written simply by arranging the pericopes in order and then explaining what conceptions on Jesus' own part led him to do first one thing and then the next. The evidence for the historical Jesus turns out to be much more problematic than either scholar thought. Holtzmann thought that Mark was a straightforward chronicle of events in Jesus' life, and Schweitzer thought that Matthew and Mark could be used to reconstruct such a chronicle. Both were wrong; they were not dealing with chronicles. Reading the pericopes in order does not produce a 'life of Jesus' in the modern sense.

This requires demonstration, especially since many readers continue to expect the gospels to be 'biographies' as we now understand them. We shall first note the degree to which they lack biographical information, and then the degree to which the material which at first blush appears to be biographical is actually not so.

1. There are numerous expectations which are met by modern historical biographies, but not by the synoptic gospels. Most important to notice is the extreme brevity of each account of Jesus' life compared to a modern biography. This brevity succeeds in making a startling impact by its succinct and narrowly focused presentation, but it leaves many gaps which the modern reader has to fill in by historical research.

For example, a modern biography should situate its subject in the cultural, economic and political realities of the time, explaining especially those matters unfamiliar to readers. Apart from Luke's dating of Jesus' birth and his introductory list of rulers in the Roman administration (3.1), no formal description of the social, religious and political life of Galilee and Judaea at the time of Jesus is provided by any of the synoptics. References are made to Pharisees, scribes, priests, Sadducees, Herodians and tax-collectors without indicating their roles, numbers or influence, apart from what can be gathered incidentally from the immediate context. Mark explains the Jewish custom of handwashing (7.3–4), but generally Jewish festivals and rites are mentioned without explanation. Similarly, the ruler of Galilee is called King Herod in Mark 6.14 without specifying that this particular Herod was Herod Antipas, the tetrarch (technically not a king). Matt. 14.1 and Luke 9.7 call him Herod the tetrarch, but none of the gospels indicates when or where he ruled. There is the same vagueness in reference to Pilate, who is seen as a man easily intimidated by Jewish crowds. Caiaphas, the High Priest, is named only in the Matthaean passion narrative and in Luke's introduction, where Annas is associated with him in an unclear way (3.2). Nowhere are the ramifications of Roman rule in Judaea and overlordship in Galilee detailed. All these matters are simply alluded to, and the historian must look to other texts from the period – especially Josephus' history (see ch. 1 n. 13) – to build up a picture of the circumstances in which Jesus lived.

The brevity of the presentation also affects characterization. The synoptic gospels provide information about what Jesus said and did, and what happened to him, but they omit a great deal of relevance to a biography, even in their depiction of the main character. Apart from Luke's general remark, echoing the description of Samuel (I Sam. 2.26), that Jesus advanced in wisdom and in favour with God and men, and his story of Jesus' visit to Jerusalem at the age of twelve (2.39–52), nothing is said about Jesus' childhood or adolescence, about the influence of parents or relatives, or about his education and interests before he embarked on his ministry. Ancients were interested in such matters, and subsequently apocryphal gospels would supply the deficiencies, but they are not described in the synoptics. One finds there neither a sense of character nor of historical development. How Jesus conceived his ministry or whether he started with a plan which was modified by experience is never made explicit: thus Holtzmann, Schweitzer and others tried to supply plans which he followed. Rather the significance of his ministry is implied by a series of anecdotes, each of which epitomizes an aspect of his task: that he showed himself to be Messiah in his healing and preaching, that he attracted followers and also met with opposition. This is why the order and context of episodes can sometimes vary from one gospel to another. The various elements are drawn together only in the final chapters, in which Jesus' opponents triumph in destroying him, and his followers desert him until their faith is revitalized by his resurrection.

The other characters in the synoptics are even less fully realized. Mostly, whether groups or individuals, they exhibit a single trait, in response to Jesus, like trust or repentance or animosity. They are not rounded characters, but flat caricatures. This is true even of the disciples, about many of whom we know nothing but their names

29

(Matt. 10.1–4; Mark 3.16–19; Luke 6.13–16). The synoptics agree that there were twelve, although the significance of the number is never discussed. Mark's disciples can be summed up as lacking both understanding and faith (e.g. 4.40; 6.52), Matthew's as having understanding but little faith (e.g. 13.51; 8.26; 28.17), Luke's as pious and penitent followers (e.g. 5.1–11,27–32). Three of the disciples, Simon Peter, James and John, are marked out as close to Jesus, but few details are provided even about them. They were fishermen, together with Simon's brother Andrew, before they followed Jesus (Matt. 4.18–25; Mark 1.16–20; Luke 5.1–11). James and John were the sons of Zebedee, and Simon and Andrew the sons of Jonah (Matt. 16.17). They sometimes accompanied Jesus when the other disciples were left behind, at healings (Mark 1.29; 5.37–43; Luke 8.49–56), at the transfiguration (Matt. 17.1–8; Mark 9.2–8; Luke 9.28–36), and in Gethsemane (Matt. 26.36–46; Mark 14.32–42).

Otherwise, little is known of James and John. Mark records that Jesus called them 'Boanerges, sons of thunder' (3.17), but the significance of the name is not clarified by further stories. Usually they say nothing. Together with Peter and Andrew, they ask when the destruction of the temple will happen (Mark 13.4), and the two of them request to sit at Jesus' right and left hand in his kingdom (Mark 10.35–40), although Matthew attributes the request to their mother (Matt. 20.20–28).

Simon, who is called Peter, the Rock, generally exhibits no rock-like qualities. Although he confesses that Jesus is the Christ (Mark 8.29 and parr.), in Matthew and Mark he immediately goes on to oppose Jesus' prediction of his own death in Jerusalem. He denies Jesus while he waits in the courtyard after Jesus' arrest (Mark 14.66–72 and parr.). Only Matthew makes sense of his nickname, by attributing to Jesus the statement, 'you are Peter, and on this rock I will build my church' (16.18). We know that he was married, because the story of Jesus healing his mother-in-law is related (Mark 1.29–32 and parr.), but we remain ignorant of his wife's name, whether they had children, or how the marriage was affected by Peter's new life as a follower of Jesus. Matthew adds two stories which involve Peter, one in which he is questioned about the (temple) tax and is told to catch a fish, remove the shekel, and pay the tax for himself and Jesus (17.24–27), and the other in which he attempts to walk on the water to Jesus (14.28–33). The second story simply illustrates the disciples' little faith. Luke tends to exonerate the disciples. He omits the request by James and John to sit at Jesus' right and left hands in the kingdom, but includes Jesus' rebuke when they suggest calling down fire from heaven to destroy the Samaritans (9.54–55). He omits Peter's opposition to Jesus and Jesus' rebuke after the first prediction of the passion, he looks beyond Peter's denial to the time when he would strengthen his brothers (22.32), and he refers to a resurrection appearance to him alone (24.34). In these ways, Luke prepares for the exemplary portraits of the disciples in the Acts of the Apostles.

There is even some disagreement among the three gospels about the names of the twelve. Matthew and Mark include Thaddaeus instead of Luke's Judas the son of James. Also, Matthew identifies the tax collector called Levi by the other gospels (Mark 2.14; Luke 5.27–28) with the disciple Matthew (Matt. 9.9). All agree that

Judas Iscariot betrayed Jesus (Matt. 26.14–16,47; Mark 14.10–11,43; Luke 22.3–6,47), but exactly why or what he betrayed is left unclear. Luke suggests that he arranged to find an opportunity to place Jesus in the hands of the temple guards away from the crowds (22.3–6). Matthew describes him returning the money, repenting for betraying an innocent man, and hanging himself (27.3–5). Luke gives a different account of Judas' death in Acts 1.18: he bought a plot of land with the money, but fell down dead upon it, bursting open so that his entrails poured out.

It is, perhaps, surprising that the gospels devote so little space to their portraits of the disciples, especially to those, like Peter, James and John, who seem to have been influential figures in the early church. Since this is so, however, we should be warned against treating other depictions of individuals or groups, especially those of Jesus' opponents, the scribes, Pharisees, Sadducees and priests, as if they were full and complete.

The synoptics, then, lack the traits which we would expect in biographies. We now turn to the next point: some of the apparently biographical material is not actually such.

2. Matthew and Luke begin with accounts of Jesus' birth, and at first glance these appear to be 'biographical'. Matthew first gives a genealogy from Abraham to Jesus, divided into three groups, said to have fourteen generations each (actually, one has only thirteen). Then comes the narrative proper: Mary and Joseph lived in Bethlehem. Wise men came enquiring about the king who would be born. Herod (the Great, who was the king) heard of this and wished to eliminate any threat to his throne, and so he decided to have the male infants of Bethlehem and its environs killed. Joseph was warned in a dream and took Mary and the baby to Egypt. When Herod died the family returned, but they also feared the new Herod who ruled Judaea (Archelaus), and so they moved to Nazareth in Galilee, which was now governed by Herod Antipas (Matt. 1–2).

Luke's narrative is much more substantial, and it also includes John the Baptist as well as Jesus. With regard to Jesus, we learn that Joseph and Mary lived in Nazareth. Caesar Augustus required a world-wide census, and Joseph had to go to Bethlehem, the city of David, to register, since he was descended from David. He took Mary, and while they were there Jesus was born. A few days later they returned to Nazareth. Later Luke also gives a genealogy, from Adam to Jesus. It has fifty-six names between Abraham and Jesus, compared to Matthew's forty-one.

The two birth narratives have many other elements, but instead of going through each gospel on its own, we may now compare and contrast them. They agree on a few points: (1) Jesus' mother was not married, but only betrothed, at the time of his birth; (2) his conception was miraculous; (3) he was born in Bethlehem; (4) he grew up in Nazareth.

On some points they do not agree, but also do not contradict each other: (1) the story about John the Baptist – his conception, his parents, and their relationship to Mary – is in Luke but not in Matthew; (2) in Luke Jesus is visited by shepherds, in Matthew by Magi; (3) Matthew but not Luke tells of Herod's slaughter of infant males; (4) the flight to Egypt is in Matthew but not Luke; (5) the presentation of

Jesus at the temple and the prophecies of Simeon and Anna are in Luke but not Matthew.

On some points the stories are contradictory: (1) the genealogies cannot be reconciled; (2) the moves between Nazareth and Bethlehem cannot be harmonized.

The last point especially is fruitful for understanding the intentions and outlooks of the authors. According to Luke, Joseph and Mary were residents of Nazareth in Galilee, they went to Bethlehem in Judaea only because of a world-wide census, and after Jesus' birth they returned to their home in Galilee. According to Matthew they lived in Bethlehem, they fled Judaea to escape Herod, and they moved to Nazareth only because they still feared Archelaus after Herod's death. How can this contradiction be explained?

We first note that the points on which each story turns cannot be reconciled with the history of the time. Luke devises a world-wide census to shift the scene from Nazareth to Bethlehem, but we may be sure that Augustus ordered no such census. The mass upheaval of virtually every resident of the Roman Empire would have left a trace somewhere other than in Luke had it actually taken place. Further, the rationale of the census offered by Luke is simply impossible. Joseph, a descendant of David, is required to go to David's city. On Luke's count David had lived forty-two generations before Joseph. Forty-two generations back every one had (and has) millions of ancestors (1,000,000 is passed at the twentieth generation). It is not reasonable to think that Augustus required people to return to the family home of *one* of their ancestors forty-two generations previously. Even if it be said that such a decree might have been made and applied only to those who could claim some royal descent, the basic difficulties do not disappear. David could have been claimed as an ancestor by thousands of Jews. What was true of Israel would also have been true of other nations within the empire, and again the upheaval would have been enormous and would have left some trace in the general histories of the period. There were censuses at different times in different places in the empire, but none ever required registration in the home town of a remote ancestor. There actually was a census *of Judaea* alone in CE 6, when Quirinius was governor of Syria. Luke 2.2 shows knowledge of this census, though the author erred in thinking that Quirinius was governor when Herod was king (see below), and also in supposing that the census was worldwide. Luke employs the theme of a census simply in order to move Joseph and Mary to Bethlehem for the birth of Jesus.

Matthew's story which shifts the scene from Bethlehem to Galilee, as well, cannot be reconciled with the history of Herod's reign. Matthew's story, unlike Luke's, does have verisimilitude. In his declining years Herod exhibited paranoid behaviour, and he killed numerous people who seemed to him to pose a threat, including his beloved wife Mariamne, two of his sons indirectly (there was a rigged trial), and a third by his direct order. We have a detailed account of Herod's reign by Josephus. He reported the atrocities of Herod's reign at some length, but there is no mention of a mass slaughter of male infants, and such a crime could hardly have passed unnoticed by every one but Matthew. Matthew, as we shall see, modelled his story of Jesus' infancy on the story of Moses, and he seems to have derived the idea of the slaughter from Exodus 1.15–22.

What motivated Matthew and Luke to devise these accounts, which serve only to shift Jesus' family from one place to another? The explanation is not far to seek. It was a 'mere' fact that Jesus was a Galilean and that he came from Nazareth. Yet Matthew, Luke and the other early Christians regarded him as the fulfilment of the biblical prophecies that Israel would be restored by a scion of the house of David. Thus they knew, on the basis of prophecy, that Jesus must have been born of David's line and in David's city. To reconcile these two 'facts', one derived from history, the other from prophecy, they chose different ways of locating Jesus' birth in Bethlehem, though he was known to have grown up in Nazareth.

One other part of Matthew's infancy narrative was derived from the Moses story. Since he thought of Jesus as the second and greater Moses, he arranged for there to be a New Exodus from Egypt, to fulfil the prophetic statement 'out of Egypt I have called my son' (Matt. 2.15, quoting Hos. 11.1), and to this end he had Joseph take the family to Egypt.

Matthew's gospel may have been shaped in part by the need to answer Jewish criticism of the Christian movement. He replied in terms effective in such a debate: he showed that Jesus fulfils biblical prophecy, which was revered both by him and his community and by non-Christian Judaism. Thus almost every step of the birth narrative is marked by the statement that a given scripture is fulfilled. The virgin birth fulfils Isa. 7.14; the slaughter of the innocents recalls the story of Moses and fulfils Jer. 31.15; the flight to Egypt and the return fulfil Hos. 11.1. The naming of Jesus is not said to fulfil scripture, but the translation of 'Jesus' as meaning 'salvation' makes approximately the same point: Jesus fulfils scriptural hopes for redemption. Only the story of the Magi is not said to fulfil scripture, although it could readily be seen as doing so. In Num. 24.17 Balaam predicts that 'a star from Jacob [will take] the leadership', and the reference to a star may have suggested to Matthew a passage in Isaiah:

> Arise, shine, for your light has come. . . . The nations come to your light and kings to your dawning brightness. . . . the wealth of the Gentiles will come to you. . . . Camels in throngs will cover you. . . . Everyone in Sheba will come, bringing gold and incense . . . (Isa. 60.1–6).

Luke's story focuses on the human drama much more than on the divine scheme. Zecharias, Elizabeth, Joseph and especially Mary are treated with sympathy and respect, and they stand out from the pages as models of Jewish piety and devotion. Luke, no less than Matthew, was concerned to show that Jesus fulfilled the hopes of his people, but he did not employ argumentative devices such as Matthew's prooftexts. Luke's warm and humane story nevertheless makes the claim that Jewish devotion to God comes to its culmination in the story of Jesus. Zechariah, in the poem now called the Benedictus, said that Jesus fulfils what was promised by the prophets, Israel's redemption (Luke 1.67–79). Gabriel told Mary that Jesus would

[handwritten margin note: ⊗ Matthew's Gospel interested in fulfilling Scripture]

[handwritten margin note: Luke interested in the Human Drama]

33

'reign over the house of Jacob' (1.32–35), and the angel told the shepherds that Jesus was the Messiah (2.8–14).

Thus Matthew and Luke do not disagree with regard to the significance of Jesus: he is the promised saviour, the son of David, the Messiah. He fulfils all the expectations of Israel's prophets, and Luke adds the hopes of humble members of Israel, such as Simeon and Anna. Yet he was destined to be not just the redeemer of Israel, but also of the whole world.

We see that the authors of Matthew and Luke had different aims and principles from those of the academic historian or biographer. They wanted their stories to present Jesus as the fulfilment of the hopes of humanity, and especially of Israel. They were sure that he had done so, and thus they could take 'information' about him directly from Hebrew prophecy.

A further consideration of the genealogies will help illuminate the authors' methods and concerns.

We saw above that Matthew probably borrowed the idea of starting with a genealogy from I Chronicles and that it is divided into three sections: there are fourteen generations from Abraham to David, fourteen from David to the deportation to Babylon, and fourteen from the deportation to the birth of the Christ (Matt. 1.17). There are not actually fourteen names for the last group, but rather thirteen. Fourteen are probably insisted on because the number has an importance of its own. Three groups of fourteen = six groups of seven. Jesus, then, would begin the seventh seven, and since seven symbolizes fulfilment (God 'rested on the seventh day from all the work which he had done', Gen. 2.2), Matthew may have called attention to the number of generations in order to claim that Jesus brought Israelite history to fulfilment. It is important to note that the focus is on Israelite history, not world history. The genealogy starts with Abraham, the father of Israel, and concludes with the Christ, Israel's Messiah.

Even more striking than the three fourteens are the four women who appear in the genealogy. The list of names consists of males ('Abraham was the father of Isaac'), but four mothers are named: Tamar (1.3), Rahab (1.5), Ruth (1.5) and the wife of Uriah, Bathsheba (1.6). Two were Gentiles: Rahab was a Canaanite (Josh. 2.2) and Ruth was a Moabite (Ruth 1.4). The other two had, at least, Gentile connections: Tamar from the context of Gen. 38.6 may have been a Canaanite, and Bathsheba was the wife of the Hittite Uriah (II Sam. 11.3). Further, questions could be raised about the sexual conduct of all of them. Rahab is straightforward: she was a prostitute. Tamar played the prostitute with her father-in-law, attempting to force him to marry her to his third son after the deaths of his first two sons, who married her successively. Bathsheba was taken into David's house after her husband, a Hittite soldier of David's, had been, in effect, murdered by David: the king had ordered that he be sent to the front lines and then left to fight alone. David had already committed adultery with Bathsheba. He had been inspired to these iniquitous deeds because she bathed within sight of his roof, where he sometimes walked. Ruth lay beside Boaz while he slept. When he awoke she urged him to take her under his protection. The behaviour of Ruth and Bathsheba may be judged to have been perfectly innocent, and Tamar's may have been justified. Rahab, who protected the Israelite spies before Israel invaded Canaan, can hardly be accused of having been interested only in money. Still, Matthew's choice of just these four women is striking.

They certainly point in the direction of taking the gospel to the Gentiles. Those are also the last words in Matthew's gospel ('Go and make disciples of all nations [Gentiles] . . .', Matt. 28.19), and so where he stood on the issue of admitting Gentiles cannot be doubted. It is possible that a second motive was at work, and that he saw the need to defend Mary against calumny. She had borne a child before she was married; and Matthew, possibly living in close proximity to a strong synagogue, may have needed to remind the non-Christian Jews, and perhaps Christians as well, about some of the chief women in Israel's history.

The main purpose of the genealogy, however, is to link Jesus first with Abraham and then with David. The Messiah should be a descendant of David, and thus we understand why David is one of the pivots of the genealogy. Yet Matthew has a bit of a difficulty. He traces the lineage of David to Joseph, and then finishes the list of names by saying that 'Joseph [was] the husband of Mary, of whom Jesus was born, who is called Christ'. That is, Matthew held that Mary was a virgin, and he traces Jesus back to David only legally: Joseph married Mary and thus acknowledged Jesus as his son, but according to Matthew Jesus was not physically descended from David.

Luke also has a genealogy, in 3.23–37. He runs it in ascending order, from Jesus to Joseph, who he says was thought to be Jesus' father, then on to David, Abraham and finally to Adam, who, the reader is reminded, was 'the son of God'. Jesus here is depicted as heir of the father of the human race rather than just the heir of Abraham and David. The reference to God recalls the heavenly voice at the baptism of Jesus, which had just preceded the genealogy: 'Thou art my beloved Son; with thee I am well pleased' (Luke 3.22).

Many of the names in Luke's genealogy between Jesus and Abraham are different from Matthew's list. If we invert Luke's order to agree with Matthew's, and begin with Zerubbabel, for example, we find this:

Matthew	*Luke*
Zerubbabel	Zerubbabel
Abiud	Rhesa
Eliakim	Johanan
Azor	Joda

The genealogies have substantial agreements for the period from Abraham to David (where they are both based on I Chronicles and Ruth), but this list exemplifies how much they sometimes differ. In the section from Zerubbabel to Jesus the disagreements are especially numerous, and there is even wide disparity in the number of generations. Matthew has twelve names and Luke has twenty-one. If the names are multiplied by twenty-five or thirty (the number of years for each generation), it will be seen that Luke has the more plausible list: there were actually

35

about 575 years from Zerubbabel to Jesus, and Luke's twenty-one names, spread over the period, would give twenty-seven years for each generation.

There are numerous other substantial differences between the two lists. After David, Matthew gives a sequence of names from Solomon to Jechoniah, while for the same period Luke has a different list, running from Nathan to Neri. The two gospels do not even agree on the name of Joseph's father, Matthew calling him Jacob and Luke offering Heli.

The genealogies cannot be reconciled. It is unlikely that either author knew the names of Joseph's ancestors in sequence. It is more likely that each had recourse to a list of the descendants of David. Different Judaean households may have kept such lists – perhaps hoping that one day the time would be right to stake a claim to the throne – and thus it may be that here we see the result of early Christian research – which did not, however, lead to assured results. Both Matthew and Luke wished to set Jesus firmly in the context of the history of salvation, which was ultimately based on a view of God's intention, not human descent: God created the world, called Abraham and his descendants, and sent the Messiah to save the world.

The birth narratives are not typical gospel material. The stories about Jesus' activities are based on quite different sorts of tradition, and they are much more reliable. We have used the birth narratives to exemplify the point that the gospels are not scientific histories or biographies. They constitute an extreme case, but they show what two of the evangelists were prepared to do in order to write *sacred history*. Matthew, in particular, was willing to follow prophecy and to learn from it 'information' about Jesus. It is not surprising that, later in the gospel, we read that Jesus rode two animals into Jerusalem, since the prophecy said 'on an ass, and on a colt, the foal of an ass' (Matt. 21.5–6). Luke sometimes wrote in imitation of the Septuagint (the Greek translation of the Hebrew Scriptures), following not only its syntax, style and vocabulary, but also using its themes (compare the song of Hannah in I Sam. 2 with that of Mary in Luke 1.46–55).[4]

• Accuracy

We are not proposing that the evangelists were creators of fairy tales. There is a great deal of space between 'fantasies' and 'academic history/biography, fully researched', and the gospels are to be put somewhere in that large intermediate area. We have already seen that they rely on 'information' selected from biblical prophecy. Luke, however, also claims to present an accurate account. We should enquire just what this means, and we begin by putting the claim in context.

We first note that the concern for accuracy was not quite the same in the ancient world as it is today, though ancient historians knew the difference between accuracy and error in reporting events. Josephus, for example, charged other chroniclers with distorting the evidence (e.g. War 1.1–2). He claimed that he presented 'the whole story in full and accurate detail' (*met' akribeias*) and that Israelite political history was described 'without error' (*Antiq.* 20.260–261). Papias commented that Mark wrote 'accurately (*akribōs*) all that he remembered', though he did not put events in

the correct order. He claimed that, despite this, Mark 'made no mistake', since he omitted nothing that he knew and made no false statement. Luke, as we saw, implicitly criticized earlier gospels for not being sufficiently accurate. He claimed that his gospel was written 'accurately' (*akribōs*) and in correct order, and he wished his readers to know 'the truth' or 'certainty' of 'the things of which you have been informed' (Luke 1.1–4).

This all sounds modern and critical enough, but in fact the standards were different. (We leave aside here the fact that modern ideals are seldom realized by people who recount history.) Josephus, for example, who was a very self-conscious historian, and who was also fairly accurate, claimed, in retelling biblical history, that he added nothing and omitted nothing (*Antiq.* 1.17; cf. *Antiq.* 4.196; 20.260–261). In fact he omitted a great deal and added numerous items. He attributed to Moses, for example, the commandment to gather each week to study the law (*Against Apion* 2.175). This represents first-century practice but cannot be found in the Bible; and Josephus, if pressed, would have granted that to be true. He knew the Bible extremely well, and further he knew that many of his readers were equally well versed in it. Then why ascribe to Moses new commandments? We cannot precisely recapture his mental processes, but perhaps they went like this: It is an established tradition in our religion that we gather in synagogues on the sabbath to study the Scripture; this has been true as far back as anyone can remember; Moses himself must therefore have intended it; I shall use a shortcut and say that he commanded it.

Ancient historians regularly supplemented their narratives with freely created material of various kinds. They paid especial attention to the creation of suitable speeches for their heroes. Staying with Josephus, we may comment especially on the great speech which he attributes to the rebel leader Eleazar just before he and the other defenders of Matsada committed suicide rather than be captured (*War* 7.323–336, 341–389). Eleazar's speech holds up the ideals of Josephus himself (though Josephus did not live up to them); and this, the concluding event of the last battle of the great revolt, is marked by a suitable oration, though Josephus could not have known what Eleazar had actually said.

We should not exult too much over ancient historians. Below the very top level of academic biography modern authors frequently attribute statements to their subjects when, in the nature of the case, there could be no possible line of transmission. Most modern readers accept this, since the story is presented smoothly and authoritatively, without noting the absence of evidence. Ancient authors wrote in this way – only more so.

We have been considering the case of historians. Of our authors only Luke shows knowledge of the standards of Hellenistic historiography. Besides his claim of accuracy in his preface, we may also note his concern to establish dates (e.g. Luke 2.2; 3.1–2). He did not, however, carry this sort of historiographical concern through his gospel, and the body is written just as are Matthew and Mark: a collection of individual events and sayings put together in a convenient way, usually without substantial links from one to the next. Thus in most of Luke, and in Matthew and Mark, we are dealing with writing at a more 'popular' or 'folk' level than in the case of Josephus and other contemporary historians. Scholars often refer to the authors of the gospels as 'redactors', a term which points towards 'editing' rather than towards 'composition'. They gathered and arranged material, and they used what they found suitable. They did not, as far as we can tell, conduct research, cross-examine witnesses, compare accounts, and then offer only what was verified. They were a long way from being modern scholars. They were not even historians by the ancient standard (except, to a small degree, Luke).

Put another way, they were interested in the homiletical impact of their work, and their standards of 'accuracy' were more like those of ancient rhetoricians than those of ancient historians. The 'truth' of a given event or saying would be assessed according to the impact it made. If it testified to the value of faith, or inculcated high morals, or exemplified the Christian way of life, it would be used as true. And, in a very real sense, it may so be judged today. Numerous values are higher than empirical accuracy.

If we read ancient authors with the assumption that either they told the literal and verifiable truth or they lied, we shall badly misconstrue them. Ancient authors passed on legends, invented edifying speeches, and engaged in wishful thinking to an even greater degree than do modern 'popular' biographers and historians – which is saying a good deal. On the other hand, they also made use of good material, accurately remembered and transmitted. If we seek historical information – which is a valid quest – we must sift our sources critically. The only question, as we noted above, is our own critical breaking point. At some point doubts arise, at some point they become overwhelming. Scholarly reconstructions of ancient history are as artistic as they are scientific, and the principal aspect of the art is 'good judgment'. We must be neither too credulous nor too dismissive with regard to our sources. This topic will engage us in the final chapters.

In considering 'accuracy', we have raised two questions which deserve further mention: (1) Did the authors of the gospels do research? If they did, what information was available to them? (2) Why did they write? And how did they understand 'truth'?

• The authors' difficulties

When the authors of the present gospels came to write them, they faced a formidable task. Let us consider the situation of Luke. Of the early Christians known to us, he is most likely to have done historical research, and he explicitly wrote that he had worked at composing an accurate account.

Luke was probably a Gentile. There is no reason to think that he knew either biblical Hebrew or Aramaic, the language of Jesus and his first followers. The knowledge of geography shown in the gospel and Acts points to Asia Minor as his homeland. He does not know the geography of Palestine very well, but he correctly describes the paths across Asia Minor which Paul and other missionaries would have taken. It is the year 80 (let us say). Jesus' disciples are dead, most having met their end before the year 70. There has been a great war. The Jews rebelled, and the consequence was that parts of Galilee were ravaged, Jerusalem laid waste and the temple destroyed. Thousands had died, and more thousands had been sold as slaves.

Whatever records there had been had vanished, as had virtually all of the eyewitnesses of deeds done 50 years before.

Luke, having at least some of the instincts and interests of a Hellenistic historian, wanted to get things right, and to recount 'the things which have been accomplished among us' (1.1). What material did he have to work with? He had Mark, possibly a different short proto-gospel, possibly Matthew, one or more collections of sayings – and the Bible, that is, the Greek version of the Jewish scripture, which Greek-speaking Christians accepted as their Scripture. He did not have much else. He did not, for one thing, have access to Roman archives. Josephus, his contemporary, who wrote the account of the first Jewish war (66–73 or 74), did have such access, since his work was commissioned by the Flavians (Vespasian, who left the war to become Emperor, and Titus, who finished the war and shortly succeeded his father as Emperor). A comparison of Luke and Josephus, when they tell of the same event, inevitably shows that Josephus has the superior account.[5] He had not only Roman archives, but also Greek assistants to help him with research and writing.

Conceivably Luke could have gone to Palestine to enquire there about Jesus, his family, birth and childhood. This sort of research was not necessarily beyond an ancient historian. About a hundred years after Luke wrote, Philostratus, wishing to write the life of the sage Apollonius of Tyana, claimed to have travelled to find out more:

> I have gathered my information partly from the many cities where he [Apollonius] was loved, and partly from the temples whose long-neglected and decayed rites he restored, and partly from the accounts left of him by others and partly from his own letters (Philostratus, *Life of Apollonius of Tyana* I.2).

Subsequently we learn that Philostratus did not visit every important place in Apollonius' life (see V.3), but nevertheless we see that an ancient knew the value of on-site research. In the case of Luke, however, it appears that he did not go to Galilee: as we just said, his knowledge of the geography of the area was faulty. A substantial part of the gospel of Luke takes as its setting a journey from Galilee to Judaea. The way, Luke knew, would include Samaria. All three terms refer to geographical regions of the country: Galilee to the north, Samaria just below it, and Judaea immediately south of Samaria. In Jesus' lifetime Galilee was governed by Herod Antipas, while the geographical and ethnic region Samaria was administratively part of the Roman province of Judaea, ruled by the Roman prefect, at that time Pontius Pilate. Thus geographically Jesus went more-or-less straight south, from Galilee through Samaria to Judaea. When he entered Samaria, however, he changed jurisdictions, from that of Antipas to that of Pilate. Luke has Jesus enter Samaria at 9.51–56. Yet in 13.31–33 he is evidently in Galilee, since Pharisees warn him about Antipas. According to 17.11 while on the way to Jerusalem he 'passed along between Samaria and Galilee'. In 18.35–43 he is near Jericho, which is in Judaea, and he reaches the city in 19.1. He then arrives at Bethany and Bethphage, on the Mount of Olives, just outside Jerusalem (19.29). The only part of this itinerary which is natural and obvious is the trip from Jericho to Jerusalem via Bethany. It is

39

notable that Luke derived the route to Jerusalem via Jericho, Bethany, Bethphage and the Mount of Olives from a source: it is in Matt. 20.29–21.1//Mark 10.46–11.1.

A minor problem with Luke's itinerary is that Jericho is not on the direct route from Galilee to Jerusalem. There were three roads: (1) the westernmost route was through the hill country; (2) somewhat to the east, a road went along the west bank of the Jordan river; (3) farther to the east was a road on the east bank of the Jordan. It would be natural to go through Jericho if one took either route (2) or (3), and Matthew and Mark have (3): Jesus crossed the Jordan (Matt. 19.1//Mark 10.1), went south, then turned west, crossing the Jordan again, and thus went through Jericho and entered Jerusalem from the east. This is a reasonable and straightforward itinerary. Luke, however, depicts Jesus as going through the villages of Samaria, most of which were in the hill country. Thus, according to this itinerary, he went south into Samaria and only then turned east, took the road along the west bank of the Jordan farther south, passed through Jericho and so came to Jerusalem. This is by no means impossible, but it is not an obvious route.

The greater difficulty is that Luke seems to have been misinformed about the physical relationship of Galilee and Samaria. He depicts Jesus as being in Antipas' territory (Galilee) after he entered Samaria, which would make him retrace his steps from south to north. This is apparently not what Luke thought, as the statement that he 'passed *between* Samaria and Galilee' on his way south shows. Luke apparently thought, as Conzelmann pointed out, 'that Judaea and Galilee are immediately adjacent, and that Samaria lies alongside them, apparently bordering on both the regions'.[6] If Luke thought that Samaria lay mostly east of Galilee, rather than south, all his references become clear. Jesus headed generally south, from Galilee to Judaea, but wandered a bit back and forth between east and west, thus being sometimes in Galilee and sometimes in Samaria. This explains how he could be threatened by Antipas after he entered Samaria (13.11–13): he had not retraced his steps north, as the actual geography would require, but rather was walking south through two adjacent regions, being sometimes in Galilee and sometimes in Samaria. On Luke's geography, Jesus could walk south to Judaea by hugging the supposed north–south border between the other two regions (17.11).

It appears, then, that Luke had not travelled in Palestine. That he did not have access to accurate maps is equally true, and completely unsurprising. The wide distribution of accurate maps is an extremely modern enterprise. The Roman army, but perhaps few others apart from traders, had the advantages of good maps. Even Josephus, who lived in Palestine, shows the best and most detailed knowledge of those places where the Roman army fought: he had access to the commanders' accounts and notes.[7] Luke's knowledge of Palestinian geography also varies: in parts of Acts it is better than in the gospel, and this probably reveals the use of a source.[8]

Thus Luke's research did not include a personal tour of Galilee and Judaea and the gathering of local evidence. But even if he had made the trip it would have done little good. Who, 80 years later, would know about Jesus' birth and childhood? Looking back, it seems to moderns that Luke lived so near the time of Jesus' birth and infancy that his information must have been accurate. But 80 years is a long time, the people who had known Mary and Joseph were dead, and village records would probably not have survived the war. Even if he had undertaken research in the modern sense he probably could have discovered nothing. Luke had a few memoirs, but not full accounts of Jesus' life, and there was simply no way he could get them. So, he took what he had and did the best he could.

Sometimes, as we have seen, the best he could do was to pattern a narrative on biblical stories, but in other instances he could come closer to writing history according to the standards of his day. The clearest instance of his concern to meet the expectations of Hellenistic historiography is seen in his efforts to give chronology. John the Baptist, he writes, was conceived when Herod was king (1.5,24), and Jesus was conceived a few months later (1.26). According to 2.1–7 Jesus was born at the time of a census ordered by Augustus, while Quirinius was governor of Syria. This listing of official figures was one way of indicating dates and chronologies. There was no one standard way of counting the years, no one firm chronology, no counting of years BCE (or BC) and CE (or AD). Some authors dated the events from the time of the mythical founding of Rome, but many employed the method seen in Luke: in a certain year of a certain king or emperor, when a certain man was governor. One consequence of this situation was that it was easier to confuse dates then than now.

In the present case, Luke made a mistake. Herod died in the year 4 BCE and Quirinius was governor of Syria in the year CE 6–7; that is, ten years later.[9] It is not difficult to discover why Luke thought that Quirinius' census and Herod's reign overlapped. When Herod died in 4 BCE there were riots, which were not uncommon when there was a change of government. The Romans decided not to give all of Herod's kingdom to any one of his heirs. It was divided among several, and Judaea was given to Archelaus, who was granted the title not of king but 'ethnarch', 'head of the people'. He proved unsatisfactory, and in the year 6 CE he was deposed and exiled. Judaea then passed under direct government from Rome, and a census was taken for tax purposes. Censuses for such purposes were not popular, and there was again a riot.

Luke, looking back, having heard of great events but having no independent chronology, no standard system for saying what year something happened, simply got the two occasions confused. Jesus was born about the time of Herod's death, when there were riots, and that became conflated with the census and the riots in the year 6 – when, in fact, Quirinius was governor of Syria. Modern historians, with archives at their disposal, often make more serious mistakes.

Thus the situation is clear: Luke tried to write accurate history, even by our standards, at least some of the time; but his information was not adequate to the task. It describes him better, however, to say that he wished to write history according to the standards of the day. By those standards, he should have got the chronology right, and we may be sure that he would have been chagrined to know that he confused the two dates 4 BCE and CE 6.

We should emphasize again, however, that standards of his day involved other things than accurate chronology. They included 'propaganda': the effort to make a story turn out in such a way as to lead to a pre-formed conclusion. Luke wanted readers to believe that Jesus was the Christ, the Son of God, and he shaped his material towards that end (as we shall see more fully below). Further, the standards of the day allowed the creation of appropriate material. Historians, as we saw above, readily wrote speeches which they considered appropriate to the person and the occasion, without a shred of information, and Luke did the same, especially in Acts.

Finally, Luke shared with most other ancient historians a grave defect: a failure to understand and pursue cause and effect. Ramsey MacMullen put it this way:

> Vegetius and Jerome, discussing matters that seem to require the drawing of parallels to their own times from the 200s A.D., go back instead to the 200s B.C. They are not ignorant. They have their books. History is spread out before their eyes, but they see only events and persons floating loose in a timeless past, without caused links between them – a gallery of isolated portraits and anecdotes made classical by remoteness.[10]

This can readily be exemplified by studying Josephus, who was close in time and ability to Luke – though, as we saw, he had greater resources. One can derive from his pages information about why the Jews revolted against Rome, but his own comments on cause and effect show that he could not form sound judgments. Thus, for example, he wrote that in the year 65 the lesser clergy, the Levites, asked to be allowed to wear the white robes of the greater clergy, the priests. The request was allowed, and Josephus attributes the approaching doom to this break with tradition (*Antiq.* 20.216–218). A study of his work reveals much more likely causes, such as the greed and dishonesty of some of the Roman administrators, and the lack of concern which some showed for Jewish religious sensitivities. Pilate, for example, provoked the Jews by bringing into Jerusalem troops bearing Roman standards, which some thought transgressed the commandment prohibiting graven images. These real causes stand in Josephus side by side with explanations of the coming destruction which we can no longer consider sound.

When we study the gospels we shall see this same defect with regard to cause and effect. They offer no clear answer to an obvious question, 'Why was Jesus executed as a would-be king?', and here they simply share the weaknesses of their contemporaries.

We have chosen Luke for the discussion of the gospels as histories or biographies because he at least knew something of the writing of history in the Hellenistic world. The authors of the other gospels desired even less to write what we would call 'history'. They had other concerns. We noted above that the gospels can be compared to certain rhetorical forms, and Philip Shuler has argued that Matthew is modelled on one of these, the *encomium*.[11] An encomium has as its essential aspect the shaping of material so as to praise or blame the subject. Biographical material is used, but there is no attempt to achieve a dispassionate and objective portrayal. On the contrary, the aim is to praise or condemn.

This ends the long discussion of what the gospels are not. The authors had concerns which were far greater than those we have been considering, and we now turn to a brief account of them. The full description of what each gospel *is* and of how its goals are pursued will be taken up in Part III.

• Why they were written: fact and truth

We have been emphasizing that the gospels are not 'history' or 'biography' in the modern scientific sense. The authors were interested in conveying the 'truth' about Jesus, but it did not occur to them to equate 'truth' simply with 'matters of fact'. It will be helpful here to sketch some of the motives behind the composition of the gospels – the concerns which the authors put well ahead of conveying raw data.

The gospels were written in part to evangelize on behalf of the Christian movement and in part to instruct those who were already converted in correct Christian behaviour and belief. They also offered members of the early movement 'ammunition' to use against opponents, both for offensive and defensive purposes. These aims are easily illustrated.

1. Evangelization. At the end of Mark we read that a Roman centurion, standing by at the crucifixion of Jesus, said 'Truly this man was the Son of God!' (Mark 15.39). The author doubtless intended this to be the response of the reader of the gospel, and along the way one sees the same purpose at work. Early in Mark a heavenly voice proclaims Jesus as 'Son of God' (Mark 1.11), and he is addressed as 'Son of God' by a demon in 5.7. Proclamation by a heavenly voice and by enemies (the demons and one of his executors) serves the function of persuading the reader that what they said was true.

2. Instruction. The teaching function of much of the material in the gospels can best be illustrated from Matthew. In Matt. 18 Jesus admonishes his followers (and in this way the author admonishes the readers) to be humble, as are children (Matt. 18.4), to deal carefully with those who wrong them (18.15–20), and to forgive a transgressor not just seven times, but seventy times seven (18.22).

3. Offence and defence. The third purpose for the writing of the gospels – ammunition against opponents, or sometimes a defensive shield – is seen especially in the controversies over the sabbath. The early Christians considered Jesus to be the Messiah of Israel, yet in many parts of the Christian movement, and finally in most forms of Christianity, observance of parts of the law was given up. The opponent could say to the church: 'If Jesus is the Messiah of Israel, Son of the God of Israel, why do you not obey all the laws given by God to Israel?' This is a much stronger argument than moderns immediately realize. Selectivity in obeying the Mosaic law is now centuries old, and most modern Christians do not feel the force of the argument of first-century Jews: 'You Christians say that our Bible is Scripture, yet you act as if you are free to obey it or not.' The actual history which resulted in allowing parts of the law to lapse is complicated, and it will suffice to say here that the issue led to serious disputes within the Christian movement itself, as can be seen especially in Gal. 1–2. The synoptic gospels, however, do not trace the history and the debates. They are content when they have attributed to Jesus, their Lord, a statement which defends church practice: the Messiah himself allowed his disciples to transgress the sabbath and food laws (Mark 2.23–28; 7.14–23). In ch. 20 we shall deal briefly with the passage on food in Mark 7, and there we shall point out that it is Mark's setting which leads to the conclusion that Jesus 'abolished' the Jewish food laws, not

necessarily the sayings which are attributed to him. It appears that Mark has created a defence of the non-observance of this aspect of the law.

Matthew 23, above all, shows that the Christian movement could go on the attack. If the passages on the sabbath and law for the most part are defensive, justifying Christian non-observance, many other comments are critical of the way other Jews observed the law. The scribes and Pharisees are accused, for example, of obeying minor parts of the law and neglecting 'weightier matters' (Matt. 23.23). Scribes and Pharisees are accused of not obeying the law well enough in Matt. 5.20. Whether or not this material ultimately goes back to Jesus, the way it is collected in Matthew probably shows that at some period a Christian community had assembled material which could serve as ammunition in its debate with non-Christian Judaism.

Thus we see that the gospels were not written primarily to convey facts, but to achieve different ends. There is, however, another side to the matter. There is hard historical evidence in the gospels, and the material which the evangelists used for their own purposes may *also* be historically true. In studying the synoptics we must beware of two extremes. Against modern fundamentalism we argue not only that it is incorrect to think that everything in the Bible is historically accurate, but also that it is equally wrong to judge it by the standard of historical and biographical accuracy as moderns perceive it, a standard with which the biblical authors themselves would not have agreed – though Luke would have appreciated the clarification of dates.

Against the other extreme we argue that the gospels contain a good number of historically accurate matters of fact. One generation of liberal scholarship renounced the possibility or even the desirability of finding historical information about Jesus in the gospels. In our opinion it was wrong to do so. In many places it has been the vogue to teach the synoptics as 'novels' or 'dramas'. This has merit for understanding the gospels as literary works, but it is often resorted to by people who think that there is no history in them; and there, we are sure, they are mistaken. In this book we shall get to the historical Jesus only in the final chapters, but we want to emphasize that we think that the gospels provide information about him.

It is important to note that the authors chose, as the medium for conveying their message, a narrative about Jesus. Their purposes – evangelizing, instructing and the like – could have been served in another way. Paul, for example, whose letters constitute our earliest sources for knowledge of the new movement, had all the aims of the authors of the gospels: to convert, to instruct, to strengthen, to attack opponents and to defend himself. But he did not, as far as we know, try to achieve them by writing a narrative about Jesus' life and teaching. A few times he attributes a saying directly to Jesus, but his letters are noteworthy for the small amount of information about Jesus which can be gleaned from them. His most extended narration of the basic facts of his gospel, I Cor. 15.3–10, begins with the death of Jesus and does not mention his life. What is true of Paul is true of the rest of the New Testament. James has lots of moral instruction, but no information about Jesus. I Peter counsels and comforts Christians in distress, but not by quoting Jesus.[12]

The gospels, then, stand out as accomplishing their aims by telling about Jesus. We must, therefore, attribute to the authors the intention of conveying information about Jesus of Nazareth. Further, they succeeded in doing so. That was not their only success. Teaching by means of telling stories about Jesus has proved to be extremely effective. People who find Paul convoluted and irritating, and I Peter dull and unimaginative, are interested and intrigued by the gospels. We refer here to both believers and non-believers. Jesus, throughout the centuries, has had a good press. People who actively dislike organized Christianity often admire Jesus. The Jesus whom they admire, of course, is the Jesus of the evangelists. The gospels deserve the closest attention.

- Why we study them

We study the synoptic gospels for reasons which are different from those which led their authors to write them. It is certainly possible to read them in ways that accord with their own purposes: proclaiming the Christian faith, instructing believers, defending the institutions of Christianity and inspiring public and private worship. Academic study, however, has its own aims, which, while not inimical to worship and evangelism, are different from them. The modern university – and consequently all study which, in the modern world, can be called 'scholarly' – aims at *disinterested* inquiry. 'Disinterested' does not mean either 'uninterested' or (we hope) 'uninterest-ing', but rather this: not committed to conclusions in advance of the study of the evidence. It cannot be an aim of the academic study of the gospels to establish the truth of Christianity, nor the truth of one version of it over another. We cannot intend in advance to show that the supreme ethicist of The Sermon on the Mount (Matt. 5–7), or the somewhat pedantic teacher of Matt. 18, or the fiery proclaimer of the end of all things (Mark 13) or the friend of widows and orphans (Luke 7.11–17), or the callous friend of Lazarus (John 11.1–6) is the 'real' Jesus. We cannot intend in advance to show that Mark is a theological drama, or that Matthew can be stratified into three layers of composition. Jesus may have been correctly caught in one or more of the mini-portraits of him just referred to; the compositional history of the gospels may be 'dramatic' or 'geological', or some of both. To start with we must study with open minds.

- Topics

Most people who have read the gospels have read them with the desire to know about Jesus, and that remains the case today. Jesus is one of the most important figures of history, the gospels tell about things he did and words he said, and so naturally people read them to find out about him. 'The quest of the historical Jesus' has been one of the main activities of New Testament scholars for two hundred years, it remains a major activity, and it is a substantial interest of this book (Part V).

While searching the gospels for the historical Jesus, scholars discovered that they could identify material which was developed (that is, either created or altered) between the death of Jesus and the composition of the final gospels. If such material can be identified, it is very valuable, since we have little information about the earliest forms of Christianity. There is a 'tunnel period' between the death of Jesus and the Pauline letters, that is, from about CE 30 to 50, about which we know very little – unless it is embedded in the gospels. We shall consider 'form criticism', which offers the hope of finding information about the early church as well as about Jesus (Part III).

We shall discuss attempts to discover the theology of each of the final evangelists. Their theology may be directly expressed, but usually it is not. Hints of theological shaping must come from the study of arrangement of passages, the quantity of certain types of material and the like. Looking for hints of this type is a less obvious effort than looking for the historical Jesus, and an example may help. Martin Gilbert has just completed the official biography of Winston Churchill. He has been faced with a problem quite different from that faced by New Testament scholars, but still instructive for them: he has had too much evidence. He had Churchill's own voluminous writings, speeches and minutes; public information (newspapers, Hansard); references to things he said and did in diaries and private letters of many who knew him. Gilbert adopted the tactic of letting Churchill speak for himself, and the direct voice of the historian and biographer is seldom heard. That means neither that he has no views nor that they cannot be identified. For example: Churchill was and is known to have drunk alcohol frequently, throughout the day. It has been proposed that sometimes he was not up to his normal powers because of drink. Gilbert obviously thinks this not to be true, but he says nothing about it directly, in his own voice. He does, however, repeatedly insert, in a noticeable place, material which bears on the question and which shows that Churchill did not often drink too much. (It is of interest to note that this illustration was composed in 1987, before the publication of the last volume, and before an interview in which Gilbert made precisely this point. We correctly inferred his view from his arrangement and treatment of evidence.)

In a similar way the gospels can be canvassed for hints as to the views – or theologies – of their final authors, even though they do not often speak in their own voice (Redaction criticism, ch. 14).

Finally, we shall give accounts of efforts to find, through literary analysis, the 'meaning' or 'meanings' of the gospels. This is not a quest for theological truth, but for the meaningfulness of the texts as literature. Here another example will be helpful. In Shakespeare's Richard II, John of Gaunt gives a stirring and well-known speech about England. One could ask whether John of Gaunt ever said anything of the sort, where Shakespeare got the idea for the speech, and even whether it is correct, from the medical and military points of view, that the sea has protected England from disease and war. But a literary critic would ask about such topics as the function of the speech in the play as a whole and audience response to it. Scholars have studied the gospels as literature, and in chapters on Structuralism, Rhetorical criticism and Genre (chs 15–19) we shall discuss some of these efforts.

• Terminology

New Testament scholars have adopted the practice of speaking of different kinds of 'criticism'. 'Source criticism' is the effort to find the earliest gospel, or sources now lost but used by one or more of them. 'Form criticism' is the analysis of individual passages (called 'pericopes'), to determine their origin, development and use. 'Redaction criticism' is the study of the theology and compositional habits of the evangelists. 'Literary criticism' investigates the meaning of the gospels as literature.

The first three of these are mutually interdependent and mutually useful for understanding (1) the historical Jesus; (2) the earliest forms of Christianity; (3) the theology of the evangelists.

To understand the synoptics we must analyse them closely. They pose the most difficult technical problems in the study of early Christianity, but the expenditure of effort is well repayed. The first problem which meets the attentive reader is also the most complex: the question of how they are related to one another and to prior collections of material about Jesus. To this question, called 'the synoptic problem', we now turn.

Part Two
The Synoptic Problem

3 The Basic Relationships and the Common Solution

Matthew, Mark and Luke are remarkably alike. There are examples from mediaeval literature of works which agree as closely[1], but from ancient literature no other examples of such close similarity are known. F. Gerald Downing, making the reasonable assumption that Luke's method may have been much like Josephus', has noted that, in rewriting biblical sources, Josephus never copied as closely as did Luke in rewriting the story of Jesus.[2] The motives for such close copying are difficult to ascertain, but the first assumption is respect for their sources or predecessors. Whatever the reasons, the synoptics are so close to one another that virtually all students of them have concluded that the relationship depends on direct literary copying from one gospel to another, or from common sources. It is especially to be noted that there is extensive verbatim (word-for-word) agreement in Greek, which can hardly be explained by independent knowledge of the sayings of Jesus in Aramaic.

People have been studying the interrelationships of the synoptics for centuries. Eusebius, the church historian of the early fourth century, devised a system for finding the parallel passages, and these reference numbers, called 'the canons of Eusebius' may still be found in the Nestle-Aland text.[3] In 1774 J. J. Griesbach made public a new and superior way of comparing the synoptic accounts. Gospel harmonies had previously been devised (a single running account which conflates the gospels where they agree and intersperses material where they disagree), and the gospels had even been printed in parallel columns before, but Griesbach's was the first critical synopsis which enabled scholars to study the literary relationships among the gospels.[4] Griesbach's synopsis, like the many other synopses published subsequently, allows all three gospels to be studied side by side and thus simultaneously. The use of a synopsis is crucial for the study of the synoptic gospels.

The principal synopses now in current use – of which all but the first are now in print – are these:

1. Albert Huck, *Synopsis of the First Three Gospels*, 9th ed. revised by Hans Lietzmann, Eng. ed. by F. L. Cross, 1935.

2. Kurt Aland, *Synopsis Quattuor Evangeliorum*, 1964 and subsequent years; Greek-English ed., *Synopsis of the Four Gospels*, 2nd ed., 1975.
3. Albert Huck, *Synopsis of the First Three Gospels*, 13th ed., revised by Heinrich Greeven, with the addition of the Johannine Parallels, 1981. This synopsis, which will be referred to as Greeven, is a superb technical achievement, though the arrangement of the parallels makes it often difficult to follow.
4. B. H. Throckmorton, *Gospel Parallels. A Synopsis of the First Three Gospels*, 1949 and subsequent years. This is an English version of no. 1, using the RSV. Now that the Greek text to which this is parallel is out of print, its usefulness will decline, but it remains an inexpensive and convenient way of seeing how the synoptics parallel one another.
5. H. F. D. Sparks, *A Synopsis of the Gospels. The Synoptic Gospels with the Johannine Parallels*, London, 1964 and subsequent years. This is an English synopsis, and it offers some advantages over Throckmorton.
6. J. B. Orchard, *A Synopsis of the Four Gospels*, 1983. This synopsis is available in both Greek and English. Passages are given in the order of Matthew, and this is very inconvenient if one starts with a reference to Mark or Luke.
7. Robert W. Funk, *New Gospel Parallels*, 2 vols, 1985. This is an English synopsis, using the RSV, and including the Gospel of John, the Gospel of Thomas, and parallels in other early Christian literature. Each gospel is presented in its own order in the left-hand column, with parallels given to the right. Agreements with the lead gospel are in bold type. Unfortunately, these are agreements in the English of the RSV, not necessarily agreements in Greek.

The best synopsis overall is, in our view, Aland's, despite the extra space and money required by the inclusion of all of John; and the text of Aland will be followed for our examples. We shall, however, also give the pericope numbers of Greeven and Throckmorton (which are the same as those of Huck-Lietzmann, for those fortunate enough to own it).

It is necessary that students be able to see for themselves how the synoptics relate to one another. Summary generalizations do not fully reveal the situation, and some direct marking of the text is required. The use of coloured pens to show agreements and disagreements is the simplest means of allowing them to be seen, and the student is urged to mark in a synopsis the sample pericopes in this and the following chapters.

Studying 'the synoptic problem' is a difficult and intricate task, one that requires close attention to minutiae. It was once hoped that solving the relationships among the gospels would reveal the source or sources which were closest to the raw material about Jesus, and that a life of Jesus could be written on the basis of the earliest written source[s]. This hope has long since been given up, and it has been realized that the way to get back to Jesus is to delve behind *each passage* – to use, that is, form criticism (Part III). But to get behind each passage, one needs to know its earliest form, and studying the synoptic problem is a means towards that goal. A solution to the synoptic problem is also necessary if one is to study the theology of each gospel and overall tendencies of each gospel. One learns something about the various ways in which the same pericope was used in different branches of the church (Redaction criticism, Part IV).

The close study of the text which marking requires pays off in a further way: it requires attention to *what is there*. There is no better discipline for learning the details of the gospel material.

There are various colour schemes, and one is not necessarily better than another. We find this one to be convenient:

red	agreements between Matthew and Mark
blue	agreements between Mark and Luke
green	agreements between Matthew and Luke
any combination of two colours	agreements among all three
broken lines	agreement in the word, in the word root, or other substantial agreement, but not agreement in precise form

Because printing in colours is prohibitively expensive, we shall mark a sample pericope by using **bold type**, underlining and slanted (*italic*) characters. We shall not continue to mark pericopes, however, partly again because of the cost, but partly because black and white marking is harder to follow than is marking in colour. Readers should mark the pericopes which follow, using colour. This helps to make sense of the discussion, and it also encourages close attention to the text.

- Summary of synoptic relationships

When the entire synopsis is studied, a few basic facts stand out. We shall later see that there are exceptions to many of the following generalizations, but these eight points represent the majority of cases.

1. The same passages often appear in all three synoptics. These passages constitute **the triple tradition**.

2. In the triple tradition all three synoptics often agree in the placement of the material. When all three do not agree, Mark's arrangement is supported by either Matthew or Luke. The easiest way to see this is by looking at the coloured chart prepared by Allan Barr.[5] One may also, however, simply turn the pages of a synopsis, most of which have some way of indicating what is in the same sequence and what not. In Aland's synopsis pericopes in the same sequence are in ordinary type and the headings which indicate where the pericope is are in bold type. The headings of pericopes out of sequence are in light type. In Greeven's synopsis pericopes in the same sequence are in ordinary type and the headings are in bold type. Pericopes which are out of sequence are in light italics.

3. With regard to substance, about 90% of Mark is also found in Matthew and more than 50% also in Luke. Overall contents cannot be exemplified by individual passages, but the point will be seen if one studies an index of the gospel parallels (printed at the back in Aland and Greeven, at the beginning in Throckmorton, and at the beginning of each gospel in Funk). The statistic will be discussed further below

53

(p. 62). In pericopes which are in common, verbatim agreement varies, but on average is about 50%.

4. In the triple tradition, besides verbatim agreements among all three, there are substantial agreements between Matthew and Mark against Luke, and between Mark and Luke against Matthew, but relatively few agreements between Matthew and Luke against Mark. Another way of putting this is to say that, when either Matthew or Luke disagrees with Mark, the other agrees.

5. It is especially noteworthy that agreement between Matthew and Luke begins where Mark begins and ends where Mark ends. Mark's gospel starts with John the Baptist. Matthew and Luke both have birth narratives before the appearance and preaching of John, but they do not agree. They begin to agree with the first passage about the Baptist. Similarly Mark ends with the women fleeing from the empty tomb. Matthew and Luke have resurrection accounts after the discovery of the empty tomb, but they do not agree with each other.

6. This same phenomenon occurs within individual pericopes.

Points 2 through 6 show that, in the triple tradition, **Mark is the middle term**. It is closer to both Matthew and Luke than they are to each other. All solutions to the synoptic problem must reckon with this fact. We shall see below that it leads many to think that Mark was the first gospel, some to think that it was third. This will become clearer when examples have been studied. Now, however, we turn to another large body of material.

7. Matthew and Luke have in common a good deal of material which is not in Mark, approximately 200 verses. Virtually all of it is sayings material. Verbatim agreement varies a great deal, from 100% to very little. This material is called **the double tradition**.

8. The material in the double tradition is not arranged the same way in the two gospels.

These facts, as we said, are true in the majority of cases, though we shall see in the next chapter that there are exceptions to each rule and complications of various kinds. Before dealing with complications and possible explanations of them, we shall exemplify some of the basic general points which have just been listed. In giving individual passages we shall first of all concentrate on **verbatim agreement**. The points about the arrangement of pericopes (nos. 2, 5 and 8) will be illustrated as far as is possible, but some can be seen only by looking at a synopsis.

• Sample pericopes

Our procedure will be first to restate the rule and then to give one or more examples. The first example will be printed in full, in both Greek and English, to help the reader get started. As we proceed, the manner of presentation will be simplified, and usually we shall print the pericope only in English. The translation used is the RSV, altered where necessary to show agreements and disagreements in the Greek which are not apparent in the RSV. English even when altered will sometimes be misleading with regard to precise agreements and disagreements. The marking in the English version of the first pericope represents agreements in Greek. Readers are again urged to mark their own synopses or the samples in this book in colour. The black and white code used in the first pericope is this:

underlining	agreement between Matt. and Mark
bold type	agreement between Mark and Luke
both (in text of Mark)	agreements among all three
italic type	agreements between Matt. and Luke only

Points 1 and 4: Often all three gospels agree; there are further substantial agreements between Matthew and Mark and between Mark and Luke, but only a few between Matthew and Luke.

Pericope 1: 'If Anyone would Come after Me', *Mark 8.34–9.1 and parr.*
Aland 160; Greeven 137; Throckmorton 123

Matt. 16.24–28	Mark 8.34–9.1	Luke 9.23–27
²⁴Τότε ὁ Ἰησοῦς εἶπεν τοῖς μαθηταῖς αὐτοῦ εἴ τις θέλει ὀπίσω μου ἐλθεῖν, ἀπαρνησάσθω ἑαυτὸν καὶ ἀράτω τὸν σταυρὸν αὐτοῦ καὶ ἀκολουθείτω μοι. ²⁵ὃς γὰρ ἐὰν θέλῃ τὴν ψυχὴν αὐτοῦ σῶσαι ἀπολέσει αὐτήν· ὃς δ' ἂν ἀπολέσῃ τὴν ψυχὴν αὐτοῦ ἕνεκεν ἐμοῦ εὑρήσει αὐτήν. ²⁶τί γὰρ ὠφεληθήσεται ἄνθρωπος ἐὰν τὸν κόσμον ὅλον κερδήσῃ, τὴν δὲ ψυχὴν αὐτοῦ ζημιωθῇ; ἢ τί δώσει ἄνθρωπος ἀντάλλαγμα τῆς ψυχῆς αὐτοῦ;	³⁴Καὶ προσκαλεσάμενος τὸν ὄχλον σὺν τοῖς μαθηταῖς αὐτοῦ εἶπεν αὐτοῖς· εἴ τις θέλει ὀπίσω μου ἀκολουθεῖν, ἀπαρνησάσθω ἑαυτὸν καὶ ἀράτω τὸν σταυρὸν αὐτοῦ καὶ ἀκολουθείτω μοι. ³⁵ὃς γὰρ ἐὰν θέλῃ τὴν ψυχὴν αὐτοῦ σῶσαι ἀπολέσει αὐτήν· ὃς δ' ἂν ἀπολέσει τὴν ψυχὴν αὐτοῦ ἕνεκεν ἐμοῦ καὶ τοῦ εὐαγγελίου σώσει αὐτήν. ³⁶τί γὰρ ὠφελεῖ ἄνθρωπον κερδῆσαι τὸν κόσμον ὅλον καὶ ζημιωθῆναι τὴν ψυχὴν αὐτοῦ; ³⁷τί γὰρ δοῖ ἄνθρωπος ἀντάλλαγμα τῆς ψυχῆς αὐτοῦ; ³⁸ὃς γὰρ ἐὰν ἐπαισχυνθῇ με καὶ τοὺς ἐμοὺς λόγους ἐν τῇ γενεᾷ ταύτῃ τῇ μοιχαλίδι καὶ ἁμαρτωλῷ, καὶ ὁ υἱὸς τοῦ ἀνθρώπου ἐπαισχυνθήσεται αὐτόν, ὅταν ἔλθῃ ἐν τῇ δόξῃ τοῦ πατρὸς αὐτοῦ μετὰ τῶν ἀγγέλων τῶν ἁγίων.	²³Ἔλεγεν δὲ πρὸς πάντας· εἴ τις θέλει ὀπίσω μου ἔρχεσθαι, ἀρνησάσθω ἑαυτὸν καὶ ἀράτω τὸν σταυρὸν αὐτοῦ καθ' ἡμέραν καὶ ἀκολουθείτω μοι. ²⁴ὃς γὰρ ἂν θέλῃ τὴν ψυχὴν αὐτοῦ σῶσαι ἀπολέσει αὐτήν· ὃς δ' ἂν ἀπολέσῃ τὴν ψυχὴν αὐτοῦ ἕνεκεν ἐμοῦ οὗτος σώσει αὐτήν. ²⁵τί γὰρ ὠφελεῖται ἄνθρωπος κερδήσας τὸν κόσμον ὅλον ἑαυτὸν δὲ ἀπολέσας ἢ ζημιωθείς; ²⁶ὃς γὰρ ἂν ἐπαισχυνθῇ με καὶ τοὺς ἐμοὺς λόγους, τοῦτον ὁ υἱὸς τοῦ ἀνθρώπου ἐπαισχυνθήσεται, ὅταν ἔλθῃ ἐν τῇ δόξῃ αὐτοῦ καὶ τοῦ πατρὸς καὶ τῶν ἁγίων ἀγγέλων.
²⁷μέλλει γὰρ ὁ υἱὸς τοῦ ἀνθρώπου ἔρχεσθαι ἐν τῇ δόξῃ τοῦ πατρὸς αὐτοῦ μετὰ τῶν ἀγγέλων αὐτοῦ, καὶ τότε ἀποδώσει ἑκάστῳ κατὰ τὴν πρᾶξιν αὐτοῦ. ²⁸ἀμὴν λέγω ὑμῖν ὅτι	9 ¹καὶ ἔλεγεν αὐτοῖς· ἀμὴν λέγω ὑμῖν ὅτι	²⁷λέγω δὲ ὑμῖν ἀληθῶς,

Matt. 16.24-28	Mark 8.34-9.1	Luke 9.23-37

εἰσίν τινες τῶν ὧδε ἑστώτων
οἵτινες οὐ μὴ γεύσωνται θανά-
του ἕως ἂν ἴδωσιν τὸν υἱὸν τοῦ
ἀνθρώπου ἐρχόμενον ἐν τῇ βα-
σιλείᾳ αὐτοῦ.

εἰσίν τινες ὧδε τῶν ἑστηκότων
οἵτινες οὐ μὴ γεύσωνται θανά-
του ἕως ἂν ἴδωσιν

τὴν βα-
σιλείαν τοῦ θεοῦ ἐληλυθυῖαν ἐν
δυνάμει.

εἰσίν τινες τῶν αὐτοῦ ἑστηκότων
οἳ οὐ μὴ γεύσωνται θανά-
του ἕως ἂν ἴδωσιν

τὴν βα-
σιλείαν τοῦ θεοῦ.

Pericope 1: 'If Anyone would Come after Me', *Mark 8.34–9.1 and parr.*
Aland 160; Greeven 137; Throckmorton 123

Matt. 16.24–28	Mark 8.34–9.1	Luke 9.23–27

Matt. 16.24–28

24Then Jesus said to his disciples,
'If any one
would come after me, let him deny
himself and take up his
cross and fol-
low me. 25For whoever would
save his life will
lose it, and whoever loses
his life for my sake

will find it. 26For what
will it profit a man, if
he gains the whole world
and forfeits his life?
Or what shall a man give in return
for his life?

27For
the Son of man is to come
with his angels in the glory
of his Father, and
then he will repay every man for
what he has done. 28Truly, I say to

Mark 8.34–9.1

34And he called to him
the multitude with his disciples,
and said to them, 'If any one
would follow after me, let him deny
himself and take up his
cross and fol-
low me. 35For whoever would
save his life will
lose it; and whoever loses
his life for my sake
and the gospel's
will save it. 36For what
does it profit a man,
to gain the whole world
and forfeit his life?
37For what can a man give in return
for his life? 38For
whoever is ashamed of me and of
my words in this adulterous
and sinful generation,
of him will the Son of man also
be ashamed, when he comes
in the glory
of his Father with the holy angels.'

91And
he said to them, 'Truly, I say to

Luke 9.23–27

23And he said
to all, 'If any one
would come after me, let him deny
himself and take up his
cross daily and fol-
low me. 24For whoever would
save his life will
lose it; and whoever loses
his life for my sake,

he will save it. 25For what
does it profit a man
if he gains the whole world
and loses or forfeits himself?

26For
whoever is ashamed of me and of
my words,

of him will the Son of man
be ashamed when he comes
in his glory and the glory
of the Father and of the holy angels.

27But I say to you truly,

56

Matt. 16.24-28	Mark 8.34-9.1	Luke 9.23-27
you, there are some standing here who will not taste death before they see the Son of man coming in his kingdom.'	you, there are some standing here who will not taste death before they see that the kingdom of God has come with power.'	there are some standing here who will not taste death before they see the kingdom of God.'

In this example (which in Greeven skips from p. 131 to p. 134) we see that many of the words appear in all three gospels. The introductions, however, are a bit different. In Matthew the sayings are addressed to disciples, in Mark to the crowd with his disciples, and in Luke to all [the disciples]. We shall discuss the significance of different 'settings' in Form Criticism.

In addition to the triple agreements Matthew and Mark have some words in common which are not in Luke: e.g. 'to his disciples' in Mark 8.34; 'what can a man give in return for his life' in Mark 8.37. Against Matthew, Mark and Luke have 'will save' where Matthew has 'will find' (Mark 8.35); 'whoever is ashamed of me and my words' in Mark 8.38; 'the kingdom of God' in Mark 9.1, against Matthew's 'the Son of man in his kingdom'. Matthew and Luke agree against Mark in having 'if anyone' in the first verse, against Mark's 'whoever' (though this agreement depends on a disputed reading, and in some texts, including Aland, all three have 'if anyone'), and they have 'come' instead of Mark's 'follow' (Mark 8.34). They also agree in not having Mark's 'and the gospel's' (8.35) or 'this adulterous and sinful generation' (Mark 8.38). Finally, we note that Luke 9.23 has 'daily' after 'take up his cross'; this is important for redaction criticism, for it indicates Luke's concern to shift the saying from a crisis situation to one of everyday life.

Pericope 2: Plucking Grain on the Sabbath, *Mark 2.23–28 and parr.*
Aland 46; Greeven 81; Throckmorton 69

Matt. 12.1–8	Mark 2.23–28	Luke 6.1–5
[1]At that time Jesus went through the grainfields on the sabbath; his disciples were hungry, and they began to pluck heads of grain to eat. [2]But when the Pharisees saw it, they said to him, 'Look, your disciples are doing what is not lawful to do on the sabbath.' [3]He said to them, 'Have you not read what David did, when	[23]One sabbath he was going through the grainfields; and as they made their way his disciples began to pluck heads of grain. [24]And the Pharisees said to him, 'Look, why are they doing what is not lawful on the sabbath?' [25]And he says to them, 'Have you never read what David did, when	[1]On a sabbath, while he was going through the grainfields, his disciples plucked and ate some heads of grain, rubbing them in their hands. [2]But some of the Pharisees said, 'Why are you doing what is not lawful to do on the sabbath?' [3]And Jesus answering said 'Have you not read what David did when

Matt. 12.1-8	Mark 2.23-28	Luke 6.1-5
he was hungry, and those who were with him: [4]how he entered the house of God and ate the bread of the Presence, which it was not lawful for him to eat nor for those who were with him, but for the priests alone? [5]Or have you not read in the law how on the sabbath the priests in the temple profane the sabbath, and are guiltless? [6]I tell you, something greater than the temple is here. [7]And if you had known what this means, "I desire mercy, and not sacrifice", you would not have condemned the guiltless.	he was in need and was hungry, he and those who were with him: [26]how he entered the house of God, when Abiathar was high priest, and ate the bread of the Presence, which it is not lawful for any but the priests to eat, and also gave it to those who were with him?'	he was hungry, he and those who were with him: [4]how he entered the house of God, and took and ate the bread of the Presence, which it is not lawful for any except the priests alone to eat, and also gave it to those with him?'
	[27]And he said to them, 'The sabbath was made for people, not people for the sabbath; [28]so the Son of man is lord even of the sabbath.'	[5]And he said to them, 'The Son of man is lord of the sabbath.'
[8]For the Son of man is lord of the sabbath.'		

We shall comment less fully on the second pericope and point out only that Matthew and Luke agree four times against Mark: they have 'and eat' in the first verse, which may be considered a natural expansion, independently made by each. In Matt. 12.4 they share the word 'alone', also perhaps an obvious expansion. In Matt. 12.3 they have 'he said' for Mark's 'he says'; both avoid the historic present. Most importantly, Matthew and Luke agree against Mark in not having Mark 2.27, 'the sabbath was made for people, not people for the sabbath'.

Points 2 and 4: Where Matthew or Luke do not both support Mark, one of them does. This includes both verbatim agreement (point 4) and agreements in the arrangement of material (agreements in order, point 2).

Pericope 3: True Greatness, *Mark 9.33–37 and parr.*
Aland 166; Greeven 143; Throckmorton 129

Matt. 18.1–5	Mark 9.33–37	Luke 9.46–48
	[33]And they came to Capernaum; and when he was in the house he asked them, 'What were you discussing on the way?' [34]But they were silent; for on the way they had discussed with one another who was the greatest.	
[1]At that time the disciples came to Jesus, saying, 'Who is the greatest in the kingdom of heaven?'		[46]And an argument arose among them as to which of them was the greatest.

Matt. 18.1-5	Mark 9.33-37	Luke 9.46-48
	³⁵And he sat down and called the twelve; and he said to them, 'If any one would be first, he must be last of all and servant of all.'	
²And calling to him a child, he put him in the midst of them, ³and said, 'Truly, I say to you, unless you turn and become like children, you will never enter the kingdom of heaven. ⁴Whoever humbles himself like this child, he is the greatest in the kingdom of heaven.	³⁶And he took a child, and put him in the midst of them; and taking him in his arms, he said to them,	⁴⁷But when Jesus perceived the thought of their hearts, he took a child and put him by his side, ⁴⁸and said to them,
⁵Whoever receives one such child in my name receives me;'	³⁷'Whoever receives one such child in my name receives me; and whoever receives me, receives not me but him who sent me.'	'Whoever receives this child in my name receives me, and whoever receives me receives him who sent me; for he who is least among you all is the one who is great.'

Pericope 4: Jesus Blesses the Children, *Mark 10.13–16 and parr.*
Aland 253; Greeven 202; Throckmorton 188

Matt. 19.13–15	Mark 10.13–16	Luke 18.15–17
(18.3)		
¹³Then children were brought to him that he might lay his hands on them and pray. The disciples rebuked the people; ¹⁴but Jesus said, 'Let the children come to me, and do not hinder them; for to such belongs the kingdom of heaven.' (18.3)	¹³And they were bringing children to him, that he might touch them; and the disciples rebuked them. ¹⁴But when Jesus saw it he was indignant, and said to them, 'Let the children come to me, do not hinder them; for to such belongs the kingdom of God.	¹⁵Now they were bringing even infants to him that he might touch them; and when the disciples saw it, they rebuked them. ¹⁶But Jesus called them to him, saying, 'Let the children come to me, and do not hinder them; for to such belongs the kingdom of God.

59

Matt. 19.13-15	Mark 10.13-16	Luke 18.15-17

³and said, 'Truly, I say to you, unless you turn and become like children, you will never enter the kingdom of heaven.'

¹⁵And he laid his hands on them and went away.

¹⁵Truly, I say to you, whoever does not receive the kingdom of God like a child shall not enter it.'
¹⁶And he took them in his arms and blessed them, laying his hands upon them.

¹⁷Truly, I say to you, whoever does not receive the kingdom of God like a child shall not enter it.'

Both pericopes have material about 'a child' or 'children'. One of these verses ('like a child [children] . . . will not enter') appears in pericope 3 in Matthew (Matt. 18.3), but in pericope 4 in Mark and Luke. Luke, that is, supports Mark's placement of the verse against Matthew (point 2). The conclusion to pericope 3 in Mark ('whoever receives me . . . receives the one who sent me', Mark 9.37b) is also supported by Luke but not Matthew. Matthew has the saying elsewhere, in 10.40. On the other hand, the conclusion of pericope 4 in Mark (Mark 10.16, 'laying his hands on them') is in Matthew but not in Luke. If one looks at pericope 4 in Mark, Mark 10.13–16, one sees that Mark's first two verses are in both Matthew and Luke, the third verse is in Luke (in Matthew it is in pericope 3), and the last verse is in Matthew but not Luke. Thus: mostly they all agree, but where either Matthew or Luke disagrees, the other supports Mark. There are only minor agreements of Matthew and Luke against Mark: in pericope 3 *ean* for Mark's *an* (a different 'ever' in 'whoever', Mark 9.37 and parr.), and a slight agreement in order in the same verse: Matthew and Luke place 'child' after the verb 'receive' (not visible in English), Mark has the opposite order. Matthew and Luke also agree in not having Mark 9.35 or the lengthy introduction, Mark 9.33.

• The nature of the agreements among the synoptics

At this point the student has seen some of the basic facts of the synoptic gospels, and we have illustrated one important conclusion, not about how to solve the synoptic problem, but about its character: as we pointed out at the beginning, the relationship among the gospels is literary. It is the result of either direct copying from one to the other, or of common dependence on the same source or sources. The agreements, we have seen, are in Greek. They cannot be explained by appeal to an oral tradition in Aramaic (presumably the language spoken by Jesus and his followers). Memorized but unwritten texts in Greek might possibly account for the phenomena, if we could imagine schools of professional or semi-professional memorizers. What evidence there is, however, is against this: ch. 9. The simplest explanation, and the one almost universally accepted by scholars, is that the relationship was literary, based on copying written texts.

We need now to illustrate only one further point in order to begin the examination of solutions of the synoptic problem.

60

Point 5: Agreement between Matthew and Luke begins where Mark begins, or ends where Mark ends. We noted that this is the case in the gospels as wholes, and now we give an example within an individual pericope.

Pericope 5: Jesus Foretells His Betrayal, *Mark 14.18–21*.
Aland 310; Greeven 247 and 249; Throckmorton 235

Matt. 26.21–25	Mark 14.18–21	Luke 22.21–23
	[18]And as they were at table eating,	
[21]and as they were eating, he said, 'Truly, I say to you, one of you will betray me.' [22]And they were very sorrowful, and began to say to him one after another, 'Is it I, Lord?'	Jesus said, 'Truly, I say to you, one of you will betray me, one who is eating with me.' [19]They began to be sorrowful, and to say to him one after another, 'Is it I?'	
[23]He answered, 'He who has dipped his hand in the dish with me, will betray me. [24]The Son of man goes as it is written of him, but woe to that man by whom the Son of man is betrayed! It would have been better for that man if he had not been born.' [25]Judas, who betrayed him, said, 'Is it I, Master?' He said to him, 'You have said so.'	[20]He said to them, 'It is one of the twelve, one who is dipping bread into the dish with me. [21]For the Son of man goes as it is written of him, but woe to that man by whom the Son of man is betrayed! It would have been better for that man if he had not been born.'	[21]'But behold the hand of him who betrays me is with me on the table. [22]For the Son of man goes as it has been determined; but woe to that man by whom he is betrayed!'
		[23]And they began to question one another, which of them it was that would do this.

Here triple agreement stops with the sentence 'woe to that man by whom the Son of man is betrayed'. Matthew and Mark have one more sentence, 'it would have been better for that man if he had not been born'. Now Mark ends entirely. Matthew and Luke both have conclusions, but they do not agree. Matthew attributes a question to Judas, while Luke says that they (the disciples) began to question one another. (This is almost impossible to see in Greeven's synopsis.)   61

The common explanation of the phenomena thus far: the priority of Mark

This review of aspects of agreement and disagreement in the triple tradition allows us to see why many scholars think that Matthew and Luke **independently** copied Mark. This view has been held by most for more than a hundred years.[6] The reasoning is as follows:*

    1. In the triple tradition Matthew and Luke agree with each other only when Mark is present (with very minor exceptions). Therefore they have no relationship except by way of Mark. Had one known the other, they would have agreed against Mark, either in the wording of passages or in inserting the same new material at the same place. Especially telling is the fact that they stop or start agreeing with each other when the text of Mark stops or starts. This points to independent copying of Mark by Matthew and Luke.

    2. The relationships of the contents of the gospels are also usually taken to prove Mark's priority. Most of Mark is in Matthew (Matthew has the substance of 600 of Mark's 661 verses, *c.* 90%), and a high percentage in Luke (Luke has the substance of 45% of Mark).[7] But, since Matthew and Luke are much longer than Mark, a smaller percentage of each of them is found also in Mark: for example, 600 of Matthew's 1070 verses are also in Mark, 56%. It is intrinsically likely that Matthew and Luke copied Mark, since no author would have left out so much good material as Mark would have omitted had he been dependent on Matthew or Luke or both.

This reasoning results in accepting the priority of Mark in the triple tradition, as represented by the following diagram:

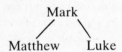

Mark

Matthew   Luke

- ### Alternative explanations

Logically, however, there are other possibilities for explaining the relationships among the three gospels in the triple tradition.

One is that Mark was third. Matthew was the original gospel and was used by Luke. Luke sometimes, however, altered Matthew or inserted new material. Mark copied them both, taking care to copy them precisely where they agreed. If they disagreed, he would copy one or the other, or he would omit both. This would lead to the results that we have just surveyed: substantial agreements among all three; few agreements between Matthew and Luke against Mark (since Mark copied them both or alternated between them); substantial agreements between Matthew and Mark against Luke, and between Mark and Luke against Matthew. This view is called the

---

*In this chapter indented summaries of 'the reasoning' or 'the argument' are not our own views, but an attempt to summarize arguments put forward by others. The reader may wish to compare Streeter's summaries in *The Four Gospels*, pp. 159–169.

Griesbach hypothesis after J. J. Griesbach, inventor of the synopsis, who first formulated it (sometimes confusingly called 'the two-gospel hypothesis'). It held the field for about a hundred years, from *c.* 1774 to *c.* 1863 and has now been revived.[8] It is diagrammed thus:

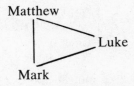

There is a third possibility: that Matthew copied Mark and that Luke copied both. Luke, however, preferred Mark, and so did not often follow Matthew when he disagreed with Mark. Thus Luke often agrees with Mark against Matthew, seldom with Matthew against Mark. Sometimes Luke went his own way, and this resulted in agreements between Matthew and Mark against Luke. This hypothesis, championed by a few, may be called Mark without Q:[9]

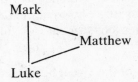

Logically it is possible that Mark was second. In this case Mark copied Matthew and Luke copied them both. Luke decided to be truer to Mark and used Matthew in a different way from the way he used Mark. We shall see below that the distribution of Matthew–Luke double tradition material makes this extremely unlikely. B. C. Butler in 1951 proposed this solution,[10] but it has won few adherents, and we shall drop it from consideration.

There are also more complicated theories, involving multiple sources and criss-cross copying, to some of which we shall return. It is time now to look more closely at another aspect of the basic synoptic relationships.

- The double tradition

Point 7: There is a substantial body of material common to Matthew and Luke which is not in Mark. The amount of verbatim agreement varies considerably from pericope to pericope.

Pericope 6: Jesus' Lament Over Jerusalem, *Matt. 23.37–39 and par.*
Aland 285; Greeven 181; Throckmorton 167

Matt. 23.37–39	**Mark**	**Luke 13.34–35**
[37]'O Jerusalem, Jerusalem, killing the prophets and stoning those who are sent to you!		[34]'O Jerusalem, Jerusalem, killing the prophets and stoning those who are sent to you!

How often would I have gathered your children together as a hen gathers her chicks under her wings, and you would not! [38]Behold, your house is forsaken and desolate. [39]For I tell you, you will not see me from now, until you say, "Blessed is he who comes in the name of the Lord."'		How often would I have gathered your children together as a hen gathers her brood under her wings, and you would not! [35]Behold, your house is forsaken. And I tell you, you will not see me until you say, "Blessed is he who comes in the name of the Lord!"'

Here we see an instance of almost 100% agreement. There are only a few disagreements: Matthew has 'chicks' where Luke has 'brood'; there is a slight difference in the form of the verb 'gathered' (*episynagagein / episynaksai*) in Matt. v. 37, and Matthew repeats the verb whereas Luke does not. Matthew has a few words not in Luke: in 23.38 'desolate' (omitted in many manuscripts), and in 23.39 'from now'. Since the placement of pericopes will prove to be important, we should note that Matthew's passage comes after Jesus' entry into Jerusalem, but Luke's before. Thus in Luke the saying is fulfilled by Jesus' entry into Jerusalem, where the crowds say 'Blessed is the king who comes in the name of the Lord' (Luke 19.38), while in Matthew the saying looks forward to a future, eschatological return of Jesus.

Pericope 7: The Parable of the Great Supper, *Matt. 22.1–10 and par.*
Aland 279; Greeven 184; Throckmorton 170

In this pericope, which it is not necessary to print, we see very few agreements. In the early verses, apart from 'kingdom' and 'man' (necessary to the parabolic form), one finds only 'and he sent servant[s]', 'those called', 'ready' and 'field'. At no point is really close agreement to be observed. One may also compare The Parable of the Talents (*talanta*) or Pounds (*mnas*) (Matt. 25.14–30//Luke 19.11–27), where there are some striking agreements near the conclusion, but otherwise appreciable diversity – including disagreement on the unit of money.

The range of agreement has suggested to many that Matthew and Luke were dependent on different versions of the same source but that neither knew the other. Had one copied the other, the argument runs, there would be more consistency in the amount of verbatim agreement. Alternatively the variety can be explained by appealing to the different interests of the authors. It is also possible that one copied the other, but did not always have the scroll open, sometimes copying from memory. The amount of agreement itself will not establish one case or the other.

Point 8: The Matthew–Luke double tradition is arranged differently in the two gospels.

This fact is widely regarded as decisive for understanding the relationship of Matthew and Luke. We may consider the order of the double tradition material by focusing on Woes Upon Cities of Galilee (Luke 10.13–15//Matthew 11.20–24). In Luke the passage appears in this sequence:

True Greatness (Luke 9.46–48)	Triple
The Strange Exorcist (9.49–50)	Mark–Luke
Decision to go to Jerusalem; Rejection by Samaritans (9.51–56)	Luke single
On Following Jesus (9.57–62)	Matt.–Luke
Commissioning the Seventy [Matt.: Twelve] (10.1–2)	Matt.–Luke
Woes on Galilean Cities (10.13–15)	**Matt.–Luke**
'He Who Hears You, Hears Me' (10.16)	Matt.–Luke
The Return of the Seventy (10.17–20)	Luke single

The same passage appears in Matthew (11.20–24) in this sequence:

The Harvest is Great (Matt. 9.35–38)	Triple
Commissioning the Twelve (10.1–16)	Triple
The Fate of the Disciples (10.17–25)	Matt. single
Exhortation to Fearless Confession (10.26–33)	Matt.–Luke
Division within Households (10.34–36)	Matt.–Luke
Conditions of Discipleship (10.37–39)	Matt.–Luke
Rewards of Discipleship (10.40–41)	Matt. single
Continuation of Journey (11.1)	Matt. single
John The Baptist's Question (11.2–6)	Matt.–Luke
Jesus' Witness concerning John (11.7–19)	Matt.–Luke
Woes on Galilean Cities (11.20–24)	**Matt.–Luke**
Jesus' Thanksgiving to the Father (11.25–27)	Matt.–Luke
'Come unto Me . . .' (11.28–30)	Matt. single

A study of these lists will show how true it is that Matthew and Luke do not place the same double tradition in the same place.

There is an important further aspect to the arrangement of the double tradition: *Matthew's arrangements are often highly logical, but different arrangements appear in Luke*. Thus, for example, Matthew puts back-to-back The Time of the Parousia ['appearance'] (a warning that the end is near); The Need of Watchfulness; The Watchful Householder (being alert for a coming 'appearance') (Matt. 24.34–44). The arrangement is appropriate and forceful. Luke has all three passages, but in three different places. The Time of the Parousia, which is a triple tradition passage, he has where both Matthew and Mark place it: in the discourse on the end and the parousia of the Son of man (Luke 21.32–33). He has The Need of Watchfulness in ch. 17 (vv. 26–27; 34–35), and The Watchful Householder in 12.39–40.

• The common solution

We now have before us the rest of the data which support the widely held **two-source hypothesis** – belief in the priority of Mark and the existence of 'Q', a symbol for the source which supposedly lies behind the Matthew–Luke double tradition. ('Q' is usually thought to come from the German word Quelle, 'source'.[11]) According to this view Matthew and Luke both copied Mark, following its narrative framework, and inserted sayings from Q here and there. We shall call this the two-*source* rather

65

than two-*document* hypothesis because many have not regarded 'Q' as a document. The hypothesis is diagrammed like this:

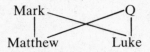

The explanation of the diagram is this:

1. Mark is the earliest gospel (as argued above, pp. 26f).
2. Neither Matthew nor Luke knew the other; otherwise they would more often agree in the placing of their common material. Luke especially could not have known Matthew, or he would have followed his logical arrangement. Yet a lot of the Matt.–Luke double tradition is in very close agreement, so that it is necessary to posit a source. On the other hand, some passages differ significantly. It appears either that the source was available to Matthew and Luke in two different versions; or that it consisted of 'floating' material, without a fixed context; or that they simply treated it differently from the way they treated Mark, paying little attention to its arrangement and sometimes re-writing it appreciably.

The second point – in the double tradition there is great variety in the amount of verbal agreement between Matthew and Luke, but no agreement in the order of the material – is an argument for the existence of 'Q' primarily because of **the argument from order**. This argument is the strongest support of the 'two-document hypothesis' (Mark and Q).

Mark's order is generally supported by both Matthew and Luke. Where one departs the other maintains support. Yet they show no agreement in the placing of the Matt.–Luke double tradition. Their agreement in order (and in wording) in the triple tradition was mediated via Mark. Their agreement in wording alone in the double tradition was mediated via Q. Their failure to agree in the placing of Q material in the Markan outline shows that both of them used that outline as well as other material, which was inserted into the Markan framework, but that they combined these two sources *independently*. Had one author known the work of the other, he would sometimes have been influenced by the other's arrangement of the material in the double tradition.

It will be seen that this is a powerful argument and that it makes the best sense of the material which we have thus far considered, though there are other possible explanations. The two-source hypothesis has dominated the field for a hundred and twenty years, and it has done so for good reason.

There are, however, exceptions to all the rules which we have just considered, and we have already begun to see that there are competing hypotheses. It will turn out that the compelling force of the two-source hypothesis rests in part on *the level of generality* with which it is presented. Once one studies the synopsis in complete detail incongruences and difficulties will appear, and they will call the two-source hypothesis into question. We turn now to complications and their significance.

4   Complexities and Difficulties

In this chapter we begin to examine evidence which counts against the two-source hypothesis, at least in its simple form.

The worst problems for the two-source hypothesis are caused by evidence which counts against the independence of Matthew and Luke. The two-source hypothesis requires that they be completely independent. If one knew the other, the whole house of cards comes down. In that case Q, the sayings source, is not needed, and Markan priority itself is called into question: if Luke did know Matthew, he could have taken both the double and triple tradition from that gospel rather than from Mark and Q, even though the argument from order constitutes a difficulty for this view. There are two types of agreement between Matthew and Luke which challenge the two-source hypothesis: minor agreements in the triple tradition and certain kinds of major agreements in the double tradition.

• Minor agreements between Matthew and Luke against Mark

Matthew and Luke, according to the two-source hypothesis, copied Mark independently. Thus in the triple tradition they should agree with each other against Mark only occasionally. The number and variety of agreements which in fact exist raise problems for the two-source hypothesis and lead sometimes to more complicated forms of it, sometimes to different hypotheses. The minor agreements between Matthew and Luke against Mark in the triple tradition have always constituted the Achilles' heel of the two-source hypothesis. There are virtually no triple tradition pericopes without such agreements; and even in the pericopes in the previous chapter, which were chosen to demonstrate triple agreements, there were noteworthy agreements between Matthew and Luke against Mark (see ch. 3, Pericopes 1 and 2). Now we consider two of the most striking passages.

Point 1: There are numerous minor agreements of Matthew and Luke against Mark in the triple tradition.

Pericope 1: The Healing of the Paralytic, *Mark 2.1–12 and parr.*
Aland 43; Greeven 64; Throckmorton 52

Underlining in Matthew and Luke = positive agreements against Mark
Bold in Mark = agreements in 'omission' against Mark

Matt. 9.1-8	Mark. 2.1-12	Luke. 5.17-26
¹Καὶ ἐμβὰς εἰς πλοῖον διεπέρασεν καὶ ἦλθεν εἰς τὴν ἰδίαν πόλιν.	¹Καὶ εἰσελθὼν πάλιν εἰς Καφαρναοὺμ δι' ἡμερῶν ἠκούσθη ὅτι ἐν οἴκῳ ἐστίν. ²καὶ συνήχθησαν πολλοὶ ὥστε μηκέτι χωρεῖν μηδὲ τὰ πρὸς τὴν θύραν, καὶ ἐλάλει αὐτοῖς τὸν λόγον.	¹⁷Καὶ ἐγένετο ἐν μιᾷ τῶν ἡμερῶν καὶ αὐτὸς ἦν διδάσκων, καὶ ἦσαν καθήμενοι Φαρισαῖοι καὶ νομοδιδάσκαλοι οἳ ἦσαν ἐληλυθότες ἐκ πάσης κώμης τῆς Γαλιλαίας καὶ Ἰουδαίας καὶ Ἰερουσαλὴμ καὶ δύναμις κυρίου ἦν εἰς τὸ ἰᾶσθαι αὐτόν. ¹⁸καὶ ἰδοὺ ἄνδρες φέροντες
²Καὶ ἰδοὺ προσέφερον αὐτῷ παραλυτικὸν ἐπὶ κλίνης βεβλημένον.	³καὶ ἔρχονται φέροντες πρὸς αὐτὸν παραλυτικὸν **αἰρόμενον ὑπὸ τεσσάρων** .	ἐπὶ κλίνης ἄνθρωπον ὃς ἦν παραλελυμένος καὶ ἐζήτουν αὐτὸν εἰσενεγκεῖν καὶ θεῖναι [αὐτὸν] ἐνώπιον αὐτοῦ. ¹⁹καὶ μὴ εὑρόντες
	⁴καὶ μὴ δυνάμενοι προσενέγκαι αὐτῷ διὰ τὸν ὄχλον ἀπεστέγασαν τὴν στέγην ὅπου ἦν, καὶ ἐξορύξαντες χαλῶσι τὸν κράβαττον ὅπου ὁ παραλυτικὸς κατέκειτο.	ποίας εἰσενέγκωσιν αὐτὸν διὰ τὸν ὄχλον, ἀναβάντες ἐπὶ τὸ δῶμα διὰ τῶν κεράμων καθῆκαν αὐτὸν σὺν τῷ κλινιδίῳ εἰς τὸ μέσον ἔμπροσθεν τοῦ Ἰησοῦ.
καὶ ἰδὼν ὁ Ἰησοῦς τὴν πίστιν αὐτῶν εἶπεν τῷ παραλυτικῷ· θάρσει, τέκνον, ἀφίενταί σου αἱ ἁμαρτίαι .³καὶ ἰδού τινες τῶν γραμματέων εἶπαν ἐν ἑαυτοῖς·	⁵καὶ ἰδὼν ὁ Ἰησοῦς τὴν πίστιν αὐτῶν λέγει τῷ παραλυτικῷ· τέκνον , ἀφίενταί σου αἱ ἁμαρτίαι . ⁶ἦσαν δέ τινες τῶν γραμματέων ἐκεῖ κάθημενοι καὶ διαλογιζόμενοι ἐν ταῖς καρδίαις αὐτῶν ⁷τί	²⁰καὶ ἰδὼν τὴν πίστιν αὐτῶν εἶπεν. ἄνθρωπε, ἀφέωνταί σοι αἱ ἁμαρτίαι σου.
οὗτος βλασφημεῖ.	οὗτος οὕτως λαλεῖ; βλασφημεῖ· τίς δύναται ἀφιέναι ἁμαρτίας εἰ μὴ εἷς ὁ θεός; ⁸καὶ εὐθὺς	²¹καὶ ἤρξαντο διαλογίζεσθαι οἱ γραμματεῖς καὶ οἱ Φαρισαῖοι λέγοντες· τίς ἐστιν οὗτος ὃς λαλεῖ βλασφημίας; τίς δύναται ἁμαρτίας ἀφεῖναι εἰ μὴ μόνος ὁ θεός;
⁴καὶ ἰδὼν ὁ Ἰησοῦς τὰς ἐνθυμήσεις αὐτῶν εἶπεν· ἱνατί ἐνθυμεῖσθε πονηρὰ ἐν ταῖς καρδίαις ὑμῶν; ⁵τί γάρ ἐστιν εὐκοπώτερον, εἰπεῖν· ἀφίενταί σου αἱ ἁμαρτίαι, ἢ εἰπεῖν· ἔγειρε	ἐπιγνοὺς ὁ Ἰησοῦς **τῷ πνεύματι αὐτοῦ** ὅτι οὕτως διαλογίζονται ἐν ἑαυτοῖς λέγει αὐτοῖς· τί ταῦτα διαλογίζεσθε ἐν ταῖς καρδίαις ὑμῶν; ⁹τί ἐστιν εὐκοπώτερον, εἰπεῖν **τῷ παραλυτικῷ** ἀφίενταί σου αἱ ἁμαρτίαι, ἢ εἰπεῖν· ἔγειρε **καὶ ἆρον τόν**	²²ἐπιγνοὺς δὲ ὁ Ἰησοῦς τοὺς διαλογισμοὺς αὐτῶν ἀποκριθεὶς εἶπεν πρὸς αὐτούς· τί διαλογίζεσθε ἐν ταῖς καρδίαις ὑμῶν; ²³τί ἐστιν εὐκοπώτερον, εἰπεῖν· ἀφέωνταί σοι αἱ ἁμαρτίαι σου, ἢ εἰπεῖν· ἔγειρε

Matt. 9.1-8	Mark 2.1-12	Luke 5.17-26
καὶ περιπάτει;	**κράβαττόν σου** καὶ περιπάτει ;	καὶ περιπάτει;
⁶ἵνα δὲ εἰδῆτε ὅτι ἐξουσίαν ἔχει	¹⁰ἵνα δὲ εἰδῆτε ὅτι ἐξουσίαν ἔχει	²⁴ἵνα δὲ εἰδῆτε ὅτι ὁ υἱὸς τοῦ ἀν-
ὁ υἱὸς τοῦ ἀνθρώπου ἐπὶ τῆς γῆς	ὁ υἱὸς τοῦ ἀνθρώπου ἀφιέναι	θρώπου ἐξουσίαν ἔχει ἐπὶ τῆς γῆς
ἀφιέναι ἁμαρτίας - τότε λέγει	ἁμαρτίας ἐπὶ τῆς γῆς - λέγει	ἀφιέναι ἁμαρτίας - εἶπεν
τῷ παραλυτικῷ·	τῷ παραλυτικῷ· ¹¹σοὶ λέγω,	τῷ παραλελυμένῳ· σοὶ λέγω,
ἐγερθεὶς ἆρόν σου τὴν κλίνην	ἔγειρε ἆρον τὸν κρά βαττόν	ἔγειρε καὶ ἄρας τὸ κλινίδιόν
καὶ ὕπαγε εἰς τὸν οἶκόν σου.	σου καὶ ὕπαγε εἰς τὸν οἶκόν σου.	σου πορεύου εἰς τὸν οἶκόν σου.
⁷καὶ ἐγερθεὶς	¹²καὶ ἠγέρθη	²⁵καὶ παραχρῆμα ἀναστὰς ἐν-
	καὶ **εὐθὺς** ἄρας τὸν **κράβαττον**	ώπιον αὐτῶν, ἄρας ἐφ᾽ ὃ κατ-
ἀπῆλθεν εἰς τὸν οἶκον	ἐξῆλθεν **ἔμπροσθεν πάντων,**	έκειτο, ἀπῆλθεν εἰς τὸν οἶκον
αὐτοῦ. ⁸ἰδόντες δὲ	ὥστε	αὐτοῦ δοξάζων τὸν θεόν. ²⁶καὶ
οἱ ὄχλοι ἐφοβήθησαν καὶ	ἐξίστασθαι πάντας καὶ	ἔκστασις ἔλαβεν ἅπαντας καὶ
ἐδόξασαν τὸν θεὸν τόν δόντα ἐξ-	δοξάζειν τὸν θεόν	ἐδόξαζον τὸν θεὸν καὶ ἐπλή-
ουσίαν τοιαύτην τοῖς ἀνθρώποις.	λέγοντας ὅτι	σθησαν φόβου λέγοντες ὅτι
	οὕτως οὐδέποτε εἴδομεν.	εἴδομεν παράδοξα σήμερον.

Matt. 9.1–8	Mark 2.1–12	Luke 5.17–26
¹And getting into a boat he crossed over and came to his own city.	¹And when he returned to Capernaum after some days, it was reported that he was at home. ²And many were gathered together, so that there was no longer room for them, not even about the door; and he was preaching the word to them.	¹⁷On one of those days, as he was teaching, there were Pharisees and teachers of the law sitting by, who had come from every village of Galilee and Judea and from Jerusalem; and the power of the Lord was with him to heal. ¹⁸And behold, men were bringing on a bed a man who was paralysed, and they sought to bring him in and lay him before Jesus; ¹⁹but finding no way to bring him in, because of the crowd, they went up on the roof and let him down with his bed through the tiles into the midst before Jesus. ²⁰And when he saw their faith he said,
²And behold, they brought to him a paralytic, lying on his bed;	³And they came, bringing to him a paralytic **carried by four.** ⁴And when they could not get near him because of the crowd, they removed the roof above him; and when they had made an opening, they let down the pallet on which the paralytic lay.	
and when Jesus saw their faith he said to the paralytic, 'Take heart, my son; your sins are forgiven.' ³And behold, some of the scribes said to themselves,	⁵And when Jesus saw their faith, he said to the paralytic, 'My son, your sins are forgiven.' ⁶Now some of the scribes were sitting there, questioning in their	'Man, your sins are forgiven you.' ²¹And the scribes and the Pharisees began

'This man   is blaspheming.'

| | hearts,   [7]'Why does this man speak thus? It is blasphemy! Who can forgive sins but God alone?' [8]And immediately Jesus, perceiving **in his spirit** that they thus questioned within themselves, said to them, | to question, saying, 'Who is this   that speaks blasphemies? Who can forgive sins but God only?' [22]When Jesus perceived |

[4]But Jesus, knowing

their thoughts, said,

'Why do you think evil in your hearts? [5]For which is easier, to say, "Your sins are forgiven," or to say, "Rise

and walk"?

[6]But that you may know that the Son of man has authority on earth to forgive sins' – he then said to the paralytic –

'Rise, take up your bed and go home.'

[7]And   he rose

and went away into his house.
[8]When the crowds saw it, they were afraid,   and they glorified God, who had given such authority to men.

'Why do you question thus in your hearts? [9]Which is easier, to say **to the paralytic**, "Your sins are forgiven," or to say, "Rise, **take up your pallet** and walk"? [10]But that you may know that the Son of man has authority on earth to forgive sins' – he   said to the paralytic – [11]'I say to you, rise, take up your pallet and go home.' [12]And   he rose, and **immediately** took up **the pallet** and went out **before** them **all**;   so that they were all amazed and glorified God,

saying, 'We never saw anything like this!'

---

their questionings, he answered them,

'Why do you question   in your hearts?   [23]Which is easier, to say, "Your sins are forgiven you," or to say, "Rise

and walk"?

[24]But that you may know that the Son of man has authority on earth to forgive sins' – he   said to the man who was paralysed – 'I say to you, rise, take up your bed and go home.' [25]And immediately he rose before them, and took up that on which he lay, and went away into his house, glorifying God. [26]And amazement seized them all, and they glorified God and were filled with fear, saying, 'We have seen strange things today.'

Matthew and Luke have the following **positive agreements** against Mark:

Matthew's verse number

2   behold / idou
    on a bed / epi klinēs
3   and / kai (Mark's 'and' in English is de)
6   bed [little bed] / klinēn [klinidion]
7   went away into his house / apēlthen eis ton oikon autou
8   fear / phob-

These are minor, but there are a lot of them. Especially noteworthy is the *kai* ('and') in Matthew and Luke for Mark's *de* (also 'and'). It is often said that Matthew and Luke both thought that Mark used *kai* too often and changed it to *de*. Here the 'change' goes the other way, and they agree on it.

There are also important **agreements in 'omission'**: words and phrases in Mark but in neither Matthew nor Luke.

> Mark's verse number
> 3   carried by four / airomenon hypo tessarōn
> 8   in his spirit / toi pneumati autou
> 9   to the paralytic / tōi paralytikōi
>   and take up your pallet / kai aron ton krabbaton sou
> 12 immediately / euthus
>   the pallet / ton krabbaton
>   before them all / emprosthen pantōn

We should pay special attention to Matthew's verse 2 and the parallels. Here Matthew and Luke have three words in agreement (behold, upon, bed), and they agree in 'omitting' three words in Mark ('carried by four'). Thus in a verse of only eight to ten words (in Greek) they agree six times against Mark. The two-source hypothesis must maintain that Matthew and Luke agreed so closely in their editorial policies that, in this pericope, they made the same minor change in a total of twenty-nine words in Greek (counting both agreements in commission and omission).

Pericope 2: Healing in a Lonely Place, *Mark 6.31–34 and parr.*
   Aland 145, 146; Greeven 125; Throckmorton 112

Agreements of Matthew and Luke against Mark:

> Mark's verse number
> 32 departed / anechōrēsen [hypechōrēsen]
>   the crowds followed him
> 34 healed / therap-

Agreements in omission:

> Mark's verse number
> 33 many saw them coming and going
> 34 they were as sheep without a shepherd
>   he began to teach them many things

In this passage Luke hardly agrees with Mark at all, while there are numerous and substantial agreements between Matthew and Luke against Mark. We shall return to this passage in considering Boismard's hypothesis in a later chapter (ch. 6, Pericope 4).

• Explanations of the minor agreements between Matthew and Luke

The statement that in the triple tradition Matthew and Luke do not agree against Mark is not literally true, and the proponents of the two-source hypothesis have always had to cope with the numerous agreements of Matthew and Luke against Mark. They have argued that the minor agreements are the result of coincidence, accident or textual corruption. Often the argument is that Matthew and Luke have independently improved Mark by making identical changes. They are often said to have agreed coincidentally in improving Mark's grammar or syntax. Agreements in omission result from their common desire to reduce Mark's verbosity. Substantial agreements between Matthew and Luke have other motives, such as showing increased respect for Jesus and the disciples. And so on – and on. Many scholars, however, have felt that the minor agreements cannot all be explained away and that they require radical revision of the theory or a different theory.

With regard to Pericope 1, for example, the supporters of the two-source theory have argued that Matthew and Luke independently decided to improve Mark by deleting the word pallet/krabbatos, which is 'vernacular and dialectic'.[1] This accounts for several of the agreements listed above. Yet one must ask how it happened that two authors, each wanting to eliminate a word, independently agreed so often on what to do about it, whether to substitute another word or to omit it. The following table shows agreements and disagreements about the bed or pallet:

Matthew	Mark	Luke
9.2 klinēs	—	5.18 klinēs
—	2.4 krabbatos	klinidion
—	2.9 krabbatos	—
klinēs	2.11 krabbatos	klinidion
—	2.12 krabbatos	on which he lay

According to the two-source hypothesis in one instance Matthew and Luke independently decided to use *klinēs* where Mark had nothing; in one instance they independently agreed to omit *krabbatos*; in one instance Matthew omitted while Luke changed the word; in one instance they made the same change (Luke's *klinidion* is a diminutive of *klinē*); and in one instance Matthew omitted while Luke paraphrased. Perhaps this is possible by chance, but of a total of five occurrences of 'bed' or 'pallet', they agreed three times.

Here we should make a more general observation. Many of the explanations of the minor agreements depend on a view about what would count as an 'improvement'. It is generally said that Mark's Greek is not as good as that of Matthew and Luke, and thus it is easy to think of them as improving the Greek. The Griesbach hypothesis requires us to think that Mark very frequently altered the relatively good Greek of Matthew and Luke, and this is often regarded as unlikely. In fact, however, the entire notion of 'improvement' or its reverse is very shaky. People who rewrote material rewrote it in their own style. If a later author liked elegance and knew how to achieve it, the product would be more elegant. But the reverse could and often did happen. Many of the apocryphal gospels of the second and subsequent centuries are written in 'worse' Greek than Mark – that is, worse by the Attic standard. Many authors, and no doubt many readers and hearers, preferred more colloquial and less elegant prose. One can imagine many modern analogies. A sermon or lecture directed to a university audience might not go down very well if given before another audience.

Since there are no universal rules of change which account for the minor agreements between Matthew and Luke against Mark, they do not help us very much with problem number one of source criticism, whether or not Mark is the first gospel. It is possible that Mark was third and conflated Matthew and Luke, often copying them when they agreed, usually following one or the other when they disagreed, sometimes altering them even when they agreed. These small alterations would produce the 'minor agreements' between Matthew and Luke. It is also possible that Matthew and Luke copied Mark independently, coincidentally agreeing in altering their source. It is also possible that one – let us say Matthew – copied Mark and that the other – Luke – copied both. In this case Luke generally preferred Mark, but occasionally preferred Matthew.

Leaving aside the question of Mark's priority, let us ask whether the minor agreements between Matthew and Luke help us settle the problem of their relationship to each other. Were they independent, or did one know the other?

Intelligent people who have spent time and effort studying the minor agreements have disagreed among themselves. Thus we must say that the minor agreements do not decisively prove or disprove the independence of Matthew and Luke. Statistics seem not quite to settle the question. One is not dealing with random probability, but with editorial choice. Two people might have the same editorial policy. In the triple tradition there are, however, about a thousand minor agreements between Matthew and Luke against Mark, if we include both positive agreements and agreements in omission. It is our judgment that this is too many to attribute to coincidence and similar editorial policies, and that thus we should posit *some relationship between Matthew and Luke in addition to or instead of their independent use of Mark*.

• Complicated forms of the two-source hypothesis

The minor agreements are significant enough that they have led to a complication of the two-source hypothesis: the further hypothesis that the Mark which was copied by Matthew and Luke was a different edition of Mark from the one we now have. This different edition is usually thought to be earlier than our Mark. It is often called Ur-Mark, the German for 'primitive Mark'. **Proto-Mark** is a better choice.

There is a variation: that the other edition of Mark was an improved, later version: **Deutero-Mark**. In this case Matthew and Luke copied the improved version.

The full evidence for the existence of more than one version of Mark is not yet before us, but we shall point out the aspects of agreement and disagreement which have produced these theories: (1) Agreements between Matthew and Luke in 'omission' make some scholars suspect that they copied an earlier version of Mark, which was then supplemented. Our Mark is the supplemented version. Thus in Mark 2.27–28 there are two sayings on the sabbath: 'the sabbath was made for people, and not people for the sabbath'; 'the Son of man is Lord of the sabbath'. Neither Matthew nor Luke has the first saying, though presumably both would have agreed with it. The Proto-Mark theory holds that their copy of Mark did not contain the saying, but that it was added later. (2) Agreements in 'improvement' between Matthew and Luke have led to the theory that they copied a version of Mark which had already been 'improved' and that our Mark is the earlier, unimproved version. This is the Deutero-Mark theory: the second Mark is the one used by Matthew and Luke.

These two points would lead to one of the following diagrams. The third is a combination of the first two.

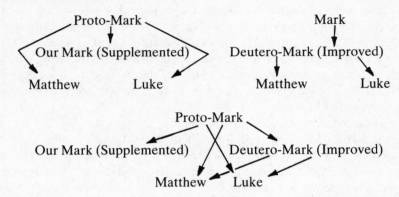

We shall return to the question of Proto-Mark and Deutero-Mark, and thus we do not evaluate these possibilities here, except by acknowledging that, between them, they can take care of all the minor agreements of Matthew and Luke against our Mark: they simply used one or more different Marks. Now we press on with another major fact in inter-synoptic agreement.

• Major agreements between Matthew and Luke in the double tradition

Point 2: There are major agreements between Matthew and Luke in the arrangement of their double tradition (the 'Q' material).

Pericope 3: John's Preaching of Repentance, *Matt. 3.7–10 and par.*
Aland 14; Greeven 14; Throckmorton 2

Pericope 4: The Temptation, *Matt. 4.1–11 and parr.*
Aland 20; Greeven 20; Throckmorton 8

The arrangement of these two pericopes in each gospel should be examined in a synopsis. They are the two most obvious passages which contradict the rule that Matthew and Luke do not place the 'Q' material in the same place vis à vis Mark. Both put John's Preaching of Repentance immediately after The Appearance of John the Baptist and before John's Messianic Preaching (both triple tradition), and both place the specification of three temptations after the statement that Jesus went into the desert to be tempted. Proponents of the two-source hypothesis argue that Mark and Q overlapped. Part of the material about John the Baptist was in both, as well as part of the temptation account. Matthew and Luke either conflated in the same way, or they simply copied Q, which overlapped with Mark. In any case the subject matter imposed its own order. If Matthew and Luke had more material about

John the Baptist and the temptation of Jesus than appears in Mark, they would have had to put it in where it now appears.

These passages, though easily explicable in themselves, raise the question of **overlapping sources**, a question which the next passages make more pressing.

Pericope 5: The Parable of the Leaven, *Matt. 13.33 and par.*
Aland 129; Greeven 111; Throckmorton 98

Both Matthew and Luke put The Parable of the Leaven, 'Q' material, immediately after The Parable of the Mustard Seed, triple tradition. According to the two-source hypothesis, The Parable of the Mustard Seed was in both Mark and Q. Matthew and Luke copied Q for both parables, and put them together because that was already their arrangement in Q. The problems which this explanation pose will be dealt with immediately below.

Pericope 6: On Collusion with Satan (Beelzebul) and The Sin against the Holy Spirit, *Mark 3.22–30 and parr.*
Aland 117–118; Greeven 99; Throckmorton 86

| Matt. | | Mark 3.22–27 | Luke 11.14–15, 17–23 |
12.22–30	9.32–34		
	³²As they were going away, behold, a dumb demoniac was brought to him.		¹⁴Now he was casting out a demon that was dumb;
²²Then a blind and dumb demoniac was brought to him,			
and he healed him, so that the dumb man spoke and saw. ²³And all the people were amazed, and said, 'Can this be the Son of David?'	³³And when the demon had been cast out, the dumb man spoke; and the crowds marveled, saying, 'Never was anything like this seen in Israel.' ³⁴But the Pharisees		when the demon had gone out, the dumb man spoke, and the people marveled.
²⁴But when the Pharisees heard it they said, 'It is only by Beelzebul, the prince of demons, that this man casts out demons.'	said,	²²And the scribes who came down from Jerusalem said,	¹⁵But some of them said,
	'He casts out demons by the prince of demons.'	'He is possessed by Beelzebul, and by the prince of demons he casts out the demons.' ²³And he called them to him, and said to them in parables, 'How can Satan cast	'He casts out demons by Beelzebul, the prince of demons;' . . .
²⁵Knowing their thoughts, he said to them,			¹⁷But he, knowing their thoughts, said to them,

75

'Every kingdom
divided against itself
  is laid waste,

         and no city
or house divided against
itself
will stand; [26]and if
Satan casts out Satan,
he is divided against himself; how then will his
kingdom stand?

        [27]And if
I cast out demons by
Beelzebul, by whom do
your sons cast them out?
Therefore they shall be
your judges. [28]But if it is
by the Spirit of God that I
cast out demons, then the
kingdom of God has come
upon you. [29]Or how can
one enter a strong
man's house and plunder
his goods,

        unless
he first
binds the strong man?

       Then indeed
he may plunder his house.
[30]He who is not with me
is against me, and he who
does not gather with me
scatters.'

out Satan? [24]If a kingdom
is divided against itself,
that kingdom cannot
stand.   [25]And if
a house is divided against
itself, that house will not be
able to stand. [26]And if
Satan has risen
up against himself and is
divided, he cannot stand,
but is coming to an end.

       [27]But no one
can enter a strong
man's house and plunder
his goods,

       unless
he first
binds the strong man;

      then indeed
he may plunder his house.'

'Every kingdom
divided against itself
  is laid waste,

and a divided household
falls.

      [18]And if
Satan
  also is divided against himself, how   will his
kingdom stand? For you
say that I cast out demons
by Beelzebul. [19]And if
I cast out demons by
Beelzebul, by whom do
your sons cast them out?
Therefore they shall be
your judges. [20]But if it is
by the finger of God that I
cast out demons, then the
kingdom of God has come
upon you.

      [21]When
a strong man, fully armed,
guards his own palace,
his goods are in
peace; [22]but when one
stronger than he assails
him and overcomes him, he
takes away his armor
in which he trusted, and
divides his spoil.
[23]He who is not with me
is against me, and he who
does not gather with me
scatters.'

The Sin against the Holy Spirit

Matt. 12.31–37 (7.16–20)	Mark 3.28–30	Luke 12.10; 6.43–45

[31]'Therefore I tell you, every sin and blasphemy will be forgiven men,
 	
            but the blasphemy against the Spirit will not be forgiven. [32]And whoever says a word against the Son of man will be forgiven; but whoever speaks against the Holy Spirit will not be forgiven, either in this age or in the age to come.
	[28]'Truly, I say to you, all sins
	               will be forgiven the sons of men, and whatever blas-phemies they utter;
		12.10
		     [10]'And every one who speaks a word against the Son of man will be forgiven; but he who blasphemes against the Holy Spirit will not be forgiven.'

	[29]but whoever blasphemes against the Holy Spirit never has forgiveness, but is guilty of an eternal sin' – [30]for they had said, 'He has an unclean spirit.'	
[cp. v. 33b]		[cp. v. 44] 6.43–45

[33]Either make the tree good, and its fruit good; or make the tree bad, and its fruit bad;
        for the tree is known by its fruit.
		[43]'For no good tree bears bad fruit,
		        nor again does a bad tree bear good fruit;
		      [44]for each tree is known by its own fruit. For figs are not gathered from thorns, nor are grapes picked from a bramble bush. [45]The good man out of the good treasure of his heart produces good, and the evil man out of his evil treasure produces evil; for out of the abundance of the heart his mouth speaks.'

[cp. v. 35] [34]You brood of vipers! how can you speak good, when you are evil? For out of the abundance of the heart the mouth speaks. [35]The good man out of his good treasure brings forth good, and the evil man out of his evil treasure brings forth evil. [36]I tell you, on the day of judgment men will render account for every careless word they utter; [37]for by your words you will be justified, and by your words you will be condemned.'		[cp. v. 45]

This is one of the most interesting passages in the synopsis. Matthew takes the role usually assumed by Mark, since Mark and Luke alternate in supporting Matthew. Running the eye down Matthew's column, we find this: Matthew's vv. 25–26a are (in general) in all three gospels; 26b in Luke not in Mark; 27–28 in Luke not in Mark; 29 in Mark not in Luke; 30 in Luke not in Mark; 31 in Mark; 32a in Luke, but differently placed; 32b in both; 33–35 in Luke, but differently placed; 36 in Matthew alone. Luke's parallels to the Matthaean material thus appear in three different places.

Critics of the two-source hypothesis argue that this is simply an extreme example of the general fact that Matthew and Luke often agree against Mark. Griesbachians propose that Luke copied Matthew, rearranging the sayings material as he usually does (on their hypothesis), and that Mark also copied Matthew, with possibly a side glance at Luke, but that he uncharacteristically abbreviated. (Mark is generally longer than Matthew or Luke in parallel passages.) Supporters of Markan priority without Q would simply say that Matthew expanded Mark and that Luke used both, rearranging the material.

From the point of view of defenders of the two-source hypothesis, this pericope is an example of an overlap between Mark and Q. They propose that Luke best represents Q, and that his having bits of the material in three different places points towards the unordered sayings source, Q. Mark had a parallel and partially identical tradition. Matthew shows his skill in organizing material. He brings it all together and carefully conflates, producing a coherent whole, while incorporating virtually all of both Mark and Q.

Matthaean priorists object that Matthew's supposed conflation would be too difficult. How could he gather four separate bits (one in Mark, three in Q) and combine them so effectively? It is easier to think that here Mark and Luke copied selectively.

It is hard to say who has the better of this argument, which readers may evaluate for themselves. The passage is regarded as crucial by both two-source supporters and by Matthaean priorists (e.g. B. C. Butler). The former see the existence of Q as being proved by the fact that Matthew conflated it with Mark. 'Conflation' by Matthew is proved by the fact that the double tradition is scattered in Luke. Matthaean priorists argue that Matthew could not have conflated so successfully and that the pericope in Matthew is integral, not the result of an artificial combination of verses.

It is more important to see that we are thrown here into the midst of a large and difficult question which we must now examine more closely.

• Mark–Q overlaps

B. H. Streeter, whose influential book on the gospels helped to establish in the English-speaking world the success of the two-source hypothesis, proposed that there are five principal instances of a Mark–Q overlap: the passages on John the Baptist; the Temptation; Collusion with Satan; the Parable of the Mustard Seed (in Q followed by the Parable of the Leaven); and Commissioning the Disciples. In these cases, he wrote, it is clear that 'Matthew and Luke had before them a version of these items considerably longer than that of Mark'. Further, the distinctions between the

Markan version of these passages and the Matthaean–Lukan are so great that one must grant that Matthew and Luke knew 'certain items' in a version 'decidedly different' from Mark's. 'In fact, to put it paradoxically, the overlapping of Mark and Q is more certain than is the existence of Q' (p. 186).

It will now turn out that the two-source hypothesis has two Achilles' heels. The first is the minor agreements between Matthew and Luke in the triple tradition, the second, the 'Mark–Q overlaps'. The 'overlaps' pose several difficulties for the two-source hypothesis.

1. We note, first, that these five passages do not all represent 'decidedly different' material in Matthew and Luke from that in Mark. The Parable of the Mustard Seed (Mark 4.30–32 and parr.) exists in basically only one form. There are minor variations from gospel to gospel, but there are not two different forms of the parable. The Mustard Seed and the Leaven are both assigned to Q, and the Mustard Seed called a Mark–Q overlap, only because there are several minor agreements between Matthew and Luke and, more important, Matthew and Luke agree in putting the Leaven after the Mustard Seed – a major exception to the rule that they do not agree in order against Mark. Putting the Mustard Seed into Q, thus, is only an effort to avoid a difficulty.

The other passages named by Streeter do contain substantial material which is in Matthew and Luke but not in Mark. Streeter spoke of Matthew and Luke being 'considerably longer' than Mark as well as 'decidedly different' (ibid.). 'Considerably longer' is the more accurate phrase. Streeter's 'decidedly different' reflects *a major supposition behind the two-source hypothesis: Everything is from a source, and no one would leave out anything important.* If Matthew has more material on The Sending of the Twelve than Mark, he had a different source for it. Mark could not have known the material, or he would not have left it out. This important and major assumption will be explored at the conclusion of Part II. Here we note, however, that it accounts for saying that Matthew and Luke had a further source whenever they have more material than Mark.

In any case, on Streeter's criterion that 'more = different', we see that four of his five cases qualify, but one (The Mustard Seed) does not. Here the theory of a Mark– Q overlap has been introduced because of an important agreement in order between Matthew and Luke against Mark.

2. There is a second objection to the theory that Mark and Q overlapped: as one studies the agreements between Matthew and Luke in triple tradition passages, it is tempting to say in more and more cases that Mark and Q overlapped, and thus Q keeps growing. Streeter's list of five major passages is minimal. In fact, his own full tabulation was much larger. Besides the passages already listed (John's Preaching, The Temptation, The Mustard Seed, Collusion with Satan and Commissioning the Twelve), it included the following:

Mark 4.21–25	5 sayings
9.42–50	Sayings collection
12.28–34	The Great Commandment
12.38–40	Denunciation of Pharisees

79

Streeter also added some further small units, for a total of sixteen passages.[2] We shall discuss the Great Commandment below, and here we note only the tendency of Q to grow to account for agreements between Matthew and Luke. Other scholars oppose putting so many passages in Q, since soon Q becomes as large as Matthew, and Markan dependence on Q becomes ever more likely. The expansion of Q and the possibility that Mark knew Q shake the foundations of the two-source hypothesis. One might as well say that Mark knew Matthew. But if the agreements between Matthew and Luke are not attributed to overlaps between Mark and Q, it becomes difficult to maintain that neither Matthew nor Luke knew each other. Proponents of the two-source hypothesis must maintain (1) that Matthew and Luke did not know each other; (2) that they used Mark and Q independently; (3) that they do not agree against Mark; BUT (4) that there are only a few minor agreements, which can be explained; (5) that the few major agreements are the result of an overlap of Mark and Q; (6) that Q was not too big. But the last three points cannot stand: there are actually a lot of minor agreements; there are a lot of major agreements; Q must therefore keep growing.

3. The theory of Mark–Q overlaps creates a still more serious difficulty for the two-source hypothesis: if there really were two separate sources, it appears that there was verbatim agreement in Greek between them. We recall that in the pericope on the Temptation Matthew and Luke have a large section not in Mark at all: the account of the three temptations. But all three have in common the basic statement that Jesus went into the desert to be tempted; this, then, is an overlap. We should have the opening two verses, where the overlap occurs, before us:

Matt. 4	Mark 1	Luke 4
[1]Then *Jesus was led* up by **the Spirit** into **the wilderness** to be **tempted** by the *devil*. [2]And he fasted **forty days** and forty nights, *and* afterward he *was hungry*.	[12]**The Spirit** immediately drove him out into **the wilderness**. [13]And he was in the wilderness **forty days**, **tempted by** Satan; and he was with the wild beasts; and the angels ministered to him.	[1]And *Jesus*, full of the Holy Spirit, returned from the Jordan, and *was led* by **the Spirit** [2]for **forty days** in **the wilderness**, **tempted by** the *devil*. And he ate nothing in those days; and when they were ended, he *was hungry*.

Here it is seen that the gospels agree and disagree in these ways:

triple agreements (in **bold**)	Matt.–Mark	Mark–Luke	Matthew–Luke (in *italic*)
the Spirit	into	and	Jesus
the wilderness			was led*
tempted by the			devil
forty days			and
			was hungry

*The form of the verb is different in Matt. and Luke.

According to the two-source hypothesis, Matthew and Luke copied Q, thus agreeing with each other against Mark. Mark and Q overlapped, since there are triple agreements. But we note that the overlap produces verbatim agreement in Greek between the two sources, Mark and Q. It is not reasonable to think that Matthew and Luke copied Mark 1.12–13 down to 'tempted by', and then switched to Q for 'the devil' (for Mark's 'Satan') and 'he was hungry'. They were presumably copying Q throughout. In this case the words in the triple agreements column above were in both Mark and Q. The situation is the same throughout the 'overlap' passages. Streeter acknowledged that the 'overlap' theory requires verbatim agreement between Mark and Q. Thus, commenting on the John the Baptist material, he pointed out that

> Mk i.7–8 occurs almost word for word in Mt iii.11 = Lk iii.16, but it is clear that Matthew and Luke did not derive the verse from Mark but from the same source whence they derived the preceding and following verses

– that is, from Q.[3] Otherwise we would have to suppose that Matthew and Luke copied Mark 1.7–8 to the phrase 'holy Spirit', and then both turned to Q for 'and fire', adding then another verse from Q. The two-source hypothesis does not ask this of us, and so proposes that Matthew and Luke were copying Q, producing incidentally triple agreements since Mark and Q agreed with each other.

The number of 'overlap' verses in which there is verbatim agreement between Mark and Q (taking Q to be best represented by Luke) is, by Streeter's count, about fifty.[4] This is the list from the principal five passages:

John the Baptist	Mark 1.2–4, 7–8
The Temptation	Mark 1.12–13
Collusion with Satan	Mark 3.22–30
Mustard Seed	Mark 4.30–32
Commissioning the Twelve	Mark 6.6b–11

Verbatim agreement in Greek naturally leads one to ask if there was a literary relationship between Mark and Q. Neither an affirmative nor a negative answer is helpful to the two-source hypothesis, as we shall explain.

No one who has investigated the issue has thought that Q used Mark. In 1911 Streeter argued forcefully that Mark used Q. In 1924 he urged that they were independent. If the second position is maintained, then we have a mystery: the difficulties of the synoptics are pushed into the unknown territory of the original development and transmission of the material. How can there be substantial verbatim agreement in Greek between two independent sources? The answer seems to be that we do not know, but apparently the material underwent quite diverse development (the hypothetical Q and Mark are not very similar), while in a few passages only retaining a common core between two different streams of transmission. If one maintains that Mark and Q were independent, yet have substantial verbatim agreement, one must posit this sort of diagram:

Original material in Greek

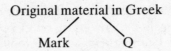

Mark   Q

We then are left with a great difficulty: why did the tradition divide into Mark (mostly narrative) and Q (mostly sayings)? The verbatim agreement between Mark and Q is too great for chance and must be attributed to a common source. But in this case the source looks very much like Matthew or Luke; it combined narrative and sayings. If one maintains that it was not Matthew or Luke, one must just shove the complexities of the synoptics to another level, and one where almost anything is possible: that of the imagination. Mark and the compiler of Q must independently have taken from a common source narrative and sayings, only very occasionally choosing the same material.

If the answer to the question of copying is affirmative, that Mark used Q, then one of the main principles of the two-source theory is surrendered: that Mark would not have left out sayings material had he known it. One of the principal objections to the view that Mark copied Matthew is that he would not have omitted the Lord's Prayer and the Beatitudes just to give space for verbal expansion of pericopes. But if he knew Q, that is just what he did. Streeter's earlier view, that Mark used Q, means the defeat of the two-source hypothesis – which of course he saw, and thus retracted the conclusion of a detailed and excellent study. The denial that Mark knew Q, in *The Four Gospels*, is made without the detailed and sharp analysis which marks the article in which he showed that Mark did know Q.

• Consequences

Thus far we have seen that agreements between Matthew and Luke against Mark put the two-source hypothesis into difficulty:

1. The minor agreements in the triple tradition are hard to explain if Matthew and Luke copied Mark completely independently. If they did not copy independently, both the existence of Q and the priority of Mark are put in jeopardy.

2. Major agreements between Matthew and Luke lead to the theory of Mark–Q overlaps. On the one hand, this theory solves everything: any uncomfortable agreements between Matthew and Luke can be attributed to their copying overlapping sources independently. On the other hand, the theory leads to difficulties. Either it pushes the hardest problems into the realm of an unknown large body of material in Greek (if Mark and Q are held to be independent), or it leads to the conclusion that Mark might willingly have left out a rich body of sayings material (if Mark knew Q), which would mean that one of the objections to the dependence of Mark on Matthew (or Luke) is eliminated.

The passages which count as Mark–Q overlaps according to the two-source hypothesis are not much of a problem for other hypotheses. Griesbachians, we have seen, regard Collusion with Satan as counting on their side, though the different placement of some of the material in Luke is a bit of a difficulty for them. They can only say that he moved it as he wished. In the other 'overlap' passages they say that

Mark abbreviated and that Luke was more faithful to Matthew, though he
sometimes rearranged material (or even repeated it, in the case of the Sending Out of
the Twelve). Mark–without–Q proponents see no difficulty in these passages: Mark
was first and shortest; Matthew expanded; Luke often followed Matthew, but
sometimes rearranged Matthew's expansions of Mark.

The issue is still not decided, but the Mark–Q overlaps lead us to a consideration of
one of the greatest puzzles in the study of the synoptics, the instances in which
Matthew instead of Mark is the middle term. We turn to this and the issue of
alternating support for Mark in the next chapter.

5 Further Complexities and a Different Solution

- Matthew as middle term

It is a fundamental feature of the synoptic gospels that usually Mark is the middle term. We saw that this fact does not necessarily decide whether Mark was first or third, but any solution must explain why there are lots of triple agreements, lots of Mark–Matthew agreements, lots of Mark–Luke agreements, but relatively few Matthew–Luke agreements. Yet in a few passages Matthew takes the place of Mark: there are triple agreements, Matthew–Mark agreements, Matthew–Luke agreements, but very few Mark–Luke agreements.

Point 1: Sometimes Matthew not Mark is the middle term.

Pericope 1: On Collusion with Satan, *Matt. 12.22–37 and parr.*

In the previous chapter (Pericope 6) we pointed out that Matthew is supported alternately by Mark and Luke. Griesbachians propose that Mark and Luke copied Matthew selectively, while supporters of the two-source hypothesis say that Matthew conflated Mark and Q (represented by Luke). In any case Matthew is the middle term.

Pericope 2: The Great Commandment, *Matt. 22.34–40 and parr.*
Aland 222; Greeven 222; Throckmorton 208

Matt. 22.34–40	Mark 12.28–34	Luke 10.25–28
(22.46)		(20.40)
[34]But when the Pharisees heard that he had silenced the Sadducees, they came together. [35]And one of them, a lawyer, asked him a question,	[28]And one of the scribes came up and heard them disputing with one another, and seeing that he	[25]And behold, a lawyer stood up

84

Matt. 22.34-40	Mark 12.28-34	Luke 10.25-28
to test him. [36]'Teacher, which is the great commandment in the law?' [37]And he said to him,	answered them well, asked him, 'Which commandment is the first of all?' [29]Jesus answered, 'The first is, "Hear, O Israel: The Lord our God, the Lord is one;	to put him to the test, saying, 'Teacher, what shall I do to inherit eternal life?' [26]He said to him, 'What is written in the law? How do you read?' [27]And he answered, 'You shall love the Lord
'You shall love the Lord your God with all your heart, and with all your soul, and with all your mind.	[30]and you shall love the Lord your God with all your heart, and with all your soul, and with all your mind, and with all your strength."	your God with all your heart, and with all your soul, and with all your strength, and with all your mind;
[38]This is the great and first commandment. [39]And a second is like it, You shall love your neighbor as yourself. [40]On these two commandments depend all the law and the prophets.'	[31]The second is this, "You shall love your neighbour as yourself." There is no other commandment greater than these.' [32]And the scribe said to him, 'You are right, Teacher; you have truly said that he is one, and there is no other but he; [33]and to love him with all the heart, and with all the understanding, and with all the strength, and to love one's neighbor as oneself, is much more than all whole burnt offerings and sacrifices.' [34]And when Jesus saw that he answered wisely, he said to him, 'You are not far from the kingdom of God.'	and your neighbor as yourself.' [28]And he said to him, 'You have answered right; do this, and you will live.'
22.46		20.40
[46]And no one was able to answer him a word, nor from that day did any one dare to ask him any more questions.	And after that no one dared to ask him any question.	[40]For they no longer dared to ask him any question.

In this passage there are numerous minor agreements between Matthew and Luke against Mark, several agreements between Matthew and Mark against Luke, but virtually no agreements at all between Mark and Luke. Matthew has in common with Mark, for example, 'he asked him' and 'which commandment'. He agrees with Luke in having 'lawyer', 'to test', 'teacher' and 'in the law'. We note that the result is **alternating support** for Matthew:

Matthew's verse	Agreement with
34 heard / akousantes	Mark
35 one asked / epērōtēsen heis	Mark
a lawyer testing / nomikos peirazōn	Luke
36 teacher / didaskale	Luke
which commandment / poia entolē	Mark
in the law / en tōi nomōi	Luke
37 and he to him / ho de autōi [pros auton]	Luke

Whereas in Collusion with Satan Griesbachians argue that Mark and Luke copied Matthew, happening sometimes to copy alternating verses, in the Great Commandment they propose that they both copied but happened not to pick the same words. There are no agreements between Mark and Luke, except for the opening 'and' and the biblical quotations which give the great commandments. (According to some manuscripts, however, in the quotations they agree with each other against the biblical passages quoted. This is a vexed issue, and little weight can be put on it.[1])

The passage is very difficult to explain on the basis of the two-source hypothesis. It might be proposed that Matthew and Luke depended on a Proto–Mark, but some consider this passage a Mark–Q overlap. Luke's version, in any case, could not have come from our Mark – thus the theory of a Proto–Mark or an overlap with Q. For our present purposes, we note that Matthew is the middle term, agreeing with both Mark and Luke, though they do not agree with each other.[2]

Pericope 3: Warnings concerning Temptations, *Matt. 18.6–9 and parr.*
    Aland 168; Greeven 145; Throckmorton 131

In this passage, which we do not print, Matthew's v. 6 is largely in agreement with Mark, though the word 'these' agrees with Luke (v. 2b). Luke agrees with both in the words 'mill . . . around his neck' ('stone' in Luke is a different word from 'stone' in Matthew and Mark). Matthew's v. 7 is largely in agreement with Luke, not at all with Mark. For the rest of the passage Luke has no parallel, and Matthew and Mark agree, though Mark has material not in Matthew. The only agreements of Mark and Luke against Matthew are 'if . . . were hung . . . around . . . into' (Matthew's prepositions are 'on' and 'in').

Thus again Matthew is supported alternately by Mark and Luke, and there are few agreements between Luke and Mark. It is difficult to know, as in the previous case, how Luke could have derived his passage from Mark if he did not also have Matthew.

Pericope 4: Healing in a Lonely Place, *Mark 6.32–34 and parr.*
    Aland 146; Greeven 125; Throckmorton 112

We have already noted the agreements between Matthew and Luke against Mark in this passage (ch. 4, Pericope 2). Further, we shall return to it in discussing Boismard's theory in the next chapter, where it will be printed in full (ch. 6, Pericope 4). Here we note that in it Matthew is the middle term. Most synopses do not segregate these verses as a separate passage, but it should be considered one, and

Funk correctly treats it as one. It now stands as the introduction to the Feeding of the Five Thousand in other synopses.

There are agreements between Matthew and Mark and between Matthew and Luke, but virtually no triple agreements and very weak agreements between Mark and Luke. Matthew is the middle term, and Luke's version cannot be derived from Mark. The following table shows the alternating support for Matthew:

Matthew's verse	Agreement with
13 withdrew / anechōrēsen [hypechōrēsen]	Luke
in a boat to a desert place	Mark
alone / kat' idian	Both
the crowd followed him	Luke
on foot from the city	Mark
14 and going out he saw a great crowd and felt	
compassion for them	Mark
healed / etherapeusen [therapeias]	Luke

To defend the two-source hypothesis, it is best to appeal to a Proto– or Deutero– Mark – some version of Mark other than ours – to explain the passage. It is simpler to think that Luke used Matthew.

While appeal to complicating factors – Mark–Q overlaps, Proto–Mark or Deutero–Mark – can always 'save' the two-source hypothesis, it seems to us best to grant that in pericopes 2–4 we have, at the very least, evidence that Luke knew Matthew. It is hard to be definite about the relationship between Matthew and Mark. The Griesbachians will say that in passages in which Matthew is the middle term, Mark and Luke simply copied different bits of Matthew. Goulder and others will say that in these cases Luke, with Matthew and Mark both before him, preferred Matthew – contrary to his usual choice.

We should note how two-source proponents and Griesbachians regard the question of **the middle term**. Both see that the gospel which is the middle term is most probably first or third. According to the two-source hypothesis, Mark is usually the middle term because it was first and was copied selectively by the later gospels. When Matthew is the middle term it is because it conflated Mark and Q. Luke is (almost) never the middle term because it remained true to Q in 'overlap' passages, not conflating as did Matthew.

According to the Griesbach hypothesis Mark is usually the middle term because it was third and conflated Matthew and Luke. When Matthew is the middle term it is because it was copied selectively. Mark sometimes chose not to conflate Matthew and Luke, thus producing no Mark–Luke agreements. Luke is not the middle term because it had nothing to conflate. Luke copied one source (Matthew) and was copied by one (Mark). Thus it could never stand between them, at the apex of a pyramid or an inverted pyramid.

Goulder's view is that Mark, usually the middle term, was first. Matthew became the middle term when Luke preferred Matthew to Mark.

• Alternating support for Mark

We have seen that the Griesbachians propose that Mark conflated Matthew and Luke. We now turn to their strongest argument: Mark is the middle term, and this means among other things that either Matthew or Luke supports Mark. Sometimes they alternate in their support. The alternation becomes so marked that the simplest explanation is that it was Mark who did the alternating, not Matthew and Luke. He copied first one then the other, rather than being copied by first one then the other.

Point 2: There is too much alternation of support of Mark's sequence of pericopes by Matthew and Luke.

The chief instance of alternating support is the section Mark 4.10–6.52. The following chart shows the pattern of agreements in order. It is seen that generally Matthew and Luke agree with Mark: the sequence runs from Matthew 13.10 to 14.23 and from Luke 8.9 to 9.17. Yet there are numerous changes of support. The chart puts passages which are in the same order under the main headings and those which are out of order to the side.

	Matt.		**Mark**	**Luke**	
	13.10–15		1. 4.10–12	8.9–10	
	13.16–17		–		10.23–24
	13.18–23		2. 4.13–20	8.11–15	
13.12			3. 4.21–25	8.16–18	
	–		4. 4.26–29	–	
	13.24–30		–	–	
	13.31–32		5. 4.30–32		13.18–19
	13.33		–		13.20–21
	13.34–35		6. 4.33–34	–	
	13.36–43		–	–	
	13.44–46		–	–	
	13.47–50		–	–	
	13.51–52		–	–	
12.46–50		3.31–35		8.19–21	
8.18,23–27			7. 4.35–41	8.22–25	
8.28–34			8. 5.1–20	8.26–39	
9.18–26			9. 5.21–43	8.40–56	
	13.53–58		10. 6.1–6a		4.16–30
9.35;10.1ff.			11. 6.6b–13	9.1–6	
	14.1–2		12. 6.14–16	9.7–9	
	14.3–12		13. 6.17–29	–	
	14.13–21		14. 6.30–44	9.10–17	
	14.22–23		15. 6.45–52	–	

There are several striking alternations of support for Mark from Matthew to Luke, and from Luke to Matthew. The following list will make them clear. Numbers refer to the Markan passages as given above.

1. Matthew and Luke
2. Matthew and Luke
3. Luke
4. Neither
5. Matthew
6. Matthew
7. Luke
8. Luke
9. Luke
10. Matthew
11. Luke
12. Matthew and Luke
13. Matthew
14. Matthew and Luke
15. Matthew

One gospel stops supporting Mark and the other starts at these points: 3–4; 6–7; 9–10; 10–11. The Griesbach argument is straightforward: there are too many alternations of agreement to be explained as arising accidentally from the independent copying of Mark by Luke and Matthew.

Point 3: There is the same alternation of agreement within several triple tradition pericopes. We give a few examples:

Pericope 5: Jesus Blesses the Children, *Mark 10.13–16 and parr.*
   Aland 253; Greeven 202; Throckmorton 188

In this passage, which is printed above (ch. 3, Pericope 4), Mark looks very much like Matthew in the Beelzebul Controversy. Most of Mark's v. 13 is in both Matthew and Luke, but 'children' is in Mark and Matthew, 'touched' is in Mark and Luke. Mark's v. 14 is in both; v. 15 is in Luke; v. 16 in Matthew.

Pericope 6: The Sick Healed at Evening, *Mark 1.32–34 and parr.*
   Aland 38; Greeven 26; Throckmorton 14

Matt. 8.16–17	Mark 1.32–34	Luke 4.40–41
[34]When evening came they brought to him many who were possessed with demons;	[32]When evening came, when the sun set, they brought to him all who were sick or possessed with demons. [33]And the whole city was gathered together about the door.	[40]Now when the sun was setting, all those who had any that were sick with various diseases brought them to him;
and he cast out the spirit with a word, and healed all who were sick.	[34]And he healed many who were sick with various diseases, and cast out many demons;	and he laid his hands on every one of them and healed them. [41]And demons also came out of many, crying,
[17]This was to fulfil what was spoken by the prophet Isaiah, 'He took our infirmities and bore our diseases.'	and he would not permit the demons to speak, because they knew him.	'You are the Son of God!' But he rebuked them, and would not allow them to speak, because they knew that he was the Christ.

89

Here we see one of Mark's famous double expressions: 'when evening came, when the sun set'. Matthew has 'when evening came', Luke 'when the sun was setting'. Further, in Mark 1.34 we find 'who were sick with various diseases'. Matthew has 'who were sick', Luke has 'various diseases' (Luke 4.40).

We briefly note a few other cases of alternation in support: Mark. 1.42 – 'the leprosy left him' (Luke 5.13), 'and he was cleansed' (cf. Matt. 8.3); Mark 14.37 – 'Are you asleep?' (cf. Luke 22.46) 'are you not able to watch one hour?' (Matt. 26.40).

The Griesbach hypothesis accounts for these and other cases by proposing that Matthew wrote (for example) 'when evening came', that Luke altered it to 'when the sun was setting', and that Mark combined the two phrases.

Markan priorists argue that Mark had a double expression and that Matthew and Luke both wished to avoid the repetition. By chance they dropped different halves of Mark's expression. Griesbachians then reply that Matthew and Luke 'agree' in choosing alternate expressions from Mark too often for it to be accounted for by chance. If Matthew and Luke copied Mark independently, and if they shared the desire to avoid Mark's repetitiveness, one would expect them more often to have dropped the same half of a double expression. David Dungan put it this way:

> Just when Luke goes off into a special passage, there appears at Mark's side faithful Matthew, as if by magic, and just when Matthew suddenly departs on an errand of his own, in the nick of time back comes Luke, as if in response to a providential bath qol [heavenly voice]. How is it possible?[3]

Dungan, of course, thinks that it is not possible, and that alternating support is created by Mark's copying Matthew and Luke alternately. Christopher Tuckett, speaking for Markan priorists, replies that Mark has a great number of duplicate expressions. By one count there are 213. In only seventeen of these cases does Matthew have one half and Luke the other. That is not 'significantly high'.[4]

The argument could be continued. One could examine the 213 cases to determine where there is true redundancy. Not all the cases are as obvious as 'when evening came, when the sun set', and if the total number of duplicate expressions were reduced, the percentage of times in which Matthew has one half and Luke the other half would increase. One could also apply statistical analysis, attempting to establish the parameters of coincidence: how often could one expect two independent copyists to drop the same half, how often different halves?[5]

Frans Neirynck, who has done a major study of double expressions and similar aspects of Mark, has offered another defence of Mark's priority against the charge of 'too much alternation'. Matthew and Luke both, he proposes, tended 'to reduce reduplications, but in so far as the phrase each evangelist adopts proves to be in harmony with his personal redactional manner, one cannot say that the agreements or disagreements in the selection happened by chance'. Neirynck opposes statistics: one should not count instances and weigh probabilities, but rather explain each choice by Matthew and Luke. It turns out, however, that the 'personal redactional manner' of Matthew and Luke consists simply of what each must have done had he been copying Mark, and Neirynck's study remains locked in circularity. It depends on the opening assumption, that Mark was copied by Matthew and Luke.[6]

Finally the student is involved in an 'artistic' judgment. The problem of the duplicate expressions in Mark, and the large problem of other cases of alternating support, are rather like the problem of minor agreements. How much coincidence is too much coincidence? Do these problems cause one to look for another solution to the synoptic problem than the two-source hypothesis, or is it possible to handle each problem, repairing the basic hypothesis and making special arguments to account for difficulties?

• Consequences for the two-source hypothesis

Let us now return to the two-source hypothesis and ask if it has been discredited by the problems which have led some to prefer other solutions.

It is our own judgment that the two-source hypothesis in its simple form cannot be maintained. Its simple form is this:

1. Matthew and Luke both copied Mark and Q.
2. Q was a document.
3. Q consists of material common to Matthew and Luke.
4. Neither Matthew nor Luke knew the other.
5. The 'minor' agreements between Matthew and Luke against Mark are to be explained as largely the result of coincidence.
6. The major agreements between Matthew and Luke against Mark are the result of overlaps between Mark and Q.
7. Mark did not know Q; the overlaps are coincidental.

This hypothesis seems to us *unsatisfactory* for the following reasons:

1. The 'minor' agreements are too many and too substantial to be explained away.
2. There are instances in which Matthew is the middle term, and in which the simplest explanation is that Mark and Luke copied Matthew.
3. The defence of the two-source hypothesis by appeal to overlaps between Mark and Q is not satisfactory. This proposal simply shifts some of the principal problems of the hypothesis to the relationship between Mark and 'Q'. 'Q' then keeps growing to explain numerous agreements of Matthew and Luke against Mark. Further, the theory of overlaps results in extensive verbatim agreement between Mark and Q, which itself is hard to explain on the two-source hypothesis, except by more appeal to an unknown process of development and transmission of the material. The question here as elsewhere is whether or not there are fundamental complications to which there are no clear answers. Appeal to unknown documents and unknown relationships between them will in a sense solve everything. We return to this problem below.

The two-source hypothesis, then, must maintain the independence of Matthew and Luke – against the strong evidence that one knew the other; and the independence of Mark and Q – despite the verbatim agreements. It is not adequate to the task.

• Results for the Griesbach hypothesis

If the two-source hypothesis is not fully satisfactory, can we give the nod to the Griesbach hypothesis? It seems to us mechanically feasible. Mark could have written his entire gospel by conflating Matthew and Luke. In this sense the Griesbach proposal has an advantage over the two-source hypothesis. The latter simply cannot account for all the agreements between Matthew and Luke, and thus must be modified and complicated in numerous ways in order to be maintained at all. But Mark could have done what the Griesbach proposal has him do.

The question is, why would he? The strongest arguments against the Griesbach hypothesis are general, not technical. Why would anyone write a shorter version of Matthew and Luke, carefully combining them, and leaving out so much – such as the Lord's prayer and the beatitudes – while gaining nothing except perhaps room for such trivial additions as the duplicate phrases and minor details ('carried by four' and the like)? Further, if someone had undertaken this task, why would the church have preserved the gospel at all?

The Griesbachians do not have to have a full answer for these questions. Why an ancient would do what Mark is said to have done is unrecoverable. Perhaps he wrote to synthesize competing gospels and thus achieve harmony. Perhaps he enjoyed the puzzle aspects of his task. In the Graeco–Roman world epitomes and abbreviated documents did exist, and possibly Mark should be seen as an epitome which achieves a dramatic impact, based on the miracle stories and the emphasis on 'immediacy'. Yet the epitome theory leaves most people unsatisfied. Why would Mark bother? Matthew is not all that long. While we agree that we cannot fully recover an ancient author's intention, and thus that we cannot say that Griesbach's Mark is impossible, still it must be granted that, to the modern mind, there is a very strong objection to putting Mark third.

Let us go back now to the general problem. There are substantial difficulties in the way of accepting the two-source hypothesis or the Griesbach hypothesis. There are basically three ways out: (1) getting rid of the facts which most plague the two-source hypothesis (e.g. explaining away the agreements of Matthew and Luke against Mark); (2) offering more complicated varieties of the two-source hypothesis; or (3) devising a new hypothesis which will handle all difficulties yet also give a better explanation of Mark than does the Griesbach hypothesis. We reject (1): the difficulties with the two-source hypothesis in its simple form will not go away. We shall now consider (2) and (3), beginning with an alternative simple hypothesis.

6 Further Hypotheses: Simple and Complex

• Mark without Q

Since the worst difficulties for the two-source hypothesis come from the relationship between Matthew and Luke, one obvious solution is to eliminate 'Q' and to make either Matthew or Luke dependent on the other. We have already seen considerable evidence for the use of Matthew by Luke. The hypothesis that there was no Q, and that Luke copied Mark and Matthew (Mark without Q) was first proposed by Austin Farrer and has now been developed and explained more fully by Michael Goulder.[1] Goulder has argued that Matthew and Luke had no further sources: Matthew had only Mark and the Old Testament; Luke had only Mark, Matthew and the Old Testament. Thus the material attributed by many to Q and other sayings sources was composed by Matthew and Luke.

The first question is whether or not it can be proved that Luke knew Matthew – rather than a source containing some material now also in Matthew. The question is whether or not there are Matthaeanisms in Luke; that is, peculiarities of Matthew's own editorial or redactional activity.

Point: There are Matthaeanisms in Luke.

Pericope 1: Many from East and West, *Matt. 8.11–12 and par.*
  Aland 85; Greeven 58; Throckmorton 46

After the saying about 'Many coming from east and west', Matthew 8.12 reads thus: 'But the sons of the kingdom will be cast out into the outer darkness, and there will be weeping and gnashing of teeth'. Each of these phrases is Matthaean: that is, in the New Testament each phrase occurs only in Matthew, and occurs two or more times – except for one, 'weeping and gnashing of teeth', which occurs in the Lukan parallel. Luke 13.28 reads 'and there will be weeping and gnashing of teeth, when you see Abraham . . . in the kingdom of God'. (Besides the present passages, the Matthaean phrases occur as follows: 'sons of the kingdom' for Jews, Matt. 13.38; cf. 21.43;

'outer darkness' 22.13; 25.30; 'wailing and gnashing of teeth' 13.42, 50; 22.13; 24.51; 25.30).

The two-source explanation is that the saying appeared in Q, was copied by Matthew and partly by Luke, and that Matthew liked the terminology and repeated it elsewhere. The more obvious explanation is that Luke copied a Matthaean saying, picking up one of Matthew's pet phrases.

Pericope 2: Commissioning the Twelve, *Mark 6.6b–13 and parr.*
Aland 142; Greeven 122; Throckmorton 109

Matt. 9.35; 10.1,7–11,14	Mark 6.6b–13	Luke 9.1–6
	(3.13–15)	

Matt. 9.35; 10.1,7–11,14

9.35
[35] And Jesus went about all the cities and villages, teaching in their synagogues and preaching the gospel of the kingdom, and healing every disease and every infirmity.
10.1,7–11,14
[1] And he called to him his twelve disciples
and gave them authority over unclean spirits, to cast them out, and to heal every disease and every infirmity.
[7] And preach as you go, saying, "The kingdom of heaven is at hand." [8] Heal the sick, raise the dead, cleanse lepers, cast out demons. You received without payment, give without pay. [9] Take no gold, nor silver, nor copper in your belts, [10] no bag for your journey,
nor two tunics, nor sandals, nor a staff; for the laborer deserves his food. [11] And whatever town or village you enter, find out who is worthy in it, and stay with him until you depart.
[14] And if any one will not receive you or listen to your words, shake off the dust from your feet as you leave that house

Mark 6.6b–13

[6b] And he went about among the villages teaching.

[7] And he called to him the twelve, and began to send them out two by two, and gave them authority over the unclean spirits.

[cp. v. 12f.]

[8] He charged them to take nothing for their journey except a staff; no bread, no bag, no copper in their belts; [9] but to wear sandals and not put on two tunics.
[10] And he said to them, 'Where you enter a house,
stay there until you leave the place.
[11] And if any place will not receive you and they refuse to hear you, when you leave, shake off the dust that is on

Luke 9.1–6

[1] And he called the twelve together and gave them power and authority over all demons and to heal diseases,

[2] and he sent them out to preach the kingdom of God and to heal.

[3] And he said to them, 'Take nothing for your journey, no staff, nor bag, nor bread, nor silver; and do not have two tunics.

[4] And whatever house you enter, stay there, and from there depart.
[5] And wherever they do not receive you, when you leave that town shake off the dust from

There are several agreements between Matthew and Luke against Mark:

Mark's verse number

7   and to heal disease (therapeuein; RSV has 'cure' in Luke)

8   not a staff (for Mark's 'except a staff'; Luke 9.3,
    difficult to see in Greeven)

8   nor silver (arguron / argurion; difficult to
    see in Greeven; RSV has
    'money' in both Mark and Luke)

10 into whatever

11 leave . . . that town . . . dust (ekserchomenoi for
    Mark's ekporeuomenoi)

The last agreement is especially important, since Luke's phrase 'coming out of *that* city' has no antecedent in Luke. Above, Luke had written 'into whatever house you enter' (Luke 9.4). Now he writes, 'leave that town' (Luke 9.5), as if a town had previously been mentioned. Where it was previously mentioned was in Matthew, who has first 'into whatever town or village you enter' (Matt. 14.11), and then 'leave . . . that town' (14.14). It appears that Luke's 'that town' was taken from Matthew.

On the two-source hypothesis this is a Mark–Q overlap, and we must suppose that Q contained 'into whatever city or village' (as Matthew) and 'leave . . . that town (so both Matthew and Luke). (Mark overlapped Q with extensive verbatim agreement and was partially combined with Q by both Matthew and Luke.) This is unlikely, and it is much simpler to think that Luke used Matthew.

Pericope 3: John the Baptist, *Mark 1.2–3 and parr.*
  Aland 13; Greeven 13; Throckmorton 1

Pericope 4: Jesus' Testimony to John, *Matt. 11.10//Luke 7.27*
  Aland 107; Greeven 77; Throckmorton 65

This is a complicated example, the force of which can be seen fully only by comparing Pericopes 3 and 4 in Greek. Mark attributes to 'the prophet Isaiah' the following quotation: 'Behold I send my messenger before your face, who will prepare (*kataskeuasei*) your way; a voice crying in the wilderness . . .' (Mark 1.2–3). The first   95 part, 'behold I send . . .', is from Malachi (or Exodus) rather than Isaiah; 'a voice crying . . .' is from Isaiah. Neither Matthew nor Luke at this point has the quotation from Malachi, and they both begin the scriptural quotation with 'a voice crying . . .'. They do, however, have the quotation from Malachi elsewhere, in the passage where Jesus is said to have commented on John: he is the one of whom it was said 'behold I send . . .' (Matt. 11.10//Luke 7.27, Pericope 4).

Thus far we have an agreement in order between Matthew and Luke against Mark: they put 'behold I send' in the same place. Then we note that the quotation 'behold I send' in Mark is not a precise quotation of either Exodus 23.20 or Malachi 3.1: the verb in the first phrase, 'prepare your way' is *kataskeuazō* rather than *phylassō* (Exodus) or *epiblepō* (Malachi). When in the later passage Matthew and Luke quote 'behold I send my messenger . . . who will prepare the way', they agree with Mark rather than with Exodus or Malachi. Finally, Matthew and Luke have their own version of the quotation, ending *emprosthen sou*, 'before you'. *Emprosthen* is a favourite word of Matthew. It is in neither Exodus nor Malachi nor Mark; here Luke agrees with Matthew against them all.

On the basis of the two-source hypothesis it would have to be said (1) that there was an overlap between Mark and Q in the first section about John the Baptist; (2) that 'Q' had only the Isaiah quotation, while Mark had a conflated quotation; (3) that Matthew and Luke, independently, looking back and forth between Mark and 'Q', preferred 'Q'; (4) that their quotation of the saying later depended on a passage (Jesus' Testimony to John) which was in 'Q' but not in Mark; (5) that Q had Mark's variant verb, *kataskeuasei*; (6) that Q's quotation of the Malachi/Exodus passage agreed with Matthew's own preferred word choice. This is all perhaps conceivable, though more than slightly strained.

It is improbable that what we have here is a series of coincidences: Mark and 'Q' varied the 'behold I send' quotation in the same way; Matthew and Luke each decided to quote the passage in one place rather than another; Q happened to vary the quotation by using one of Matthew's favourite words. Copying among the evangelists is much simpler: either that Matthew is first and that Mark, copying it, but wanting to leave out one long story about John the Baptist, put a pertinent quotation in his opening passage about John; or, more likely, that Matthew copied Mark, recognized that 'behold I send' is not from Isaiah, and put the quotation later. Luke then simply followed Matthew both times. Whether Matthew is before Mark or Mark before Matthew, it is highly probable that Luke copied Matthew. It would have been Matthew who knew that 'behold I send' is not in Isaiah, and Matthew who put the quotation partly in his own vocabulary.

Conclusion: Mark without Q

Do these and similar arguments prove Goulder's hypothesis? It is our judgment that they prove at least part of it: Luke knew Matthew (or, as we shall point out below, a Proto–Matthew). A few examples cannot show that Luke had no other sources than Matthew and Mark. For that, one has to undertake a full redactional analysis of Luke (which Goulder has now completed but which is not yet published). We shall shortly take up the question in general of whether or not this simple and obvious proposal accounts for all difficulties.

We shall briefly mention that the opposite case – that Luke was copied by Matthew – cannot be made out. Luke's priority has been proposed, on the ground that his Greek can often be turned into Hebrew more easily than can that of the other gospels.[2] That, however, shows little, for the Hebrew which emerges is often classical biblical Hebrew, not first-century Hebrew. Luke, that is, imitated the biblical style, and he appears to have imitated it in Greek. In any case the Hebraisms of parts of his gospel show nothing about priority.

Further, there have been no successful attempts to find 'Lukanisms' in Matthew. If a simple hypothesis will prevail, it will be that Luke copied Matthew, not the reverse.

In favour of complicated solutions

The real question, however, is whether or not a simple hypothesis should prevail. Let us return to the question of which gospel is the middle term. We saw above that Mark is usually the middle term and is thus probably either first or third. Yet this is not always the case. In a considerable number of instances Matthew is the middle term. This alternation of which gospel is the middle term can be explained on the basis of the two-source hypothesis only with difficulty. Its defenders have to appeal to Mark–Q overlaps to explain these passages. The Griesbach hypothesis must maintain that in these cases Mark followed only Matthew (not conflating it with Luke), but that he usually left out those parts of Matthew chosen by Luke, since there are few Mark–Luke parallels at all, either against Matthew or in agreement with Matthew. This attributes to Mark a curious procedure. Goulder has a similar difficulty: he must say that in these passages Luke, contrary to his general practice, followed Matthew rather than Mark, except when Matthew agrees with Mark, when Luke chose to follow neither. Thus all three hypotheses are forced into strained explanations of the passages in which Matthew is the middle term.

This inclines us to look to a complicated solution. If there was a simple relationship among the gospels, we would expect each gospel to be related to the others in a consistent way. But they are not. *There are exceptions to every rule, including the most basic rule of all: that Mark is the middle term.*

A second factor which makes us prefer a complex solution is the *variety of agreement in the Matthew–Luke double tradition*. We recall that the Parable of the Pounds or of the Talents, for example, seems to be the same parable, yet Luke's version is not a copy of Matthew's (Matthew 25.14–30//Luke 19.11–27). Luke could, of course, have chosen sometimes to copy Matthew, sometimes to re-write. But it is difficult to see a system at work, and a *continued evolution of tradition* seems a strong possibility.

There is a third major argument. *Sometimes it appears that one gospel is the earliest, sometimes another.* Which one 'looks' earliest, of course, is a matter of subjective judgment, but there are enough cases in favour of each of the gospels to make us doubt that one has a monopoly on priority. We shall very briefly give some examples of arguments for priority in wording or presentation, focusing especially on arguments for the priority of Matthew or Luke.

1. It is often said that the later evangelists made the material more reverent towards Jesus. According to Mark 3.21 those around Jesus took hold of him, for others were saying 'he is beside himself'. Neither Matthew nor Luke has the passage, and Markan priorists reasonably propose that they omitted it out of reverence for Jesus.

Yet if one applies rigorously the criterion of 'reverence', one will see that the argument does not always cut the same way. According to Mark 6.3 the people of Nazareth asked, 'Is this not the carpenter, the son of Mary and the brother of James. . . ?' In Matthew's parallel (13.55) they ask, 'is this not *the son of* the carpenter, is his mother not *called* Mary and his brothers James. . . ?' Arguably Matthew – who has the virgin birth story – is here less reverent, not only in calling Jesus 'the son of the carpenter', but also in using the term 'called' for Mary – as if his origins were a bit dubious. The defender of Markan priority can say that Matthew did not like the Messiah to have a trade, but on balance Matthew here looks less pious.

Further examples: in Mark 10.17 the young man who approaches Jesus is said to kneel before him, a sign of reverence omitted by both Matthew and Luke. Both Mark and Luke emphasize the fame which Jesus attracted by healing a leper and curing the Gerasene demoniac, and they make the cured people early missionaries on behalf of Jesus. These pious conclusions are not in Matthew (Mark 1.45 and parr.; Mark 5.20 and parr.). Matt. 12.32b//Luke 12.10a state that whoever speaks against the Son of man will be forgiven. The next half-verse is in Mark, but not the saying about speaking against the Son of man. Since all the evangelists identified Jesus with the Son of man, Mark is more pious towards him than are Matthew and Luke.

2. Matt. 5.23–24 is often regarded as parallel to Mark 11.25 (so Greeven 34; Aland 55). These are the texts:

Matthew	*Mark*
If you are offering your gift at the altar, and there remember that your brother has something against you, leave your gift there before the altar and go; first be reconciled to your brother. . . .	And whenever you stand praying, forgive, if you have anything against anyone . . .

Rudolf Bultmann proposed that Matthew is 'a more original form, which presupposes the existence of a sacrificial system in Jerusalem'.[3]

3. In the Confession at Caesarea Philippi (Aland 158; Greeven 135; Throckmorton 122) Matthew's verses 16.17–19 are in neither Mark nor Luke. ('Jesus said, blessed are you Simon Bar Jonah . . . on this rock . . .'). Yet Bultmann thought that they contain the original ending of the pericope. He proposed that these verses go back to 'an old Aramaic tradition' and that they would have no place outside the Palestinian church, 'where Peter was looked up to as the founder and leader of the church'. The

rebuke of Peter ('get behind me, Satan') in Mark 8.32f. is 'a polemic against the Jewish-Christian point of view . . . from the sphere of the Hellenistic Christianity of the Pauline circle' (pp. 258f.). It is noteworthy that Matthew but not Luke has the rebuke. Bultmann's view leads to the following sequence: There was an early tradition (Bultmann thought an early post-resurrection tradition) in which Peter confessed Jesus as Messiah and was said to be the rock on whom the church was built. Matthew had independent access to that tradition and included the saying that Peter was 'the rock'. Mark dropped it and put in the rebuke to Peter. Our Matthew copied the rebuke from Mark, as well as the older tradition commending Peter. Luke followed Mark but chose not to include the rebuke.

4. There is a total of four passages in the synoptics which contain the prohibition of divorce: Matt. 5.32; 19.1–12; Mark 10.1–12; Luke 16.18. This fact in and of itself is evidence for two sources, generally held to be Mark and 'Q'. In this case Matt. 5.32 and Luke 16.18 are from 'Q', while Matt. 19.1–12 and Mark 10.1–12 are from Mark. Yet in the Markan passage there is, at the end, a statement that women should not divorce their husbands. The other passages mention only men who divorce their wives. Bultmann and others have thought that the prohibition directed to women, which in any case seems just to be tacked on at the end of Mark's pericope (Mark 10.12), is a later addition and that the Q form is earlier (p. 132). But in this case Matthew avoided the later addition, which does not appear in his parallel to Mark. It might be proposed that Mark 10.12 was added after Matthew copied Mark.

5. We saw above that in the passage on Plucking Corn on the Sabbath, Mark has two concluding sayings: 'the sabbath was made for people, not people for the sabbath'; 'the Son of man is Lord of the sabbath' (Mark 2.27–28). Neither Matthew nor Luke has the first saying, and many scholars have proposed that they did not have it in their text of Mark.[4]

These examples, which could be multiplied several times, indicate that scholars who accept the two-source hypothesis are not completely bound by it. In studying the details of the gospels, many scholars have been led to offer exceptions to Mark's priority. Some of the arguments are now no longer convincing, but scholars of all periods, using diverse criteria, have found exceptions to the general rule of Markan priority. These exceptions point in two different directions: (1) Mark had sources which maintained an independent life and which could be drawn on by Matthew and Luke, even while they were copying Mark. This accounts for instances such as nos. 2 and 3 above, in which Matthew (on Bultmann's view) had independent access to the pericopes about forgiving one's brother and about Peter's confession. (2) Matthew and Luke copied a text of Mark which was earlier than our Mark. This proposal covers nos. 1, 4 and 5 above, in which it is proposed that Matthew copied a version of Mark which was in part less pious than our Mark (no. 1) and which did not have Mark 10.12 (the woman divorces) and Mark 2.27 (sabbath made for people). These are two different ways of offering complications of the two-source hypothesis.

These two views are not in opposition to each other. They could be combined, and they were combined by Rudolf Bultmann. He could envisage Matthew's having access to a Markan pericope independently of Mark, and he also thought it likely that the text of Mark was slightly edited after Matthew and Luke had copied it, though the changes were not very substantial (338f.).

The second of these possibilities leads to the Proto–Mark theory, which has been mentioned previously. Most supporters of the two-source hypothesis have been willing to accept this view, though they have generally held, as did Bultmann, that Proto–Mark was not very different from our Mark. A slightly different Proto–Mark especially helps to explain some of the 'agreements in omission' between Matthew and Luke against Mark: the passages are later insertions into Mark. Others, however, have viewed Proto–Mark as very appreciably different, and in earlier years there were attempts to reconstruct it and to specify numerous additions by a later redactor. Emil Wendling, for example, reconstructed an early gospel which runs to about 18 pages, while the 'insertions' by the final redactor occupy about 11½ pages.[5]

We also saw above that the minor agreements of Matthew and Luke against Mark can be explained by the view that they copied a Deutero–Mark. We shall shortly lay out in full what these various complications look like when diagrammed. Just now we should note that it is quite reasonable to think in terms of a Proto–gospel or a Deutero–gospel or both: the original gospel material was not printed and distributed in hundreds of copies; it was passed on by hand, and it would have been simple for an individual copiest to become also an editor, making various and sundry changes. *We must allow for evolution of the gospel material at all stages of its transmission, including after it was shaped into a distinctive gospel.*

Complicated versions of the two-source hypothesis

We have several times glimpsed aspects of complicated versions of the two-source hypothesis, and now fuller evidence is in hand. We shall enumerate the arguments, beginning with those which we have already outlined, and then diagram the results:

1. The numerous minor agreements between Matthew and Luke, many of which are 'improvements', lead some scholars to the view that they used **Deutero–Mark**, an improved second edition.

2. In some passages scholars think that Matthew or Luke (usually Matthew) had access to an *earlier form of an individual pericope* than that now in Mark.

3. Sometimes both Matthew and Luke seem to have used an earlier form of Mark than the one we now have, a **Proto–Mark**, which lacked some of the verses in our Mark.

These three views lead to this diagram for the triple tradition:

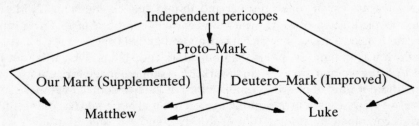

Independent pericopes

Proto–Mark

Our Mark (Supplemented)   Deutero–Mark (Improved)

Matthew   Luke

4. The wide variety of agreement between Matthew and Luke in their double

tradition has led to the view that there were two editions of Q. We may again cite Bultmann as having held this view.

5. Matthew and Luke have considerable material which is not paralleled in either of the other two gospels. This has led to the proposal that they had further sources: M (special Matthaean tradition) and L (special Lukan tradition).

6. Much of Luke's 'L' material, together with most of his 'Q' material, appears in a long section of Luke (9.51–18.14) which has very little material in common with Mark. The alternation of 'Q' and 'L' is best seen in the colour chart by Alan Barr, *Diagram of Synoptic Relationships*, though it can also be shown in tabular form. We reproduce here a portion of a table prepared by F. C. Grant[6] which shows the proposed combination of L and Q:

Q	L
12.2–12	
	12.13–21
12.22–31	
	12.32,33a,[35–38],47,48
12.33b,34,39,40,42–46,49–53,[54–56],57–59	
	13.1–17

If one looks at a synopsis it will be seen that Luke's long passage called Cares about Earthly Things (Luke 12.22–34) has a lot in common with two passages in Matthew (Matt. 6.25–33; 6.19–21), but also has further material, such as 12.32, 'Fear not, little flock, because your father pleases to give you the kingdom'. This saying, according to the theory we are now considering, comes from L, though most of the passage is from Q. Since the Q and L material is interwoven in this long section of Luke, while the Markan material is hardly represented at all, many scholars have thought that Q and L were combined before the Markan material was incorporated. This combination of Q and L came to be called 'Proto–Luke'. The theory of Proto–Luke, of course, depends on the general validity of the two-source hypothesis. It simply adds another level of editorial activity in order to account for the arrangement of material in Luke. It is noteworthy that the Proto–Luke hypothesis requires very close interstitching of the two sources; the author must have alternated between them more than once in some verses.

The theory is diagrammed as follows:

Q   L

↓   ↓

Proto–Luke

Thus we see that many scholars, while maintaining the two-source hypothesis, have complicated the theory in order to meet numerous difficulties. Besides those listed above, we recall that the hypothesis requires overlaps between Mark and Q,

101

either because Mark knew Q or because, when the tradition divided into what became Mark and Q, some passages went in both directions.

If we add all these together, we see that the simple two-source hypothesis is no longer simple, and that, in order to maintain it, many scholars have complicated it. We may diagram these various proposals as follows:

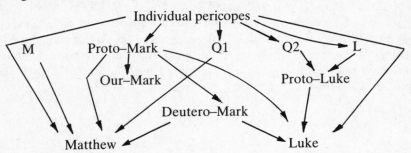

This arrangement makes almost all things possible. According to it, any one of the three synoptics may have the earliest form of a tradition, and *the two-source hypothesis does not entirely determine which of the gospels is earlier in any given pericope.*

We should emphasize that the five-stage diagram immediately above is not the concrete proposal of any individual scholar, but a composite based on various widely held views. Some might thus object that the chart offers an unreasonably complex portrait of modified two-source theories. We first note that combinations of the major complications have been proposed by leading scholars. Streeter, for example, the 'codifier' of the two-source hypothesis in English-language scholarship, actually offered a four-source and three-stage theory: M, Q, L and Mark, followed by Proto–Luke (conflating Q and L), and only then by the canonical gospels. Bultmann, we have seen, accepted both a Proto–Mark and independent access on the part of Matthew to independent pericopes. Variety in defining Q has naturally been very great, since the document is hypothetical. Q1 and Q2 is a mechanical way of expressing the common view that the Q material was fluid.

We should also note that many scholars who claim allegiance to the two-source hypothesis often hold complicated forms of it without laying out and diagramming the implications of various individual comments. Commentators on Matthew, for example, having accepted the two-source hypothesis in their introductions, not infrequently intersperse the commentary with references to 'independent traditions' and the like. The actual variety in views held by those who accept the two-source hypothesis is probably greater than the chart indicates.

Finally, we offer two diagrams to illustrate the great flexibility which formal holders of the priority of Mark and the existence of Q have put forward. The first is by F. C. Grant, who proposed a 'Multiple Source Theory' which is even more complicated than Boismard's (see the next section), but which is more closely tied to the two-source hypothesis. It may profitably be compared with our own diagram of complications of the two-source theory above:[7]

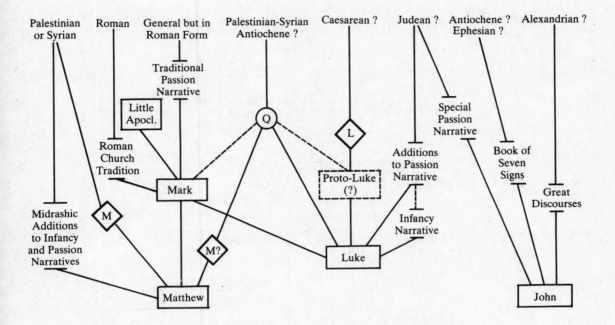

In addition, Grant proposed, the gospels also had access to oral traditions. Here we see exemplified the view that all the gospel material has a source, and we also see the logical extension of the two-source theory once all the exceptions to the rule are fully taken into account.

The next chart (on p. 104), by Robert Funk, presents the transmission of gospel material as a process in which a continuing oral tradition could influence the written gospels at any point:[8]

The net effect of this chart is to allow what we diagrammed above as 'individual pericopes' to re-enter the gospel tradition after Mark and Q. This, again, makes it possible to find, in any individual case, that one of the later gospels has the earlier tradition. We should note here that we do not share the view that memorized texts were passed down orally in Greek. For the present we allow the point to pass; it will be discussed in ch.9.

Is the two-source hypothesis, if altered and made more flexible in one or more of these ways, convincing? Complexity can account for the agreements of Matthew and Luke against Mark, for instances in which Matthew is thought to be earlier than Mark, and for the range of agreement between Matthew and Luke in their double tradition. Yet the basic hypothesis is still vulnerable on the two counts that have always been its weak spots: (1) The agreements between Matthew and Luke are still best explained by the view that Luke knew Matthew. The evidence for Luke's use of

103

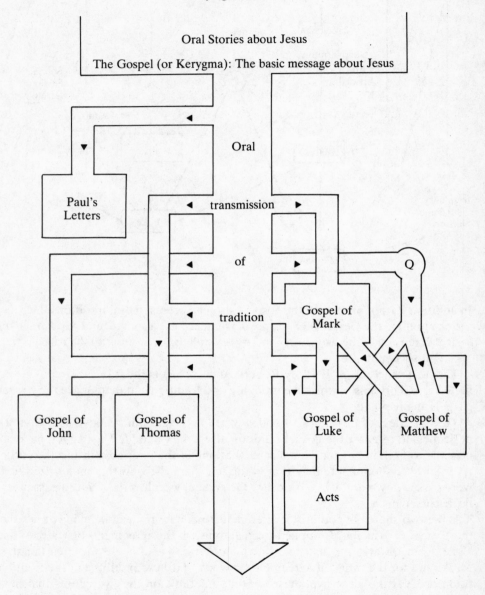

Crucifixion of
Jesus
30 CE

50 CE
Scribal or written
activity begins

70 CE
Fall of Jerusalem

90 CE

JESUS

Sayings and Parables

Oral Stories about Jesus

The Gospel (or Kerygma): The basic message about Jesus

Oral

transmission

of

tradition

Paul's
Letters

Gospel of
Mark

Q

Gospel of
John

Gospel of
Thomas

Gospel of
Luke

Gospel of
Matthew

Acts

Matthew leads to a rejection of Q as a document, or even as a closely maintained body of oral texts. To accept this one need not follow Goulder in holding that Matthew and Luke had no sources for their sayings material, just that the evidence is against the existence of Q as traditionally defined: the sayings material common to Matthew and Luke. (2) The problem of the Mark–Q overlaps still remains. The verbatim agreement between Mark and the hypothetical Q is very difficult to explain on the two-source hypothesis, even complicated forms of it. It is hard to defend the view that Mark and Q overlapped, and that there is verbatim agreement between them, but that they were entirely independent. Continuing oral tradition will not account for word-for-word agreement in Greek. If they were not independent, one cannot explain Mark's omission of so much of the Q material.

These two points are complementary. The evidence which, in our judgment, shows that Luke used Matthew can be answered only by appealing to more and more Mark–Q overlaps. But the theory of overlaps, when extended beyond two or three pericopes, up to 15 to 20 (required to take care of the Matthew–Luke agreements), means that Q was very like a whole gospel.

We shall now consider another complex solution to the synoptic problem: that of M.-E. Boismard.

• Boismard's solution

Boismard has offered a different kind of complicated solution, one which envisages multiple documents and also multiple editions of each gospel. *The final form of each gospel was dependent on the earlier version of at least two of the gospels.* In diagrammatic form his proposal looks like this:[9]

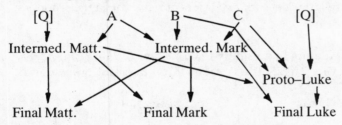

The letter Q appears twice in brackets in order to indicate that Boismard thinks of there being only one Q. The duplication is only for ease of line-drawing. The source A he defines as a Palestinian proto-gospel; B is a Gentile–Christian revision of it (and the primary source of Intermediate Mark); C is independent and old, probably of Palestinian provenance. Intermediate Mark and Q play the roles assumed by Mark and Q in the two-source hypothesis: Intermediate Mark supplies the narrative framework of the synoptics, while Q provides the sayings material common to Matthew and Luke.

Boismard's theory allows for all possibilities even better than do complicated versions of the two-source hypothesis. Final Matthew may have an earlier version of a pericope than Final Mark, because it may more faithfully represent the source A – and so on.

105

Boismard's theory has four advantages:

1. It satisfactorily deals with the evidence that Luke knew Matthew, since Intermediate Matthew was used by Proto–Luke.

2. It allows for 'Matthaeanisms' in Mark, 'Markanisms' in Matthew, and the like.

3. It explains the verbatim agreement when Mark and Q overlap. Final Mark used both Intermediate Matthew and Proto–Luke, which in turn had used Q.

4. It combines some of the strong points of the two-source hypothesis and of the Griesbach hypothesis:

(*a*) As does the two-source hypothesis, Boismard's view explains the different arrangement of the sayings material in Matthew and Luke. Intermediate Matthew and Proto–Luke combined a narrative source and a sayings source independently, and they combined them in two different arrangements.

(*b*) As does the Griesbach hypothesis, Boismard's theory accounts for the signs of conflation in Mark. We recall that Mark often agrees alternately with Matthew and Luke. This is explained if Final Mark used Intermediate Matthew and Proto–Luke.

One substantial general problem remains unsolved. Why do we have a Final Mark at all? On Boismard's hypothesis Final Mark knew Intermediate Matthew and Proto–Luke, both of which already included Q. Why would he leave out such good material? This general problem is, we recall, one of the strongest arguments against the Griesbach hypothesis.

How does Boismard's theory work in detail? We take two sample pericopes, the first of which he has singled out as being one of his strongest examples.[10]

Point: There is evidence for two layers of redaction in the synoptics.

Pericope 4: Healing in a Lonely Place, *Mark 6.31–34 and parr.*
Aland 146; Greeven 125; Throckmorton 112; + Boismard, *Synopse* §151

Matt. 14.13–14	Mark 6.31–34	Luke 9.10b–11
	[31]And he said to them, 'Come away by yourselves to a lonely place, and rest a while.' For many were coming and going, and they had no leisure even to eat.	
[13]Now when Jesus heard this, he withdrew from there in a boat to a lonely place apart.	[32]And they went away in the boat to a lonely place by themselves. [33]Now	[10b]And he took them and withdrew apart to a city called Bethsaida.

106

Matt. 14.13-14	Mark 6.31-34	Luke 9.10b-11
But when the crowds heard it, they followed him on foot from the towns.	many saw them going, and knew them, and they ran there on foot from all the towns, and got there ahead of them.	[11]When the crowds knew it, they followed him;
[14]As he went ashore he saw a great throng; and he had compassion on them,	[34]As he went ashore he saw a great throng, and he had compassion on them, because they were like sheep without a shepherd; and he began to teach them many things.	and he welcomed them and spoke to them of the kingdom of God, and cured those who had need of healing.
and healed their sick.		

Boismard first notes that Luke has important agreements with Matthew against Mark, but only minor agreements with Mark against Matthew. Luke and Matthew agree against Mark:

Matthew's verse numbers

13 he withdrew / hypechōrēsen [anechōrēsen] (against Mark's 'they went away');
'the crowds . . . followed him' (against 'they got there ahead of them,' etc.);
14 healing / therap- (missing in Mark)

Luke and Mark agree against Matthew:

Mark's verse numbers
33 they knew / gnontes/epegnosan (missing in Matthew);
34 teaching, though expressed differently (see Luke 9.11b)

The agreements between Luke and Matthew are stronger than those between Luke and Mark, and Boismard says that the defender of the two-source hypothesis 'must concede that Luke, without knowing the text of Matthew, has reworked the Markan text in such a manner that it no longer yields more than vague contacts, while it agrees essentially with Matthew' (p. 2). There are, further, substantial agreements between Luke and Matthew in 'omission'.

This, of course, is just more evidence that Luke knew Matthew – a point which can be repeatedly demonstrated. What favours a complicated solution?

First Boismard observes that when Matthew is generally in agreement with both Mark and Luke, 'his text is closer to Luke than to Mark' (p. 11). But when he agrees with Mark alone, his text is nearly identical to Mark's: thus, in Matt. 14.13c–14 we read 'on foot from towns. As he went ashore he saw a great crowd and had compassion upon them'. That is all in precise agreement with Mark, though Mark has a few additional words. How to account for this alternation in Matthew, from agreeing largely with Luke when all three have basically the same material, to agreeing precisely with Mark when Luke does not have the material at all? Here Boismard proposes a double level of redaction.

If one notes the phrases in Matthew which largely agree with Luke, and omits the words and phrases where Matthew agrees with Mark, one reads a coherent short account: 'Jesus withdrew to a lonely place apart, and the crowd followed him, and he healed [them].' Boismard proposes that here we have Intermediate Matthew (relying on source A), and that Proto–Luke copied Intermediate Matthew. Luke then relied on Proto–Luke: thus the agreements between Matthew and Luke against Mark, agreements which, moreover, make up a coherent story. Final Matthew, however, had Intermediate Mark, and conflated it with Intermediate Matthew: thus the precise agreement with Mark in the phrases quoted above from Matt. 14.13c–14. Luke's weak agreements with Mark (teaching, 'knowing') show that Final Luke knew Intermediate Mark, but did not much use it in this passage (unlike Final Matthew, who quoted it extensively).

Final Mark conflates two different though partially parallel sources:

Mark 6.32, 33b,c, 34b
[32] And they went away to a lonely place by themselves. [33b,c] [Many] knew them, and they ran there from all the towns. [34b] And he began to teach them many things.

Mark 6.31, 32a, 33a, 33d, 34a
[31] And he said to them, 'Come away by yourselves to a lonely place, and rest a while.' For many were coming and going . . . [32a] And they went away in the boat. [33a] Now many saw them going; [33d] and on foot they got there ahead of them. [34a] As he went ashore he saw a great throng, and he had compassion on them.

Boismard notes that in Mark there are two complete *sequences*, each starting with a withdrawal to a lonely place. He proposes that the shorter sequence, printed above in the left-hand column, is from Source A, while the longer is from Source B. Mark's version of Source A concludes with teaching, while Matthew's version concludes with healing. This, Boismard proposes, reflects redactional tendencies, and the same variation is seen in Matt. 19.2//Mark 10.1.

The numerous agreements in 'omission' between Matthew and Luke against Mark are explained in this way: Final Matthew's story-line was set by Intermediate Matthew, which did not have Source B. The same is true of Luke (following Proto–Luke). Final Matthew copied some of Final Mark, and thus incorporated some of Source B. The parts not incorporated are 'agreements in omission'.

This is a complicated example, and we shall offer a summarizing list of the points and Boismard's explanation of them:

1. Luke has very few and quite weak agreements with Mark, but substantial agreements with Matthew. The Luke–Matthew agreements arise because Proto–Luke copied Intermediate Matthew. The few Mark–Luke agreements show that Final Luke knew Intermediate Mark. Final Luke basically followed Proto–Luke.

2. Intermediate Matthew, in turn, used Source A, a short account of withdrawal and either teaching or healing.

3. Once this short account is deleted from Final Matthew, we see that the other words in Matthew are in precise agreement with Mark. This shows that Final Matthew conflated Intermediate Matthew and Intermediate Mark.

4. There are two full sequences in Mark: One of them basically agrees with the Matthew–Luke common version (Source A via Intermediate Matthew), except that it has teaching rather than healing. This variation is redactional (either Intermediate Matthew or Intermediate Mark). The second, longer sequence is from Source B.

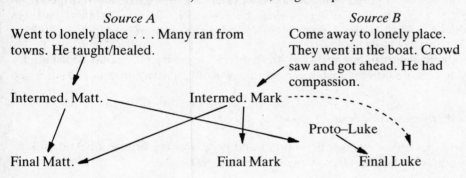

Source A
Went to lonely place . . . Many ran from towns. He taught/healed.

Source B
Come away to lonely place. They went in the boat. Crowd saw and got ahead. He had compassion.

Intermed. Matt.   Intermed. Mark

Proto–Luke

Final Matt.   Final Mark   Final Luke

Pericope 5: Jesus' True Kindred, *Mark 3.31–35 and parr.*
Aland 121; Greeven 102; Throckmorton 89; Boismard 122

Matt. 12.46–50	Mark 3.31–35	Luke 8.19–21
[46]While he was still speaking to the people, behold, his mother and his brothers stood out-side, asking to speak to him.	[31]And his mother and his brothers came; and standing out-side they sent to him and called him. [32]And a crowd was sitting about him; and they said to him, 'Your mother and your brothers [and your sisters] are outside, asking for you.' [33]And he replied, 'Who are my mother and	[19]Then his mother and his brothers came to him, but they could not reach him for the crowd. [20]And he was told, 'Your mother and your brothers are standing outside, desiring to see you.' [21]But he said to them,
[[47]Some one told him, 'Your mother and your brothers are standing outside, asking to speak to you.'] [48]But he replied to the man who told him, 'Who is my mother, and who are		

109

Matt. 12.46-50	Mark 3.31-35	Luke 8.19-21

my brothers?' ⁴⁹And stretching out his hand toward his disciples, he said, 'Here are my mother and my brothers! ⁵⁰For whoever does the will of my Father in heaven is my brother, and sister, and mother.'

my brothers?' ³⁴And looking around on those who sat about him, he said, 'Here are my mother and my brothers! ³⁵Whoever does the will of God is my brother, and sister, and mother.'

'My mother and my brothers are those who hear the word of God and do it.'

Boismard first of all notes that a version of the saying also appears in The Gospel of Thomas (it can be seen in a footnote in Greeven, in an appendix in Aland), and that version is closest to Luke. This he takes as evidence for the existence of two versions of the saying. He then observes that there seem to be two different passages combined in Mark. In Boismard's analysis one version is found in Mark. 3.32b,35:

> Behold! your mother and your brothers and your sisters are outside asking for you. [Jesus answered]: whoever does the will of God is my brother and sister and mother.

The other version is in Mark 3.33–34:

> And he replied, 'who is my mother and [who are] my brothers'? And looking around . . . he said, 'behold my mother and my brothers'.

Luke, it is to be noted, has material parallel to Mark 3.32b,35, not to Mark 3.33–34. The first story Boismard attributes to source B, which was used by Proto–Luke as well as by Mark, and Final Luke's version comes via Proto–Luke, not Intermediate Mark.

On text-critical grounds Boismard excludes Matt. 12.47 from the authentic text. The result is that Matthew does not have an equivalent to Mark v. 32. Intermediate Matthew, he proposes, had only 12.48–49, which is parallel to Mark 3.33–34, and which Boismard attributes to source A. Matt. 12.50 was added by Final Matthew in dependence on Intermediate Mark. Thus:

Matt.		Mark		Luke	From
		32b	=	20	B
48–49	=	33–34			A
50	=	35	=	21	B

Intermediate Mark conflated A and B; Final Matthew conflated Intermediate Matthew (source A) and Intermediate Mark; Final Luke followed Proto–Luke; Proto–Luke followed B.

This is all possible, and it is argued with a wealth of detail and is based on sharp observations. What counts against Boismard's theory is that it combines complication, precision and hypothetical documents in a way that defies evidence. On the one hand, relationships are complicated. There were sources, the sources were shared by intermediate redactors, and the final redactors drew on more than one intermediate redaction. On the other hand, we are required to think that these steps can be precisely traced and that the hypothetical documents Q, A, B, and C really existed and can be reconstructed. In explaining everything, Boismard takes us into the realm of conjecture, where everything is possible.

Further Hypotheses:
Simple and Complex

111

7   Conclusion

It has become clear that no one solution to the synoptic problem is without objection. Boismard is correct in noting that both the two-source hypothesis and the Griesbach hypothesis have strengths, but his own attempt to combine them requires such a precise reconstruction of hypothetical sources and intermediate editions, and such a complicated pattern of interrelations among them, that it cannot be confirmed in detail. We have seen reason, further, to accept some aspects of Goulder's very simple solution.

All the other proposed solutions have their own merits. The two-source hypothesis is the best solution to the arrangement of Luke, and the Griesbach the best explanation of why Mark is the middle term. But, it seems to us, they both break down. The two-source solution must deny what is very probable: that Luke knew Matthew. The Griesbach proposal attributes an inexplicable procedure to Mark. Further, it has some difficulty with many of the passages in which Matthew is the middle term. At first these seem to support Matthew's priority, but they make Mark's editorial procedure even harder to understand, since in some of these cases he preferred the parts of Matthew not already chosen by Luke.

There have been numerous other proposed solutions, and they all have their merits. This constitutes a general argument for a complicated solution, but one which cannot be precisely described. The fact that each solution has its strong point may indicate that no one of them is right in all cases. Uncertainty is also recommended by the fact that the evidence is often patient of more than one interpretation, while some passages seem to point definitely in one way or the other. The problem is that they do not all point in any one way.

The solutions proposed by Goulder and Boismard are especially worth considering in general terms. They stand at opposite poles on an important question: the use of sources and the degree of free composition. Boismard sees our evangelists and their immediate predecessors (the editors of the intermediate redactions) as basically conflators, not authors. Goulder sees Matthew and Luke especially as authors, able to write excellent material, especially parables and ethical teaching. Our own inclination is to accept some of each hypothesis but to avoid the extremes. The evangelists were authors, though perhaps not quite as inventive as Goulder thinks, but in any case authors rather than only wielders of scissors and paste. On the other hand Boismard is probably on the right track in thinking of different editions and in allowing for criss-cross copying.

It is entirely reasonable to think of different editions of one or more of the gospels. At the social and economic level at which they were first published and circulated, it is unlikely that they were published professionally. Some books were: a large room of scribes would copy simultaneously while the text was read, and the result would be several copies with only minor variations.[1] But if one of the gospels were copied only once, and the copy passed on, it would be very easy for modifications to be made. Some of these modified versions then might survive and the original perish. Thus theories of Proto– and Deutero–Mark, or of Intermediate Matthew and Mark, are not in the least unlikely, and we may have here the explanation of some of the difficulties of the problem as we meet it today.

Ultimately the issue between Boismard and Goulder can be resolved only by complete redactional studies of each gospel. Goulder has offered such a study of Matthew and has now completed his study of Luke. It will take some while before the latest work can be evaluated, and meanwhile we can best briefly state that we find his explanation of the composition of Matthew not to be fully convincing. It depends on the theory that the Old Testament was read in the churches in a one-year lectionary cycle. Matthew, he has argued, composed his gospel by using Mark and the Old Testament in its lectionary sequence. Thus Goulder finds connections between successive pericopes in Matthew and the proposed lectionary. The evidence, however, is against the hypothesis of a one-year lectionary cycle, and in any case some of his proposed connections seem strained. Thus far, it seems to us, he has not succeeded in giving a full explanation of Matthew, and it is better to continue to think that the gospels had sources for at least some of their sayings material. Goulder has, however, advanced the study of Matthaean style and compositional habits, and his work on how to identify the Evangelist's 'hand' is extremely useful though criticisms can be made (see Kenneth Newport, cited below). The book on Luke will, we do not doubt, prove to be equally rewarding.

We shall not undertake here to say in just which passages we follow Goulder in thinking that the entire composition is the work of Matthew or Luke, but we can indicate in general that his best case is the parabolic material.

Boismard's theory of criss-cross copying seems the best explanation of the fact that sometimes Mark, sometimes Matthew is the middle term. Mark probably did sometimes conflate material which came separately to Matthew and Luke (so the Griesbach hypothesis), and Matthew probably did conflate material which came separately to Mark and Luke (so the two-source hypothesis).

Thus we think that Luke knew Matthew (so Goulder, the Griesbachians and others) and that both Luke and Matthew were the original authors of some of their sayings material (so especially Goulder). Following Boismard, we think it likely that one or more of the gospels existed in more than one edition, and that the gospels as we have them may have been dependent on more than one proto- or intermediate gospel.

113

The great strength of the two-source hypothesis is that it explains why Luke's narrative framework is the same as that of Matthew and Mark, while in the 'Q' material its order is different from Matthew's. If Luke used Matthew, why this distinction? The situation is not as straightforward as it often seems. In a very large section of Luke, about nine chapters, there is virtually no Markan material (Luke 9.51–18.14). Moreover, Mark 6.45–8.26 does not appear in Luke. The author of Luke broke with Mark to a very considerable degree. When he did so, he strung sayings passages along a narrative line, the story of Jesus' journey to Jerusalem. This meant that the sayings material was not presented in large blocks as it is in Matthew. He had his own views, that is, about both the narrative framework and the distribution of the sayings material, and he did not wish to treat them as Matthew did.

At the end of ch. 3 we wrote that the compelling character of the two-source hypothesis depends in part on the level of generality with which it is presented. If one says that Luke's order in the triple tradition agrees with that of Mark, while in the double tradition it does not agree with Matthew, the conclusion seems reasonable that Luke used Mark but not Matthew: the double tradition came from a loose collection or from a source with a different order from the one used by Matthew. Streeter expressed this view in telling phrases. If Luke derived the Matthew/Luke double tradition from Matthew,

> he must have gone through both Matthew and Mark so as to discriminate with meticulous precision between Marcan and non-Marcan material; he must then have proceeded with the utmost care to tear every little piece of non-Marcan material he desired to use from the context of Mark in which it appeared in Matthew – in spite of the fact that contexts in Matthew are always exceedingly appropriate – in order to re-insert it into a different context of Mark having no special appropriateness. A theory which would make an author capable of such a proceeding would only be tenable if, on other grounds, we had reason to believe he was a crank.[2]

This depends on one value judgment and some incorrect generalizations. Streeter thought that Matthew had made a good arrangement of the sayings material and that no one would have changed it. We can, however, imagine that an author would like more action and fewer long monologues – and so on. But it is over-generalization which gives Streeter's statement its persuasive power. In fact, Luke does not always follow Mark; and in fact one can find numerous agreements in *relative* order between Matthew and Luke in their placement of double tradition material – not agreement with regard to which part of Mark it is close to, but agreement in the order of the double tradition itself.

This last fact is essential to all efforts to reconstruct 'Q', one of which was made by Streeter. He opposed the idea that 'Q' was a loose body of floating material and argued that it was a document. Crucial to this argument was his observation that one can 'detect behind the great variety of order a certain original unity of arrangement'. The order of the 'Q' material in Luke, he proposed, is very like the order of the Markan: '. . . if we compare the first thirteen chapters of Matthew and Luke as regards the sections which they derive from Mark, there is found to be an even greater variation in their respective orders' than there is in the arrangement of the double tradition. Moreover,

> if Mark had been lost instead of Q a precisely similar objection would have been made to the hypothesis that these Marcan sections in Matthew and Luke could have come from a single written source.[3]

This destroys the argument that the order of the double tradition proves that Luke did not use Matthew. If its order is close enough to prove common use of *one* written source, it is close enough to allow direct copying from one gospel to the other. If Luke used Matthew, he re-arranged the double tradition with about the same liberty as he re-arranged Mark. The overall Markan outline is preserved, to be sure: the story starts in Galilee at the time of John the Baptist, there is one trip to Jerusalem, and at the end Jesus is crucified. The double tradition has no such chronological markers, and so groups of two or three pericopes could be moved from the beginning to the middle. Despite this, 'if we confine our attention to the more salient features we find that the order of the Q sections in Matthew and Luke is very much the same'.[4] The order of pericopes in Luke does not prohibit the idea that Luke used Matthew.

Once one thinks that Luke could have used Matthew, it is easy to see the Third Gospel as in part a correction of the First. The number of generations in the genealogy is altered so as better to fill the number of years. The place of one of Jesus' discourses is changed, from the Mount to the Plain (Matt. 5.1; Luke 6.17), and the other Mosaic elements in Matthew's depiction of Jesus are also eliminated. If one grants that Luke used Matthew *and* was an author, the question of why he handled the double tradition as he did can be met by reasonable answers. The fact that it is arranged differently in the two gospels has often been posed as a mechanical or technical problem: if Luke knew Matthew, how could he have marked out the double tradition and re-arranged it, while not re-arranging the narrative source, Mark? But, to a considerable degree, Luke did re-arrange Mark, and, to a considerable degree, he preserved Matthew's order of the sayings material. If one adds to this that the author objected to Matthew's large blocks of sayings, and especially to the Sermon on the Mount, one will see that the problem has been posed in the wrong terms.[5]

It leaves something to be desired not to 'know' 'the solution' to the synoptic problem. But New Testament scholars have lived with uncertainty for a long time, an uncertainty masked by lip-service to 'the two-source hypothesis'. Few scholars have accepted the simple form of the hypothesis without exception, and once it becomes complicated, and exceptions are made, one is in fact accepting uncertainty. We think that this situation should simply be admitted.

There is, however, a corresponding gain. When scholars give up the mechanical application of the two-source theory they are free to look for other sources. An early source might well be embedded in the synoptics, but rendered invisible because part of it is triple tradition and part double tradition. H.-D. Betz has proposed that the Sermon on the Mount was an edited, coherent source.[6] The modified two-source

115

hypothesis which accepts M and L (thus requiring four sources) attributes much of the Sermon on the Mount to M, some to Q and a small number of sayings to Mark. This requires Matthew himself to have put it all together. Betz proposes that the Sermon on the Mount was edited much earlier than the time of the final evangelist. His argument is powerful and, at least at this early date, persuasive. Betz has not clarified how his source relates to Q (which he does not renounce), but the hypothesis seems destined to give proponents of Q a good deal of trouble. It will require Q to have developed in two quite different ways at a very early date.

Similarly David Wenham has proposed that there was a very early eschatological discourse.[7] As he reconstructs it, it was more a proto–Matthew than a proto–Mark, though Mark 13 is included within it. On his hypothesis Matthew had access to one of Mark's sources and used more of it than did Mark.

Finally, Kenneth Newport, in an as yet unpublished Oxford DPhil. thesis, finds a special source, closely related to the Sermon on the Mount, behind Matt. 23, instead of distributing the material to Mark, Q and M.[8]

These proposals all seem fruitful to us. We think that the gospels should be searched for sources, and one of the worst results of the dogmatic commitment to the two-source hypothesis is that such research has not been able to flourish.

We have remarked several times that most scholars who have worked closely on the synoptic gospels have, often without admitting it openly, rejected parts of the two-source hypothesis, whose official status was close to canonical for a hundred years (1860s to 1960s). We should be remiss, however, not to note that there are true believers. We have above cited Frans Neirynck and Christopher Tuckett as staunch defenders of the priority of Mark and the existence of Q as a document, and there are many others. In particular, there are believers in Q. Historically most scholars have been conscious that 'Q' is a scholarly convention which explains the Matthew–Luke double tradition, and they have deliberately remained vague about whether or not it was one document, a loose assemblage of passages, or simply a convenient name for oral or 'floating' traditions. For many decades the effort to reconstruct Q, like the effort to reconstruct Proto–Mark, was abandoned.[9] Now a few scholars are again attempting to define Q as a document: it really existed, it directly reflects *the* theology of *a* community, and one can even make a concordance of it. This work is mostly of curiosity value, since it shows how far a hypothesis can be pushed despite its lack of fundamental support. How dubious reconstructions of Q are will be readily recognized if we consider how much of Mark we could reconstruct from Matthew and Luke without having the text of Mark. For example, we would be ignorant of the existence of Mark 6.45–8.26, which does not appear in Luke and we could not be sure that Mark contained a passion narrative, since the versions in Matthew and Luke are so different. Some of the studies of Q, however, have independent value. We may mention ch. 7 of John Kloppenborg's *The Formation of Q*, on ancient sayings collections. There are other good sections of the work, especially the destruction of the notion that ancient materials possessed innate 'trajectories' that pushed them on a pre-determined course.

To summarize the conclusions of these chapters: We think that Matthew used Mark and undefined other sources, while creating some of the sayings material. Luke used Mark and Matthew, as well as other sources, and the author also created sayings material. There are probably complicating factors in the interrelationships among the gospels, and it is not unlikely that there was criss-cross copying among them – or, better, from one edition of one to one edition of another, and back the other way at a later stage.

It is our judgment that this shows that the literary relations are in fact complex. Those who have defended the two-source hypothesis by complicating it, and those who have proposed other complicated solutions, have seen something. They have seen that there is no one answer which easily solves everything. We should review the theories discussed:

1. The two-source theory – when complicated by the addition of Proto– and Deutero–Mark, further sources, two versions of Q, Mark–Q overlaps and Proto–Luke – can handle most of the material. Yet even with these complications difficulties remain. The two fatal ones are (1) the evidence that Luke knew Matthew (which not even the theories of Proto–Mark and Mark–Q overlaps entirely meet) and (2) the verbatim agreement between Mark and 'Q' in the supposed overlap passages. Of all the solutions, this one, which remains the dominant hypothesis, is least satisfactory.

2. The Griesbach hypothesis (Matthew was copied by Luke, and Mark conflated them both) is technically possible. It suffers from the inability to explain Mark. It may be that here we face only a failure of imagination: why would anyone carefully conflate parts of Matthew and Luke, while omitting so much of both? Nevertheless, scholarship cannot accept a theory of literary relationship which it cannot comprehend. Moreover, what is known of ancient authors who conflated indicates that they did so by incorporating their sources in blocks, rather than by switching back and forth from phrase to phrase.[10]

Goulder's hypothesis (Mark without Q) is also technically possible. Accepting it depends on being able to explain how Matthew and Luke were composed if the only sources were (in Matthew's case) Mark, Scripture and imagination; and (in Luke's case) Mark, Matthew, Scripture and imagination. Thus far Goulder has not persuaded us that one can give up sources for the sayings material. With this rather substantial modification, however, we accept Goulder's theory: Matthew used Mark and Luke used them both.

4. Boismard's multiple source theory is also technically possible. What is dubious is that such fine detail in the reconstruction of hypothetical documents can be correct. It certainly cannot be validated. We have noted, however, that his theory of criss-cross copying has much to commend it in general.

• Omission and creation of material

We should now comment on a basic but, we think, erroneous view which has long plagued study of the synoptic problem. Boismard's theory shares with the two-source theory, especially in its complicated forms, the view that *nothing was ever omitted*

117

and nothing was ever created. Defenders of the two-source hypothesis have long sought a separate source for each category of synoptic material. They have often denied in theory the view that a documentary source can be defined as consisting of material which has been preserved in both Matthew and Luke, Matthew alone, or Luke alone; but they have nevertheless put that view forward: Q is material common to Matthew and Luke, M is material peculiar to Matthew, and L is material peculiar to Luke. The accident of preservation defines the source. The theory of Proto–Luke depends entirely on the assumption that material was neither discarded nor created. The long central section of Luke (9.51–18.14) contains negligible Markan material, but a lot of it is paralleled in Matthew. A more or less equal amount is not. Thus the theory: Someone here combined two sources. Why cannot the entire section be from Q? Because Matthew would not have omitted the material now only in Luke. Why cannot Luke be thought to have rewritten Q and supplemented it? Because no one ever invented anything.

We see the same logic at work in the analysis of Matthew. G. D. Kilpatrick, in a fine study of Matthew, posed to himself the question which we are now pursuing: do sources correspond to our categories of the synoptic material, so that there was a source for the triple tradition, one for the Matthew–Luke tradition, and so on?

> We cannot say that, because there are four categories of material in Matthew, that common to all three synoptic Gospels, that appearing in Matthew and Mark, that shared by Matthew and Luke, and that peculiar to Matthew, therefore the evangelist used four documents in compiling the Gospel. It may be that the material which a mechanical analysis would reveal as peculiar to Matthew might show signs of being derived from more than one document or, in part, of not being derived from written sources at all. More than mechanical analysis on the basis of one criterion is needed.[11]

Yet Kilpatrick's study concluded that, among other things, Matthew combined M and Q in the Sermon on the Mount, that Q consisted of the material also in Luke, and that M consisted of the rest. We should add, however, that Kilpatrick attributed to M only the sayings material peculiar to Matthew, not the peculiar narrative material.

We note how firmly entrenched is the view that nothing was discarded when we consider the arguments over the priority of Mark and the overlaps with Q. A major argument against placing Mark second or third is that he would not have left out so much material had he known Matthew or Luke. Similarly one of the reasons for denying that Mark knew Q is that his omission of material would be inexplicable. We have, in fact, accepted part of this reasoning: Mark cannot be held to be third unless the composition of the gospel can be explained. We do not intend, however, to argue that no one would have omitted anything, but only that the procedure ascribed to Mark on the Griesbach hypothesis is difficult to explain. The omission of material in the course of transmission should be accepted as a general possibility. We should here affirm one of the general principles of form criticism, which will be discussed below: the church kept what was useful. This principle should apply at all stages in the transmission of the gospel material. An individual gospel presumably contained what the author or authors found useful. Much that now interests us, or that may have interested other first-century Christians, was discarded. That this is so is seen clearly if one asks how many details of Jesus' personal life were preserved. The gospel material is notoriously short of them, not because the material was entirely transmitted by people who knew none of them, but because knowledge about personal habits, friendships and the like was not needed by the church.

The view that no one created anything also influences Boismard's theory: for everything there is a source. The 'authors' of our gospels wrote a few introductions, but for the most part simply conflated sources. Of course creativity is not entirely denied: someone wrote Source A. But it is clear that Boismard does not think of creativity on the part of the communities, transmitters, or authors.

The discussion of the creation, alteration and omission of material leads us to the question of how the material was treated between the time of Jesus and the composition of the gospels. Form criticism undertook to explore this issue. We shall first define it and then take up further the question of the 'creation' of material in the early church.

Further Reading

A. J. Bellinzoni, with J. B. Tyson and W. O. Walker (eds), *The Two-Source Hypothesis. A Critical Appraisal*, Macon 1985

William R. Farmer (ed.), *New Synoptic Studies*, Macon 1983

Joseph A. Fitzmyer, 'The Priority of Mark and the "Q" Source in Luke', *Jesus and Man's Hope*, vol. 1, Pittsburg 1970, pp. 131–170

John S. Kloppenborg, *The Formation of Q*, Philadelphia 1987

Frans Neirynck, with T. Hansen and F. Van Segbroeck, *The Minor Agreements of Matthew and Luke against Mark with a Cumulative List*, Leuven 1974

John M. Rist, *On the Independence of Matthew and Mark*, SNTSMS 32, Cambridge 1978

Robert H. Stein, *The Synoptic Problem. An Introduction*, Grand Rapids 1987, Part I, The Literary Relationship of the Synoptic Gospels

G. M. Styler, 'The Priority of Mark', in C. F. D. Moule, *The Birth of the New Testament*, 3rd ed., London 1981, pp. 285–316

Part Three
Form Criticism

8 Introduction

• Definition and basic principles

Form criticism is the study ('criticism') of individual pericopes, separated from their present contexts in the gospels, with special attention to their formal characteristics. The first aim is to recover the pre-gospel use of each passage in the life of the early church, the second to uncover the setting of the passage in the life of Jesus (assuming that there is one). In using form criticism, the student first finds several pericopes which share common literary and stylistic features. These constitute a 'form', and once the 'form' is identified and analysed the passages can be better understood. Thus, for example, there are numerous passages in which an opponent is represented as putting to Jesus a question or as challenging him. Jesus then responds, and the reader is to understand that the response was effective. These passages collectively constitute the 'form' which is called 'controversy dialogues'. 'Criticism' or study of the form involves study of the form in other bodies of literature; comparison of all the examples of the form in the synoptics; analysis of each individual passage, noting especially its component parts; observations about the passage's integrity (whether composite or unitary); and estimations about earlier possible contexts. 'Criticism' in this case means especially analysis of the *history* of the passage. 'Form criticism' translates the German term *Formgeschichte*, literally 'form history'. The intention is to understand the development of each pericope, and of each group, with the dual aim pointed out above: understanding the history of the communities which transmitted the material and getting back to the most primitive layer – and thus to recover authentic material about Jesus.

Form criticism is based on a few main observations and principles:

1. The pericopes can be separated from the narrative framework which introduces and often concludes them. The Parable of the Lost Sheep, for example, is in both Matthew and Luke. In Matthew (18.10–14) it is said to be directed to the disciples, in Luke (15.4–7) it is told against the Pharisees. It is evident that the parable had a life of its own and could be used in different ways. In discussing the synoptic problem we noted instances in which the introductions to pericopes vary (e.g. ch. 3, Pericope 1), and turning the pages of a synopsis will show that this is often the case.

123

The distinction of pericope from framework was made easier by the work of William Wrede in *The Messianic Secret* (originally published in 1901). Before Wrede it had been thought that the framework of the gospels, or at least of Mark, was historical (see above, pp. 25–28). The Markan framework was relied on to sketch Jesus' spiritual development. Wrede showed to the satisfaction of most scholars that main elements of the structure of Mark are the result of post-Easter theology and do not belong to the history of Jesus.[1]

In 1919 K. L. Schmidt proposed that all the framework material of the synoptic gospels – the links between pericopes – was added at a late stage.[2] The gospel material should be considered to be like 'pearls on a string'. The string was provided by the evangelists, the pearls – the pericopes – make up the material which can be analysed to find out about Jesus and the history of the earliest Christian communities. Schmidt based his view in part on an analysis of the genre of the gospels. He proposed that they are not 'real literature' (*Hochliteratur*) but 'popular' or 'unsophisticated literature' (*Kleinliteratur*). He compared them to later collections of anecdotes and sayings about saints, in which new stories kept being added and material altered or deleted. There were, in his view, no real 'authors' of the gospels. The gospels were simply assembled by 'redactors'. Similarly Martin Dibelius wrote that 'we must assume unliterary beginnings of a religious unpretentious "literature"'.[3] This view of the gospels' genre made it easier to separate pericopes from their narrative framework: the synoptics were not creations of authors who had a comprehensive grasp of the material and who wrote them as free compositions (Dibelius, pp.59–60). One can still see their component parts, the individual pericopes.

In an important respect, the results of Wrede's proposals are quite different from those of Schmidt. Wrede's work leads to examining the framework for theology, while Schmidt's points towards dismissing it as being mere 'string' – the editorial work of hacks.* Yet with regard to the present topic, their proposals led to the same result: a separation of the individual pericopes from the narrative framework. We shall later see that Schmidt's view in particular may be questioned; he was probably wrong about the genre of the gospels and about the lack of intellectual control on the part of the final evangelists. But his arguments gave a powerful impetus to a rewarding way of studying the gospel material.

2. Another principal view of the form critics was that each form grew out of a specific activity of the early church. A study of the forms shows their purpose, and the purpose can be related to a need of the church. Material was not kept if it was not useful. Thus each form was said to have a *Sitz im Leben*, a 'setting in the life' of the church. The church engaged in typical practices, and each practice produced an appropriate 'form'. This view agrees with the conclusion that the evangelists were 'assemblers' rather than 'authors': the pericopes were shaped not by the final evangelists, but rather by communities as they were used in diverse social settings of the church's life (Dibelius, pp. 59–60).

*Wrede's view, modified, prevailed: see ch. 14.

For example, in discussing the synoptic debates about the law, Rudolf Bultmann proposed that their 'setting' was either internal strife within the church or arguments between Christians and non-Christian Jewish opponents. The church, or one wing of it, needed material in which Jesus himself justified its practice (cf. above, pp. 43f., on the need for 'ammunition'). Christians debated Jews about the necessity of observing the sabbath, and in doing so they developed 'conflict dialogues' in which 'the Pharisees' accuse the 'disciples' of not observing the sabbath, and in which 'Jesus' defends church practice. In the story about plucking corn on the sabbath (Mark 2.23–28 and parr.), 'Jesus' defends the 'disciples' for working on the sabbath. Bultmann noted that it is the 'disciples' who are accused, not 'Jesus' himself. He then proposed that in the passage 'the disciples' simply stand in for the church, 'the Pharisees' stand in for the subsequent Jewish opponents of the church, and 'Jesus' steps in to the defence. The sayings which defend non-observance of the sabbath ('the sabbath was made for people, not people for the sabbath', and 'the Son of man is Lord of the sabbath', Mark 2.27–28) may have been said by the historical Jesus, but perhaps in another context. The event as it is told in the synoptics is 'an ideal scene', created by the church so as to give the saying the context which was subsequently appropriate. It is to be noted that in Mark the sayings are prefaced by 'and he said'. According to Bultmann, this shows that they were originally independent and were added, the addition being indicated by the introduction, 'and he said'. The sayings, whether authentic or not, have been made to serve later circumstances.[4]

The church had needs other than defence, such as the teaching of new church members. Out of this need grew 'didactic dialogues', in which the questioners are disciples rather than opponents. Thus in Matt. 18.21–22 Peter (standing in for later disciples) asks how many times to forgive. The setting or narrative frame is again seen as a church creation.

3. The history of each pericope can be traced by analysing how close it is to the 'pure form'. To determine this, the form critics studied similar forms in other literature. Miracle stories, for example, exist elsewhere, as do didactic dialogues and conflict dialogues. (We give examples below.) When the form is studied elsewhere, one can see that there is such a thing as a 'pure form', which consists of just the essential elements. Dibelius and Bultmann both thought that pericopes started out in the 'pure form' and acquired further material. In the example used just above, the pericope defending working on the sabbath has two sayings in Mark, one in Matthew and Luke. The first saying in Mark ('the sabbath was made for people . . .') may have been added to Mark after it was used by Matthew and Luke, and thus the passage in our Mark may have acquired an additional saying. Alternatively, a pericope might be supplemented by material which belongs to another form, and then it would be said to be 'mixed'. For example, in Matt. 9.2–8 we find first that Jesus starts to heal a paralytic by pronouncing the forgiveness of sins, then that he is challenged by opponents, and then that he performs the cure, leading to the conclusion: he was wondered at. Here a miracle story and a conflict dialogue are combined, and a common form-critical judgment would be that originally the elements existed separately. Dibelius and Bultmann, the leading German form

125

critics, sought earlier forms of material by eliminating material which could be seen as additions to the 'pure form'.

Making use of these simple principles, the 'classical' form critics – Dibelius and especially Bultmann – produced studies which made an enormous impact and which put scholars to work for decades. Form criticism offered a great prize: scientific knowledge both of the historical Jesus and of the early Christian movement. By distinguishing the 'pearls' from the 'string', one could partially free the Jesus-tradition from its captivity. In the previous century, scholars had separated the Jesus of the gospels from the Christ of the fourth- and fifth-century creeds, and then the synoptic Jesus from the Christ of John, and form criticism promised a third rescue operation. The encrustations around the Jesus-traditions could be removed, and one would be closer to the real man. The 'encrustations', though, were not to be thrown away. They were the result of the church's activity, and study of them would throw light on earliest Christianity.

Neither Dibelius nor Bultmann was naïve, and Bultmann in particular was cautious. He knew that authentic material could not be recovered simply by peeling off a few words or lines from each pericope. He did think, however, that it was possible to work backwards through each passage, separating layer from layer, and that in this task some material would be found which could be called 'authentic'. Bultmann's caution has often been regarded as excessive scepticism about the tradition, but in many ways he was very optimistic about the outcome of form criticism. The layers in the gospels 'on the whole [can] be clearly distinguished', even though 'at some points' the separations are 'difficult and doubtful'. The earliest layer cannot be proved to be 'the exact words . . . spoken by Jesus'. Bultmann offered to the sceptical reader of his book on Jesus the option of putting 'Jesus' in inverted commas or quotation marks, as a term which stands for the earliest layer, though he himself was willing to think that Jesus really was the speaker of the oldest sayings.[5]

Dibelius and Bultmann did not invent the critical, painstaking analysis of individual passages, but they gave it apparently scientific grounding. To this day scholars work on, revising the pericopes by peeling off layers and proposing different settings in life from those offered in the gospels. The student who learns to look at the material through the lens of form criticism will see things previously unnoticed and will pose sharp questions. *Why* are only the disciples accused of breaking the sabbath and of not washing their hands (Mark 7.5)? Could it be supposed that, in the lifetime of Jesus, he washed his hands before eating but his followers did not? This is difficult to accept. Then could it not be that the accusation against the followers came after Jesus' lifetime, that its setting is the Jewish–Christian debate in the first decades of the movement? By following such lines of questioning one is given the sense of discovery: there is something hidden, waiting to be discovered.

Yet not quite everyone has gone along. We may divide criticisms into two categories: difficulties noted by scholars who have basically accepted form criticism, and more fundamental objections.

• Difficulties within form criticism

1. Bultmann and Dibelius, we noted, thought that, at the earliest stage of each pericope's life, it existed in a 'pure' form. Vincent Taylor, the leading British form critic, argued just the reverse: that the material originally was not in pure forms, and that one tendency of the tradition was to conform it to well-known and popular forms.[6] The German form critics saw the gospel material as being somewhat like snowballs – gathering further sayings, events and details as it rolled along. Taylor, in contrast, proposed that the synoptic pericopes were like stones on the sea shore, being rolled smooth – into pure forms – with time.

Taylor here raised a very important issue. The form critics, by identifying typical forms, showed that individual pericopes in the gospels have been shaped or moulded into their present state. It is not really true that Jesus' ministry consisted of a series of events in which either someone ill was presented to him to be healed, or a foe asked him a challenging question – as a simple reading of Mark 2.1–3.6 might suggest. Each unit in that section has been shaped or formed so as to make its point in an economical and clear way. These stories or particular events are presented as typical: as if the author wrote, 'this is the sort of thing which he said and did, the sort of thing which won admiration and a following'. Thus at some level Taylor was surely right: in real life events are not cast in pure forms. There is give and take; the speaker might hesitate, repeat and expand; opponents are not always silenced by a shrewd reply.

But were Dibelius and Bultmann right with regard to the literary development of the material? That is, should we think that preachers or teachers used remembered sayings, 'rough' and varied in form, then cast them into economical (and therefore pure) forms, and that subsequent telling and retelling led to their amplification and development? In this case, the mixed forms which we see are not original, but literary developments of pure forms – which were themselves developed from the original material. The original eyewitness details and settings cannot be recovered. They were stripped off, and only later were the details and mixtures which we now see added. Taylor, in other words, thought more simply than Bultmann and conceived of only two possibilities: detailed, early material; pure, later material; therefore details prove 'authenticity'. Bultmann thought of more layers: original accounts (now lost for the most part), accounts as first used by the church and cast into 'pure' forms (recoverable behind the present gospels), the rough and mixed material which we now have. We may put the issue like this: are the minor details in Mark (e.g. the paralytic was carried by four people, Mark 2.3) eyewitness details which have not yet been rounded off (so Taylor), or supplementary details put in by later hands for the sake of verisimilitude and colour (so Bultmann)?

We shall not be able to come to a decisive answer to this question, and for the present we must leave it to the reader to judge. (See further the analysis of 'authentic' material in chs. 20–21 below.)

2. All the form critics thought that the synoptic material changed in regular ways, governed by 'laws', such as the rule that it became increasingly detailed – or decreasingly detailed. It is the supposition that these laws worked which allows

127

scholars – as it allowed Bultmann – to revise the gospel material by stripping away what are thought to be later accretions. Bultmann attempted to give scientific support to his view of how the material changed by appealing to research on fairy tales, which he said confirmed his analysis (p. 7). Unfortunately for his view, and his reputation, that turns out not to be true. Students of folk literature know no rules of change. Thus we cannot settle our question by referring to research in other fields.[7] We should note that the view that the gospel material is 'folk' literature, transmitted orally, may be and has been challenged, but for our present point we still do not need to discuss fully the genre of the literature. Whether the synoptic material is 'folk' or not, there are no general laws which governed its transmission.

When we study in detail the form critical 'laws' of the development and change of the material, we discover that none of them holds good.[8] A comparison of the quotations of Jesus' sayings in second- and third-century literature with the synoptic versions does not reveal that the sayings tended to become longer and more detailed, or shorter and less detailed. Individual retellers might expand or abbreviate, might elaborate or epitomize. There are no general laws about length and detail. This negative judgment applies to Taylor's proposals as well as to those of Dibelius and Bultmann. His view that the material tended to be 'smoothed' has no more support than does the opposite view, that it tended to become more complex.

Taylor and Bultmann agreed on one law of change, and here they have been joined by dozens of scholars: the gospel material shifted from the world of those who spoke Aramaic to the Greek-speaking world. Therefore, it is reasoned, forms of the material which contain more **Semitisms** are more likely to be early than are forms which are in better Greek. (A 'Semitism' is a syntactical or grammatical usage which is typical in Aramaic or Hebrew but not in Greek.) At first this sounds like a self-evidently reasonable view, but it too will not stand examination. Many early Christians spoke Aramaic or the closely related Syriac; and Greek-speakers knew and were influenced by the grammar and syntax of the Bible, which in the Greek translation retains strong marks of its Hebrew origin. Both groups could have introduced Semitisms into the gospel tradition. Further, many apparent Semitisms may be only the signs of vulgar Greek. 'Semitisms' abound in some of the later apocryphal gospels. They do not show that material is early.

3. There are numerous minor worries about the devices employed by the form critics. We may take one example: Is it a sound principle that introductory phrases ('and he said') indicate that new material has been added? This seems reasonable, and it may often be true. But such a phrase as 'and he said' might have the meaning, 'and he also said', or 'and he further said', and be simply the kind of emphasis which any reteller of a saying might add to give the saying more force. Thus we cannot be sure that deleting material for which there is a separate introduction will give us an earlier version.

• Fundamental criticisms of form criticism

128 We have thus far described the main principles of form criticism and indicated

reservations about concrete points. The method has, however, been subject to more thorough-going criticism, which has been directed against its basic assumptions.

1. When form criticism was still in its youth scholars challenged the theory that the synoptic gospels are to be compared to folk literature. The idea that the gospel material was produced collectively and by communities was doubted, on the grounds that committees seldom produce worthwhile literature. The analogy is not fully justified, for the form critics had not supposed that the church members sat as a group and wrote stories together, but that in the collective activities of the church diverse forms were used for diverse occasions. It was always recognized that the churches had leading preachers and teachers. Nevertheless, the general theory that the gospels are folk literature is dubious, principally for the second reason brought forward as an objection to form critical theory: the doubt that the material was transmitted orally long enough to develop in the way supposed by the theory. It was not handed down orally through numerous generations, like true folk literature; our gospels were written in the second or third generation, and they probably relied in part on earlier written sources.

2. The question of how the material was transmitted has been pressed especially by Birger Gerhardsson. In a series of books and articles, beginning with *Memory and Manuscript* (1961), he has discussed the various ways in which synoptic tradition could have been handed down in general terms, and he has also proposed specific analogies.[9] The general thrust is conservative: he looks for analogies which allow one to think that the Jesus-tradition was faithfully and accurately transmitted. He does not, however, deny that changes were introduced and that some material was created. The most recent statement of his general stance towards the material is this:

> We have already underlined two basic facts: that our sources tell us that Jesus taught with the aid of short, artistically formulated texts, and that the extant material in the synoptic sayings tradition is a series of such texts. . . . These texts were presumably transmitted as memorized texts in roughly the same way as the Jewish mashal-tradition [mashal=parables and the like], with roughly the same technique as Jewish material of similar types (note that the haggadic material had somewhat freer wording than the halacha-rules) . . .*
>
> I have also stressed the fact that all verbal tradition has a very wide sector of flexible words.[10]

This summary recalls Gerhardsson's original proposal in *Memory and Manuscript*: that the synoptic material was handed down in a way analogous to the transmission of rabbinic material – at least as subsequently described. In the Talmud one reads of professional memorizers of rabbinic law and of various mnemonic techniques. Rabbis were said to repeat a section of law forty times until their students had it by heart. Gerhardsson proposed that the Jesus material was handed down in a similar way. Jesus himself, he argued, would have taken care to see that his teachings were memorized, and after his death his disciples would have supervised the transmission of the sayings of the Lord.

Halakha is legal material, *haggadah* is non-legal (in rabbinic terminology).

As is the case with many theories about the gospels, this sounds eminently plausible. Yet it has not persuaded many scholars. Doubts start with the Rabbis' descriptions of their techniques. They are usually thought to have been exaggerated, and many scholars of rabbinic literature think that its transmission was not purely oral, but was aided by notes. But the principal objection to Gerhardsson's view is that the synoptic material does not in fact show itself to have been transmitted verbatim. In the preceeding section we examined numerous pericopes which diverge from each other in ways not explained by the theory of precise memorization. Gerhardsson had anticipated this objection, and he proposed that the variations among the gospels are to be accounted for by the hypothesis of various schools – again on the rabbinic model. This has also been unpersuasive, since the variations among the gospels do not seem to reflect the sort of changes that organized schools would introduce.

If we examine rabbinic material and note changes which schools actually made, we see that much of the discussion is the same, but that the conclusion or application is different. This sort of variation is not entirely missing from the gospels. In the pericope on divorce, for example, Mark ends by forbidding wives to leave their husbands, a prohibition not in Matthew or Luke (Mark 10.12 and parr.). Matthew has an 'except clause', 'except in the case of [prior] sexual immorality' in both his versions of the saying on divorce (Matt. 5.32; 19.9), a variation not in the other gospels or in Paul (I Cor. 7.10–11). These may justly be considered 'school' alterations, but there is relatively little of this sort of change in the synoptics. Parallel passages have lots of variations, but not many which seem to correspond to different Christian schools of interpretation.

Gerhardsson has more recently proposed that parts of the synoptic material were transmitted as was the text of scripture – that is, by professional scribes copying it carefully. Parts were probably transmitted in a looser way, in partially extemporaneous and partially prepared comments on a reading of scripture or of Jesus-material in the early churches. In this case transmission would be analogous to the passing on of targumic tradition (synagogal paraphrases and explanations in the vernacular of the scripture, which was read in Hebrew). But, again, it is hard to find in the synoptics material which was transmitted precisely (like the text of scripture), or as explanations of precisely formulated texts (like the Aramaic targums to the Hebrew scripture).

As a final and general explanation of how the material could have been memorized and yet have ended up fairly diverse, Gerhardsson proposed 'a very wide sector of flexible words' (quoted above).

Gerhardsson, as we shall see more fully below, has done much to make us more aware of just how unique the synoptics are in their handling of material. It appears that there was both freedom to alter and limits on creativity. He has not yet, however, provided us with an analogy which helps explain these characteristics of the material – and we do not have one to offer. We think that his efforts have proved that there is no one model which accounts for the synoptics. In a sense he explains everything: some things were passed on with no alteration (like Scripture); in some cases there were different views among different Christian groups (no divorce, or none except for sexual immorality); some of the material was passed on in a 'targumic' or paraphrastic way; some was altered homiletically (like *haggadah*); in some cases there was only minor verbal change, as is true of all oral tradition.

We finally end without an explanation which will tell us what Gerhardsson and the form critics have all wanted to know: in general, how carefully was the material preserved and transmitted? In general, how authentic is it? There is no general answer; the synoptics conform to no model which will tell us *how much* the material changed, nor *what directions* the changes took.

We can offer only a vague generalization. The material was subject to alteration but was not treated with reckless abandon. We shall illustrate this by taking as examples the material which should have changed least, for this is the material which Gerhardsson's models should explain best. The earliest and best-attested passages which are attributed to Jesus are the prohibition of divorce and the sayings over the bread and wine at the last supper, and they will be discussed in more than one context. These two traditions occur not only in the synoptics but also in Paul, where they are explicitly attributed to 'the Lord' (divorce, I Cor. 7.10) or 'the Lord Jesus' (the supper, I Cor. 11.23). Here if anywhere we should expect complete agreement, but we do not get it. There are very substantial disagreements.

In the case of the legal or semi-legal text on divorce all of the differences among the five passages can be considered 'school' disagreements, precisely because of the legal character of the saying. What should be recognized is that in this case the schools disagreed quite widely. According to the version in Matt. 19, for example, a man who divorces his wife for sexual immorality is allowed to remarry. That is not the case in the other versions. Similarly two versions (Paul and Mark) take into account the possibility of the woman initiating separation or divorce, while those of Matthew and Luke do not. These and many other disagreements are laid out in detail below (pp. 324–29), where we attempt to recover the earliest form of the tradition. Just now we must worry about the mere fact that the passages disagree. Gerhardsson correctly pointed out that in general legal material is less subject to change than homiletical, but here we have a text which is at least semi-legal and which was changed a great deal. 'No divorce' is quite different from 'divorce permitted on grounds of sexual immorality', and 'no remarriage' is even further away from 'the man's remarriage is permitted if the wife was adulterous'. If the Christian 'schools' disagreed this much, and were as willing to change material as this example indicates, we must be prepared to think that in other cases Jesus' own view has been so overlaid that one cannot recover it. Since we have five versions of the passage on divorce, it is possible to examine them and come to a view as to the earliest. But we are not always this lucky. We do not very often have versions which lend themselves so readily to analysis. There is an even more haunting question: What if the earliest of our five versions was as different from the lost original as the last existing version is from the first?

In the case of Jesus' words at the last supper, the reader must ask, Did Jesus say of the cup, 'this is my blood' (Matthew and Mark) or 'this is the new covenant in my blood' (Paul and Luke)? The two versions are not different comments on a stable core; rather the core itself varies.

A third passage which one would expect to have been transmitted with care is another liturgical text, the Lord's Prayer. Here again there are noteworthy variations. Luke (11.2–4) differs in wording from Matthew (6.9–15), but also lacks entirely some of Matthew's clauses ('thy will be done . . .'; 'deliver us from the evil one').

There are virtually no instances of agreement among the gospels which are so close as to justify Gerhardsson's comparison between transmission of the Jesus-material and verbatim copying of the text of Scripture, and the other analogies (rabbinic memorization; school variations of legal material; targumic expansions) also seem not to explain very many passages.

Gerhardsson's proposals show that the **manner of transmission** is both important and hard to recover. He has not yet persuaded scholars that his analogies solve the problem of the transmission of the gospel material, but he has succeeded in exposing a basic flaw in form criticism, and to this we now turn.

3. We recall the second main principle of form criticism: that each form corresponds to a typical activity of the church. Controversy dialogues have the purpose of refuting Jewish criticism, and they grew out of the need to have 'Jesus' defend church practice; didactic dialogues grew out of the need to instruct church members; and so forth. Gerhardsson has pointed out that we can see the church responding to these various situations, but that substantial texts about Jesus are not used. We shall return to this point, and here give only two very short examples:

(*a*) Paul argued with Peter and the other Jerusalem disciples about whether or not his converts (and other Gentile converts) had to observe the laws of circumcision, food and 'days'. This topic is the occasion of Galatians, where the case against these parts of the law is argued extensively, and it comes up again as a major part of Romans. Yet Paul on the issue of the law does not quote Jesus, much less tell stories in which Jesus defends his followers for not observing (for example) the sabbath.

(*b*) In I Peter there is a good deal of exhortation to bear up under suffering. Thus the author writes, 'yet if you should suffer for your virtues, you may count yourselves happy' (I Peter 3.14). How appropriate it would have been to have written: 'Jesus said, "Blessed are those who are persecuted for righteousness' sake, for theirs in the kingdom of heaven"' (Matt. 5.10)! The beatitude may have been in the author's mind, and it is appropriate to his theme, but he does not take the opportunity of quoting it – much less a full text of beatitudes. Similarly Paul sometimes seems to echo one of the beatitudes (e.g. Rom. 12.14), but lists of beatitudes are quoted only in Matthew and Luke. There – against the theory of precise transmission – the lists are different; but it is nevertheless noteworthy that Paul and the author of I Peter did not carry out their exhortations by manufacturing Jesus-texts. A text was not simply invented, nor even cited, each time a 'setting' seemed to require it.

Thus we see that Gerhardsson is right in a very substantial part of his critique of form criticism. There were 'typical situations' which did not necessarily produce full texts attributed to Jesus. This argues in favour of some special setting in which texts of Jesus-tradition were needed. On the other hand, he has not yet successfully identified those settings. We are left with even more question marks about the transmission of the material than before Gerhardsson's arguments against the basic assumptions of form criticism. Jesus-material was transmitted and used, but the wording and even the substance were not precisely maintained, and we do not know the setting in the church in which the tradition was passed down.

4. Willi Marxsen and Erhardt Güttgemanns argued that the form critics erred in assuming continuity between the oral period when the material was passed down in small individual units and the literary period, represented by our gospels, when it was brought together in much larger arrangements. The form critics assumed that the evangelists for the most part were compilers, with the result that the individual units were not very greatly altered when they were plucked from the (supposed) stream of oral material and arranged in a gospel. In fact, however, the evangelists were authors, and their transformations of the material may have been more far-reaching.[11]

We agree that form criticism does not give an adequate account of the gospels as finished works – which, of course, it did not aim at. On the other hand the present synoptics do in fact preserve the material in largely self-enclosed pericopes. If one compares them with John, it will be seen to what degree this is true. One should not emphasize that the synoptic evangelists were 'authors' so much that one thinks that they digested the material and then sat down and wrote their own theological meditations on it. The individual units are clearly visible.

5. In recent years Klaus Berger has offered a 'new' form criticism, which differs from the old principally in these ways:[12]

(a) He expands the categories to take the entire New Testament into account.

(b) He emphasizes that the synoptic forms as we have them are fully literary, and he seeks their parallels in neither folklore nor oral tradition, but rather in Graeco–Roman rhetoric.

(c) The idea of a setting in life as *generating* a certain form is decisively dismissed. That given passages were used in fixed settings can be demonstrated only exceptionally, as in the case of liturgical units (e.g. the last supper).

(d) Berger holds that it is seldom worthwhile to rewrite individual passages. The follower of the new form criticism will do less 'tradition history' – the search for earlier layers – than the practitioner of the old.

(e) Corresponding to (b) and (d), emphasis is laid on the study of groups of passages and the rhetorical function of each form, not on individual pericopes.

The negative aspects of points (b) and (c) come as no surprise. We have thus far resisted the notion that the synoptic gospels can be *explained* by combining these two ideas: there were typical settings which produced certain forms; passages were handed down according to laws of oral transmission, and we can retrace the steps and recover the earliest traditions. That one should look to common Hellenistic or Graeco–Roman literary conventions for parallels to the gospels ((b) and (e)) is also now widely held. This has long been said with regard to the genre 'gospel' itself, and Berger proposes that the individual units should be examined in the same light. As we shall note in the discussion of *chreiai*, the first form-critical category, other scholars have been working in the same direction. What new understanding a new set of proposed parallels will bring is not yet certain, but studying Graeco–Roman literary forms will certainly help us understand how the gospels were read by Greek-speaking readers. (See further chs. 17–19.)

It would be truly revolutionary, however, were New Testament scholars to stop rewriting and re-setting the synoptic pericopes. Our own response to this is mixed. Davies, the author of 'Holistic Readings' (Part IV), is no longer very sympathetic to the search for hypothetical earlier versions; Sanders, the conductor through Form Criticism and the section on the Historical Jesus, has argued that secure information about Jesus cannot be obtained by rewriting individual pericopes, and that if by chance the rewriting were successful, there would be no way of proving it.[13] Despite this basic agreement with opposition to revising and re-setting, we shall, both here and in Part V, try to dig behind the present text of some individual passages.

There are two reasons for attempting this. (1) The secondary literature requires it. The student who picks up a book on Jesus or the gospels will almost inevitably run into detailed examinations of one or more passages which endeavour to open the passage up and recover an original version. We wish to explain the principles and illustrate various techniques, so that the student will be able to read the work of practitioners with a critical eye. (2) It is in theory possible and therefore in practice must be attempted at least sometimes. That is, the material really did change. It started at point a and ended up at point x, with an unknown number of stages in between. Once we know that it changed, we must put our minds to work analysing it, to see if we can discover how it changed. In the endeavour, we shall be forced to learn whatever we can about both Jesus and the early Christian movement. To be able to say, This passage fits better Here than There, we must know things about Here and There. If we study a lot of passages, we may begin to make sense of sizeable pieces of evidence.

No one knows better than the author of the preceding paragraph that hypothetical reconstructions do not lead to firm knowledge. But if we will not dig, we know even less than if we do. Thus here and in the final chapters of the book we shall become literary archaeologists and consider some examples of spade craft.

• Preliminary assessment of form criticism

How shall we assess the viability of form criticism overall, once we have seen that telling criticisms have been made of its basic theories? We shall consider the three principal features of the method.

1. On one point the form critics were surely right. They correctly observed that in the gospels one can see *individual and originally independent units*. The pericopes do not flow along smoothly in chronological order. One notes what Dibelius called 'external rounding off' (pp. 44f.). Each pericope has a beginning and an end, and one does not run on to the next as would be the case if they originated as part of a coherent and consecutive narrative. Thus the basic form critical insight is to be confirmed: the individual pericopes can and in fact must be studied apart from their present settings if one is to get behind the gospels as we have them to earlier situations, whether in the early church or in the lifetime of Jesus.

The degree to which the gospels are not biographies was discussed above (pp. 28–36), but we should return to the point in this discussion; for the self-enclosure of the individual pericopes is one of the most important facts to perceive if one wishes to understand the synoptics. We may note the degree to which the only continuity is provided by the chief actors – Jesus himself and the disciples. Most other characters appear only once. Mary Magdalene, for example, is an extremely important person. She witnessed the crucifixion of Jesus and his burial in the tomb; she found the empty tomb, and to her the risen Lord first appeared (so Matthew and Mark, except that Mark does not have the appearance of the risen Lord: Matt. 27.56,61; 28.1,9; Mark 15.40,47; 16.1). Luke also records Mary Magdalene as one of the witnesses to the empty tomb (24.10). Only Luke attempts to explain her appearance at the crucifixion/resurrection by placing her in an earlier story: she was healed by Jesus according to Luke 8.2. It is remarkable that Mark and Matthew show that Mary and other women followed Jesus from Galilee to Jerusalem, but give them no role in the Galilean ministry. They are not to be suspected of anti-feminism on this account. They seem to have had only isolated stories, not a connected account, which would surely have mentioned the women. Luke, we suspect, recognized the problem and retrojected Mary and other women into stories of Jesus' own ministry.

Similarly the gospels make no connection between the Pharisees, who are depicted as opposing Jesus in Galilee, and the chief priests, who were instrumental in his trial and execution in Judaea. The various parts of the synoptics are, to repeat, self-enclosed.

We also observed above that the characters in the gospel – including to a large extent even Jesus himself – lack characterization and development. Nothing *moves* from one incident to the next; motives, frustrations, changes of plan and the like have been found in the gospels, but they have to be read into them – as we saw above in discussing Holtzmann and Schweitzer. The problem in all these cases is that the evangelists were limited by their materials – individual pericopes with no apparent causal links. Comparison of the synoptic *chreiai* with those of other literature, we shall see, drives home how limited is the information which can be gleaned from biographies which depend on isolated units (pp. 161f. below).

2. The second main principle of form criticism was that material was kept only if it was useful to the church and that the church's need actually shaped it: social settings generated the various forms. The first half of this view is to be confirmed. Material which was superfluous to the needs of the earliest communities did not survive. One may pose simple questions and see that they are not answered: What happened to Mary? Was Jesus short or tall? How did he wear his hair? Where did he study and learn the Bible? Who influenced him in his youth?

With regard to the proposed settings in the life of the church, however, time has not been kind to the original form critics. We should first note that here they did not agree among themselves. Dibelius began with the form which he called 'the paradigm' ('example'). Bultmann named the form 'apophthegm' (from apoph-thegma, -mata, meaning 'terse saying', 'pithy maxim'), and Taylor attempted a simpler and more descriptive term, 'pronouncement story'. It is best called the *chreia*, as we shall see in ch. 10. The form consists basically of a challenge to the subject (in the case of the gospels, Jesus) and a brief reply. Sometimes there will be a prefatory setting. In any case, Dibelius proposed that the setting in life of this type of story was the sermon. The preacher needed examples on which he could draw when he wished, and this need was met by the existence of 'paradigms', exemplary short narratives with a strong and clear conclusion.

Bultmann gave no such primacy to the sermon. He distinguished apophthegms according to basic thrust and assigned them to different needs. His three major categories were 'biographical apophthegms', 'controversy dialogues' and 'didactic dialogues'. Biographical apophthegms he saw as originating in the need for 'edifying paradigms for sermons' (*Synoptic Tradition*, p. 61), here thinking that Dibelius was right. But, he urged, the church had other needs than edification, namely apologetics, polemics and discipline. Apologetics and polemics gave rise to controversy dialogues and discipline to didactic dialogues. By being so specific with regard to use, Bultmann laid himself open to Gerhardsson's criticism. Those needs of the early church did not necessarily generate stories about Jesus.

We have seen that we must grant the force of the criticism. 'Need', based on 'setting in the life of the church', is not the sole and sufficient explanation for the existence of the synoptic accounts. The success of Gerhardsson's criticism, however, when coupled with the unpersuasiveness of his positive proposals, means that we cannot say precisely why the church saved or created the Jesus-tradition, nor precisely how each bit was used. We are left with questions which we cannot precisely answer: how was the material transmitted? Why were the diverse types either preserved or created?

3. What about the use of comparative material, especially to establish 'pure' forms? Dibelius and Bultmann employed hypothetical pure forms to establish or reconstruct a pre-synoptic form of various pericopes, since they thought that folk literature developed away from pure forms. Here we must be even more agnostic than about the life-settings and grant that all possible forms of change took place. It is not to be doubted that sometimes additional sayings were added and that originally independent stories were combined into one. Yet it is also likely that the material was often pared down, reduced to essentials, so as to gain greater point and dramatic punch. Here we must simply study the passages on their own merits, and see what we can make of them.

For the first time in a long while, scholars are now turning again to the study of the synoptic forms on a comparative basis. There is a new interest in rhetoric, especially as taught in the schools of the Graeco–Roman world, and in the literary forms which were employed. A few of these studies will be cited when we turn to the separate forms. It is too early to write a progress report, since much of the work is preliminary. We may be sure, however, of one use which will *not* be made of comparative material. Bultmann, following his teacher, Wilhelm Bousset, thought that there was a great chasm between Jewish Palestine and the Greek-speaking Hellenistic world, and he assigned material to 'the Palestinian church' or to 'the Hellenistic church' with great confidence. The apophthegmata (*chreiai*), for example, he regarded as Palestinian, since he knew Hebrew parallels but not many in Greek literature (p. 48). His knowledge was deficient, and examples of the form abound in Greek literature. More important, the overall view of a great dichotomy between Aramaic/Hebrew Palestine and the Greek-speaking West has now been largely given up. The result of this increase in knowledge, as in other cases, is greater uncertainty rather than less. Bultmann, so long regarded as too sceptical, now often looks overly optimistic.

Before proceeding to study the various forms, we must pause to give attention to two prominent problems. (1) Form critics (and most scholars before and since) have thought that not everything in the synoptics goes back to Jesus or to his lifetime. As we have seen, the material was altered from gospel to gospel – and thus, presumably, in the pre-synoptic period as well. Yet we have also judged it to be unlikely that the evangelists and others invented with complete freedom. We must, then, discuss the issue of creativity and try to clarify it. (2) The problem of the transmission of the material remains opaque. We cannot solve it, but we should explore in slightly more detail the question of oral tradition. Both of these problems are brought to the fore by form criticism and its critics, Gerhardsson in particular.

9   Creativity and Oral Tradition

• Creativity

Our discussion thus far has revealed differences from gospel to gospel (the synoptic problem) and change and development (form criticism). These require us to assume some degree of creativity in the early church or parts of it. The question will also arise when we discuss the use of the material to find out about the historical Jesus. Did early Christians, besides altering and reapplying stories about and sayings of Jesus, also simply make up material and attribute it to him? The answer is 'Yes', though 'simply make up' mis-states their own perception. We should consider the situation in which material was created.

The early Christians needed guidance on all sorts of issues. They could turn to Scripture or to their leaders, and they did so. Their queries resulted in letters, then in collections of them, and finally in pseudepigraphical letters – written by others in the apostles' names. This we know from the Pauline corpus. When the resolution of a hard problem was reached, it appears that nevertheless many wanted assurance that the Lord himself approved the solution. The best-documented dispute from the early church is that over food: should Christians, especially Gentile converts, be required to keep the Jewish dietary laws? Thanks to the survival of Galatians, we know that Paul fought bitterly with the Jerusalem apostles over this issue (and the connected ones, circumcision and sabbath) (Gal. 2.11–14; on food cf. Rom. 14.2–3), and the author of Acts offers two passages which deal with it: Peter's vision of all kinds of food, which he was commanded to eat (Acts 10.9–16), and a conference in Jerusalem at which a compromise solution was worked out (Acts 15).

The real decision-making was long, laborious and contentious. It was simpler to have Jesus himself declare 'all foods clean', and Mark or a predecessor either created a saying which had this effect or gave an authentic saying a context in which this was its meaning (Mark 7.15–19; see below p. 314).

This is not to say that everyone was willing to create or discover a new meaning in a saying of Jesus each time there was a difficulty. The passages on food in Acts, Galatians and Romans – where Jesus is not appealed to – show this not to be the case. On the other hand, it did happen.

People who 'discovered' a new saying or a new meaning were presumably sincere. They believed in revelation – that the Spirit of God spoke through inspired humans or that the Lord spoke directly to them – and thus could honestly attribute to Jesus things which came to them from some source other than his pre-crucifixion teaching. Paul's discussion of 'gifts of the Spirit' in I Cor. 11–14 presupposes that some Christians prophesied (11.28–29; 14.3,5). We cannot say that those who prophesied in the Spirit all quoted 'the Lord', and that these became sayings which were attributed to Jesus. We do, however, see that this was a possibility. Prophets subsequently became a problem for the church, since they sometimes prophesied in the Spirit that they should be supported financially (Didache 11.12), as do many modern evangelists who speak by the Spirit; and the words of those who spoke by the Spirit had to be tested (Didache 11.3–13.7). Already in Paul's day there had to be warnings against excesses of spiritual enthusiasm (I Cor. 12). No one, however, seems yet to have worried that those who spoke by the Spirit would actually misquote the Lord, and it almost certainly happened that some who had the Spirit were inspired to offer a saying of the Lord which they had recently learned by revelation. Paul at first appears to be an example which points the other way, since he was not inclined to create 'sayings' by Jesus freely. He quoted him only a few times (in the extant correspondence), and he argued out numerous cases without appeal to Jesus' teaching. In discussing celibacy, marriage and divorce, he distinguished between a 'word of the Lord' and his own advice (I Cor. 7.10,12). Yet we can see in his letters part of the process which resulted in new sayings by Jesus. God, he wrote, had revealed to him and others 'What no eye has seen'.

> For what person knows a man's thoughts except the spirit of the man which is in him? So also no one comprehends the thoughts of God except the Spirit of God. Now we have received not the spirit of the world, but the Spirit which is from God, that we might understand the gifts bestowed on us by God. And we impart this in words not taught by human wisdom but taught by the Spirit. . . . (I Cor. 2.9–13)

He continued by saying that he had 'the mind of Christ' (v. 15). We note that he imparted 'in words' things which he learned from the Spirit. Since he had the Spirit of God (I Cor. 7.20) he expected his converts to accept his advice on almost the same level as that of the Lord. The statement 'I think I have the Spirit of God' backs up his advice to single people to remain celibate. This is not a command, but the advice of one who knew the will of God. There were potential conflicts, since he thought that the Spirit of God dwells in other Christians (I Cor. 7.20). Were others who imparted in words things revealed by the Spirit always careful to make the source clear, and to distinguish the Spirit from the Lord and the Lord of revelation from the historical Jesus?

Paul also believed in revelation during times of ecstasy. He knew a man (presumably himself) who was caught up into Paradise and 'heard things that cannot be told' (II Cor. 12.1–4). But sometimes in prayer Paul heard things which could be told. He had a 'thorn in the flesh' – some physical ailment – and three times he asked

139

that it be removed. The Lord replied, 'My grace is sufficient for you, for my power is made perfect in weakness' (II Cor. 12.9). Here we have a 'saying of the Lord', newly coined for the occasion. We do not know whether 'the Lord' in the passage is 'the Lord Jesus Christ' or 'the Lord God', but for our present purposes it does not matter. Paul could say to one and all that the Lord said, 'my grace is sufficient for you'.

The cool eye of the academician sees this as a saying of the Lord which has been created in the history of the early church. It is clear that Paul's view of it was different: it was something that the Lord said to him during prayer. Scholars who say that sayings have been 'made up' sound at least a bit impious. Christians want them to be 'true'; and 'made up', 'invented', 'created' and the like sound as if a charge of fraud is being levelled. That is not the case. The devotion and religious experience of those who spoke by the Spirit, or to whom the Lord continued to speak from heaven, are not in question. The hard-and-fast line between 'the historical Jesus' and 'the Risen Lord' is a modern idea. Once it is accepted, however, and it is agreed to discuss the historical Jesus, it is necessary to try to distinguish a saying by Jesus from a saying by the Risen Lord or by the Spirit.

When we read Paul we can distinguish quite well between sayings which go back to the historical Jesus and new sayings from the Lord, or from Paul himself speaking in the Spirit. If all early Christian teachers and preachers had left us letters, we would doubtless see that many of them made the distinction. But some individuals would not have maintained it. The boundary between 'Jesus said this to his disciples while in Galilee' and 'the Lord revealed this to me last night' was a bit porous at the best. People believed that the Lord really did speak directly to them. But let us imagine a Christian prophet who, in preaching, used sayings without emphasizing their source, perhaps only mentioning it quickly: 'The Lord said "Do not divorce", the Spirit says "If celibate remain so", and the Lord said to me "My grace is sufficient".' If the preacher emphasized 'the Spirit says', both the word Spirit and the present tense would be a clue that this was not the historical Jesus. Similarly 'said *to me*', if spoken by someone who had not followed Jesus during his ministry, would point to an origin in prayer or some other form of revelation. But how long would such nice distinctions be made? And can we suppose that everyone meticulously made them?

It is worth noting that today, when we have written texts to study and compare, some people still attribute to Jesus sayings which are not ascribed to him in the gospels. In a radio interview (BBC radio 4, 26 June, 1988), a professional tennis player was asked how she reconciled being a Christian with the enormous financial rewards which come to the successful athlete. She replied quite sensibly, and backed up her defence of earning money by saying, 'Jesus said, "Run the race to win"'. She had in mind a statement by Paul, not Jesus (I Cor. 9.24). It is impossible to see that this happens today and then to deny that it happened in the first century – when people who heard Christian preachers did not have written accounts of the teaching of Jesus to compare.

The form-critical assumption is that as the material was used it was altered and supplemented. All scholars agree that this happened to some extent. To grant one case is to grant them all *in principle*. But on the other hand all scholars agree that the church used material which originated from Jesus and thus preserved it. To grant one case is to grant them all *in principle*. Since both cases must be granted in principle, what is required is good judgment in deciding each particular passage. This means that it is necessary to study all the passages. In the last chapter of the book we discuss extensively the problem of authenticating the material. In the following discussions of form criticism, we shall mostly just note that Bultmann (for example) thought that a given passage was created after Jesus, without trying to decide individual cases. At this stage the reader is asked to follow the discussion and to suspend judgment about authenticity.

• Oral tradition

Everyone accepts oral transmission at the early stages of the gospel tradition. Almost no one, that is, thinks that Peter and the others had notebooks of Jesus' sayings. The problem is that we do not know how to imagine the oral period, neither how long it lasted nor how oral transmission actually functioned.

We are offered 'scenarios'. Dibelius proposed primarily sermons, in which examples from Jesus' lifetime were cited. Bultmann thought of a variety of settings, including debate and instruction. Gerhardsson has made various proposals, such as strict memorization beginning in Jesus' lifetime.

We should start by making a basic distinction between 'oral tradition' and 'oral history'. The latter, or at least a version of it, is well known today. It is possible to take a tape recorder and interview people who lived through certain events. Their accounts will usually be rambling and ill-formed, and they will lack a bird's eye view – or the view of the recording angel. An official history will usually start with a comprehensive review: 'A storm centre gathered in the Atlantic and cut across parts of northern Europe before sweeping into the southeast coast of England, where it destroyed over a million trees, seriously damaged thousands of houses and disrupted electricity supply, travel and emergency services.' One who lived through it will ordinarily begin with something like this: 'I awoke at . . .' and continue with his or her personal experience.

Oral tradition in a minor sense is also known today. A short story about someone who is well known may circulate orally and be fairly well maintained, although variations will develop. Usually the story will include a memorable saying, or the tradition may consist only of the saying. That the battle of Waterloo was won 'on the playing fields of Eton' was probably not said by the Duke of Wellington, but it was widely thought that he said it, and it was the kind of thing that he would have said. It was eventually written down, and thus it is a familiar saying to this day, but at first it was an oral tradition: common to everyone who retold it, quite unlike oral histories.

In the ancient world both were known, as was a further form of oral tradition, the sort appealed to by Gerhardsson: memorization of extensive teaching material. Two types of oral tradition, however, should be dismissed. (1) We should not think that Jesus lived in a pre-literate society where everyone memorized everything. Documents abounded. Memorization was no more automatic then than now; it required discipline and drill. Short oral 'texts' could be remembered easily, as they

141

can now, especially if they included a pointed saying, though variations and misattributions would occur. (2) In Jesus' day the time of oral epics was long past. First-century Jews did not sit around campfires telling and re-telling stories, making them ever more colourful and poetic.

While these forms of memorization had vanished, the intentional memorization of material had not. We cannot now know how widespread was the practice of memorizing large blocks of material, nor whether or not any groups actually tried to maintain a purely oral tradition. The first century knew all about 'handbooks', both collections of teaching material and summaries and digests of it. Sages, both in Israel and in pagan society, knew about writing and publishing. Students knew about taking notes; Aristotle's 'writings' as we know them are from notebooks of his students. Committing to memory was prized, but usually the admonition to memorize referred to written texts: memorize them so as to interiorize them.[1] The digests and handbooks of teaching material simply reveal the degree to which students did not rely only on memory.

No one has recognized all this more clearly than Gerhardsson. He has realized that, unless a specific setting can be found in which early Christians deliberately committed Jesus-material to memory, he will have to grant the case of the form critics: bits and pieces go back to Jesus, and of course some stories about him go back to the personal memories of his disciples, but the oral period of the gospel material was like that of today – *if* one subtracts newspapers, TV, radio, and recorders, *as well as* universal literacy and cheap and plentiful writing materials. We do not know if Jesus' disciples were fully literate – able both to read and to write. Many people could do the former but not the latter. While documents abounded, they were often written by professional scribes. Even people of property sometimes could not sign their names, though they could probably read the legal documents which scribes prepared.[2]

Thus if we cannot imagine Jesus drilling his disciples in the repetition of his sayings, we cannot come up with a believable environment in which extensive teaching material was precisely transmitted. Even if the disciples could write, they probably did not carry writing materials with them. And Gerhardsson, we think, has thus far failed to find that environment or 'setting'.

Two passages in the church fathers have made some suppose that the Jesus-material was memorized and preserved orally. Both actually point the other way. We take them in turn.

1. According to Eusebius, Irenaeus wrote this about Polycarp, a Christian in Asia Minor who died *c*. 155:

> I [Irenaeus] remember the events of those days more clearly than those which happened recently, for what we learn as children grows up with the soul and is united to it, so that I can speak even of the place in which the blessed Polycarp sat and disputed, how he came in and went out, the character of his life, the appearance of his body, the discourses which he made to the people, how he reported his intercourse with John and with the others who had seen the Lord,

how he remembered their words, and what were the things concerning the Lord which he had heard from them, and about his miracles, and about [his] teaching, and how Polycarp had received them from the eyewitnesses of the word of life, and reported all things in agreement with the Scriptures. I listened eagerly even then to these things through the mercy of God which was given me, and made notes of them, not on paper but in my heart, and ever by the grace of God do I truly ruminate on them. . . .[3]

It is noteworthy that Irenaeus does not say that he was trained to remember what Polycarp taught. On the contrary, he remembered Polycarp because old men can remember what they experienced as children – a fact which all those who have had or who have elderly friends or relatives can confirm. This is not 'oral tradition', but 'oral history'. Further, Irenaeus does not say that Polycarp himself repeated what he had memorized, but rather that he told everything 'in accordance with the Scriptures'. There is no evidence from this passage that, around the turn of the first century, there was a body of memorized oral tradition for Christians to draw on. There were occasional reminiscenses (Polycarp had met 'eyewitnesses'), not a carefully controlled body of orally transmitted texts.

2. The second passage is from our old friend Papias. According to Eusebius, Papias wrote that

. . . if ever anyone came who had followed the presbyters [elders], I enquired into the words of the presbyters: what Andrew or Peter or Philip or Thomas or James or John or Matthew, or any other of the Lord's disciples, had said, and what Ariston and the presbyter John, the Lord's disciples, were saying. For I did not suppose that information from books would help me so much as the word of a living and surviving voice.[4]

Papias, we learn, was not too discriminating. He did not have a completely firm fix on who was a disciple of Jesus and who was 'an Elder' (in Greek, presbyter) but not an original disciple. That is, we should not take Ariston and the second John (John the Elder) actually to be disciples of Jesus in the strict sense, though they doubtless were followers of his way. What we learn from this is (1) that Papias listened avidly to anyone who knew something about what Andrew or one of the others said; (2) that therefore there was probably not a body of oral tradition from which he could learn. He sought 'oral history' about the disciples or 'elders'; or he sought 'oral tradition' in the minor sense – short sayings and stories – either about the disciples or via them about Jesus.

These passages help defeat the hopes of those who look for a scholastic oral tradition which transmitted an extensive body of material. The principal hindrance to that view, however, we sketched in the previous chapter: considerable variation in the surviving material is the rule.

Throughout this discussion we have referred to the kind of oral tradition which doubtless did exist: short stories and sayings. Ian Henderson has recently demonstrated the prominence in the gospel of the **gnomic** saying.[5] These sayings are (1)

analogical in structure, (2) normative and (3) independent. First some examples and then the explanation:

> Those who are well have no need of a physician, but those who are sick. (Mark 2.17a and parr.)
>
> Can the wedding guests fast while the bridegroom is with them? (Mark 2.19a and parr.)
>
> For there is nothing hid, except to be made manifest; nor is anything secret, except to come to light. (Mark 4.22 and parr.)
>
> The measure you give will be the measure you get. (Mark 4.24 and parr.)

These sayings are 'analogical' because an analogy is expressed or implied. Analogies may be negative or positive: In the third example hid = secret; made manifest = come to light. In the first the relationship is negative: well ≠ sick; implied non-physician ≠ physician. In the second example the analogy is negative and implied: 'wedding guests do not fast when the bridegroom is with them' implies that they may fast when he is absent. Thus fast ≠ not fast; bridegroom present ≠ bridegroom absent. The analogy in the fourth example is positive. This expressed or implied four-part analogical structure is the form of the gnomic saying.

The sayings are 'normative' because there is an implied requirement or a description of how things should be. 'The measure you give will be the measure you get' implies 'take care how you measure, there is a law of retribution'. The norm implied by the third example is a bit more difficult: possibly it refers to the correct behaviour which God will display when all secrets are revealed.

The sayings are 'independent' because they can fit many different situations. The Matthaean parallel to Mark 4.22 appears in a different context (Matt. 10.26), and both the parallels to Mark 4.24 are in other contexts (Matt. 7.2//Luke 6.38). There is also a closely related saying in Matt. 25.29//Luke 19.26.

In the following chapters we shall often see that a saying can be detached from its context, and that the form critics, especially Bultmann, thought that the separate sayings are more likely to be authentic than the stories in which they are found. Henderson's study partly confirms this guess, since the gnomic form makes the saying resistant to change. He points out, however, that this does not necessarily mean that the original speaker was Jesus.

• Conclusion

The discussion of creativity and oral tradition ends with a series of cautions and qualifications: The first Christians, or rather some of them, could 'create' sayings by Jesus in numerous ways, including hearing them in prayer, receiving them as revelations, and attributing to him excellent and appropriate sayings which may have originated with someone else. On the other hand, they seem not to have been wildly creative. We shall see evidence of this from time to time in the discussion of form criticism and also in subsequent chapters (14, 20–22).

The early Christians did not have professional or semi-professional schools of memorizers who meticulously passed down oral tradition. On the other hand, many things which Jesus said and did were striking and were remembered. This is likely to be the case with short stories and sayings, especially gnomic ones. But we cannot suppose that even the gnomic sayings are necessarily authentic, since gnomai are well-attested throughout the Mediterranean world.

Creativity and Oral Tradition

10 Chreiai

We shall go through the main categories of pericopes as the form critics organized them, mostly following Bultmann's arrangement, and also relying largely on Bultmann for detailed comments, such as which verses are redactional, which are interpolations of originally different passages, which are creations just for the pericope at hand, and the like. Bultmann is the one who had views on all these matters, and who assigned more-or-less every verse in the synoptics to some point of origin or another. More recent critical work will be drawn on to provide balance. In terms of detail and thoroughness, however, there is no parallel to Bultmann's work, and the reader who wishes to study individual pericopes in detail will learn much from his discussions.

It will not be possible to quote in full all the pericopes discussed, and the reader will have difficulty following the discussions in this and the following chapters if a synopsis is not used. First, though, we shall quote two examples. We shall have to spend several lines defining the form, and it will help if synoptic passages are in mind at the outset.

> And the scribes of the Pharisees, when they saw that he was eating with sinners and tax collectors, said to his disciples, 'Why does he eat with tax collectors and sinners?' And when Jesus heard it, he said to them, 'Those who are well have no need of a physician, but those who are sick; I came not to call the righteous, but sinners.' (Mark 2.16–17).

> And the scribes who came down from Jerusalem said, 'He is possessed by Beelzebul, and by the prince of demons he casts out the demons'. And he called them to him, and said to them in parables, 'How can Satan cast out Satan? . . .' (Mark 3.22–23)

• Terminology

The name of this form has proved difficult to decide on; though what the name, if one were found, would signify is not difficult. In mind are short stories in which something happens, or someone says something, which provokes an illuminating response from the chief actor. Dibelius, we saw above, called it 'the paradigm',

Bultmann 'the apophthegm', Taylor 'the pronouncement story'. Dibelius' term was intended to describe the supposed paradigmatic or exemplary function of these stories in sermons. Taylor sought a brief and commonsense descriptive term. Bultmann's term, 'apophthegm', is from the Greek *apophthegma*, which means 'speaking forth' and which is often used in Greek literature for succinct and pointed statements.

In giving Greek analogies to the Paradigm, Dibelius proposed 'chreia' as the most appropriate. He regarded the chreia as distinguished 'from the larger group of "Apophthegmata" by its connection with a particular situation', and from the Gnome because it is always connected with a person (pp. 152f.). These neat distinctions do not reflect the range of ancient usage, as we shall see, but it does appear that chreia is the most appropriate word. Berger prefers it for the passages in the gospels, though he gives 'apophthegm' as an alternative.[1] He titles the independent short and pointed statement, for which apophthegm would be a good word, a *Sentenz*, a 'sententious saying'.

The issue of terminology is murkier yet. A recent study clearly demonstrates that ancient literary scholars frequently used the term 'chreia' for a short saying without a provoking action or statement.[2]

We can pin the blame solidly on the ancients: they did not use the terms consistently themselves, and modern scholars have not yet agreed on what will be called what. With regard to the pointed saying, without an explicit statement or incident which calls it forth, we may cite Plutarch as using the term 'apophthegm': Brutus when writing in Greek 'affected the brevity of the apophthegm and the Spartan' (Spartans were famous for their economical and effective remarks). Once, for example, Brutus wrote to the Pergamenians:

> I hear that ye have given money to Dolabella; if ye gave it willingly confess that ye have wronged me; if unwillingly, prove it by giving willingly to me.[3]

Similarly Plutarch wrote that Lycurgus trained Spartan boys to answer 'apophthegmatically', which he defined as combining 'pungency with grace' (*Lycurgus* XVIII.1).

The grammarian Theon of Alexandria, however, called such statements chreiai. This is one of his examples of chreiai:

> Epameinondas, as he was dying childless, said to his friends: 'I have left two daughters – the victory at Leuctra and the one at Mantineia.'[4]

The 'apophthegmatic' statement by Brutus and the chreia by Theon are, formally, indistinguishable. There is a setting which calls forth the saying in each case: the Pergamenians had given money to Dolabella; Epameinondas was dying childless, and to keep others from feeling sorry for him he indicated that he actually had 'daughters'. In neither case, however, is there an explicit saying or action which provokes the response. It is the fuller form – with an initiating action or word by someone other than the chief figure – which is so prominent in the gospels, but

147

ancients sometimes used the principal terms on offer – chreia and apophthegm – for the saying itself or for the saying with only an implied setting.

There is no 'correct' terminology, and a certain amount of arbitrariness is required. The present discussion is not intended to solve the problem, and we have wanted only to explain why the student will run into first one term and definition and then another, and to clarify our usage in this chapter. We shall follow Berger and others[5] in calling the longer form, Taylor's 'pronouncement story', the chreia. The terminological problems of naming independent, pointed statements will be largely avoided by adopting Bultmann's titles which describe their contents ('woes', etc.), rather than purely formal ones. The reasons for choosing the term chreia are these:

1. When the gospels employ common forms, the passages should not be categorized under unique headings. For this reason an ancient term is desirable.

2. Etymologically and (we believe) in general Greek usage, chreia is more appropriate than apophthegm. The latter term is best reserved for the response of the chief character or for a saying with an implied setting.

3. Ancient grammarians and rhetors who discussed the chreia, and whose work has now been presented and explained by Hock and O'Neill, used the term to cover a variety of forms, all of which are closely related to the one which we are discussing. 'Chreia' is sometimes used for the pungent remark alone, but often for a remark which is given a context, but in which there is no other speaker – like the two passages cited above, one called a chreia and one an apophthegm. The ancient chreia, in other words, was often presented from the chief figure's point of view, and the circumstances were given without anyone else appearing as the subject of a finite verb: 'when Socrates heard . . . he said. . . .' This sort of chreia would conform to synoptic usage if the other speaker were made the subject of an independent clause: 'Thrasymacus said . . . Socrates replied. . . .'

4. One of the grammarians studied by Hock and O'Neill, Theon of Alexandria, had a sub-category called 'the responsive chreia', in which there is another speaker, who makes a statement instead of merely asking a question. This sufficiently expands the category to include the passages which scholars customarily place in it.

'Chreia', then, as defined by the grammarians, covers a broader range of material than that discussed here, but it does include it; and no other ancient term is equally satisfactory.

Bultmann made sub-divisions of the form according to content, and it is helpful to have these in mind. His categories were controversy dialogues, didactic dialogues and biographical 'apophthegmata'. The two synoptic passages with which we began are both 'controversy dialogues' or, in our terminology, controversy chreiai.

• Examples

We begin with a series of pericopes in Mark 2.1–3.6. Not all of these are pure chreiai, but working our way through the list will help us see how form criticism defines 'forms' and what uses the method has. The individual pericopes are these:

	Mark	*Matthew*	*Luke*
Healing of Paralytic	2.1–12	9.1–8	5.17–26
Teaching by Sea	2.13	—	—
Call of Levi	2.14	9.9	5.27f.
Eating with Sinners	2.15–17	9.10–13	5.29–32
Question about Fasting	2.18–22	9.14–17	5.33–39
Plucking Grain on Sabbath	2.23–28	12.1–8	6.1–5
Man with Withered Hand	3.1–6	12.9–14	6.6–11

We shall begin with general observations about the collection of passages.

1. There has long been wide agreement that we find here a collection of pre-synoptic origin. This was proposed by Martin Albertz (1921), who was followed by several scholars, including Vincent Taylor (1933) and W. L. Knox (1953). Recently Arland Hultgren has supported this view (1979). Scholarship never reached unanimity on the question of whether Mark or a source first assembled these passages in sequence, and the latest publication argues that it was Mark rather than a pre-Markan source (Kiilunen, 1985).[6] Despite this challenge we shall treat the section as a pre-Markan block. Doing so will help us demonstrate how the synoptics are analysed and studied. The arguments in favour of the pre-Markan composition of this unit are these:

(*a*) The conclusion to the series, in which the Herodians and Pharisees are said to plot to have Jesus killed (Mark 3.6), comes too early and is in fact awkward. It appears that Mark felt the awkwardness and had to reintroduce this plot closer to the trial narrative (Mark 12.13). When it comes to the arrest and trial, however, neither Pharisee nor Herodian appears. In the other synoptics, Herodians appear only in Matt. 22.16, the parallel to Mark 12.13, and otherwise play no role. Pharisees are mentioned by neither Matthew nor Luke in connection with the trial; and, after the point in the narrative represented by Mark 12.13, appear only once more, in Matt. 27.62, after the execution.

Thus the plot in 3.6 (Pharisees and Herodians) does not represent a view which the evangelists wanted to make central. In Matthew there is a good deal more anti-Pharisaic material, and it would be easier to believe that he introduced the plot in his parallel to Mark 3.6 (Matt. 12.14). But in this case where did Mark get 'the Herodians'? It seems that no one knew quite who they were, and they appear only in three passages we have named: Mark 3.6; 12.13; and Matt. 22.16, the parallel to Mark, 12.13. They are probably not redactional and presumably therefore come from a source.

(*b*) The conclusion comes too early if we consider the rest of the gospel material. After the decision to have Jesus killed (Mark 3.6; Matt. 12.14) nothing in fact happens for several chapters. The Pharisees are sometimes present, and there is mutual hostility; but one does not see that there is a blood feud. It is entirely reasonable that Mark 3.6 is the conclusion to a pre-synoptic collection.

2. The purpose of the collection. Knox proposed that 'the original collection of stories ended with the plot for the simple reason that at one time it stood by itself as an introduction to the story of the Passion' (p. 12). Knox held a 'tractate' view of the

pre-synoptic sources: that individual pericopes had been gathered into small collections before the gospels were composed. If this is so, each collection could have been more or less complete: that is, it might give an account of how it came to be that Jesus was crucified. Knox proposed that this was the motive behind the collection in Mark 2.1–3.6, and here he was on good ground.

That the source served a specific purpose is better seen if we dwell for a moment on the artificiality of the construction. There is a rapid series of events, none very serious, which culminates in a decision to execute. Life is not like this. Knox pointed out that the stories 'do not belong to any period in the ministry of Jesus that can be definitely fixed' (p. 14). Diverse stories have been put together, and it is even possible that 'scribes and Pharisees' were not originally opponents in these stories (Hultgren, p. 159). It is also possible that not all the stories were originally conflict dialogues. Bultmann speaks of the 'productive power of the controversy dialogue' (p. 51): stories tended to be turned into controversy dialogues when they may have been previously only simple stories of, for example, healing (e.g. The Man with the Withered Hand).

3. Albertz and Taylor proposed that one can see an intentional escalation of the conflict for dramatic purposes (Taylor, p. 177):

Paralytic	latent opposition: complaints to one another, 2.7
Eating with Sinners	criticism addressed to disciples, 2.16
Question of Fasting	criticism of disciples to Jesus, 2.18
Grain on Sabbath	Jesus responsible for transgression, 2.24
Withered Hand	plot to kill, 3.6

We are not entirely convinced that the conflict escalates smoothly through each pericope, but in general terms it does. The construction is artificial and not historical.

4. On the question of the historicity of the material, however, many have held that there is a kernel of truth in the collection. Knox proposed that the artificiality does not entirely cancel historicity. Jesus, he thought, would first have attempted to win the Pharisees to his side, and the early opposition by Pharisees he considered unhistorical. Yet he thought that conflict with the Pharisees actually did take place (pp. 14f.). Bultmann put it this way: 'If any part of these controversy dialogues does go back to Jesus himself, it is, apart from their general spiritual tenor, the decisive saying' (p. 49). The stories have 'an inward spiritual truth'. That does not mean, he continued, that there is no 'outer historical truth', but only that this is something that 'is no longer possible to establish' (ibid.). We shall not press the question of historicity here, but only observe that form criticism is not opposed to the search for information about the historical Jesus. It is, rather, one of the main tools of those who undertake that task.

5. Finally, we should note the significance of our collection for the synoptic problem. Discovery of the collection rested upon the two-source hypothesis, but it may also support it. The passages follow in uninterrupted sequence in Mark and Luke, but not in Matthew. Matthew has substantial bodies of intervening material, principally a collection of miracle stories and more material about the twelve

(perhaps put here because of The Call of Levi/Matthew). The student studying only Matthew would not identify the stories which we are discussing as a pre-synoptic source. Once the identification has been made, however, it can be seen to be reasonable. The sequence in Mark (and Luke), interrupted by Matthew, constitutes an argument in favour of Markan priority. Agreement that the material in Mark 2.1–3.6 is a pre-synoptic collection, however, does not entirely rule out the Griesbach hypothesis, or a variant of it. One would have to say that Luke used not only Matthew but also a pre-synoptic source containing this collection of passages, that he here preferred the arrangement of the independent collection, and that Mark decided to follow Luke's arrangement rather than Matthew's. Here as elsewhere we would have to see a complicating factor: the continued existence of one of the sources of the earliest gospel. On balance, though, the theory of a pre-synoptic collection counts in favour of Markan priority, at least in this section of the gospels.

Now we shall examine the stories one-by-one:

Pericope 1: The Healing of the Paralytic, *Mark 2.1–12 and parr.*

Bultmann proposed that we should divide the pericope into two component parts: the miracle (2.2–5a,11–12) and the saying about forgiveness (2.5b–10). The dialogue in 2.5b–10 has been inserted into the miracle story, which can be seen to 'skip' from 2.5a to 2.11. An editor has done no more than insert the saying and perhaps add 'I say to you' in v. 11. Bultmann further proposed that the saying about forgiveness in 2.5b–10 was composed for the purpose. He saw at work here the church's claim to be able to forgive sins, and he thought that it wished to establish the claim by first attributing it to Jesus.

In this entire analysis we see operating the theory that the original material consisted of simple and pure forms. A healing and a dialogue now appear together; Bultmann and many other form critics assume that they were originally separate.

Berger with some justice characterizes this scissors-and-paste view of editorial work as assuming 'a naïve scheme of development' (p. 84). He treats the passage as a dramatic chreia, a category which contains several other passages which involve either healing or the call of disciples (p. 85), and he resists the suggestion that it should be broken into two parts. The two parts rather make it a 'mixed' chreia, since it contains both an action and a saying (most chreiai consist of one or the other, but mixed chreiai are otherwise known). Whether a passage with as many exchanges as occur in Mark 2.1–12 should be called a chreia may be doubted, but this is largely a question of definition.

Taylor would say that the fact that the passage does not perfectly fit a known form shows that it has not yet been rounded down. It is indeed possible that in Jesus' lifetime a healing led to a controversy. We think it more likely, however, that it was an early Christian who shaped a healing story so that it led to a controversy over Jesus' authority – shaped it not by cutting an action-chreia open in the middle and inserting a saying-chreia, but rather by composing the passage as a whole so that one thing led to another. One notes the artificiality of the scene: the scribes grumble to

151

themselves, but Jesus knows what they say and replies to them. This is stage one in the escalating conflict of this series of passages, and it probably owes more to the author's sense of drama than to anything else. The right to announce the forgiveness of sins was, as Bultmann saw, an important theological claim, and the church's claim is here made not by argument but by a concrete story. This is the usual way in which the synoptics 'argue' cases. This would mean that the description of the conflict with the scribes is probably part of the author's work as he composed the present pericope.

This is not to say that nothing lies behind the story. Jesus very likely did heal a paralytic; he obviously saw himself as imbued with divine authority. All this has been neatly packed into a single forceful story.

Pericope 2: Teaching by the Sea, *Mark 2.13*

This verse is obviously an editorial summary. One notes that no teaching is actually given. This is often the case in Mark: see also 1.39; 6.6b; 6.34. A partial collection of such passages is printed in parallel columns in Greeven, §28. A similar saying in Mark 4.1, however, is followed by teaching material.

Pericope 3: The Call of Levi, *Mark 2.14 and parr.*

Bultmann denominated the chreia 'biographical' (p. 28). Berger points out that all chreiai are in a sense biographical, but those with an explicit self-reference (in this case 'follow me') can be separated from the others (p. 85). Mark 1.16–18 and 1.19–20 are variants of the same theme, the call of disciples. All these passages Bultmann regarded as being 'ideal scenes' and probably of 'unitary construction'.

Let us pause for a moment to note these two terms. Bultmann, we have seen, regarded many chreiai as having been based on a pre-existent saying, with the story being a later setting. The users of the material, he further explained, preferred the setting to be marked by a single action which gives rise to a question or a challenge, which in turn is followed by the decisive saying. These actions which initiate chreiai, while lifelike, are 'ideal' or 'imaginary'. They give 'lively expression to some idea in a concrete event' (p. 39). It is an especially acute observation when, in discussing the action which begins a chreia, Bultmann says that its specificity shows its typical character. 'The typical character of a controversy dialogue is most marked when a single action like plucking corn or healing on the sabbath constitutes the starting-point rather than when the opponent merely fastens on some general attitude of the person he criticises' (p. 39). That is, we think, precisely correct. Popular presentations in all times and cultures tend to rely on the anecdote, but the anecdote is often tailor-made for the point which it illustrates.

Thus in describing The Call of Levi as an ideal scene Bultmann meant in part that it is an imaginary creation which dramatically portrays what the author wishes to present as typical: people did or should give up everything to follow Jesus.

The term ideal means more than just 'imaginary' in the sense of 'fictitious'; some passages are 'ideal' in that they point beyond themselves and become symbolic (cf. p. 56). Thus Bultmann's view of the Call of Levi was that it is an 'ideal scene' in two senses: the story as a concrete event has been made up; but, more, it presents in short form an ideal of wider application: this is how one should respond to Jesus. All of the scenes of Jesus' call of disciples are ideal in both senses: they are imaginary and they represent a Christian ideal.

We must emphasize that, in Bultmann's view, an ideal scene might contain a kind of history. It might portray 'the general character' of Jesus' life, and portray it 'on the basis of historical recollection' (p. 50, on controversy dialogues). Further, some chreiai contain sayings which are authentic.

By the term 'unitary', however, Bultmann intended to rule out the possibility of an authentic saying in the present instance. 'Unitary' means that the entire scene, saying and all, was composed as a unit. There was no saying which went floating around until it was embedded in the present story. In the present passage the saying is only 'follow me', not a very substantial saying, and not one which could have circulated independently. Yet even here Bultmann would not deny that sometime, somewhere, Jesus asked or told someone to follow him. He wished to conduct a methodologically strict analysis of the material. In doing so he occasionally would point out that this or that must have been really true of Jesus, but in *The History of the Synoptic Tradition* that was not his focus. He performed a socio-literary analysis according to rules, and by those rules The Call of Levi is ideal in the sense of 'imaginary' and 'paradigmatic'; and it is also unitary – made up all at once, not composed of independent bits.

Pericope 4: Eating with Sinners, *Mark 2.15–17*

The fairly full setting which v. 15 provides goes beyond the norm for chreiai, and Berger considers the chreia to be only vv. 16f. In this case, v. 15 is an editorial development of the setting given in the chreia itself: Jesus was eating with sinners and tax collectors.

Bultmann held that the saying was originally unattached (note what 'originally' must mean: not originally in Jesus' lifetime, but originally in the early tradition). The story has been designed for the saying. The appearance of 'the scribes of the Pharisees' is impossible historically (p. 18).

Hultgren's analysis is more acute. He calls attention to the fact that Mark 2.17 contains two different sayings, and that they are also formally different. 'Those who are well have no need of a physician, but those who are sick' (2.17a) is a proverb, while 'I came not to call the righteous, but sinners' (2.17b) is an 'I saying' which assigns a statement of Jesus' purpose to Jesus himself. Hultgren, correctly in our view, doubts the authenticity of this kind of 'I saying'. 'All come under suspicion of being the products of Christian reflection on the historical appearance of Jesus. They are summaries of his total impact and significance for Christian faith' (p. 110). The first saying (not the well but the sick) is also inauthentic; it is a proverb based on the Christian view of Jesus as a healer of sinners.

Thus Hultgren's overall view of the pericope is that it was entirely composed 'in a time and place in which the church was attacked by opponents on the grounds that its fellowship was suspect . . .' (ibid.).

This is, again, not to say that the theme of eating with sinners is unhistorical. As we shall see in ch. 20, that is almost certainly an accusation against Jesus which was made in his lifetime. Once accepted as a theme, however, it was expanded by concrete stories, and we see this development in some of Luke's special material as well as in the present pericope. We should also note that the opposition to Jesus on the part of scribes and Pharisees (Matthew, 'Pharisees'; Mark 'the scribes of the Pharisees'; Luke, 'The Pharisees and the scribes') has been expanded as well.

Bultmann's view that the appearance of 'the scribes of the Pharisees' when Jesus was dining is historically impossible deserves comment. W. L. Knox regarded it as believable that these supposedly 'accredited religious leaders of the nation' would make special inspection tours (p. 14). Here we see that the question of whether the setting is 'ideal' in the sense of 'imaginary' requires not just formal and literary judgment, but also historical research. We think that it is much more probable that Bultmann was right than Knox: no one, certainly not Antipas nor the chief priests, had 'accredited' the Pharisees to inspect people's dining companions. This does not mean that Jesus was not criticized for the company he kept, but rather that the scene in the gospels is imaginary: it puts into one dramatic event of a few lines what was probably a much longer process.

The form-critical assumption is that, if the pericope does not reflect the lifetime of Jesus, it comes from the life of the early church and reveals something about the early Christian communities and the context in which they lived. It is possible that the theme (or the saying) goes back to the lifetime of Jesus, but that the pericope itself was composed later; thus it should reflect (in Hultgren's words) 'a time and place in which the church was attacked by opponents on the grounds that its fellowship was suspect . . .'. Following this view, we would conclude that the church continued to compose material in which Jesus opposed scribes and Pharisees and included sinners. This would mean that opposition from those strict with regard to the law continued for some period of time.

The problem with this is that it is hard to find a time and place in which scribes, Pharisees or some combination of the two harrassed the church for admitting sinners. These were not the opponents of Peter, John and the others in Jerusalem (at least, not according to Acts), and the evidence of Paul's letters is that the Jerusalem church was dominated by those who were strict according to the law. Thus it is unlikely that the pericope was from Jerusalem Christianity. Then from where? We shall not cast around trying to find a place and time. The point is that using form criticism to discover the history of early Christianity is a demanding task, at least as demanding as the search for the Jesus of history. On the immediate point of the Pharisees as the opposition to Jesus and to the early church we shall only comment that, the more that is known about Pharisaism, the less it appears that it actually dominated any place during any part of the first century. The tendency to exaggerate the Pharisees' role in the lifetime of Jesus is clearly marked in the gospels themselves: thus, for example,

Matthew often changes Mark's 'scribes' to 'Pharisees'. But the motivation for this development poses an appreciable historical problem, one which is much greater than used to be perceived, when it was thought that the Pharisees controlled Palestine.[7]

Pericope 5: The Question about Fasting, *Mark 2.18–22*

Bultmann noted that v. 18 is divisible. The opening statement, they were fasting (18a), can be entirely derived from the question of 18b (cf. the relationship of 2.15 and 2.16). In this case the chreia was originally 2.18b–19a. Bultmann considered it more likely, however, that 2.19a was originally unattached and was given its present setting at a time when the Christian movement was troubled about its relationship to the followers of John the Baptist (p. 19). The saying, in this case, was originally part of a debate, but the original debate has been lost. Bultmann next noted that it is the disciples who are accused, not Jesus, and he saw 'the disciples' as standing in for the later church: it is the church's behaviour which is actually in dispute. Verses 19b and 20, which refer to the 'bridegroom' and his departure, are secondary. They correspond 'neither to the style of an apophthegm nor to the situation of the Church' (which is the setting of 18b and 19a). They may have been added by Mark himself (pp. 18f.).

Yet these verses must have some setting. It appears that they provide reflection on the difference in behaviour before and after Jesus' death (cf. Hultgren). While the bridegroom is present his attendants do not fast, but they do fast when he is gone. We appear to have here the memory that Jesus and his disciples were not ascetic (see especially Matt. 11.7–19), though some portions of the church practised fasting after Jesus' death and resurrection. We see reference to this practice in Matt. 6.16–18: 'When you fast . . .'.

The concluding saying, about the futility of patching old cloth and the advisability of using new wineskins for new wine (2.21–22), is hard to evaluate. Bultmann asked whether or not the sayings were 'secular meshalim' (parables or metaphors), and he granted that one can do no more than make a subjective judgment (pp. 98, 102). The main point is that, whether or not Jesus said them, we cannot know their precise force and nuance without their context. Small parabolic sayings of this sort point to the appearance of something 'new', and the reader of the gospels 'knows' that what is new is Jesus and his message; and, further, that the old religion cannot be patched up. This is the meaning which the sayings have in their present setting. Conceivably Jesus himself thought that minor repair work would not fix up Judaism; but that would have to be shown on other grounds. If so, these sayings could be added as supplementary evidence. But, once we grant that the setting in this passage is church practice with regard to fasting, and thus that it has no authentic setting in Jesus' lifetime, we must admit ourselves unable to know the precise meaning of the sayings about new and old.

In the present case, we do not wish to deny Bultmann's intuition that the passage can be broken into component parts. While it probably was 'naïve' of Bultmann to think that pericopes were composed by means of scissors and paste, we nevertheless know that sometimes sayings *were* moved from one setting to another. It would be naïve to think that this happened only when we can prove it by making comparisons among the gospels. Any reader can see that Mark 2.18a could be derived from 2.18b, and this may be taken to be a weak attempt to provide a historical context for the saying. Further, the sayings about new and old have no necessary relationship with the question of fasting. It is most important, however, to see that these sayings have the particular meaning which they have *only* because of their context: the 'old' religion, symbolized by *the* fasting of *John the Baptist's disciples and the Pharisees*, needs to be replaced. What would the sayings mean if attached to Jesus' instructions to his own disciples about how to fast (Matt. 6.16–18)?

Pericope 6: Plucking Grain on the Sabbath, *Mark 2.23–28*

Here again 'Jesus' defends the practice of the later church: 'Jesus is questioned about the disciples' behaviour; why not about his own?' (Bultmann, p. 16). 'And he said to them' in 2.27 shows that this saying is a later addition (Bultmann). We should also note that the sudden appearance of Pharisees in a grainfield on the sabbath is historically unlikely (even more unlikely than their appearance in a house where Jesus was dining, Pericope 4 above), and that the setting therefore is 'ideal'.

Hultgren has offered a reconstruction of the earliest form of the pericope, making use of Mark 2.23, 24, 27:

> [23]One sabbath he was going through the grainfields; and as they made their way his disciples began to pluck ears of grain. [24]And the Pharisees said to him, 'Look, why are they doing what is not lawful on the Sabbath?' [27]And he said to them, 'The sabbath was made for people, not people for the sabbath'.

This makes the argument based on the behaviour of David (2.25–26) secondary, as well as the second saying, 'The Son of man is lord of the sabbath' (2.28). Hultgren further proposed that even his reconstructed early pericope is not unitary. The saying in Mark 2.27, 'The sabbath was made for people . . .', is independent of its setting, and originally it was 'free-floating'. The story about the grainfield was composed just to provide a setting for the saying. Thus according to Hultgren the pericope as we have it consists of two stages of development beyond the original saying ('the sabbath was made for people'). First, the story of the grainfield was created (vv. 23–24), and then the Scriptural argument (vv. 25–26) and the second saying (v. 28) were added.

It is our own judgment that we cannot be sure about what is earlier and what later. The absence of Mark 2.27 from the parallels in Matthew and Luke should give us pause before accepting Hultgren's view that this is the basic saying around which the passage was developed. We cannot know whether Jesus uttered both sayings (the sabbath was made; the Son of man is lord), one of them, or neither. The general form-critical judgment that the setting has been composed and is 'ideal', however, is to be confirmed.

Pericope 7: The Man with the Withered Hand, *Mark 3.1–6*

The final verse is 'biographical' and is not related to the main point of the story.

Otherwise the pericope is 'organically complete' (Bultmann). Since this is a healing story, Berger classifies it as a 'dramatic chreia' (see above, on Pericope 1). Bultmann also noted that in Luke 6.7 the opponents are introduced into the story itself and that Matthew adds a saying (12.11f.). This shows a possible tendency of the tradition: to add sayings and to develop traditions into controversy dialogues.

These views are generally accepted. The saying ('Is it lawful to do good on the sabbath, or to do ill; to save life or destroy it?') could not have circulated independently, but must always have been connected to some action or other (cf. Hultgren). Yet it is important to note that the healing of a minor ailment, a withered hand, cannot be considered 'saving life', and in the pericope as it stands the action is not directly supportive of the saying. Further, the healing is not against any interpretation of the sabbath law of which we have independent knowledge: no work is performed, since speaking does not count as work. Finally the view that one may save life on the sabbath would have been accepted by even the most rigorous interpreters of the law.

Thus there are several incongruities in the passage: (1) the saying about 'saving life' does not correspond to the minor healing; (2) the healing does not run counter to any known interpretation of the sabbath law; (3) all would accept the principle articulated in the saying. This means that the conflict with Pharisees is artificial. Pharisees would probably not have objected to a healing which did not require work, and they would have granted – in fact, insisted – that life may be saved on the sabbath. It is dubious that either the saying or the healing would have offended them.

Our view of the pericope is that we cannot be certain how it originated. The saying could not have been independent of some action, we agree, but it could originally have been attached to a different one. The present context is clear: the church is in a dispute about the sabbath law, or it remembers that there were such disputes, but it may have been a bit out of touch with actual Pharisaic practice. If this is a historical event, the actual conflict would have been minor.

In any case all agree that the conclusion in v. 6 (the Pharisees and Herodians plotted to kill Jesus) is editorial, probably having been added by the collector of these conflict stories in order to lead up to the conclusion of the story of Jesus: his execution at the behest of Jewish leaders.

• Observations on main points

We shall now review what we have found, grouping the material under large headings:

1. *Forms*. The Gospel of Mark makes use of the chreia, but it is not infrequently developed. Sometimes an opening sentence is added to emphasize the setting; sometimes the form is complicated by including more than one exchange; sometimes there are additional sayings.

2. *Healings*. The Paralytic and The Man with the Withered Hand. We shall take up healings and other miracles in the next section, and here make only two comments, one formal and one historical. In terms of form, they are 'mixed', but it is better to

use that term in Berger's sense than in Bultmann's. Bultmann meant 'two different forms (miracle and chreia) mixed together'. Berger speaks of mixed chreias as a standard category which includes both an action and a saying. In terms of historical analysis, it is generally accepted now that Jesus was known as a miracle-worker, and there is no reason to challenge these healing stories. What is doubtful is that they were historically set in a conflict between Jesus and the Pharisees.

3. *Conflict.* We should suppose that conflict has been partially created and partially emphasized in the development of the passages in this section. Emphasis on conflict is, we have seen, the rationale for the collection of these pericopes into their present form and sequence. The conflict may be totally created in The Healing of the Paralytic, The Grain on the Sabbath, and The Man with the Withered Hand. Eating with Sinners is probably a church creation in its entirety, but the theme is doubtless authentic. The Question of Fasting is similar: Jesus probably was really criticized for his 'libertine' lifestyle (as for consorting with sinners), and this is seen in Matt. 11.7–19; but the story in Mark 2.18–22 and parallels is a construction of the early church. Thus there really was conflict, both in Jesus' lifetime and in the early church, but the stories in this section seem to reflect the situation of the later church.

We must distinguish, however, between the conflict over sinners and the conflict over the sabbath. The sabbath stories (Grain and Withered Hand) are noteworthy for their artificiality and superficiality. When we turn to historical reconstruction (chs 20–21), we shall see that conflict over sinners is more firmly embedded in the tradition than conflict over the sabbath.

We must further note the tendency to introduce the Pharisees (and the scribes) as opponents. They are probably the author's work in The Healing of the Paralytic; they are part of the unitary composition, Eating with Sinners; they appear in the editorial introduction and the 'ideal' setting of The Question about Fasting (see Mark 2.18–19); they appear in the imaginary setting of the Grain on the Sabbath; and they appear in the editorial conclusion of the collection, where they are said to engage in a plot against Jesus (Mark 3.6).

4. *Discipleship.* The Call of Levi has been created as another example of the right response to Jesus: to give up all and follow him. Again, this is doubtless an authentic theme, but the present passage is a creation of the church.

5. *Editorial work.* The most obvious example is Mark 2.13, where Jesus is said to teach but no teaching is given. It is noteworthy that this bit of Markan redaction is in neither Matthew nor Luke. We have identified the concluding verse, Mark 3.6, as the editorial work of a pre-synoptic redactor. Mark 2.15 and 2.18a are probably redactional introductions, and an editor or author has composed The Healing of the Paralytic as we now have it, as well as the unitary pericopes.

6. *Unitary and composite.* The most clearly composite passages are The Question about Fasting and Grain on the Sabbath. The editorial Teaching by the Sea and The Call of Levi are probably unitary constructions. The Man with the Withered Hand is usually regarded as 'unitary', but we noted above that the saying does not entirely

harmonize with the action, and that it may originally have been attached to a more substantial event. Against Bultmann, we are inclined to Hultgren's view that Eating with Sinners is unitary, which means that the saying ('I . . . came to call sinners') did not circulate independently. On this matter, though, we cannot speak with assurance, and it is possible that 'I . . . came to call sinners' was independent (as well as authentic in general tenor).

7. *Independent sayings.* The strongest contenders are the two sayings about the sabbath in Mark 2.27–28. We have just noted that the saying about calling sinners may have been independent, and this applies also to the sayings about new and old.

8. *Historical information about Jesus.* We cannot with certainty attribute any one of the passages as such to the lifetime of Jesus, though there is no objection to the two healing stories. The theme of calling sinners is certainly authentic, but the passage in Mark 2.15–17 is a later creation which gives life to the theme. There was almost certainly conflict between Jesus and others about the place of the sinners, and possibly also about observance of the sabbath.

9. *Historical information about the church.* Here form criticism is perhaps most helpful. We have seen that the later church had to work out its stance towards sabbath (Grain on Sabbath and Withered Hand) and fasting. It maintained that Jesus had authority to announce the forgiveness of sins, and it claimed the same authority for itself (The Paralytic). It continued to teach that people must be willing to give up all and follow Jesus (The Call of Levi). It maintained Jesus' view that sinners were to be welcomed into fellowship (Eating with Sinners). We write that 'the church' had these concerns, but in the one case where we pressed the question (Eating with Sinners), we saw that we cannot easily identify 'the church'. Scholars often say, 'Mark's community', regarding it as more specific; but we must even doubt whether or not everything in Mark (for example) reflects the evangelist's community. Form criticism offers material for the study of the early church, and in that sense it aids us in understanding church history. We cannot always tell, however, whether we are learning about what one individual, the evangelist, wished Christianity to be; or about how it actually was in the community from which the gospel sprang; or about broader movements and developments within the church.

• Chreiai in other literature

Bultmann gave numerous examples from Billerbeck's collection of rabbinic material in order to illustrate the form of the chreiai. He pointed out that in the rabbinic examples one finds counter-questions, the quotation of Scripture, and sometimes parables given in reply. The study of chreiai in other literature is important for assessing the relative ability of stories about Jesus to catch an audience's attention, and it may also allow us to consider the cultural level of the audience. We shall give several chreiai from both rabbinic literature and from Greek literature. The first passage was one of Bultmann's examples:

1. A matron expressed doubts to R. Joseph b. Halaphtha about God's righteousness, because God chooses whom he will. The Rabbi answered, as he offered her a basket of figs from which she chose the best: 'You know how to choose the good figs from the bad ones: and you maintain that God doesn't know whom he has chosen as the best of his creation?' (Numbers Rabbah 3.2; Bultmann, p. 44)

2. It happened that a certain heathen came before Shammai and said to him, 'Make me a proselyte, on condition that you teach me the whole Torah while I stand on one foot.' Thereupon he repulsed him with the builder's cubit which was in his hand. When he went before Hillel, he [Hillel] said to him, 'What is hateful to you, do not to your neighbour: that is the whole Torah, while the rest is commentary thereof; go and learn it.' (Shabbath 31a)

3. Once as Rabban Johanan ben Zakkai was coming forth from Jerusalem, R. Joshua followed after him and beheld the Temple in ruins. 'Woe unto us!' R. Joshua cried, 'that this, the place where the iniquities of Israel were atoned for, is laid waste!' 'My son,' Rabban Johanan said to him, 'be not grieved; we have another atonement as effective as this. And what is it? It is acts of lovingkindness, as it is said, "For I desire mercy and not sacrifice"' (Hos. 6.6). (Aboth de R. Nathan 4; Goldin, p. 34)

4. At a time when R. Simon and R. Ishmael were led out to be killed, R. Simon said to R. Ishmael: Master, my heart fails me, for I do not know why I am to be killed. R. Ishmael said to him: Did it never happen in your life that a man came to you for a judgment or with a question and you let him wait until you had sipped your cup, or had tied your sandals, or had put on your cloak? (Mekilta Nezikin 18; Lauterbach III, pp. 141–142)

5. Darius begged for peace and offered Alexander (the Great) 10,000 talents and also half of Asia Minor. Parmenio said, 'If I were Alexander, I would take it.' Alexander replied, 'So would I, by God, if I were Parmenio!' (Plutarch, *Morals* 180C, paraphrased)

6. Among the arrivals from Athens there was a youth who asserted that the goddess Athene was very well disposed to the Emperor [Domitian], whereupon Apollonius said to him, 'In Olympia please to stop your chatter of such things, for you will prejudice the goddess in the eyes of her father'. (Philostratus, *Life of Apollonius of Tyana* 8.16)

7. and 8. See the passages about Brutus and Epineinondas quoted above (p.147).

9. The Athenians were once asking contributions for a public sacrifice, and the rest were contributing, but Phocion, after being many times asked to give, said: 'Ask from these rich men; for I should be ashamed to make a contribution to you before I have paid my debt to this man here', pointing to Callicles the money-lender. (Plutarch, *Phocion* 9.1)

Examples 4 and 6 may require short explanations. The story of R. Ishmael and R. Simon reflects the time after the second major Jewish revolt, when Hadrian forbade aspects of Jewish life, and this led to the execution of some Jewish leaders. In Jewish religion generally, as in early forms of Christianity, it was thought that premature death was punishment for sin. R. Simon is depicted as not being able to explain his own execution in that way, until urged by R. Ishmael to think of very minor transgressions.

Apollonius was a known enemy of Domitian and had been arrested by him, but escaped. In the story he objects to the youth who, in Olympia, sacred to Zeus, said that Zeus' daughter, Athene, favoured Domitian. Apollonius assumes that he and Zeus agree about Domitian! This example is possibly a bit misleading as to form. It introduces a longer dialogue, and longer dialogues are the rule in Philostratus' account.

Bultmann, influenced principally by the rabbinic stories, argued that most of the chreiai in the synoptics developed in the Palestinian church. 'This is shown by the parallelism with rabbinic stories, as well as by the intellectual content of problems and arguments, where we can only seldom find any trace of Hellenistic influence' (p. 48).

We now know that most or perhaps even all of the rabbinic passages which Bultmann cited are later – most appreciably later – than the gospels. And, further, we are very cautious about relying on a clear distinction between 'Hellenistic' and 'Palestinian'. Yet these critical observations do not altogether destroy the force of Bultmann's point. The rabbinic stories, like those about Jesus, come from a popular culture in which the Bible was known and quoted. Further, the ability to give a decisive or conclusive reply was valued in both. Thus it is reasonable to think that the stories came from similar worlds, and to that degree we can see the value of reading the rabbinic stories in order to gain insight into the form of the chreiai, especially their variety and development.

We doubt, though, that we should follow Bultmann in thinking that the synoptic passages must have developed in Palestine. That is possible, but it should be asserted with less confidence. The form, as we have seen, is parallel in secular or pagan Greek literature, and the stories about Jesus differ only because of their Jewish content. Diaspora Jews, however, were as good at quoting the Bible and giving quick answers as were Palestinian ones.

Thus, as is often the case, the result of our critical reservations about Bultmann's work is more uncertainty than he had, not less.

The chreiai show that the Christians employed a form which enjoyed great popularity throughout the Mediterranean. Plutarch wrote in part for the intelligentsia, but he also intended his work to be influential at the popular level. The rabbinic stories may derive in part from sermonic material, directed to one and all. People from all walks of life could appreciate the synoptic chreiai, in which Jesus is shown as decisively speaking in response to a question or a challenge.

Study of the chreia helps us understand the synoptics as literary works, since it points up the fact that they are *anecdotal*. One short passage follows another, and each could be placed at almost any point in Jesus' career. The use of chreiai and apophthegms was regarded by the intelligentsia of the Graeco-Roman world as rhetorically effective, especially in speech, but as belonging to a lower level of education than more polished and complicated rhetorical devices. Plutarch compared Demosthenes with Phocion by saying that the former was the more excellent rhetor, but Phocion, whose language 'had most meaning in fewest words', the more forceful speaker (*deinotatos*; *Phocion* IV.2). The socio-educational implications are brought out in the description of Brutus. In Latin he was 'sufficiently trained for narrative or pleading', while in Greek, his second language, he employed apophthegms. These were clever and effective, but they do not belong to the highest literary order. By this standard, Jesus is depicted as a popular and forceful speaker, but not highly educated. This, of course, comes as no surprise, but Plutarch's discussions allow us to state the matter with some precision.

When a whole work was composed of anecdotes (chreiai and other short forms), scholars today generally judge it to be inferior history. Readers of this book who are familiar with the gospels will not usually see just how little historical information is conveyed by their anecdotal sequences, because they are accustomed to supplying missing information. The reader of Plutarch's life of Phocion will see the point. The chreia which is given above as no. 9 is simply one of a series in which Plutarch illustrates that Phocion 'had a mind at variance with the city' (*Phocion* VIII.3). Most are introduced by a simple connective, such as 'again' or 'and', and only the barest context is given. One learns from them something of Phocion's character, but not how his relationship with the Athenians developed or changed. Reliance on the anecdote gives a static, almost timeless quality to biography. All this can be applied directly to the synoptics' depictions of Jesus.

It must also be said that the synoptic chreiai are not superior in general quality to those from Hellenistic and rabbinic literature. Jesus does not appear sharper, quicker or more authoritative than Alexander the Great or R. Ishmael. This form was so popular and widespread that the Christians could hardly improve upon it. The content of Jesus' replies is, of course, indicative of distinctively Christian positions, but the method itself does not establish him as superior to other teachers and leaders.

11 Miracle Stories

• The significance of miracles

The miracle stories of the gospels seem primarily to have the purpose of authenticating Jesus' power or authority as God's agent. Thus we read that a demon, before being exorcized, called Jesus 'the Holy One of God' (Mark 1.24//Luke 4.34). It is difficult to grasp the precise significance of miracles in the first century and especially in the gospels without noting some differences between the ancient world and the modern world.

Since the Enlightenment some people have had difficulty with the miracles in the gospels because they have understood the scientific world view to exclude the possibility of miracles. In the eighteenth century those who renounced the Christian faith often assumed that it was based on belief in miracles, which they regarded as proving it to be invalid. Its defenders often appealed to the miracles – handed down by trusty witnesses – as proving its veracity. The question of Jesus' divinity was sometimes tied to his miracles, as if they (if authentic) proved him to be a supernatural being, metaphysically 'son of God' in a way that altered what he could do physically. In Chalcedonian terms, this 'confuses' the 'two natures' – and is heretical (as, we admit, is separating them: 'neither confuse nor separate humanity and divinity' is a difficult requirement).

Surprisingly, this debate about what miracles prove or do not prove about Jesus still goes on. It is and has been ill-conceived on both sides. Miracles are believed to happen now, and they were believed by ancients to have happened – not just miracles performed by Jesus and his followers, but also by others.

People in the first century would not have thought that attributing miracles to Jesus made him divine in the sense of 'superhuman'. They knew about too many other miracle workers to make such a connection. Josephus claims that Jews inherited some of the secret wisdom of Solomon, which included how to heal, and that they were especially well known for miracles (see below). Jesus' miracles are not, and were not thought to be unique. Other miracles are attested in the gospels themselves. According to Matt. 12.27//Luke 11.19, Jesus granted that Pharisees could exorcize: 'by whom do your sons cast out [demons]?' There is also the story of 'The Strange

Exorcist', who cast out demons in Jesus' name, but who was not his follower (Mark 9.38–41 and parr.). Early Christians were also said to perform miracles (e.g. the resuscitation of Tabitha, Acts 9.36–43).

We said above that Jesus' followers saw his miracles as *authenticating* him, but not as the unique metaphysical Son of God. They were seen, rather, as authenticating him and his message in a more general sense: he was God's spokesman and had power from God. Non-believers, of course, did not see it that way. They did not necessarily deny Jesus' miracles, they simply did not grant that they authenticated him. He was accused of being in league with Beelzebul, the prince of demons (Matt. 12.24 and parr.). We can discover that this sort of division of opinion could exist about others. Shortly before the outbreak of war with Rome, would-be prophets arose, promising miracles. Two, Theudas and The Egyptian, are singled out by Josephus as being especially important. (Theudas: Josephus, *Antiq.* 20.97–99; cf. Acts 5.36; the Egyptian: *Antiq.* 20.168–172; *War* 2.261–263.) Theudas, for example, claimed to be a prophet, but Josephus called him a *goēs*, a deceiver. We do not know whether or not he actually performed any miracles, but he promised to part the Jordan river, by which he probably intended to show (1) that he was God's true spokesman and (2) that God would now take a direct hand in Israel's destiny, as he had when he parted the sea for those who fled from Egypt. Thus followers of a miracle worker saw his special actions as authenticating him, but others (such as those who accused Jesus of working with the help of Beelzebul) could remain suspicious and unpersuaded.

There are two further points to be considered in discussing the significance of miracles. One is that those who spoke for God did not have to perform miracles in order to be accredited. John the Baptist is not said to have been a miracle worker, either in the gospels or in Josephus. Yet he was widely regarded as a prophet, so widely that Jesus could answer his opponents by appealing to the authority of the one who sent John: God (Mark 11.27–33 and parr.; on John as a prophet, see also Josephus, *Antiq.* 18.116–119). The second is that there was no fixed notion that the coming Messiah would be a miracle worker. In Psalms of Solomon 17, for example, where there is a description of the coming Davidic king, he is depicted as righteous and powerful, but miracles are not mentioned. Thus we should not suppose that the Christians, to present Jesus as either prophet or Messiah, had to depict him as a miracle worker. Jewish expectation did not make this demand of one who spoke for God.

Once we recognize the setting of Jesus' miracles in the first century, we should be able to evaluate them coolly and objectively. Non-believers should be able to grant that Jesus was known as a miracle worker, as were some of his contemporaries, and thus not feel compelled to deny that there were some who saw what they could only regard as miracles; while believers should be able to agree that this or that miracle represents embellishment. The truth of Christianity does not depend on the miracle stories, and we can analyse the gospel accounts, compare them with other miracle stories, and seek to understand their history and function within their own context without being pressured to come to a particular conclusion about them.

- The collection in Matthew 8.1–9.34

We have chosen a collection of miracles in Matt. 8.1–9.34 as the sample for our study. We first note that this collection, like that of the chreiai in Mark 2.1–3.6, is the work of a redactor, in this case probably Matthew himself. In Matt. 4.23 we read that Jesus taught and preached throughout Galilee, and that he healed 'every disease and infirmity among the people'. There immediately follows a collection of teaching (the Sermon on the Mount, Matt. 5–7), and then a collection of miracles (Matt. 8–9). The collection is broken by an exchange with a would-be disciple and by three pericopes that we have already studied – The Call of Matthew [Levi in Mark and Luke], Eating with Sinners and The Question of Fasting – but still the collection of miracles can be seen to follow a plan. We note, for example, that there are ten of them. Matthew liked numbers, especially two, seven and ten. In view of the parallels which Matthew makes between Jesus and Moses, it may be that the ten miracles are meant to recall Moses' ten miracles, the plagues in Egypt.

The collection contains a wide assortment of miracles, which makes it suitable for study. They range from simple healings, to one of the major nature miracles (The Stilling of the Storm), to the most curious story of all, the Gadarene Demoniac. We shall now take them in turn.

Pericope 1: Cleansing of the Leper, *Matt. 8.1–4*

The story is very simple and unpretentious. The leper says 'if you will you can heal me'; Jesus stretches out his hand, touches the man, and says 'I will; be clean'; and the man is healed. Jesus then tells him to show himself to the priest 'as a witness to them'.

We see here three elements, all kept to a bare minimum: (1) the physical gesture, (2) the command, and (3) the demonstration of effectiveness. The demonstration takes place 'off stage', and this makes the story all the more modest. We shall see these elements in other stories in the gospels, and they are standard in Hellenistic healing stories. The concluding words in Matthew, 'for a witness to them', show the authenticating function of the story.

Since we spent so much time on the synoptic problem, we cannot resist pointing out that Bultmann regarded Mark 1.43, which is not in Matthew or Luke, as a Markan addition (i.e. a sign of Deutero–Mark). We might also suppose that the evangelistic conclusions of Mark and Luke (the healed man testified to Jesus' deed) are later additions.

We see at the conclusion of the story a motif which has been called 'The Messianic Secret': 'say nothing to anyone'. Since William Wrede scholars have regarded this motif as an invention of Mark or his sources.

Finally, a short word about the historical setting. The existence of a priesthood is presupposed, and Matthew also mentions 'the gift', presumably the offering. Conceivably this is simply a Matthaean touch. He mentions gifts for the altar in 5.23–24 and 23.18–19. The simplest assumption, however, is that we have here a Palestinian story which reflects the time when the temple was still standing.

165

Pericope 2: The Centurion's Servant, *Matt. 8.5–13*

In its present form in Matthew the story has a meaning other than 'authentication of Jesus'. It is used to proclaim the inclusion of Gentiles and threaten the rejection of Israel. The saying, 'many will come from east and west . . .; the sons of the kingdom will be cast out' (Matt. 8.11f.) may have been originally independent: the healing and the saying both appear in Luke, but in different places (Centurion's Servant, Luke 7.1–10; Many from East and West, Luke 13.28–29), and their combination could be Matthew's own.

The Healing of the Centurion's Servant is reminiscent of The Healing of a Syrophoenician Woman's Daughter in Mark 7.24–30//Matt. 15.21–28. Bultmann, in fact, proposed that they are simply variants. A Gentile requests Jesus to perform a healing; Jesus is reluctant but nevertheless grants the request, and the healing is performed at long distance. We can best take these stories as 'ideal' in both senses: imaginary and symbolic of the right response to Jesus. We should also, however, note the church's restraint. All the gospel writers believed in the Gentile mission, but they did not create a large body of material in favour of it. And, further, they expressed Jesus' reluctance to go to Gentiles.[1]

Pericope 3: The Healing of Peter's Mother-in-Law, *Matt. 8.14–15*

The story is even 'purer' than the Healing of a Leper. Jesus enters the house, sees the woman lying ill and touches her hand; she is then cured. This time there is no saying, just the touch. There is, however, a demonstration of the effectiveness of the healing: she serves him.

Mark and Luke are both more elaborate, and Bultmann (following the rule that simpler is earlier) thought that our present Mark has been re-edited under the influence of 1.16–20. We note that in Matthew Jesus seems to be alone, while in Mark James and John are with him, and the house is specified as Simon's and Andrew's. Further, in Mark Jesus does not 'see' the woman lying sick, he is told about her. And he does not just 'touch' her, he takes her hand and raises her. In Luke Jesus is said to 'rebuke' the fever.

The obvious alternative to seeing Matthew's simpler and shorter story as earlier than Mark and Luke is to say that Matthew abbreviates. Hull has noted that Matthaean miracles pay no attention to healing techniques, in contrast to some in Luke and more in Mark.[2] Matthew may have associated technique with 'magic'. Thus the 'rebuke' in Luke could be seen as magical 'technique' which Matthew softens. One notes that the only technique in Matthew is a 'touch', and this is also the case in Matt. 8.3 (parallel in Mark and Luke) and 9.25 – an interesting passage which we shall discuss below. Unlike Mark, Matthew never mentions such things as spitting (Mark 7.33; 8.23).

Pericope 4: The Sick Healed at Evening, *Matt. 8.16–17*

Like all summaries, this passage must be regarded as editorial, and we note here only the different editorial devices of the evangelists: Matthew says that the healings are in fulfilment of Isaiah's prophecy, while Mark says that the whole city crowded around the door. Luke seems to emphasize the miracles themselves: 'he laid his hands on them one-by-one and cured them' (Luke 4.40). Matthew's summary is strictly christological. The healings correspond to the prophecy, and fulfilment of prophecy shows that Jesus was the one to whom the prophet pointed. Further, we note the remarkable use made of the quotation. This is a 'Suffering Servant' passage, but in Matthew's interpretation the Servant does not suffer. He does not take upon himself the weaknesses of humanity; he takes them away by healing.

Pericope 5: On Following Jesus, *Matt. 8.18–22*

Matthew, it seems, thought it appropriate to break his healing sequence with passages on discipleship. He used the story of the Centurion's Servant to make a point about discipleship, and here he inserted an even more forceful story. Another is yet to come (The Call of Matthew, Matt. 9.9). We cannot know why one is inserted here and one a bit later. Matthew may have divided them up just in order to give narrative relief to his presentation of miracles. In any case we can see the general unity of intention: the miracle stories as Matthew presents them make 'faith' the dominant theme, and so it was appropriate to intermix them with stories which are directly about discipleship. Thus Matthew combines stories which illustrate two kinds of faith: fairly passive faith, illustrated by stories of healing; more active faith, illustrated by stories in which Jesus calls someone to follow him. It is possible that we are to understand that the disciple who was told to leave his dead father did not do so. In this case the passage serves as an admonition not to be like those who were called but who did not follow. With these few remarks we leave this interesting passage, in order to concentrate on the healing pericopes. We shall return to it in discussing the historical Jesus.

Pericope 6: Stilling the Storm, *Matt. 8.23–27*

Faith is again the point of the story, and we should especially note the contrast with the passage about the centurion's servant: the centurion has faith, the disciples do not. Further, we note that the story is unitary. It has sometimes been proposed that a nature miracle story developed from a saying, and this is easily possible with regard to Luke 5.1–11, The Miraculous Catch of Fish, which many think simply grew out of the saying about the disciples becoming 'fishers of men' (Luke 5.10 and parr.). Our present story cannot be explained in this way. 'Why are you afraid' and 'You of little faith' could not be independent sayings; they must have circulated as part of a story. It has also been proposed that some of the miracle stories grew out of Old Testament passages. Thus the feeding stories may have been based on the story of the jar of meal and the cruse of oil in I Kings 17.10–16, or on the story of the feeding of 100 in II Kings 4.42–44. For an Old Testament antecedent to Stilling the Storm one might point to Ps. 104.6–7: 'The waters stood above the mountains. At thy rebuke they fled', since the verb 'rebuke' is the same (*epitimesen*, LXX Ps. 105.9; Matt. 8.26 and parr.). In the present case, however, this seems far-fetched. The choice of the verb, of course, might have been influenced by the Psalm, but the story as a story probably has a different source. Either it is the dramatization of an actual event, or it is a wholesale creation to depict Jesus as Lord of the elements.

Birger Gerhardsson has called attention to the tightly structured literary form of Stilling the Storm. It could be called either *inclusio* or *chiasmus*. The end balances the beginning; and, furthermore, the second line is balanced by the penultimate line, and so forth. This balanced arrangement suggests artifice:

1. And when he got into the boat the disciples followed.
2. And there arose a great storm on the sea,
3. so that the boat was being swamped by the waves;
4. but he was asleep.
5. And they went and woke him, saying: 'Save, Lord . . .'
5. And he said to them: 'Why . . . afraid, men of little faith?'
4. Then he rose
3. and rebuked the winds and the sea;
2. and there was a great calm.
1. And the men marvelled, saying: 'Of what sort is this man, that even winds and sea obey him?'[3]

Pericope 7: The Gadarene Demoniacs, *Matt. 8.28–34*

Bultmann observed that the story has, in the standard sequence, all the component parts of an exorcism:

Standard form	*Gadarene demoniac(s)*
1. meeting the demons:	two (in Matthew) demoniacs, coming out of the tombs, met him
2. description of the dangerous character of the possession:	no one could pass that way
3. recognition of the exorcist:	'What have you to do with us, O Son of God?'
4. the exorcism:	'Go'
5. demonstration of success:	the herd of swine plunged into the sea

Matthew's form is, again, more succinct than Mark's and Luke's, and he also has a different ending: people beg Jesus to leave and the story ends. In Mark and Luke the former demoniac becomes a missionary for Jesus. The mention of two demoniacs rather than one is, however, Matthew's own contribution.

Matthew also changed the place name from Gerasa (Mark and Luke) to Gadara. Gerasa lay about thirty miles southeast of the Sea of Galilee, while Gadara was closer, only about six miles to the southeast; and Matthew says that Jesus came to the 'country' of the Gadarenes, which reduces the geographical difficulty: the swine could plunge into the sea from the 'country' of the Gadarenes, but not from Gadara or Gerasa. If we could be sure that this sort of search for accuracy is the explanation of Matthew's place name, we could think quite highly of his knowledge of the area.

The story is a curious one. The presence of a herd of swine indicates that the land is Gentile, and Mark and Luke thus indicate the beginning of preaching to the Gentiles. Mark explicitly says that the healed man preached throughout the Decapolis (Mark 5.20), the 'ten cities' of Greek foundation. Yet we note that nothing else is made of the trip. Jesus does not preach, and the people are not explicitly called Gentiles. The story is so difficult to reconcile with Jesus' probable history, and it conforms so completely to stories of exorcism, that it is usually recognized as a popular story, probably originally Jewish (note the connection of demons, swine and destruction), which has simply been attached to Jesus.

To illustrate why people regard this as a popular story of a common type, we shall offer two examples of exorcisms in which something happens which demonstrates that the demon has been expelled. The first story is from Josephus and is told in connection with his praise of Solomon, who, he says, left behind incantations and techniques of exorcism which some Jews still used. Eleazar, according to Josephus, performed one exorcism in the presence of 'Vespasian, his sons, tribunes' and others:

> He put to the nose of the possessed man a ring which had under its seal one of the roots prescribed by Solomon, and then, as the man smelled it, drew out the demon through his nostrils. . . . Then, wishing to convince the bystanders and prove to them that he had this power, Eleazar placed a cup or foot-basin full of water a little way off and commanded the demon, as it went out of the man, to overturn it and make known to the spectators that he had left the man.

The demon duly performed, and the wisdom of Solomon was thus clearly revealed (Josephus, *Antiq.* 8.46–49).

The second story concerns Apollonius of Tyana, a sage and miracle worker of the first century. The narrative was written early in the third century, though based on earlier sources – the precise nature of which is not known.

Once when Apollonius was discoursing on libations – offerings of wine poured out to gods – he attracted the ridicule of a young man, a 'dandy who bore so evil a reputation for licentiousness, that his conduct had long been the subject of coarse street-corner songs'. When Apollonius urged that libations be poured over the handle, since that part was least likely to have been put to mortal use, 'the youth burst out into loud and coarse laughter, and quite drowned his voice'. Apollonius recognized his behaviour as revealing demon-possession.

> And in fact the youth was, without knowing it, possessed by a devil; for he would laugh at things that no one else laughed at, and then he would fall to weeping for no reason at all, and he would talk and sing to himself. Now most people thought that it was the boisterous humour of youth which led him into such excesses; but

he was really the mouthpiece of a devil, though it only seemed a drunken frolic in which on that occasion he was indulging.

Apollonius addressed the demon as a master does a servant, and ordered him to come out and to show it by a sign. The demon promised to throw down a statue, and did so. The youth

> rubbed his eyes as if he had just woken up . . . and assumed a modest aspect. . . .
> For he no longer showed himself licentious, nor did he stare madly about, but he returned to his own self . . .; and he gave up his dainty dress and summery garments and the rest of his sybaritic way of life, and he fell in love with the austerity of philosophers, and donned their cloak, and stripping off his old self modelled his life in future upon that of Apollonius (Philostratus, *Life of Apollonius*, 4.20).

These passages show the degree to which the stories in the gospels are told in the same way as miracle stories in other literature. These two accounts are more literary than those in the gospels: the sentences are longer and more complex, and the authors have given attention to detail and verisimilitude. The basic devices, however, are the same, as are the points: the demons recognize their masters and the exorcism is proved by an external sign. Further, in the case of the young man healed by Apollonius, moral reform is the result.

After The Gadarene Demoniacs come four passages which we discussed as chreiai: The Healing of the Paralytic, The Call of Matthew (Levi), Eating with Tax Collectors, and The Question about Fasting (Matt. 9.1–17). We pass over these here and then again pick up the sequence in Matthew.

Pericope 8: A Ruler's Daughter and the Woman with a Haemorrhage, *Matt. 9.18–26*

We have here the unique instance of one miracle story sandwiched within another. The combination is often regarded as pre-synoptic, since it does not seem to serve one of the special interests of any of the evangelists, though there are other 'sandwiches' in Mark.[4] The insertion was probably for dramatic effect: it allows for a delay between the announcement to Jesus that the daughter is sick (or dead) and his arrival at the house.

We should deal first with the Markan passage. Bultmann noted in it a remarkable series of features which he regarded as typical of miracle stories:

1. The seriousness of the sickness. In the story of the woman with the issue of blood this is emphasized in two ways: the time the illness had lasted (Mark 5.25//Matt. and Luke) and the fruitless efforts of others (Mark 5.26//Luke). In the story of Jairus' daughter, the effect is heightened by the definite announcement that she has died (Mark 5.35//Luke) and by the laughter of the crowd at Jesus' apparent denial of the fact (5.40//Matt. and Luke). In Matthew's version, the girl was dead to start with. Thus the miracle is not diminished, but there is less novelistic interest.

2. Physical contact (Mark 5.28f.//Matt. and Luke; Mark 5.41//Matt. and Luke).

3. The immediacy of the cure (Mark 5.29,42//Matt. and Luke).

4. The dismissal of the crowd (Mark 5.37//Matt. and Luke).

5. The magic word (Mark 5.41//Luke) ('Talitha cumi', 'child arise').

6. The demonstration: the child gets up (Mark 5.42//Matt. and Luke); she is given something to eat (Mark 5.43//Luke).

It is clear that the typical features are most numerous in Mark and least in Matthew. This is so, first, with regard to technique. Mark follows the typical Hellenistic practice of giving the efficacious word in a foreign language. In Mark Jesus says in Aramaic, *talitha cumi*, which is then translated into Greek. In Luke the saying is given only in Greek. In Matthew there is no statement to the girl at all. The use of a foreign language probably made the readers think of incantations, but even in Luke there is still what Bultmann called a 'magic word'.

We note that the seriousness of the condition of the woman with a flow of blood is emphasized more in Mark and Luke than in Matthew. Mark and Luke refer to others' efforts to heal her. The second part of the demonstration of the cure of Jairus' daughter, that she was given food, is in Mark and Luke but not in Matthew.

Mark is in general much more detailed. It tells us the child's father's name, what Jesus said to her, and how she walked around. A glance at the synopsis will show that Mark is very much longer than Matthew and noticeably longer than Luke. It is generally said that Matthew has abbreviated the story and reduced the elements which are typical of miracle stories.

We should especially note the exchange between Jesus and the woman with a flow in Matthew and Mark. In Mark the healing takes place automatically: 'there is a miracle-working aura surrounding Jesus which the superstitious can tap' (Hull, p. 136). In Matthew the woman may expect magic ('if only I can touch his garment'), but the contact does not heal her. Jesus instead turns and says, 'daughter, your faith has saved you', before she is healed. The observation of these differences, we think, does not help us solve the synoptic problem. We learn instead about different interests on the part of the authors and, perhaps, their communities.

Mark is interested in having Jesus appear as what is often called a *theios aner*, a divine man, who possessed power in and of himself. Mark seems also to have wished to conform Jesus' miraculous or marvellous deeds to his own Gentile environment. Further, we see novelistic interest in Mark: the characters have names; there are more exchanges in conversation (e.g. Mark 5.30–31); there are more physical actions (e.g. Mark 5.32, 'looking around'; 5.41, 'she walked'); and there is more 'stage management' (Mark 5.40, 'he took the child's father and mother and those with him, and went in where the child was'). We earlier noted that the change in the report from 'she is sick' to 'she has died' adds dramatic movement and interest.

Matthew has the leanest story-line, and the points are made with extreme economy. Further, as we have seen, there is relatively slight emphasis on technique. Jesus does wondrous deeds, to be sure, but he does not have many of the traits of the Hellenistic miracle worker. We should also recall the formula quotation in Matt. 8.17: Jesus fulfils the biblical prophecies. He both teaches and heals, and the two parts of his activity are grouped and organized by Matthew to support his own view

171

that Jesus was the Messiah. Matthew gets his job done, thoroughly but with despatch.

Pericope 9: Healing of Two Blind Men, *Matt. 9.27–31*

In Matthew there are two nameless blind men, in Luke one nameless blind man, and in Mark one blind man with a name, Bartimaeus. Bultmann, thinking that names and other details tended to be added, proposed that Bartimaeus might have been inserted into Mark after Matthew and Luke copied it (p. 213). Bultmann also regarded the change from one character to two as a general law of the tradition, and he gave numerous examples (p. 316). Matthew in any case liked the number two: see also the two demoniacs (8.28) and the two blind men of 20.29–34. The second passage, in fact, is a doublet of the present one. We find there also the address 'Son of David' and the statement that Jesus touched their eyes. These two passages constitute an exception to the rule that Matthew deleted physical gestures which might remind readers of the practices of magicians.

One explanation of why Matthew has the story in 9.27–31, when apparently it belongs later (Matt. 20.29–34, which agrees with Mark's placement of it), is that he wished to have ten healings in chs. 8–9. This, as we pointed out above, makes a parallel between Jesus' healings and Moses' miracles, the ten plagues of Egypt. A more powerful motive may have been the desire to have here, before the quotation in 11.5 (see immediately below), a story of healing the blind.

Pericope 10: The Dumb Demoniac, *Matt. 9.32–34*

This passage is also probably a creation of Matthew. It illustrates the healing of the dumb. In 11.5 Matthew quotes Jesus' response to John the Baptist:

> the blind receive their sight and the lame walk, lepers are cleansed and the deaf hear, and the dead are raised up, and the poor have good news preached to them.

This depends on Isa. 35.5–6, and Matthew was probably concerned to illustrate all the points of the scriptural proof text. He already had stories of the healing of a leper (8.1–4), the healing of a lame man (9.1–8) and the raising of the dead (9.18–26), and he needed only cures of the blind and the dumb. To provide them, he wrote the last two of the ten miracles in this section. The healing of the blind he took from a passage which comes later (Mark 10.46//Matt. 20.29–34), thus creating a doublet; and the present passage he simply composed by making use of standard motifs. The dumb man was cured by casting out a demon (a common motif), the crowd exclaimed, 'Never was anything like this seen in Israel' (cf. 8.10, 'not even in Israel have I found such faith'), and the Pharisees say that '"He casts out demons by the prince of demons"' (taken from 12.24, where this charge follows the cure of a blind and dumb demoniac).

The present story, then, shows that miracle stories could be created on the basis of others. This and the previous passage served Matthew in two ways: they raised the number of miracles in this section to ten; they completed the fulfilment of Isa. 35.5–6. We also see, however, a *lack* of real creative ability. For his two new miracles Matthew simply raided others. He seems to have had a small stock of traditional healing stories, and when he needed new ones he drew on it, rather than coming up with entirely new accounts. We have often remarked on the limited creativity of most early Christians.

• Conclusion

The miracle stories in the gospels are on the whole modest when compared to similar stories about others. Formally, however, they fit into their environment, and in shaping them the church used the devices which were common to the place and time. Miracles, if accepted as true by those who heard about Jesus, would help authenticate whatever claims were made on his behalf. The evangelists claimed that Jesus was Messiah and Son of God, and they (especially Matthew) cited the miracles to support that view.

In the historical ministry of Jesus, miracles would have appeared differently. *In and of themselves* miracles were not held to prove any single point. In particular, they would not be seen as proving that Jesus was 'Messiah', since there is virtually no evidence that Jews expected a miracle-working Messiah; while, on the other hand, miracle-working magicians were well known, as were miracle-promising prophets.[5] Those well-disposed towards Jesus would have seen his miracles as *authenticating* him and what he claimed. According to the synoptics, Jesus did not publicly claim to be either Messiah or Son of God; rather, he proclaimed the coming of the kingdom. Those who were inclined to believe found in the miracles reassurance of Jesus' authority and insight into the will of God, by whose power he performed 'mighty acts'.

Some of the stories may have had no basis in Jesus' own ministry. Some scholars have suspected this to be the case in the story of the Gadarene demoniacs (or Gerasene demoniac), which may derive from a Jewish folktale; in Stilling the Storm, which may have been derived from statements about God's power in the Psalms; and in the feeding stories, which may derive from stories in I and II Kings. (The feeding stories do not appear in the section of Matthew which we studied, and so were not considered in detail.) Such suggestions can be neither proved nor disproved, and the historian must work with generalizations: Jesus was known in his own time as a miracle worker, and the early church probably elaborated on this aspect of his life, although it avoided excessive elaboration. The trappings of magic, which are sometimes visible in Mark, are not abundant in general, and they are largely absent from Matthew.

12 Parables

The parables are the most complicated and most studied form which we shall consider, and some account must be given of the main issues in parable research. At the outset we shall use the word 'parable' very generally to refer to a narrative, phrase or single word which has meaning on the everyday level, but which points beyond itself to another level of meaning, usually a theological, spiritual, inner or moral level.

• Form criticism, historical criticism and literary criticism

Joachim Jeremias argued that form criticism had not been applied to the parables fruitfully,[1] and there was some justice to the charge. Unlike the study of chreiai, formal analysis of parables had not led to their being taken apart, with some material being attributed to Jesus and some to the early church. There is an exception to this rule: allegorical explanations of parables are universally regarded as secondary to the parable itself. The prime example is the interpretation of the Parable of the Sower (Mark 4.13–20 and parr.). Apart from this, however, formal distinctions within the parabolic material seldom result in historical 'layering'.

Jeremias himself was interested precisely in the question of the settings of the parables in the life of Jesus. Although his work on this topic has been widely influential, it was based on dogmatic assertion. We shall not here dwell on the use of parables in the quest for the historical Jesus, but we should pause to illustrate this point. Jeremias observed that some parables are given two different audiences: the disciples in Matthew, the Pharisees in Luke. One of Jeremias' prime examples was the Parable of the Lost Sheep. In Matthew it is addressed to Jesus' followers (18.1), and the final sentence means, in Jeremias' words, 'It is God's will that you should go after your apostate brother as persistently as the shepherd of the parable seeks the lost sheep' (pp. 39f.). In Luke, however, the parable is directed against the Pharisees, who are said to be grumbling at Jesus for accepting sinners (Luke 15.1f.). Jeremias claimed that 'Luke has preserved the original situation', in which Jesus vindicated 'the good news against its critics and declare[d] God's character, God's delight in forgiveness, as the reason why he himself received sinners' (p. 40).

The logic is faulty. Matthew's setting may not be authentic, but that does not make

Luke's so. Jeremias simply assumed that one or the other must be. Jeremias turned the assertion of Luke's 'authenticity' into a major theological point, since he argued that throughout Jesus' career the Pharisees attacked him for believing in love and mercy, and that in the parables of grace Jesus counter-attacked. This has done much to keep alive the travesty of Pharisaism as being opposed to love, mercy and grace, and the denigration of Judaism which accompanies it.[2]

Bultmann was wiser on the question of the settings of the parabolic material:

> But since the introduction of a saying into a context is almost always secondary, we can determine, in the case of almost all the metaphors, only the most general significance, not the concrete meaning which it had in the mind of Jesus (or the Church).[3]

Historical agnosticism is not always a bad thing, and in this case New Testament scholarship would have been better served had Jeremias shared Bultmann's. This is not to say that the parables are not useful for understanding Jesus himself, but rather that we do not know enough to reconstruct their original context in more than a general way. As we shall see in ch. 22, the reconstruction of context is a major issue in the search for the historical Jesus.

There are, however, meanings other than the original one, and appreciable interest attaches to those uncovered by purely literary analysis. Within the parabolic material are sayings and stories which seem to transcend space and time and to speak directly to the individual reader or hearer.

> Or what man of you, if his son asks him for bread, will give him a stone? Or if he asks for a fish, will give him a serpent? (Matt. 7.9–11)

The hearer is directly addressed, and the rhetorical questions do not seem in need of a historical setting for their meaning to be clear. Speaking of such sayings, Günther Bornkamm wrote this:

> It is always a question aimed straight at the hearer himself, which neither demands from him knowledge or theoretical judgment, nor presupposes his goodness or education. The only presumption which is made in Jesus' parables is man, the hearer himself, man indeed in the plain, unadorned reality of his world. . . . Thus the hearer is gripped just where he really is, and the strongest appeal made to his understanding.[4]

Bornkamm, to be sure, stated this view with great naïveté. Modern literary critics do not suppose that there is such a thing as the 'plain, unadorned reality' of the world, a reality which is independent of space and time. 'Worlds' are notoriously historical realities, and one person's world is not the same as another's. One would be better advised to speak of the 'world' created by the parables themselves. Reconstructing such a 'world' is chancy, but it is better to engage in this effort than to presuppose the existence of a universal world which confronts each individual. Bornkamm was overcome by existentialist enthusiasm. Nevertheless, modern literary critics have

175

pursued the study of the parables on the assumption that significance can be found even though the precise historical setting is irretrievably lost. No reader who has found meaning in the parables can regard this as impossibly naïve.

Form criticism is helpful to literary critics, since it provides basic literary analysis as well as comparative examples from other bodies of literature. We shall return to this shortly.

To round off (though by no means to complete) this brief review of parable research, we shall mention that John Drury has recently urged that the parables be studied in the context which they indisputably have: the literary works which contain them, the synoptic gospels. He finds inadequate both Jeremias' and Dodd's historical research, which viewed the parables as 'windows upon the world behind them', and also literary criticism, which views them rather as 'tapestries whose weave can be followed and understood as the way their image is made or their story told'. In the second case he worries that the patterns which are discerned could be 'pictures in the fire, patterns out of our own imagination . . .'.[5]

It seems to us that Drury has expressed a proper concern, and that analysis of the parables should pay more attention to their meaning in each of the gospels, rather than only to the texts after they have been severed from their immediate context. We shall give attention to the parables of Matt. 13 when we discuss redaction criticism below. Now, however, we shall describe form-critical work on the parables, which requires the isolation of individual passages.

- • Basic distinctions: parables and allegory

Around the turn of the century Adolf Jülicher produced two epoch-making volumes on the parables, which together comprise *Die Gleichnisreden Jesu*, The Parabolic Speech of Jesus.[6] The main theme was that the parables should be interpreted as making only one point, not as allegories. In an allegory a story on one level is intended to have meaning on a second, and each individual element of the story which is told corresponds to an element of the message which is intended. In a parable, urged Jülicher, there are no point-to-point correspondences, but only a general point, which should be given the widest possible application.

This was generally accepted, and later scholars built on it. C. H. Dodd, before offering his own interpretation of some of the parables, illustrated the allegorical use of them. His example was Augustine's interpretation of the Parable of the Good Samaritan. We shall not give it in full, but only briefly characterize it. Each character in the parable is given a counterpart: The man who went from Jerusalem to Jericho is Adam; the thieves are the devil and his angels; the Samaritan is Jesus; the innkeeper is Paul. The places and the actions are also allegorized: Jerusalem is the heavenly city; Jericho is mortality; binding the wounds is the restraint of sin, and so on. By the time the allegory is interpreted the parable means this: Adam fell from Paradise to mortality; he was not saved by the priesthood of the Old Testament; Jesus redeemed him and entrusted him to the Church (the inn in the story), and especially to the care of Paul.[7]

This is Jülicher's summary of the parable's meaning:

The self-sacrificial practice of love receives the highest merit in the eyes of God and humanity; precedence of position and birth cannot substitute for it. The person who is compassionate, even if he is a Samaritan, deserves blessedness more than do the temple officials, who serve their own selfishness.[8]

It is easy to see that Jülicher's view, that the parables should not be interpreted as allegories, is generally sound. Jesus' parables make sense as stories, whereas intentional allegories do not make sense in and of themselves: to understand them one must know in advance what 'higher truth' they are intended to serve. If one did not already know the history of the church one would never discover it by reading the Parable of the Good Samaritan. It is much better to read the parable as a story and then to enquire what the main point is, than to attempt to find a point-by-point correspondence on another level.

In recent years, however, several scholars, such as Matthew Black and John Drury, have pointed out that there are some allegorical elements in the parables.[9] Some of them do correspond at more than one point to people and events in Jesus' own time. In the Parable of the Prodigal Son, for example, it is hard not to see the self-righteous as represented by the loyal son who protests his father's indulgence towards the prodigal, or to recognize that the father stands in for God. Similarly the shepherd in the story of the Lost Sheep represents God (and, in Matthew, the disciples, who are to imitate him), and the lost sheep represents the lost people of the house of Israel. Others argue, however, that these are not allegorical equations, but rather metaphors. 'Father', 'shepherd' and 'king' are standard metaphorical terms for God in the Hebrew tradition, as 'sheep' and 'vineyard' are common metaphors for Israel. Use of these figures of speech does not prove that the parables are allegorical.

Nevertheless Jülicher's critics have a point: his 'general applications of the widest scope' are often too broad, and some of the details of the parables were originally intended to correspond to people or groups.

The student of the parables must keep a careful eye on this issue and be neither too eager to make point-by-point equations between characters in the parables and historical people or groups, nor too insistent on drawing from each of them only one general point. If the application becomes too general the parables will be read merely as stories which illustrate basic theological points, such as the need of repentance or the virtue of mercy and forgiveness. Generalization at this level deprives them of their 'punch', and thus of part of their appeal.

• Form critical distinctions

Jülicher himself divided the parabolic sayings material into three main categories: similitudes (*Gleichnisse*), parables in the strict sense (*Parabeln*), and exemplary stories (*Beispielerzählungen*). Bultmann accepted these and also proposed further categories to be included under the general heading which we are calling 'parabolic speech' or 'parabolic material' (in German, *Gleichnisse*, 'similitudes'). We shall define and exemplify Bultmann's categories.

1. **Figurative speech**. Bultmann observed that only a few sayings of Jesus lack the use of examples from life which give concreteness and immediacy to what is said. He considered this to be typical not only of Jesus, but also of Semitic speech in general, as contrasted with Hellenistic language, which favoured abstraction. He offered numerous sub-categories of figurative speech.

(*a*) The sayings are full of **concrete images**:

> The son's request to the father in Matt. 7.9f. is concretely expressed as asking for fish or bread. . . . The most menial task is pictured in Mark 1.7 as loosing the shoe latchet. Concrete pictures describe the hypocrite at his almsgiving, his prayers and his fasting, in Matt. 6.2–18. . . (pp. 166–167)

(*b*) **Hyperbole** – overstatement – is a special form of concreteness. The commandment to pluck out one's own eye or to cut off one's own hand, rather than fall into evil (Matt. 5.29–30), is hyperbolic, as is the command to turn the other cheek and to give one's cloak as well as coat to the one who asks (Matt. 5.39f.).

(*c*) **Paradox**, in turn, is related to hyperbole and often makes use of it, as in the statement that the Pharisees strain at gnats but swallow camels (Matt. 23.24), or that the self-righteous person sees the splinter in another's eye but does not see the beam in his own (Matt. 7.3–5 and par.).

(*d*) **Images** constitute a very large category, and examples are very common. This sub-category is a kind of catch-all for concrete speech which is not otherwise categorized. The physician cares for the sick (Mark 2.17); the barren tree is cast into the fire (Matt. 3.10); new patches should not be put on old fabric (Mark 2.21–22); some are like the blind who lead the blind (Luke 6.39). These images imply comparisons, though usually there is no comparative word ('like' or 'as'). We may now say that Luke 6.39 means that some people are like blind guides, but the saying does not have the word 'like'. Full comparisons, however, do occur: 'I send you forth as sheep in the midst of wolves: be therefore as wise as serpents and as harmless as doves' (Matt. 10.16).

(*e*) **Metaphors** are terms used in a figurative sense but without the comparative words 'like' or 'as'. Many of the terms listed in the previous paragraphs are metaphorical: camels, the splinter and beam, and others. Further examples are putting one's hand to the plow (Luke 9.62), keeping the lamps burning (Luke 12.35), and good and bad treasure in the heart (Matt. 12.35).

All these sayings, and many others, are in a general sense 'parabolic': a term from everyday life is used in order to point to an attitude or attribute which could be described more literally: a splinter is a small fault, a beam is a large one; the burning lamps represent human preparedness for the future; and so on through the whole list.

2. Pure **similitudes** are different from **figurative sayings** only in degree: they are more detailed. Luke 14.28–32 contains two similitudes:

> For which of you, desiring to build a tower, does not first sit down and count the cost, whether he has enough to complete it? Otherwise, when he has laid a

foundation, and is not able to finish, all who see it begin to mock him, saying,
'This man began to build, and was not able to finish'.

Or what king, going to encounter another king in war, will not sit down first and take counsel whether he is able with ten thousand to meet him who comes against him with twenty thousand? And if not, while the other is yet a great way off, he sends an embassy and asks terms of peace.

These are more than simple figures of speech, but they are not parables in the proper sense, since there is no story. There is only a 'likeness': the hearer should be like the builder and the king. Bultmann regarded Luke's application in 14.33 as secondary: 'So therefore, whoever of you does not renounce all that he has cannot be my disciple'. The hearer was intended to apply the similitudes to his or her own life, but this is not the proper application. Neither similitude has to do precisely with giving up possessions, but rather with calculating the full cost of what is begun. The full cost might involve self-sacrifice, but the Lukan application is narrower than the similitudes themselves.

The Lost Sheep and the Lost Coin (Matt. 18.12–14; Luke 15.4–10) are also similitudes. God is like the woman or the shepherd. Again, there is no narrative story, but only extended figures which imply a comparison and an application.

A larger number of sayings which are commonly classified as 'parables' are more correctly termed 'similitudes', since they lack the narrative form of parables in the strict sense. Some of the best known passages are these:

The Treasure in the Field and The Pearl of Great Price, Matt. 13.44–46
The Fish Net, Matt. 13.47–50
The House Builder, Matt. 7.24–27

These and other similitudes juxtapose two situations or entities and shed light on one by speaking of the other. The kingdom of Heaven is like a treasure in the field or a pearl of great price: for it one will give all one has. The similitude of the Fish Net is slightly different. A fish net gathers up useful and useless fish. The coming kingdom is not precisely like that: rather the figure sheds light on the present situation, in which there are good and bad people. They will be sorted out when the kingdom comes. The person who builds a house, on the other hand, serves as a model: one should build on a firm foundation, presumably Jesus' own teaching.

3. A **parable in the strict sense**, in Bultmann's words, 'transposes the facts which serve for a similitude into a story, or, to put it in other terms, gives as its picture not a typical condition, or a typical, recurrent event, but some interesting particular situation' (p. 174). Someone who loses a coin will always look for it, and Jesus' saying refers to this general situation; it is thus a similitude. A parable could be easily created from the similitude by telling a story in which an individual lost and searched for a coin.

We should realize that these distinctions were not present in the mind of the speaker, and the boundaries between 'figurative saying', 'similitude' and 'parable in the strict sense' are not rigid. The Treasure in the Field and other similitudes have some narrative elements: a man finds a treasure. Yet the emphasis is on what is typical: anyone who finds a treasure will sell everything in order to obtain it.

It is generally said of both the similitudes and the parables that the situations are easily recognizable and are drawn from real life. This, however, may be over-emphasized, and one may miss what is surprising about them. We find the shepherd who seeks his one lost sheep to be something of a surprise. Would a shepherd actually leave ninety-nine sheep undefended in order to look for one? Surely not if predators were about.

Some of the 'parables in the strict sense' are also surprising. In the Parable of the Great Supper (Luke 14.15–24; cf. Matt. 22.2–14), the behaviour of both the man who gave the banquet and the invited guests is unusual. Those first invited prefer to do anything else rather than to be entertained at someone else's expense. When they do not come the man orders his servant to bring in 'the poor and maimed and blind and lame'. The hall still is not filled, and the servants are sent out to compel passers by to come. This is surely not typical behaviour. If Jesus told this parable, he probably intended to point out the surprising nature of God's mercy.

This parable, in fact, tends towards allegory, in which stories do not necessarily make sense in and of themselves. The man who gave the banquet is God, the servants are the prophets, the guests first invited are the Jews, those next brought in are the outcasts of Israel, and the outsiders who are brought to the feast are Gentiles. Matthew's version is even more allegorical. The guests first invited 'seized [the] servants, treated them shamefully, and killed them'. The king 'sent his troops and destroyed those murderers and burned their city' (Matt. 22.6f.). Then, the supper apparently still on the table, he invited other guests. Here the needs of the allegory, which probably refers to the destruction of Jerusalem and the Gentile mission, have gone beyond 'parabolic sense': the story no longer makes sense as a story drawn from real life. We have instead an allegorical expression of the themes that Israel rejected and killed the prophets (a common accusation, though with little historical basis), and that Jerusalem was destroyed as punishment.

Matthew's version, we see, reflects the destruction of Jerusalem in 70, while Luke's version does not, or at least not in such an obvious way. If Jesus told the parable, he probably meant to surprise his hearers, and possibly to warn them. If there was a version earlier than Luke's, we cannot say how close it was to allegory.

The Labourers in the Vineyard (Matt. 20.1–16) also describes unconventional behaviour. A man hires labourers at successive times during the day, and at the end pays them all the same. One would expect an owner to pay as little as possible. If a denarius was an adequate payment for a full day, half a denarius should be enough for half a day. The emphasis, again, is on the surprising nature of God's mercy.

Most of the rest of the parables point to recognizable behaviour. The most famous is the Parable of the Prodigal Son, Luke 15.11–32. As it now stands it is a double parable. In the first part (15.11–24) one son takes his inheritance early, squanders it and falls into poverty and disgrace – feeding someone else's swine. He returns to his father's house, and his father orders that he be given the best robe, new shoes and a ring. The fatted calf is killed, and a feast is given for the returned prodigal. In phase two (15.25–32) the elder son, who had remained by his father's side, complains that he has not been feasted and rewarded. The father rebukes him:

> Son, you are always with me, and all that is mine is yours. It was fitting to make merry and be glad, for this your brother was dead, and is alive; he was lost, and is found.

Many scholars think that the second stage of the parable was also second chronologically: it is a later expansion to develop the point in a slightly different direction. The first part, to v. 24, makes the point that God rejoices over sinners who return. The second part 'makes plain by contrast the paradoxical character of divine forgiveness' (Bultmann, p. 196). God does not punish the loyal son, but his mercy to the other son is brought out more strongly by the protest that he is being unjust. Whether or not 15.25–32 is a secondary expansion, the parabolic form is maintained. These verses do not constitute an allegorical interpretation of 15.11–24, but rather they constitute a full parable in and of themselves, though the story is dependent on what has gone before.

We shall now give the rest of Bultmann's list of parables in the strict sense:

The Importunate Friend	Luke 11.5–8
The Unjust Judge	Luke 18.1–8
The Sower	Mark 4.3–9 and parr.
The Barren Fig Tree	Luke 13.6–9
The Unjust Steward	Luke 16.1–8
The Talents	Matt. 25.14–39//Luke 19.12–27
The Ten Virgins	Matt. 25.1–13
The Wheat and the Tares	Matt. 13.24–30
The Unmerciful Servant	Matt. 18.23–35
The Vineyard	Mark 12.1–9 and parr.
The Two Debtors	Luke 7.41–43
The Two Sons	Matt. 21.28–31

4. **Exemplary stories** in one respect are not parabolic at all: they need not have a figurative, symbolic, metaphorical or representative element. They are discussed under 'parabolic material' for two reasons: (1) like parables proper they are narrative stories about one-time, non-recurrent behaviour, told as if the events actually took place; (2) they are used in the same way as are parables. One might add a third reason: they are commonly called 'parables'.

The best known exemplary story is that of the Good Samaritan (Luke 10.30–37). This is an exemplary story rather than a parable in the strict sense because the actors play themselves. In a similitude or a parable the king represents God; in the story of the Good Samaritan the priest and the levite represent the priestly and levitical clergy. Similarly the Samaritan plays the part of a Samaritan.

Luke has given the story a setting. After discussion of the commandment to love one's neighbour, a lawyer asks, 'Who is my neighbour?' (Luke 10.25–29), and in response Jesus tells the story (10.30–35). After the story, the point is made that it was the Samaritan who proved to be 'the neighbour' of the injured man (10.36). Most scholars think that the original story was not a general comment on caring for one's neighbour, but a direct rebuke of the priestly classes. It should be noted that the story has a truly Palestinian setting. The injured man appeared to be dead (10.30), and the priest and the levite are represented as wishing to avoid contracting corpse impurity. Care for the dead was a strict duty in ancient Judaism – as thoughout the world – but it did result in impurity (as did other necessary and normal activity, such as menstruation, sexual relations and childbirth). Impurity prevents one from entering the temple, and the removal of corpse impurity requires seven days. The priests themselves were forbidden to contract corpse impurity except for their nearest kin (Lev. 21.1–3), and probably the Levites also avoided corpse impurity whenever possible, so that their duties would not be hindered. Later rabbinic law reflects the requirement that even priests should care for an unburied body, and this may have been the expectation in Jesus' day. In any case the priest and Levite in the story are shown as being willing to pass by a man who, for all they knew, might be badly injured but not dead. The author of the story thought that they should run the risk of contracting corpse impurity, even though for the priest to do so would be against the law of Moses.

It is easily possible to extend the criticism of the priest and Levite so that it becomes a more general point. If this were done, the point would be this: in case of doubt, commandments which govern relations with other humans should supersede commandments which govern relations with God. Christian scholars often take the story to mean that the 'external' and 'ceremonial' aspects of the law should be rejected or downplayed in favour of its 'moral' dimension. But the service of God in the temple, as well as the action of caring for a corpse or an injured person, is 'inner' as well as 'outer'. The distinction between inward piety and outward activity is generally (not always) wrong when attributed to first-century Jews, including Jesus. The priest's job was sacrifice and the Levite's the singing of the psalms (among other things). Both were considered acts of spiritual worship, commanded by God. The entire sacrificial system, furthermore, was regarded as being beneficial to Israel and even to the whole world. It was not a selfish activity. The priest and Levite are not accused of lack of piety, or of self-service, but of choosing the wrong pious activity. The worship of God would go on even though one priest and one Levite were unable to share in it for a week. In this and similar circumstances the right thing to do was to care for one's brother.

The other principal exemplary stories, which we shall not comment on individually, are these:

The Rich Fool	Luke 12.16–21
The Rich Man and Lazarus	Luke 16.19–31
The Pharisee and the Publican	Luke 18.10–14

• Parables in other literature

The parable was widely used in antiquity. The book of Proverbs abounds in similitudes and figurative sayings, and there are true parables elsewhere in the Hebrew Bible. An example is Eccl. 9.13–17:

I observe another evil under the sun, to me a grave one. There was a small town, with only a few inhabitants; a mighty king marched against it, laid siege to it and built great siege-works round it. But a poverty-stricken sage confronted him and by his wisdom saved the town. No one remembered the poor man afterwards. Now I say: wisdom is better than strength, but a poor man's wisdom is never valued and his words are disregarded. The gentle words of the wise are heard above the shouts of a king of fools.

Here the author introduces his parable, tells it and then applies its 'moral'. Rabbinic literature abounds in parables. These are of uncertain date, but they show that the parabolic tradition lived on in Judaism. Most rabbinic parables are told in order to comment on a biblical passage. We offer one striking and forceful example:

I am the Lord Thy God (Ex. 20.2). Why were the Ten Commandments not said at the beginning of the Torah? They give a parable. To what may this be compared? To the following: A king who entered a province said to the people: May I be your king? But the people said to him: Have you done anything good for us that you should rule over us? What did he do then? He built the city wall for them, he brought in the water supply for them, and he fought their battles. Then when he said to them: May I be your king? They said to him: Yes, yes. Likewise, God. He brought the Israelites out of Egypt, divided the sea for them, sent down the manna for them, brought up the well for them, brought the quails for them. He fought for them the battle with Amalek. Then He said to them: May I be your king? And they said to Him: Yes, yes. (Mekilta Bahodesh 6)

Again we have an application immediately appended to the parable. It teaches that first God shows mercy, and only then makes demands.

Finally we may consider this similitude of Epictetus, a philosopher who lived in the late first and early second centuries:

One of [Epictetus'] acquaintances who seems to lean toward the Cynic's calling, asked, 'What kind of man ought a Cynic to be, and what is the basic conception of his vocation?' Epictetus said . . ., 'I can tell you this, the man separated from God who takes up so great a calling is hateful to God, and he wishes (upon himself) nothing other than public disgrace. For no one in a well-run household comes along and says to himself, "I ought to manage this house". If he does, the lord of the house, when he turns and sees him pompously giving orders, will drag him out and squeeze him dry. It is the same way also in this great city (the world). There is also here a Lord of the house who gives orders to each.'[10]

The application of the similitude is indicated, though not expressed in full: a philosopher, who comments on how the world should be run, should do so only on the basis of a divine call.

These examples of parabolic speech show that those attributed to Jesus are not different in kind. Jesus' teaching was on the whole not exegetical: it did not consist of commenting on the scripture, and this distinguishes his parables from many rabbinic ones, though the distinction is not absolute. Not all parables told in Hebrew were exegetical in nature, as the one from Ecclesiastes shows. It is fair to say, however, that Jesus' parables were superior: on the whole they are simply better than those found in any other body of literature. The stories are apt, clear and forceful; and the point is usually striking. The Christian church, in using the parables, employed a form which was widely popular, but they had material which was, for the most part, more striking than that of their competitors, who also exemplified their leaders' wisdom by telling parables.

• Conclusion

Form criticism plays a relatively minor but still important role in the study of parabolic material. In terms of testing for historically older material, it offers its standard solution: what is not necessary to the pure form is later.

> The *conciseness* of the narrative is characteristic. Only the necessary *persons* appear. Thus in the story of the Prodigal Son there is no mother, or in the parable of the Importunate Friend no wife of the disturbed sleeper. There are never more than three chief characters, and for the most part only two (Bultmann, p. 188)

This observation, which holds good in the majority of cases, leads to the criterion that anything beyond the pure and concise form is secondary. This general criterion can be utilized at two points: (1) Applications of the saying itself, and other interpretative comments, are often held to be secondary. (2) Elements within a similitude or parable which are not essential to it are generally ruled to be secondary elaborations. With regard to parables, as well as to all other material in the gospels, form criticism generally holds the settings to be secondary. We may consider some examples.

We saw above that Luke's *setting* of the story of the Good Samaritan is thought to be Luke's own (pp. 181f.), and that both the Matthaean and Lukan settings of the similitude of the Lost Sheep are questionable (pp. 174f.). The same applies to other settings of the parabolic material.

With regard to *applications* of the material, Bultmann held that many are secondary, but not necessarily all. We saw above that Luke 14.33 ('So therefore, whoever of you does not renounce all that he has cannot be my disciple') is probably an added application of the similitudes about Building a Tower and Fighting a War (Luke 14.28–32) (p. 179). Bultmann also regarded the applications of the parables in Luke 15 as the author's own: after the Lost Sheep and the Lost Coin Luke concludes, 'Just so, I tell you, there is joy before the angels of God over one sinner who repents' (Luke 15.10; 15.7 is slightly different). Without these applications the implication of the sayings might be hortatory: 'You too seek the lost.' Matthew gives an application of the similitude of the Lost Sheep which points in this direction: 'So it is not the will of my Father who is in heaven that one of these little ones should perish' (Matt. 18.14). This application as well must be queried, and here as elsewhere the precise context and the original point cannot be retrieved with confidence (Bultmann, p. 184, where there are further examples). The quest of form criticism for the earliest form often results in uncertainty about the meaning of sayings in the lifetime of Jesus. Secondary accretions are stripped away, but the discovery of the original meaning is more difficult and more uncertain. Jeremias' confidence in Luke's settings was not well-grounded, and the agnosticism of classical form criticism with regard to the settings of pericopes is to be preferred.

Our small sample of parables from other traditions, however, shows that applications were often attached to parables. The application may be said to belong to the form itself, and this should give pause before rejecting those in the gospels as secondary. The judgment that an application is secondary may be made on the grounds of content: some applications are not congruous with the parable itself. Further, as we have just seen, applications sometimes vary from gospel to gospel, showing that the evangelists were prepared to draw their own conclusions from the parables.

Bultmann himself regarded some applications as possibly original. He cited as possible Luke 17.10; Matt. 13.49–50; 18.35; 21.31 (p.184). Luke 17.10 reads thus: 'So you also, when you have done all that is commanded you, say, "We are unworthy servants; we have only done what was our duty".' The principle behind this decision was probably only the observation that the application is entirely appropriate to the saying and does not reveal a change of audience.

Above (p. 180) we illustrated possible *expansions within a parable* in the discussion of the Great Supper (Luke 14.15–24; in Matt. 22.2–14, the King's Wedding Feast). Matthew's verses 5–7 introduce action which is not necessary to the parable: those invited to the feast not only refuse to come (as in Luke), but seize and kill the king's messengers. In retaliation the king destroys them and burns their city. These verses are almost certainly later additions which allegorically relate the parable to the destruction of Jerusalem. Suspicion has also attached to the parable of the elder son, which is added to that of the Prodigal Son (p. 181 above). Most of the parables, however, are remarkably 'pure' in form, and the law of conciseness is seen to prevail. This is one of the principal considerations behind the widespread, though by no means universal view that the parables have been treated very conservatively in the transmission of the sayings material.

Besides aiding in the search for secondary aspects, form criticism also provides a first step for the literary analysis and appreciation of them. Simply distinguishing 'figurative saying', 'similitude', 'parable in the narrow sense' and 'exemplary story' is instructive for understanding the narrative art of the creator or creators of the material. Literary appreciation will go beyond these simple distinctions, but it will also be based on them.

Thirdly, form criticism demonstrates that a similitude, by pointing towards a 'likeness', fairly clearly implies an application. The man who wants to build a tower, and who must first count the total cost, is like –? The question mark must stand against any very specific application, but not against the general application. We do not know that the similitude originally referred to some individual, like the rich man who wished to know how to gain eternal life (Mark 10.17–22 and parr.); but we do see that it is appropriate in that case and all similar ones. The similitude points to a situation which is common or recurrent, and thus lends itself fairly easily to sensible application.

The parable in the narrow sense and the exemplary story are a bit more difficult. They are striking stories about some action or behaviour as if it really took place, and they may have had an equally precise application. Jülicher, however, was right in maintaining that they are patient of a general application. We do not know whether or not Jesus (or whoever created the story) had in mind an individual or a group to whom the Parable of the Prodigal Son was applied (despite Jeremias). One may, however, discover situations which are analogous to that of the prodigal and his father. The ability to imagine analogies helps the reader to appreciate the art with which the point is made, and consequently to see better what the point is: not just that God forgives, but that those who need forgiveness should not hesitate quickly to return to him, since his forgiveness is dependable. The exemplary story of the Good Samaritan may similarly be understood and appreciated. Some pious duties are more urgent than others and should be given precedence. Here we may be sure that the author of the story singled out the temple service as less important than caring for one's fellow.

Study of the parables of Jesus now goes much beyond the basic form critical work, as we pointed out above. They remain one of the chief topics of research for those who study Jesus, the gospels, and the message of the early church.

13   Conclusion

• Other forms

We have by no means studied all the forms discussed by the form critics. It is possible, for example, to categorize each type of saying. As an example we may take **woes and threats**.* This is a list:

> Matt. 10.33: Whoever denies me before men, I also will deny before my Father who is in heaven.
>
> Matt. 11.21–24: It will be more tolerable on the day of judgment for Tyre and Sidon than for you, etc.
>
> Matt. 12.41: The people of Nineveh will arise at the judgment with this generation and condemn it.
>
> Matt. 23: Numerous woes on the scribes and Pharisees.
>
> Luke 23.28–31: The days are coming when they will say, 'Blessed are the barren, and the wombs that never bore, and the breasts that never gave suck!' Then they will begin to say to the mountains, 'Fall on us'; and to the hills, 'Cover us'.
>
> Luke 4.25–27; 12.54–56; Matt. 7.21; 7.22–23; 8.11–12; 24.37–41; and others.

We shall not discuss these here, but only observe that once a list is made it can be studied, and the simple act of categorization allows us to focus on the topic: What setting will be assigned to woes and threats? Was Jesus the one who threatened people with destruction or damnation, or was it his followers, or both? Form criticism allows the student to give attention to the individual pericopes and to try to delve back through each one, a task that will be facilitated by studying all the examples of a form.

• Evaluation of form criticism

We recall that form criticism rests on three basic principles:

---

*As noted above (p. 148), we shall offer no formal analysis of isolated sayings, and we give here Bultmann's categorization of one group according to content.

1. The pericopes should be separated from the narrative framework of the gospels as we have them and studied independently.
2. Each type of pericope – each form – grew out of some typical activity of the early church.
3. The forms should be studied in light of similar forms in Graeco–Roman and Jewish literature. These provide information about the 'pure form', and additional elements are to be regarded as secondary.

We shall consider these points in turn.

1. *The pericopes and their settings*. We should first recall that the form critics were interested in the pre-synoptic stage of the tradition. They sought information about Jesus or about the earliest Christian communities. One may object that these emphases prevent one from seeing the meaning which the material unquestionably has in the context which survives: the written gospels (cf. Drury's remark about parable-research, above, p. 176). This fault is to be granted. Bultmann's students attempted to rectify it by concentrating on the theology of the evangelists (see the next chapter).

With regard to the questions which the form critics posed, however, they were right to separate the pericopes from their settings. When we discuss the problems of uncovering information about the historical Jesus (Part V), we shall see that ignorance of the *precise context* in which sayings were formulated often prevents the recovery of *precision and nuance* in interpreting Jesus' teaching. Meaning is determined by context, and sayings whose context is unknown cannot be pressed too hard in the quest of original meaning. Often we shall have to remain content with a more general understanding than we might wish. The need to perceive this limitation is an important lesson to be learned from form criticism.

The first fundamental principle of form criticism, then, is to be confirmed. Detailed study of the pericopes will show that their immediate settings are often not entirely congruous with the implications of the passage itself. Further, we have seen numerous instances in which the setting of sayings material varies from gospel to gospel, thus proving beyond the shadow of a doubt that settings did get changed.

Once change is proved in even a few instances, it must be granted as a possibility in all. If those who shaped and transmitted the material before our gospels were written, and the evangelists themselves, were willing to put some sayings and actions in new contexts, we must conclude that they did not intend to transmit contexts unchanged. We may not then take the position that the settings are correct unless proved not to be, but rather put the burden of proof the other way: the settings are secondary unless proved to be original. 'Proof', further, must be defined as meaning 'shown to be plausible or (at most) likely'. Historical reconstruction cannot go beyond probability in assessing the 'originality' of the settings of individual pericopes. (We shall see below that the broader context of Jesus' ministry can be reconstructed with a high degree of probability.)

The way in which context determines meaning has recently been exemplified by Morna Hooker, and we shall cite here one of her chief examples: the similitude in Mark 2.22 and parr.:

No one pours new wine into old wineskins; if he does, the wine will burst the skins, and the wine will be wasted, and the skins as well. New wine must be put into fresh wineskins.

The first readers of the gospels, she proposes, would have understood the similitude to mean that 'the new wine of the gospel cannot be contained within the confines of Judaism'.[1] The gospels were written at a time when the break had been largely accomplished: the Christian movement was no longer a movement within Judaism, and in that setting the old wineskins refer to the old religion. 'Christian discipleship and Judaism now appeared to be incompatible' (p. 24). Jesus, however, could hardly have seen matters in the same way:

> When Jesus spoke about new wine in old wineskins, and a new patch on an old garment, his words were probably intended as a challenge to his hearers to respond to his new teaching about the Kingdom of God – and as a warning of the changes in outlook which such a response will entail . . . (p. 24)

One notes that in suggesting a meaning of the parable for Jesus' own day it is necessary to become a bit vague. 'What is old' and 'what is new' can be more precisely determined for the evangelists' day than for Jesus'. One could, to be sure, propose a precise meaning of the saying in Jesus' own ministry: the coming kingdom will disrupt the existing social and political order. The problem with being precise is that we may be wrong. It is often better to offer more general and vaguer meanings of the sayings for Jesus and his immediate followers.

On the question of the pericopes and their settings, then, form criticism requires great circumspection of those who would use the sayings material in reconstructing the life and message of Jesus. The pericopes are laid bare, and one may attempt to dig back to earlier layers, but uncertainty attends the effort.

It is otherwise when we ask about the theology and outlook of the evangelists themselves. Here the distinction of setting from pericope offers the chance of firm and positive results. Once one has solved the synoptic problem, at least to one's own satisfaction, many of the settings can be assigned to one of the evangelists. Redaction criticism, the study of the work and theology of the final evangelists, is a good deal more complicated than simply analysing the settings and summaries in each gospel, but this task is an essential part of it (see the next chapter).

One of the promises of form criticism, and an exciting one, is the discovery of information about aspects of the Christian movement between Jesus and the composition of the gospels as we have them. The search for intermediate layers in the gospels is challenging and rewarding, though again results are never completely secure. The success of such efforts depends on the success of historical Jesus research and redaction criticism. Since these are two difficult tasks, it will be seen that the search for intermediate material cannot result in completely certain results. In actual practice, scholars work in a never-ending circle: assigning material at first tentatively to various layers, then running through each layer looking for coherence, altering the assignment of some passages and parts of passages, reviewing it all again – and so on.

Thus the student should not think that it is possible to go through the gospels, marking Jesus-material in red and redactional material in green, thereby successfully assigning what is left in black to the intermediate church. The categories are seldom so clear that one can say 'this verse is pure Jesus-material, this one is entirely Matthew's composition'. In some instances, however, we do see scholars making such attributions with confidence. We shall take two examples to show how such work is done and to give some idea of the range of opinions:

Luke 15 is composed of these parts:

15.1–2	Pharisees and scribes complain that Jesus receives sinners
15.3	He told a parable
15.4–6	The Lost Sheep
15.7	More Joy in Heaven over one sinner who repents
15.8–9	The Lost Coin
15.10	Joy before the Angels of God
15.11–24	The Prodigal Son
15.25–32	The Elder Brother

Different scholars assign these verses to different strata. We shall illustrate stratification by presenting schematically three possible analyses:

Verses	Analysis A	Analysis B	Analysis C
1–2	Jesus' lifetime	Luke	Intermediate church
3	Luke	Luke	Luke
4–6	Jesus	Matthew (used by Lk)	Jesus
7	Jesus	Luke	Luke or inter. ch.
8–9	Jesus	Luke	Jesus
10	Jesus	Luke	Luke or inter. ch.
11–24	Jesus	Luke	Jesus
25–32	Jesus	Luke	Intermediate church

For the sake of contrast we have chosen two extreme positions and one moderate one. Analysis A is approximately the position of Jeremias: Not only do most of the sayings go back directly to Jesus, but in this case so does the setting itself (as do many of Luke's settings). Analysis B is approximately the position of Goulder, towards which Drury also tends: Everything not taken from Mark was composed by the other evangelists. The Lost Sheep, which is also in Matthew, was derived by Luke from Matthew, who composed it. Analysis C represents in general Bultmann and numerous other scholars who accept form criticism. The material has a history. Some of it – for example the chief parables – goes back to Jesus, and some was composed by the evangelists, but the intermediate church altered, composed and reset much of the material. The second stage of the Parable of the Prodigal Son, called 'The Elder Brother' above, is a likely candidate for subsequent creation. Debate with the scribes and Pharisees was emphasized in some parts of the early church, and (according to Bultmann) some passages which were originally not polemical were made such. On this view the introductory verses are assigned to the intermediate church rather than to Luke himself. The applications of the two first parables could have been made by Luke, but the entire chapter might have come to him whole, including the applications in vv. 7 and 10.

It seems to us apparent that the stark either/or of Analyses A and B – either Jesus or Luke – by definition leaves out a great deal, and it is a major achievement of form criticism to direct our attention to what happened to the material between the lifetime of Jesus and the composition of the gospels. Surely there was some material, and just as surely something did happen to it. If the evangelists shaped it to their own purposes, how can we doubt that the earlier users of the material did the same?

Our second example is The Pericope on Divorce, which appears five times in the New Testament: (1) In I Cor. 7.10–11 it appears in the context of other rules on marriage and divorce; (2) In Matt. 5.31–32 it appears in sequence with other sayings which make the law stricter, all addressed to disciples; (3) In Matt. 19.3–12 it appears as a dispute with Pharisees, and following it is an explanation to disciples, who ask whether they should marry at all; (4) In Mark 10.2–12 it is the result of a dispute with Pharisees, but the last part of the passage is an explanation to the disciples; (5) In Luke 16.18 it is preceded by a dispute with Pharisees (16.14–15) and by the statement that the law and the prophets were until John and that not one bit of the law would pass away.

These settings offer two major possibilities: the saying is inner-group, intended to urge very strict behaviour on Jesus' followers; or it is critical of the law, and of the Pharisees, for allowing divorce and thus for not being strict enough. Matthew 19 and Mark 10 combine Pharisees and disciples: the passage is triggered by debate with Pharisees, but the rule is further explained to the disciples alone. What can be said of these settings?

First we note that in I Cor. 7 Paul finds it necessary to give his own rules, one of which allows divorce or separation (in case a pagan partner desires it), and that in Matt. 19 the disciples are clearly troubled by the prohibition: perhaps it is better not to marry at all! These settings, which reveal continuing difficulties with the commandment, are clearly secondary. Most would also regard the settings in Mark 10 as secondary: first the 'public' pronouncement in response to a question of the Pharisees, then a private explanation to Jesus' followers. The common assumption is that this and similar changes of scene are the work of the final evangelist. They reveal later church questions about hard sayings. They also achieve dramatic effect and help the narrative 'move'. The 'Q' setting (Matt. 5 and Luke 16), in context with other statements about the validity of the law, seems better.

There is, however, another possibility. Perhaps none of the five settings gives the full context in which the saying was most meaningful. We should note the part of the passage which appeals to the order of creation: 'from the beginning of creation' (Mark 10.6); 'from the beginning it was not so' (Matt. 19.8). This seems to put the saying in the context of a discussion of the New Age, which should recapture the state of paradise. This observation leads to giving the saying a general setting in Jesus' ministry: the ethics of the New Age. It may be that none of the immediate contexts is fully 'original', but that the saying itself points to a context within a general type of teaching. The general topic, in this case, would be that of this section of the Sermon on the Mount, in which the New Age is contrasted with the Mosaic dispensation. The Sermon on the Mount has been artificially put together, but it may nevertheless help us recapture the context of the Saying on Divorce within the lifetime of Jesus. If this reconstruction is followed, it is to be noted that it depends on the long form of the pericope in Matt. 19 and Mark 10. That is where the appeal to the order of creation appears. The context of the saying, however, is most closely related to that of Matt. 5, the Sermon on the Mount. Historical reconstruction seldom leaves passages precisely where they are now found.

This exemplifies how form criticism helps with research into the life of Jesus and into the life of the early church. In this case we may assume that Jesus actually did prohibit divorce or at least remarriage; here the attestation of Paul is very strong support. Did Jesus do so in the context of discussing rules for an ongoing community (I Cor. 7; Matt. 19)? Probably not. In the context of debating with the Pharisees? Possibly, but not necessarily. But even if not we see that these two contexts existed in the life of the church. With regard to Jesus himself we can make a good guess as to the general context; with regard to the church we can see precisely two contexts in which the saying was used: the continuing problems of human life and debates with opponents who are identified as 'Pharisees'.

Distinguishing pericope from setting, then, remains a necessary tool for those who wish to study the synoptic gospels. It potentially reveals information about Jesus, the final evangelists, and the intermediate church.

2. *Social settings*. We find less helpful form criticism's identification of social settings (*Sitze im Leben*): not that we doubt that the church engaged in worship, teaching, apology and attack, or that material in the gospels has been employed in these social settings. We doubt, rather, form criticism's assertion that the settings more-or-less automatically generated the material. We earlier discussed Gerhardsson's objection, which seems compelling, that the life-situations were often met without the use of Jesus-material. This results in assigning less creative power to the social settings discussed by form criticism. We take some examples in order to illustrate both the use of gospel material in certain regular activities of the church and the possibility of carrying out those activities without using Jesus-material:

(*a*) Worship. The two synoptic passages which were most obviously used in Christian worship are the Last Supper and the Lord's Prayer. The Last Supper is extremely important for the study both of Jesus and of the early church, but in the present discussion it can be treated very briefly. In this instance the church transmitted and used the immediate setting in Jesus' own lifetime: the night on which he was betrayed. The synoptic gospels put the prediction of betrayal into Jesus' mouth (Matt. 26.20–25; Mark 14.17–21; Luke 22.21–22), and Paul transmits the setting in a few words: 'on the night when he was betrayed [he] took bread . . .' (I Cor. 11.23). The use in the church is then given: 'as often as you eat this bread and drink the cup, you proclaim the Lord's death until he comes' (I Cor. 11.26). We cannot know how much more of the Passion Story may have been included in the commemoration services in Paul's churches, and it may be that the services did not include the entire account of the Passion as we now have it in the synoptics. But it is beyond doubt that here the church was very conservative. We see in both Paul and the synoptics that it set the Lord's Supper in the context of the events immediately before Jesus' death, and it used the material in worship services which remembered his death and looked forward to his return. Paul puts this expectation in his own words, addressed to the Corinthians: 'you proclaim . . . until he comes'. The synoptics attribute the prediction to Jesus: 'I shall not drink again of this fruit of the vine until that day when I drink it new with you in my Father's kingdom' (Matt. 26.29; cf. Mark 14.25; Luke 22.18).

In this instance we see that the social setting, 'worship', existed and that this was the context in which material from the gospels was used, but that worship did not generate the material; it already suited the situation of the church, which looked forward to Jesus' return. We do not know how often worship services in various churches held the commemorative meal, but presumably all commemorative services included the meal. We noted above that the precise wording of the passage varies from source to source, but the overall thrust is the same.

The Lord's Prayer, in Jesus' own lifetime, could have been set either in worship or in teaching. Matt. 6.5–15 puts it in the context of teaching the disciples and crowds how to be better than 'the hypocrites'. Luke places it in the context of Jesus' own worship:

> He was praying in a certain place, and when he ceased, one of his disciples said to him, 'Lord teach us to pray, as John taught his disciples'. (Luke 11.1)

The wording of the prayer is very different in the two gospels: Luke's version is much shorter than Matthew's. Thus we may be sure that at least one branch of the church has altered the prayer, and perhaps more than one has done so. Different branches of the church also supplied settings: catechesis in Matthew's tradition, actual prayer in Luke's. The original context cannot be known.

The church could worship without using the prayer. As we now have it, the Lord's Prayer seems to have been said collectively: '[you, plural] pray then like this' (Matt. 6.9); 'when you [plural] pray, say' (Luke 11.2). Paul's references to worship, however, do not refer to collective prayer, much less to one set prayer. In I Cor. 14.26 he writes that each person 'has a hymn, a lesson, a revelation, a tongue, or an interpretation': prayer is not mentioned at all. Paul's references to prayer usually imply individual prayer. Many refer to intercessory prayer, and therefore not to the Lord's Prayer: Rom. 1.10; 15.30; Phil. 1.9; I Thess. 1.2; 5.25. Other references are clearly to individual prayer. An example is I Cor. 11.4–5, 13, where Paul discusses praying or prophesying with uncovered or covered hair. Since 'prophecy' is to be done one-by-one (I Cor. 14.26), one must assume that prayer is expected to be done in the same way. I Cor. 14.14 refers to praying 'in a tongue', also an individual activity.

Most striking is Phil. 4.6:

Have no anxiety about anything, but in everything by prayer and supplication
with thanksgiving let your requests be made known to God.

The connection with the Lord's Prayer seems irresistible. Both Matthew and Luke
have the petition, 'Give us this day our daily bread' (Matt. 6.11//Luke 11.3). It is
remarkable that Paul did not cite it to teach the Philippians how to pray. Either he did
not know it, or he found his own admonition to be adequate. In either case the need
of the Pauline churches for instruction and example in prayer did not lead Paul to
create or use Jesus-material. (We noted above that he was not inclined to create
sayings by Jesus.) The social setting, prayer in the church, did not necessarily
generate a prayer attributed to Jesus. Further, if the setting of worship had great
generative power, we would expect more prayers to be assigned to Jesus in the
gospels. We see here a limit to the explanatory power of form criticism. It does not
fully explain how the Jesus-material was shaped or created.

(*b*) Apology and polemic. The early churches needed to defend their beliefs and
practices (apology) and to attack others (polemic). That Jesus-material was used in
these activities cannot be doubted. There are numerous examples. For apology, we
may recall the pericope on Plucking Grain on the Sabbath (Mark 2.23–28), in which
sayings attributed to Jesus defend the church for not keeping the sabbath laws. The
scribes and Pharisees are fiercely attacked in Matt. 23, which doubtless reflects real
conflict in the life of some branch of the church. Further, Jesus-material was used by
one part of the church against another. A good example is Matt. 5.19:

Whoever then relaxes one of the least of these commandments and teaches men
so, shall be called least in the kingdom of heaven; but he who does them and
teaches them shall be called great in the kingdom of heaven.

This is probably not against the Pharisees, who are mentioned in 5.20, for they
certainly taught that the law should be entirely kept (see Matt. 23.3, 'observe
whatever they tell you'). We probably have here, instead, a rebuke of a part of the
church which did not teach full observance.

This part of the church is attacked in James, where there is criticism of those who
hear the word but do not do it (James 1.22–25). More explicitly, the example of
Abraham is cited:

Was not Abraham our father justified by works, when he offered his son Isaac
upon the altar? You see that faith was active along with his works, and faith was
completed by works, and the scripture was fulfilled which says, 'Abraham
believed God, and it was reckoned to him as righteousness'; and he was called the
friend of God. You see that a man is justified by works and not by faith alone
(James 2.21–24).

There is almost universal agreement that the attack in James is directed against
Pauline Christianity. Paul himself never concluded from his argument in favour of
justification by faith, which was based on Abraham, that good deeds, including those
in the law, should not be done; and the attack in James is a bit off target. In his own

lifetime, however, Paul was suspected of overthrowing the law, and he had to defend himself against the charge (Rom. 3.8, 31; 6.1–2,15–16). James shows that, despite the defence, the charge was still levelled. The saying attributed to Jesus in Matt. 5.19 uses Jesus-material to attack antinomian Christians, but the letter of James needs no such material. The attack can be carried on without citing Jesus.

Thus the church did need to defend itself, and there were opponents within and without. It sometimes used Jesus-material for these purposes, and in doing so it doubtless changed the material in various ways. But these needs did not necessarily lead to the creation of pericopes about Jesus, and the apologetic and polemical needs of the church were less creative than the form critics supposed.

(*c*) Teaching can be dealt with very briefly. The New Testament is full of teaching, admonition, pastoral counselling and the like, but substantial Jesus-texts are seldom used outside the gospels. We may again illustrate the situation from the letters of Paul.

As we have more than once noted, there are substantial Jesus-texts at three points in Paul's letters: the teaching about divorce (I Cor. 7.10–11); the Last Supper (I Cor. 11.23–25); and the return of the Lord (I Thess. 4.15–17). There is a short text in I Cor. 9.14: 'the Lord commanded that those who proclaim the gospel should get their living by the gospel'. This seems to show knowledge of a text similar to our Matt. 10.9: 'Take no gold . . .; for the labourer deserves his food'. Mostly, however, Paul taught on his own authority. We may consider Rom. 12.17–21:

> Repay no one evil for evil, but take thought for what is noble in the sight of all. If possible, so far as it depends upon you, live peaceably with all. Beloved, never avenge yourselves, but leave it to the wrath of God. . . . No, if your enemy is hungry, feed him; if he is thirsty, give him drink; for by so doing you will heap burning coals upon his head. Do not be overcome by evil, but overcome evil with good.

This is very close, in general terms, to Matt. 5.39,43–44, where we find 'do not resist one who is evil' and 'love your enemies'. Paul either did not know these sayings or felt no need to cite them directly. Similarly, in the passages on the love commandment (Gal. 5.14; Rom. 13.8–10) Paul shows no direct use of Jesus' citation of the two great commandments (Matt. 22.34–40 and parr.).

In teaching, admonishing, and counselling, therefore, the leaders of early Christianity seem to have felt competent to speak in their own names. Jesus-material was used in these contexts, but the social settings did not necessarily lead to its creation.

Our conclusion with regard to all the categories under the general heading 'social settings' is the same. These settings did lead to the use of texts about or spoken by Jesus, and doubtless material was sometimes shifted from one context in Jesus' lifetime to another in the life of the early church. The form critics, however, overestimated the creative power of the needs of the church. The church needed defence against criticism, attacks on the practices of others (including other Christians), advice and instruction. It made use of Jesus-material in meeting these

195

needs. Its leaders, however, often spoke on their own authority, and the pressure to create new Jesus-material was probably not as great as the form critics thought. Individual prophets or teachers may have been more inclined than others to speak 'in the name of the Lord', but we cannot ascribe this tendency to 'the church' in all its branches.

3. *Parallels in other literature*. The third great principle of form criticism was that the synoptic material is better understood when it is compared with similar forms in the Graeco–Roman–Jewish world. We shall deal with this point – as did the form critics themselves – briefly, more briefly than it deserves. We may recall four passages referred to above: didactic chreiai attributed to Hillel and R. Johanan ben Zakkai (p. 160 above) and exorcisms attributed to Eleazar and Apollonius of Tyana (p. 169 above). Josephus told the story of Eleazar in order to illustrate Jewish prowess at exorcism. The other stories were told in order to persuade readers of the correctness of a point – to instruct them – or to celebrate the greatness of the subject of the story. The story about Hillel both teaches that love is central in Judaism and shows his ingenuity in teaching; the story about Johannan ben Zakkai inculcates the point that Judaism can flourish without the temple, by relying on mercy and deeds of loving kindness instead of sacrifice. It also bolsters the reputation of the man who was generally considered the chief founder of post-70 Rabbinic Judaism. Apollonius's exorcism is a demonstration of his power, but it is also didactic: boistrous and licentious youths should take the philosopher's cloak and live as did Apollonius.

The early Christians, in using chreiai and miracle stories – forms which were common and popular – did what any good teachers and propagandists would do: they spoke to their own time in ways approved by their culture. This is generally instructive for understanding the early Christian missionary endeavour and the way in which church practice was taught to those who were already believers.

There is, however, a more specific point. Studying other traditions teaches us what to expect, and this allows us to identify what is surprising or unusual in the synoptic material. We saw that the healing stories in the gospels, when compared to other healing stories, are quite modest and relatively free of magical details. The Christians did not stoop to the lowest level of Graeco–Roman culture. The chreiai, which end with a decisive saying, however, do not stand out in the same way. Jesus' replies are no more 'sovereign' or decisive than those attributed to others, and the short sayings are not necessarily more profound than those of others. It is the parables attributed to Jesus which are superior to parallels in other literature, and this is one of the principal reasons why so many scholars regard the parables as going back directly to Jesus. We are ourselves not entirely convinced, for we note the degree to which the parables in Matthew suit the gospel of Matthew, while those in Luke agree with Lukan themes. Nevertheless, the comparative material must be taken account of, and the differences from the synoptic material must be explained. Agreement and similarity with non-Christian material should be expected: distinctiveness requires

explanation.

It is clear that the work of form criticism is extremely useful in the study of the gospels. It is essential, though not always decisive, in seeking information about Jesus. It is the foundation of redaction criticism, which begins with the distinction of pericope from setting; and it is the one tool available which potentially gives information about the intermediate church. This third area we must now take leave of. The search for the historical Jesus we shall consider in Part V, but now we turn to redaction criticism.

Further Reading

Rudolf Bultmann and Karl Kundsin, *Form Criticism. Two Essays on New Testament Research*, ET New York 1934

Klaus Koch, *The Growth of the Biblical Tradition. The Form-Critical Method*, ET New York 1969

Robert H. Stein, *The Synoptic Problem*, Grand Rapids 1987, Part II, The Preliterary History of the Gospel Traditions

Part Four
Holistic Readings

14 Redaction Criticism

Redaction criticism focuses on those elements in the gospels that source and form criticism analyse as secondary, those parts that link, mould, and order traditional material, joining individual pericopes and combining sources. 'Redaction' is used rather than 'edition' because it is closer to the German *Redaktionsgeschichte*, and the discipline originally developed in Germany among Bultmann's disciples who took up and refined the final section of his *History of the Synoptic Tradition*, entitled 'The editing [German: *Redaktion*] of the traditional material'.

Works of redaction criticism assume, therefore, that both the two-source hypothesis and Bultmann's form-critical history of the synoptic tradition have produced assured results. Bultmann thought that editorial activity was a continuing process which reached its final stage in the present versions of the synoptic gospels. Collections of individual forms of sayings or miracle stories, for example, are posited, before they became parts of a larger source (p. 322). Further, source-criticism suggests that editorial developments can be discovered by studying an evangelist's use of written sources, known independently (Mark) or reconstructed (Q). H. Conzelmann discovered Luke's theology by noticing his alterations to his sources, and G. Bornkamm, G. Barth and H. J. Held discovered Matthew's in the same way.[1] Most redaction-critical studies of Matthew and Luke, therefore, are developments from source criticism, and for some time scholars who regarded Mark as our earliest source assumed that the method could not be applied to that gospel. But in 1956 Willi Marxsen published the German edition of *Mark the Evangelist*, which distinguished redaction from tradition in a gospel whose sources have to be reconstructed by taking up the suggestions already made in Bultmann's form-critical analysis.[2]

Bultmann had pictured the work of editing in largely passive terms as a mechanical process, produced by anonymous communities. His successors came more and more to see the redactors as creative theologians, preserving the past but in a form that spoke directly to their own situations. As creative individuals, the redactors are believed to exhibit intentions which can be discerned in their reworking of tradition. Although critical scholarship had made it plain that little or no reliable historical information exists about the evangelists, Matthew, Mark, Luke and John, these studies were written in a cultural context which took for granted that the meaning of literature is to be discovered only by laying bare the 'author's (or in this case, redactor's) intention'. This is why the studies are written in personalistic ways, about the intentions Matthew, Mark and Luke show in writing their gospels.

Redaction criticism is essentially an historical quest. But unlike form criticism, which discerns what typically gave rise to forms of tradition, redaction criticism seeks to define the particular situation in one of the churches which prompted the evangelist to express the theological and pastoral concerns of the final form of each gospel. It also tries to distinguish the final editing from previous edited 'layers' which may have been taken up by the final redactor, and which may express different or even contradictory interests. It is, however, difficult to make the distinction between one layer of redaction and another. If the two-source hypothesis is accepted, as it almost always has been by redaction critics, then, as far as Matthew and Luke are concerned, the editor's alterations of Mark and Q constitute the evidence for redactional style, but if more than one redactor is envisaged, it becomes necessary to distinguish the style of one from that of another. Since the evidence available is so limited, the criterion of contradiction becomes very important. When one section of a gospel seems to contradict another section, scholars often assign each to separate redactors. For example, it is sometimes argued that, since Matthew 10.5–6 envisages a mission of the disciples exclusively to Israel, other sections, like 8.5–13 or 15.21–28, which countenance a mission to the Gentiles, must stem from another redactor. There are, however, two objections to the proposal. Firstly, the evidence is open to another interpretation. Although the Gospel of Matthew limits the mission of Jesus and that of his disciples during his life-time to Israel, the post-resurrection Jesus authorizes the mission to Gentiles, and the stories of Gentile conversions within Jesus' earthly ministry may be intended as proleptic exceptions to the general rule. Secondly, since the redactor appears to have been free to make some alterations in the sources used, by omitting, rearranging and amending, the notion that new perspectives can be introduced only by adding a second layer to older material is clearly unnecessary. It is better, therefore, to try to make sense of apparent contradictions. Moreover, even if contradictions remain, this does not prove separate authorship, since contradictions within the work of a single author are commonplace. Nevertheless, in passages in which the stylistic peculiarities of the final redactor are absent, yet the section has no parallel in the other gospels, it may be the case that the work of a previous redactor has been incorporated.

Redaction criticism, therefore, undertakes to discover information about the Christian community in which the redactor wrote, through the texts produced and preserved. The individual redactor is assumed to address the needs of his own community. But the procedure is not entirely limited to reading off a situation from a text. The New Testament epistles provide independent evidence about some of the problems and concerns of some Greek-speaking churches, which may throw light on those mirrored in redactional passages of the gospels. But it is redaction criticism's interest in elucidating the distinctive theological and pastoral concerns of individual editors within their communities at the time of writing which marks an advance over form criticism. Form criticism highlights what is general and typical in the history of tradition, redaction criticism what is specific – to a time, a place and an individual.

Our procedure in this chapter will not be to describe the principal results of the major redaction critics, but rather to explore the method by discussing an example in some detail. There are two reasons for changing tactics in this chapter. One is that there already exists a competent summary of the results achieved by Conzelman on Luke; Bornkamm, Barth and Held on Matthew; Marxsen on Mark; and many others: Joachim Rohde, *Rediscovering the Teaching of the Evangelists*.[3] The second, more important reason is that we do not think that the theology of each gospel is best discovered by studying the redactors' alterations of their sources (even if we knew for sure what they are!), but rather by studying each gospel as a whole. In the plan of this book, the characterizations of each gospel will be given most fully in chs 17–19, on Genre. Redaction criticism, however, paved the way for holistic readings of the gospels, and it also contributed to understanding the particulars of each. Thus it remains a worthwhile study, though it is subject to some substantial criticisms.

An Example: J. D. Kingsbury, *The Parables of Jesus in Matthew 13*, 1969.

J. D. Kingsbury's study provides an excellent example of redaction criticism because it explicitly states the steps involved and the reasons for making judgments. Since it examines a short but centrally important part of the Gospel of Matthew, it demonstrates the ways in which the framing, arrangement and detail within the whole complex of the gospel determine the meaning of traditional elements. Although Kingsbury's study is relatively short, 180 pages, it will be impossible to discuss every detail in the space available. Readers will need to consult a copy as well as to follow the text of Matthew 13. Kingsbury's aim is not to expose the form of parables as they may have been spoken by the historical Jesus, but the meaning of the parables for Matthew, the author of the gospel, and for his community. Matthew's intention in writing this series of parables, in this order, with these details, in this context in his gospel, is to be discovered through a careful analysis which distinguishes source material from editorial work.

Since the whole endeavour hangs on the significance of details, we shall have to follow Kingsbury's arguments to assess their value for discerning the author's intention, his theology and his church's needs. Is Kingsbury correct in seeing 13.36 as a turning point in the Matthaean Jesus' ministry? Does the gospel address problems which arose from relations between church and synagogue in the Matthaean community? Has the community become rich and complacent? Does Matthew teach that the kingdom of heaven is a present or a future reality? Does he see Jesus as the exalted Lord, even when depicting his earthly ministry? We shall also have to consider the significance of those passages in Matthew which seem to come from the tradition. Are we to understand the redactor's intention only from unique wording and arrangement, or also from the repetition of traditional material?

203

• The framework

The first task undertaken in Kingsbury's study is to determine how far Matthew himself structured the chapter and how far he was dependent on a structure already provided by his sources. He assumes that Matthew used the Gospel of Mark, Q and other sources.

In the light of these assumptions, Matthew 13.1–23 is seen to be taken from Mark 4.1–20, and Matthew 13.34 from Mark 4.33–34. The structure of Matthew 13.24–33 is, however, to be recognized as the work of the redactor, for the following reasons. 13.24a and 31a repeat a formula, 'another parable he set before them', and 33c is very similar, 'another parable he spoke to them'. The formula is said to contain four favourite Matthaean terms:

(*a*) *Allos* (another) is used 29 times in Matthew, 9 times in parallel to Mark, twice in parallel to Luke.

(*b*) '*Parabolē* (parable) attests to Matthaean authorship because it signals the great "turning point" to which Matthew calls attention in 13.1–35' (p. 13).

(*c*) 'Matthew has elevated *autois* (to them) in 13.11–35 to the status of a *terminus technicus*: it is his formal designation for the Jewish crowds (cf. 13.3, 10, 13, 24, 31, 33, 34)' (p. 13).

(*d*) *Legōn* (saying) is listed by Jeremias as characteristic of Matthaean style.

It is unfortunate for the argument, however, that three of these four points are unconvincing. Like Mark, Matthew refers to the stories contained in this collection as parables. There is nothing distinctive in his use of this particular word at this point. That *autois* is used as a technical term to refer exclusively to the Jewish crowds is simply not the case. In vv. 1–9, it refers to the crowds, in vv. 10–17, since the disciples are addressed directly as 'you' it again refers to the crowds, but in vv. 24–35, it could refer either to the disciples alone, or to the disciples and the crowds, and finally in v. 52, it refers to the disciples. That Jeremias is correct in citing *legōn* as characteristic of Matthaean style is, again, doubtful.[4] It is true that Matthew uses it more frequently (112 times) than either Mark (about 20 times) or Luke (about 80 times), but it is too commonly used throughout the synoptic tradition to be distinctive.

The argument, then, has shown that the formula is not from Mark but has not been successful in proving that it is a Matthaean construct rather than a link already present before the final redaction. This could be an instance of pre-Matthaean redaction.

Matthew 13.34, 35

The same judgment can be made about Kingsbury's suggestion that Matthew 13.34 is a redactional alteration of Mark 4.33–34 (p. 88–89). Certainly, Matthew 13.34 is different from the Markan parallel in the following respects: it makes explicit links with 13.1–2 through the mention of Jesus and the crowds, and, in line with details throughout the chapter, insists that the disciples understand Jesus' teaching, whereas in Mark they do not, but no evidence is produced which demonstrates that these elements are Matthaean rather than pre-Matthaean.

On the other hand, 13.35 has no synoptic parallel and is a typical Matthaean formula quotation (cf. 8.17). The passage is attributed to a prophet although the first half quotes the Septuagint of Psalm 78.2a. Kingsbury supports Stendahl's proposal that, since the Psalm bears Asaph's name and I Chronicles 25.2 calls Asaph a prophet, the attribution makes sense.[5] In any case, Matthew refers to the whole of Scripture as 'the law and the prophets' (7.12) and has no separate category into which to fit the Psalms. The second part of the quotation, which conforms to neither the Septuagint nor the Hebrew of the Psalm, has probably been integrated into the context by Matthew, as Stendahl and Kingsbury suggest, but Kingsbury immediately raises the question whether it actually contradicts the context. Do the parables told by Jesus in chapter 13 reveal things that have been hidden since the foundation of the world, or do they conceal these mysteries from the crowds (13.1–15)? Kingsbury argues convincingly that no contradiction exists because the parables tell of these mysteries to those granted insight by God, i.e. to the disciples who do indeed understand them.

The framework in 13.36

Kingsbury goes on to propose that the framework in the second half of the chapter is Matthaean too (p. 14 and pp. 94–95). Nothing in Mark 4 corresponds to Jesus' withdrawal into the house in 13.36. The mention of Jesus' departure from the house in Matthew 13.1 is parallel to Mark 3.20, but in 13.36, as in 9.28, Matthew uses the house as a setting independently of Mark or Q. Kingsbury distinguishes the Markan perception of the house as a place of seclusion, perhaps representing the church, from the Matthaean conception of the house as a specific dwelling in Capernaum. Actually, Mark does not always picture the house as a place of seclusion, as Kingsbury is forced to recognize later (compare p. 93 and footnotes 1 and 2 with footnote 6, and see Mark 1.32–34, 2.1–12, 3.19–25). Also in Matthew it is uncertain whether it is to be inferred that the house is in Capernaum, since that place has not been mentioned since 8.5. Mark 2.1 mentions that Jesus entered Capernaum, and the house scenes in the following chapters can be understood to take place there. Since the Matthaean arrangement is different, however, just where the house of 13.36 is situated remains unclear. Kingsbury rightly goes on to point to the similarity between v. 36b and 13.10a with the distinctive combination of *proserchomai* (approach) and *legō* (say), and to the similarity between vv. 36c and 15.15b, which differs from its Markan parallel. The second instance supports not just a pre-Matthaean structure, but the work of the final redactor. Moreover, Kingsbury could have drawn attention to the presence of *tote* (then) in the verse, generally reckoned to be an indicator of the final redactor's hand.

13.51–52 The conclusion to the discourse (pp. 125–129)

Kingsbury argues that the verses are the work of the final redactor for three reasons. Firstly, v. 51 seems to hark back to the disciples' request for clarification in v. 36. Secondly, v. 51 reinforces the Matthaean picture that the disciples understand Jesus' teaching (13.11, 16, 23) although this feature could be pre-Matthaean. Thirdly, 'every scribe' in v. 52 is understood to refer to all disciples, in spite of the fact that 23.34 distinguishes a particular group in the church as scribes. Such a contradiction should suggest that v. 52 is pre-Matthaean, if Kingsbury's interpretation is correct, but his interpretation is probably wrong, and the disciples/scribes of Matthew 13 are to be understood as a special group with understanding. The first and the third of the three reasons suggest, then, that 51–52 is part of the framework of the final redactor.

13.53 'And it happened when Jesus had finished'

Finally, 13.53 is linked with the same phrase in 11.1 to indicate a major division in the gospel (p. 15). A similar formula is found in Matthew 7.28, 19.1, 26.1. But no reasons are given to show that here is the hand of the final redactor. This particular use of *egeneto* (it happened) is found only in the formula and in Matt. 9.10. It is found rarely in Mark but very commonly in Luke. The verb *teleō* (finish) is used outside the formula only in Matt. 10.23 in the same sense, and in 17.24 in the different sense of paying taxes. Perhaps Kingsbury assumes, on quite general grounds, that if this major structuring of the gospel cannot be attributed to the final redactor, then nothing can.

We should now survey the results of Kingsbury's attempt to demonstrate conclusively that the framework of Matthew 13 is not only different from Mark and Q, but also the work of the final rather than an earlier redactor. It has to be admitted that it is not wholly successful. Only 13.35, 36 and 53 can be reckoned Matthaean with any certainty.

- ### The narrative context (pp. 15–16)

The formula in 11.1 and 13.53 marks 11.2–13.52 as a subsection of the gospel, in which the collection of parables in chapter 13 appears at the end of a series of stories depicting mounting opposition to Jesus. This arrangement, Kingsbury proposes, declares Matthew's intention and reflects the experience of Matthew's church. Unfortunately, Kingsbury's anxiety to interpret every detail in terms of these presuppositions leads him to make unlikely conjectures and to overlook more obvious interpretations. For example, the doubts of John the Baptist about Jesus' identity recorded in 11.2–19 are said to reflect possible contacts between Matthew's church and the Essenes, but it is far more likely that they offer an apology for the awkward fact that, in spite of Jesus' early association with him, John did not become a follower of Jesus. Again, 11.2–24 is said to correspond to the unsuccessful missionary work of Matthew's church in Galilee, although it could be better construed as part of a narrative pre-figuring of Jesus' final rejection and death. Further, 12.1–45, the conflict discourses with the (scribes and) Pharisees, is taken to mirror the animosity between Matthew's church and the Judaism contemporary with it. This is a popular scholarly view advocated by many besides Kingsbury, and the gospel itself may provide evidence that Matthew's church suffered persecution from communities of Jews as well as Gentiles, but any one-to-one reading off of the experience of Matthew's church from the stories of Jesus in the gospel is too simplistic to be convincing. We shall come back to this point in our assessment of redaction criticism.

Finally, 12.46–50 is interpreted to mean that Matthew intended to present Jesus as dividing his audience into two groups, those who are his true relatives, who do God's will, the disciples, and the rest, including Jesus' blood relatives and the crowds who represent unbelieving Judaism. 'Previously (chapters 11–12) Jesus was depicted in conflict with only individual segments of the Jewish nation. Now, however, he faces in the crowds the whole of unbelieving Judaism' (p. 16). Surely this is an exaggeration in two directions. Firstly, accounts of rejection or expected rejection have appeared earlier in the gospel (2.7–15; 5.11–12; 8.34; 9.4, 34; 10.14–39) and secondly, the crowds change this way and that, now for Jesus, now against him, both before and after 12.46 (e.g. 12.15, 23; 14.13–14; 15.30–31; 21.8–11, 46; 23.1; 27.22–26). One of the central points of Kingsbury's interpretation, that 13.36 marks a great turning point when Jesus reacts to the rejection of Jewish leaders and Jewish crowds by turning away from them to the disciples, seems, therefore, to be based on a misleading presentation of the evidence. Insofar as the arrangement of Matthew 11–13 can be reckoned the work of the final redactor, however, it may be significant that the chapter of parables immediately follows a series of incidents, especially in chapter 12, which depicts the (scribes and) Pharisees, who take counsel to kill Jesus (12.14) and who attempt to discredit him before the crowds by the Beelzebul accusation (12.22–32). The text therefore posits groups reacting to Jesus in different ways. The (scribes and) Pharisees seek to destroy him as an evil doer, the disciples play an active role in his support (10.1–5) and the crowds follow him passively, attracted by his healings and teachings.

We shall now go on to examine the book's treatment of each of the parables in Matthew 13, since this detailed examination is what is required next by the method. Kingsbury's study places a chapter, Matthew's concept of the Kingdom of Heaven, between his discussion of the framework and context on the one hand, and detailed exposition on the other. What Matthew means by 'the kingdom of Heaven/God' and what Jesus may have meant by the 'kingdom of God' have been subjects discussed at length by many scholars, as any glance at a commentary makes clear. A careful redaction critical study of Matthew 13 could be expected to throw light on the range of meanings that the chapter provides, in the context of the whole gospel. Kingsbury's presentation, however, puts the cart before the horse. He lists his presuppositions about the meaning of 'the kingdom of heaven' before he begins to examine the parables of chapter 13, and these blind him to other possible interpretations when he reads the parables. Not only so, however, but some of his statements in chapter 3 barely make sense and need explanation. For example, it is repeatedly stated that 'the *kingdom* of heaven' or 'the *kingdom* of God' denotes God's kingly *rule* rather than God's kingly *realm*. Once in the book, he nevertheless slips into using the word 'realm' (p. 81) because the grammar of the sentence demands it. Elsewhere, he is content not to notice that statements like 'Jesus calls men of all nations into God's kingly *rule*' defeats the argument that 'rule' is better than 'realm' since 'call into' requires 'realm', whereas 'rule' goes with 'accept' (e.g. p. 120).

Again, he emphasizes that the kingdom of heaven is a present as well as a future reality, remarking that 'Matthew believes that the kingdom manifested itself in the person . . . of Jesus' (e.g. pp. 18 and 80). He never explains, however, what the nature of the kingdom is and how it could be 'manifested' in Jesus. His assumption that the teachings and miracles of Jesus constitute the presence of the kingdom is simply a mistake. Matthew makes it plain that Jesus was not alone in teaching and performing miracles. Indeed, even the Pharisees performed miracles, 12.27. And when Kingsbury cites 10.32–33, 40; 21.42–43; 25.31–46, to show that whatever attitude people assume towards Jesus is the same as the attitude they assume towards the kingdom present in him, he misrepresents the texts. The passages state that the attitude people adopt towards Jesus will affect what *God* will do in the Final Judgment.

Jesus' parables to the Jewish crowds beside the sea: 13.1–35. 13.1–3a, The setting (pp. 22–32)

In discussing the framework, Kingsbury had advanced stylistic arguments to justify his contention that the arrangement of material was the work of a final redactor, Matthew. He assumes that they are foolproof, and therefore treats Matthaean differences from Mark in the rest of ch. 13 as the work of the final redactor too. So, although it is based on Mark 4.1, 13.1 is largely a Matthaean creation which makes explicit Jesus' departure from the house (compare Mark 3.20) to sit by the sea. The introductory 'on that day' may be Matthaean (compare 22.23); but Kingsbury's suggestion that *kathēmai* (sit) is a favourite Matthaean word (19 times in Matthew, 11 in Mark, 13 in Luke) when it is used in Mark 4.1, which, *ex hypothesi*, Matthew has in front of him, is misleading. Even more so is the suggestion that since Rabbis sit to teach and God is imagined sitting on a throne, the very posture of Jesus tells us that 'Matthew's intention in v. 2 is to fashion a setting that will in itself attribute honour to Jesus and underline, not merely a Rabbinic, but even a divine dignity' (p. 23 and see p. 24). Are we to attribute the same divine dignity to Matthew the tax collector, who is described as sitting (*kathēmai*) at the tax office, 9.9? Rather, both Matthew and Mark describe Jesus sitting in the boat because sitting is an appropriate posture for anyone in a boat. The detail about the boat, Kingsbury rightly notices, however, is forgotten in the events which follow (13.10, 36).

Getting into the boat allows Jesus to address the great crowd on the beach (*ochloi polloi*/ Mark *ochlos pleistos*). The principal parties are therefore Jesus and the crowds. Kingsbury insists that *ochlos* itself, whatever its context in Matthew, means 'Jews' not 'Jews and Gentiles', in spite of 4.25, which explicitly mentions people from the Decapolis as components of the crowd, and 15.29–31, the feeding of the four thousand, which many commentators see as a Gentile feeding after the healing of the Canaanite woman's daughter. Moreover, Kingsbury assigns the Jewish crowds a role in chapter 13 which he admits they do not play generally: they 'represent the whole of unbelieving Judaism'.

Another change in detail which Kingsbury finds illuminating is Matthew's *laleō* (speak) for Mark's *didaskō* (teach). Kingsbury's view is that Matthew uses *didaskō* and *kērussō* (proclaim) when Jesus addresses the crowds only before the conflicts of chapter 12. Now he marks the change with the word *laleō*. This is untrue, however, since in 26.55 Matthew has Jesus refer to his earlier teaching in the Temple with *didaskō* (see also 21.23; 22.16). Why then does he use *laleō* here? Perhaps because 'teaching' has the narrower connotation of enabling someone to learn, whereas 'speaking' may fall on deaf ears, and that is part of the situation to be described in the rest of the chapter.

13.3b–9 The Parable of the Sower

Although there are some minor differences between the Matthaean and the Markan parable, there is substantial agreement, but Kingsbury expounds the parable as if it were a Matthaean composition. Here is a dilemma for redaction critics. On the one hand, they emphasize the changes that the redactor makes to his sources and find in them their chief interest; on the other hand, they have to admit that in reproducing material from his sources without alteration, the redactor also has some intention. What significance should be found in this reproduction? Are we to assume that what is reproduced captures the intention of the redactor as well as that of the original author? Or could it be that the redactor was not free to meddle with established tradition, even when he did not agree with it? Kingsbury appears to adopt the former view but does not discuss the issue. Since the treatment of sources in the synoptic gospels requires us to suppose that material from the source could be either altered or omitted, Kingsbury's view is probably correct.

Kingsbury describes the form of the parable of the sower as a 'fable', by which he means a story about an event of the past, not necessarily one involving animals or plants as characters. The fable is, however, allegorical. Jesus is the sower, sowing (i.e. preaching) the seed (i.e. 'the word of the kingdom' 13.19). The point of the story is to highlight the contrast between the failure and the success of the sowing/preaching. It offers a comment on what had been described in the previous chapters, in which Jesus' preaching is seen to fail with the scribes and Pharisees and to succeed with the disciples. The imagery of the parable helps to suggest that there is nothing more remarkable in this than in the failure and success of a sower. Kingsbury, however, blinded by his insistence that the Jewish crowds of Matthew 13 completely reject Jesus, sees the parable and the opposition in too simple terms. He does not notice that the parable describes remarkable failure, partial failure and extraordinary success. The partial failure seems to encompass the fate of Jesus' preaching to the crowds, who are not written off as obdurate opponents but are seen as potential disciples.

13.10–17 The reason for speaking in parables

Kingsbury sees the section as a combination of Mark and Q because of the otherwise inexplicable agreements of Matthew and Luke against Mark, if the two-source theory is accepted.

Mark changes scene at 4.10, picturing Jesus no longer in the boat addressing the crowd, but alone. Matthew overlooks the fact that he had placed Jesus in a boat, omits the Markan scene change, and has the disciples approach Jesus directly, using one of his favourite words, *proserchomai* (approach) (52 times in Matthew, 5 (6) in Mark, 10 in Luke). Because the word is sometimes used in the Septuagint when people approach God, Kingsbury suggests that the word itself has 'cultic overtones', and he goes on to pick out examples from Matthew in which the word is used of people approaching Jesus, especially those in which they then address him as 'Lord' (e.g. 8.25; 17.14–15; 18.21). But, once again, the presentation of the evidence is misleading. Are we to suppose that the Tempter approaches Jesus reverently in 4.1 because the same verb is used by Matthew but not by Luke? Or that the Pharisees do so in 15.1 or 19.3? Rather, *proserchomai* means simply 'approach' and other words and gestures define what kind of approach is described.

It is the disciples who approach Jesus in 13.10, to ask why he speaks in parables. The Matthaean disciples, suggests Kingsbury, are the Twelve. They, unlike their Markan counterparts, understand Jesus even before the final events of his life, but Kingsbury fails to note that this does not place them above Matthaean criticism. Mark criticizes the disciples for failing to understand, Matthew because, although they understand, they doubt and lack faith; for example, 8.26; 14.31; 16.8; 17.17; 28.17.

In answer to the disciples, Jesus explains that they are privileged because God has made known (the passive *dedotai*, 'has been given', indicating God's activity) the mysteries (plural in Matthew and Luke, singular in Mark) of the kingdom of heaven to them and not to others. Because of this reference to mysteries, Kingsbury supposes that each of the parables makes known a secret about the kingdom of heaven. He therefore overlooks the possibility that the mysteries are those to which Matthew had already drawn attention and to which the disciples had responded, that the kingdom of heaven is imminent (4.17 and 10.7) and that there are conditions of entry (e.g. the sermon on the mount in chs 5–7). Matthew adds to those remarks the general statement (see Mark 4.25) about more being given to the one that has. 'The more', says Kingsbury, is not more understanding but the kingdom, because the same saying recurs at the end of the parable of the talents, 25.29. The reverse statement, even what someone has will be taken from the one to whom God has not revealed the mysteries, seems to pick up the imagery from the parable of the sower about the seed falling on stony ground and among brambles. This suggests that the crowds are in danger because even what they have, they may lose.

Verse 13 then comes to the point about the parables. Jesus speaks to them in parables *because* (contrast Mark's 'in order that') seeing they do not see and hearing they do not hear or understand. What, then, is a parable? Kingsbury asserts that for Mark, a parable is a riddle *per se*, as much for the disciples as for the outsider. For Matthew, however, a parable is a riddle only for an outsider. But Kingsbury recognizes that if this is the meaning in chapter 13, 'parable' means something else in the rest of the gospel, where Jesus clearly addresses opponents in parables which they understand (e.g. 21.28–32, 33–46). So Kingsbury reaches an impasse. Perhaps he should admit that 'riddle' is an unhelpful word in this context, and to abandon it would allow a different interpretation. The short stories, called parables in Matthew 13, are depictions of events which can be understood at a trivial level by everyone.

The point about them which only the disciples grasp is that they provide metaphors about the success, failure and ultimate outcome of Jesus' preaching about the imminence of the kingdom. Only the disciples have followed Jesus, actively sharing in his mission, because only they have been given understanding by God. Once the mysteries of the kingdom's imminence and the conditions of entry into it are recognized, the parables are seen to encourage, criticize and warn the listeners about these eschatological realities depicted in commonplace images. But in chapter 21, for example, the parables about the two sons and about the vineyard need no such insight into the point of Jesus' mission to be taken as offensive by Jesus' opponents.

13.18–23 The interpretation of the Parable of the Sower

Kingsbury thinks that the minor alterations Matthew makes in the Markan version remove inconsistencies, but they do not obviate a major problem in reading the section. Is the 'seed' to be understood as 'the word of the kingdom'? Grammatically, the masculine *houtos* (this) and *ho spareis* (that which is sown) (v. 19) could refer back to *ho logos* (the word). But this reading is ruled out by v. 20, which makes it plain that '*he* who is sown' (*ho spareis*) is the one who hears the word, not the word itself. Kingsbury therefore suggests that the interpretation be read as follows: 'Just as in the case of the seed which was sown . . . so it is with the person who hears the word' (p. 53). This seems slightly unclear and less than satisfactory, though, because it gives a different reading for the same elements in the parable itself and in its interpretation. Earlier, Kingsbury had seen the sower as Jesus sowing/preaching the seed/the word of the kingdom. The interpretation might have been expected, therefore, to see various conditions of soil as different sorts of people who receive the word, but it does not. Nevertheless, contra Kingsbury, it is possible to read the interpretation as straightforwardly elucidating the parable, rather than changing it. The person is the plant produced by the effect of the seed (= the word) in various conditions of soil. The seed, then, is the word as v. 19 says, but the plant it produces is the person who has responded to the word more or less adequately. This interpretation makes sense of details like 'the Evil one comes and grabs that which is sown in his heart' (i.e. the word of the kingdom) v. 19; or 'he has no roots (i.e. a plant, not a seed) in himself' v. 21. In other words, the interpretation explains the meaning of the parable, as the text requires it to do.

Nevertheless, if the disciples have been given insight by God, why is an explanation necessary? Kingsbury notices that, whereas in Mark the explanation serves to overcome the disciples' ignorance, in Matthew it serves to confirm their understanding. Moreover, Kingsbury could have suggested that on the literary level, repetition helps to drive the message home for the readers.

Because the interpretation is addressed to the disciples, Kingsbury supposes that it applies directly to the situation of Matthew's church, indicating, for example, that the church is well-to-do. But this is an element found also in Mark and may simply have been taken over. In fact, the dangers of distraction described are so general that they can hardly be used for a reconstruction of a particular church's experience at a particular time.

13.24–30 The Parable of the Wheat and the Weeds

In Mark, the interpretation of the parable of the sower is followed by the parable of the Seed Growing Secretly, 4.26–29, which neither Matthew nor Luke includes. Kingsbury thinks it unlikely that the parable was missing from the version of Mark known to Matthew but that Matthew's chapter continues with the parable of the Wheat and the Weeds (or Tares), which he found in another source and preferred, because it helped him develop his apology against 'unbelieving Israel'.

He argues that Matthew had edited his source, adding the formulaic introduction, 'Another parable he set before them saying', and the dialogue (vv. 27–28a), which repeats in direct speech information already given in the narrative (vv. 24–26). Moreover, Kingsbury supposes that vv. 28b–30 reflect the experience of the Matthaean community: 'The servants said to him, Then do you want us to go and gather them? But he said, No, lest in gathering the weeds you root up the wheat along with them. Let both grow together until the harvest, and at the harvest time I will tell the reapers, Gather the weeds first and bind them in bundles to be burned, but gather the wheat into my barn.' Kingsbury comments, 'The subject matter in v. 28b–30 harmonizes well with the circumstances of Matthew's day' (p. 65). Before such a link can be made, however, we not only need to know more about the Matthaean community, but we need to pay attention to the narrative level of the text. The parable is addressed to the disciples in the context of the partial success and partial failure of Jesus' ministry up to this point. Since the details are rather implausible at the story level, the parable is immediately recognized as an allegory, with the Lord representing Jesus, the slaves the disciples, the reapers another group, presumably angels, and the harvest the Final Judgment. The disciples are urged not to undertake the task that the angels will perform at a later date, that is, not to separate weeds from wheat, not to drive away the unresponsive. In the narrative context, this means that Jesus and the disciples will pursue their mission as before, in spite of the failures, and the gospel depicts them acting accordingly.

Does this reflect the life of the Matthaean community? Were we in a position to give a full and independent account of the community history, we could at least attempt sensible conjectures, but in fact we do not know for certain where, when or by whom the gospel was written, and the evidence we have is derived from the gospel itself not from independent sources. Moreover, the sort of general problem treated in the parable of the wheat and the weeds is common to most communities, whether village, town, religious or political group. Kingsbury believes the verses harmonize well with the circumstances of Matthew's own day because one of his presuppositions is that Matthew's church is worried about relations with Judaism. In the light of this presupposition, Kingsbury reads the verses to mean that Matthew presents Jesus as the one who advises the church against a complete separation from Judaism. This is one possibility, but, as with most presuppositions, the light it sheds throws other possibilities into shadow. In particular, an alternative view that recognizes the need for the narrative to make sense and the constraints that this imposes on an author is completely overlooked. The meaning of the passage suggested in the previous paragraph, above, makes good sense on a narrative level.

The parable of the wheat and the weeds, like that of the sower, is followed by an explanation later in the chapter (vv. 36–43). As with the explanation of the parable of the sower, Kingsbury is at pains to show that 'explanation' is a misnomer, and that one parable is in fact being replaced by another. He adduces three reasons for this. The first is that the so-called explanation does not stand next to the parable, and the second that there has been a change in audience (vv. 1–35 addressed to crowds by the lake, vv. 36–52 to disciples in the house). This second point is slightly over-stated. The parable is addressed to the disciples in the presence of the crowds, and the interpretation to the disciples when the crowds are absent. Neither the first nor the second point shows that we should expect a new parable rather than an interpretation. The third point is, however, more weighty. The centre of the parable is the dialogue between master and slaves, whereas the interpretation omits the dialogue and draws attention to the harvest.

The parable begins with an introduction which itself needs explanation. 'The kingdom of heaven may be compared (*hōmoiōthē*) to a man (dative) who sowed good seed in his field' (v. 24). Elsewhere in the chapter Matthew uses an equivalent expression, 'The kingdom of heaven is like (*homoia estin*) a grain of mustard seed' (dative; v. 31). Although at first sight these statements seem to suggest that the kingdom of heaven is being compared directly to the person or thing described in the dative (the man, the grain of mustard seed), this is not the case. For example, if the kingdom of heaven is being compared to anything in the parable of the wheat and the weeds, it is not compared to the man, but to the whole story of a man planting good seed, discovering weeds and waiting for the harvest. Kingsbury, following Jeremias, therefore proposes that an expression like 'It is the case with the kingdom of heaven as with a man who . . .' more adequately captures the sense and avoids unnecessary misapprehensions. This means that although the parable is allegorical, no one element in it represents 'the kingdom of heaven'. Here Kingsbury makes an important point, but does not develop its implications. While advancing this argument, he fails to notice that it deals the death blow to his assertion in chapter 3 that the kingdom of heaven is present in Jesus. Since in the parable, the lord is identified as Jesus, Kingsbury's thesis, which identifies the kingdom with Jesus, requires the parable to teach that the kingdom of heaven is, in fact, like the man. That Kingsbury correctly recognizes this as a mistake should have led him to doubt the worth of his remarks in chapter 3. Moreover, his presuppositions about the kingdom of heaven occasionally lead him to bizarre readings. For example, he states (p. 67) that since *hōmoiōthē* in 13.24 is an aorist passive, it should be translated by a past tense in English. He gathers from this that the kingdom of heaven is seen by Matthew as a reality which has existed for some time in the past. But translating this aorist as a past simply asserts that 'The kingdom of heaven *was compared*', i.e. that the comparison had been made in the past, not that the kingdom of heaven existed in the past or at any time. Actually, translating this aorist as a past rather than in its punctiliar sense does not fit the Matthaean context at all. The RSV's 'The kingdom of heaven may be compared . . .' gives the sense required.

Recognizing the parable as allegorical, Kingsbury interprets 'the field' (v. 24) as 'Israel' not as 'the world' (contrast v. 38). Since Kingsbury had advanced arguments, albeit unconvincing ones, that the crowd is rejecting and rejected Israel, the interpretation seems natural to him. Given the allegorical meanings of seeds and plants already supplied in the parable of the sower and its interpretation, however, this parable need understand 'the field' only in its most general allegorical sense as 'the area of the mission of Jesus and his disciples'. So far in the gospel, this mission had been directed primarily to Israel (10.6) although some hints of a Gentile mission had already been included (2.1–12; 4.25; 8.5–13; 8.28–34). The bold statement in the interpretation 'the field is the world' (v. 38) is something of a jolt, therefore, coming as it does before the stories in chapter 15, but it helps prepare the reader for the final command in 28.19.

In the parable, the householder is addressed as *kyrie* (sir, master, v. 27). Kingsbury interprets the word to mean 'Lord' and identifies the householder not with the historical Jesus but with the exalted Lord of the church. It may be true that when suppliants or disciples in the gospel address Jesus as Lord or fall down before him, they are behaving in ways appropriate not simply to a respected teacher or miracle-worker, but to a kingly figure. Certainly, the historical Jesus of Matthew's gospel is regarded as the Messiah. Whether *kyrios* also carries connotations of divinity, however, is a difficult problem. The gospel teaches that the reader comes to know about the salvation God is effecting by recognizing the significance of Jesus' life, death and resurrection, but Matthew seems not to have puzzled about the implications of such views for his theology and christology. In any case, as far as this instance of *kyrie* in the parable is concerned, it makes perfect sense in terms of the story, since slaves habitually addressed their master as *kyrie*.

The allegorical significance of elements in the parable is obvious enough. Jesus is the householder (master) who sows (preaches) good seed (the message of the imminence of the kingdom, 4.17 and 10.7) in his field (the area of his mission), and whose enemy (the Devil) sows weeds (people influenced by the Devil). If the slaves are the disciples, the wheat must be other followers of Jesus, and the disciples are envisaged as a group with special responsibility, in line with the Matthaean portrait of them in chapter 10. Kingsbury fails to notice this point and insists that 'slaves' stand for the whole of the Matthaean church, not just its leaders (p. 69 and pp. 72–74). The parable then encourages even those who carry responsibility to leave the Final Judgment to the Messiah's angels.

Since Kingsbury interpreted 'the mysteries' of 13.11 to mean that each of the parables in the chapter would reveal a mystery, he formulates this parable's revelation as follows: 'The secret this parable reveals about the kingdom of heaven is that this kingdom, as a present reality, has confronted all Israel in the word of proclamation. But since all Israel has not responded to the word in faith and obedience, this people has come to be divided into two camps: true Israel, which lives under the kingly rule of God, and unbelieving Israel, which lives under the rule of Satan. Not until the end of the age and the coming of the Son of man is there to be any forcible change of this state of affairs' (p. 76). Kingsbury's language is influenced by

German existentialism and shares its opacity. For example, what does 'this kingdom . . . has confronted all Israel in the word of proclamation' mean? What the parable itself seems to teach is that Jesus, in his historical ministry, met with advocates, followers and opponents, and that he advised his disciples not to drive away opposition but to leave that role to the angels. Why is this story, then, called a parable of the kingdom? What relationship does the success or failure of Jesus' teaching have with the kingdom of heaven? Matt. 24–25 pictures God's establishment of his kingdom at the Parousia of the Son of man, and this vision of a future kingdom ties in with the summaries of Jesus' preaching and that of the disciples, who announce the kingdom's imminence (4.17; 10.7). Does this parable contradict these passages in declaring that the kingdom is present? It is not at all clear that it does. The seed is Jesus' preaching, not the kingdom itself. Jesus' teaching predicts the imminence of the kingdom and calls people to meet the conditions of entry, and only in that loose sense is the parable about the kingdom.

13.31–32 The Mustard Seed

There are three versions of this parable, the Matthaean, the Markan (4.30–32) and the Lukan (13.18–19). Luke's is the simplest and focuses on growth, while Mark's and Matthew's exhibit an interest both in growth and in the contrast between the small seed and the large plant (Matthew even calls it a tree, v. 32). Mark's version is a straightforward similitude, but Luke's and Matthew's versions tell stories about what a man did. Mark places the parable after his 'seed growing secretly', Matthew and Luke before the parable of the leaven. The Markan version lacks clarity and calls out for amendment, e.g. *hos* (which) is masculine agreeing with *kokkos* (grain), but *microteron hon* (it is the smallest) is neuter anticipating *sperma* (seed). There are two occurences of *epi tēs gēs* (upon the earth) in the same sentence. The scriptural allusion is slightly different in each of the versions, Mark picturing the plant providing shade for birds (Dan. 4.12, 21; Ezek. 31.6), Matthew and Luke a nesting place (drawing on different parts of Daniel 4.12, 21, and Ezekiel 31.6, and a Psalm, 104.12). In line with the two-source hypothesis, Kingsbury sees the Matthaean parable as a combination of Mark and Q.

Kingsbury draws attention to what he calls the miraculous element in the Matthaean version. He interprets the parable as apologetic directed to Jews, indicating that the kingdom of heaven had already come to Israel in Jesus and the church. The secret which the parable reveals is that 'in bringing his kingly rule in Jesus, God has chosen to manifest it in humility', but 'that his kingly rule through the agency of the church spreads itself out, embracing both Jews and Gentiles, and that God will one day unveil his kingly rule in majesty as a splendid realm' (p. 84). He cites Jeremias' contention (*Parables*, p. 147) that *kataskēnoō* (settle) is a technical eschatological term for the incorporation of Gentiles into the people of God, on the basis of Joseph and Asenath 15. This seems far-fetched. The reference to branches and birds serves rather to point up growth or the contrast between small seed and large tree. Kingsbury's acceptance of Jeremias' point alongside his own interpretation of the tree as the final eschatological kingdom

215

creates difficulties for him since it forces him to treat the tree as the Matthaean church too (p. 82).

Thus Kingsbury has identified the kingdom of heaven with the mustard seed. The introductory statement, as he has frequently made clear, does not necessarily imply such an identification, and asserts no more than that 'it is the case with the kingdom of heaven as with a grain of mustard seed'. Up to this point in the chapter, sowing seeds had represented preaching the word of the kingdom. Does the parable make sense if this meaning is retained? It does. The man is Jesus who sows the seed (preaches the word) in his field (the area of his mission). Although the seed is small (the preaching ministry is not extensive?), it produces astonishing results promoting a growth that will give shelter (gives rise to a community which becomes extensive enough to provide security). The parable may be understood to offer encouragment to the disciples who have just been told not to anticipate the Final Judgment in driving out opponents, since the preaching will be effective enough to give those who respond a secure life.

13.33 The leaven

The two parables, mustard seed and leaven, are juxtaposed in both Matthew and Luke (13.20–21) but are separated in the Gospel of Thomas (20 and 96). Kingsbury therefore considers them originally separate but combined in Q.

Once again, the introductory formula means no more than 'it is the case with the kingdom of heaven as with leaven'. Interpreting it as a companion to the mustard seed, Kingsbury thinks it is directed against the Jewish crowds while encouraging the disciples and revealing the secret 'that the kingdom of God has already appeared, but, contrary to Jewish anticipation, in lowliness; that God is enlarging his kingdom; and that at a time God himself will determine, this kingdom will be revealed in splendour' (p. 87). He has identified the kingdom of heaven with the leaven.

The parable of the leaven is one of the most opaque parables in the gospels, partly because it is so short, and partly because it is unclear which elements are most significant. Should we emphasize the leaven, or the leaven hidden and connect this with the mysteries of 13.11, or the detail that it is a woman who hid the leaven? Taken out of context, numerous meanings are possible. Taken in the Matthaean context, the effectiveness of the small amount of leaven in the large amount of flour could be read as encouragement to the disciples. Although Jesus' ministry is meeting with opposition and may seem to be in danger of failure, the preaching is in fact effective and the effect will gradually become noticeable. This interprets the parable as parallel to the mustard seed in which the sowing of the seed refers to the preaching of the word.

13.34–35

On this optimistic note, the first part of the chapter is brought to a conclusion. Matthew rounds off the scene more explicitly than Mark (4.33–34) by referring to Jesus and the crowds, as in 13.1–2. He also omits the Markan 'but privately to his own disciples he explained everything' because he goes on to describe in detail Jesus' private conversations with the disciples (13.36–52). Both Matthew and Mark stress that Jesus spoke only in parables, 'indeed he said nothing to them without a parable', to recall what had been said earlier about Jesus' reason for speaking in parables (13.10–16). Typically, Matthew completes the section with a formula quotation to show that Jesus' action fulfilled God's will expressed in scripture.

13.36

Jesus' withdrawal into the house marks a scene change. The crowds are left behind and the disciples alone follow him. If, as seems likely, Matthew's depiction of the disciples as a group of Twelve is intended to symbolize the renewal of Israel (the twelve tribes), the group can be seen as a small but representative body responding to Jesus' preaching.

13.36–43 The interpretation of the Parable of the Wheat and the Weeds

Kingsbury claims that the relationship between this explanation and the parable of the wheat and the weeds (13.24–30) 'is formal and accidental rather than real and essential' (p. 94). If this is the case, it is odd that it is introduced by the request 'Explain to us the parable of the weeds in the field' (v. 36). *Diasapheō* means 'to make clear', and the alternative reading with *phrazō* means 'explain, interpret'. That Matthew intended the chapter to be read as seven parables with two explanations, rather than as nine parables, is suggested by his liking for collections of seven, for example the seven woes in chapter 23. Kingsbury rightly accepts Jeremias' proposal that the explanation is either a Matthaean creation or a Matthaean reshaping of material, since it contains so much vocabulary that is distinctive of Matthew (Jeremias, p. 82). He also correctly points out that the explanation is interested in the future harvest, whereas the parable was interested in the present conversation between the householder and his slaves.

The explanation divides everything there is into two camps, in one, the Son of man, the sons of the kingdom, the angels and the Father; in the other, the Devil and the sons of the evil one. Many scholars, however, have been puzzled by the relationships among 'the world', 'the kingdom of the Son of man' and 'the kingdom of their Father'. Some have taken 'world' to be identical with 'the kingdom of the Son of man', which itself is equated with the church. This seems unlikely, since 'world' and 'church' are not identical elsewhere in the gospel, as Kingsbury remarks. But Kingsbury identifies 'the world' as 'the kingdom of the Son of man' in the sense, not of church, but 'the globe as mankind's place of residence' (p. 97). This reading allows him to retain his notion of a present kingdom in the person of Jesus, the Son of man. He then distinguishes 'the kingdom of the Son of man' from 'the kingdom of their Father', the latter being the kingdom established in the future at the Parousia. He does not discuss another possibility, that 'the world' is the sphere of the mission of Jesus and his disciples, and that 'the kingdom of the Son of man' is identical with 'the kingdom of their Father', established at the Parousia of the Son of man. Such an identification has the advantage that it fits the Matthaean picture of the Parousia in chapters 24 and 25, where no distinction is made between the kingdom of the Son of man and the kingdom of the Father. But it has the disadvantage that it has to read 13.41 as an imprecise expression. 'And they will gather out of his kingdom all causes of sin and all evil doers' seems to imply that there are evil doers in the kingdom of the Son of man, whereas there are none in 'the kingdom of their Father'. Is it possible that 13.41 is a loose way of describing the transformation of the world into the kingdom of the Son of man by the removal of evil doers, as depicted in chapters 24–25?

It is clear that Matthew regarded the world as God's creation, and in that sense his realm. The existence of evil in the world, however, was understood to challenge God's sovereignty. Therefore, evil's destruction must be the prelude to the future establishment of God's kingdom. But the parable seems to place 'the kingdom of the Son of man' within an evil world, and this is the strength of Kingsbury's reading. Chapters 24–25 and 13.41 can be made to coincide only if 13.41 is reckoned to be expressed loosely. But is the gospel ever guilty of imprecise expression? Actually, another example seems to occur in this same section. In v. 38, 'The good seed, these are the sons of the kingdom; the weeds are the sons of the evil one' is difficult to interpret unless it is realized that 'the good seed' should read 'the wheat'. If v. 38 is unclear, v. 41 could be too. To allow this, however, may undermine the whole enterprise of redaction criticism, which is based on a close reading of the text and the assumption that 'Matthew is a careful editor'. Recognizing these difficulties, can we nevertheless understand the main force of the passage? Kingsbury sees it as parenetic. 'Jesus, the exalted kyrios, exhorts the Christians of Matthew's church to be sons of the kingdom who do the will of God. Accordingly, this pericope reflects a strong ethical concern which comes to expression in a message put across with the aid of apocalyptic imagery' (p. 109). In this way, the disciples of the narrative are completely identified with the Christians of Matthew's church.

Since Kingsbury had argued that originally parable and interpretation had no essential connexion, he does not consider them together. As his argument is not without difficulties, however, it may be worthwhile asking whether an 'essential' connexion is possible. The parable had advised the slaves/disciples not to separate out weeds/opponents from wheat/followers, but to leave the separation to harvesters/angels. The explanation develops an element of the parable by-passed before, the harvest as the Final Judgment which would destroy all evil-doers. At this point in the narrative, it is just such an assurance which is needed by the disciples, whose mission, like Jesus', is not expected to meet with startling success in worldly eyes (10.17–39). It encourages them to look beyond their present existence to God's transformation.

13.44 and 45–46 The Hidden Treasure and the Pearl
Although these two parables are separated in the Gospel of Thomas (109 and 76), Kingsbury interprets them as companions teaching the same message. Both describe an event in the past, and both are introduced by the usual Matthaean formula 'It is the case with the kingdom of heaven as with . . .'. Again, these short parables are opaque. Kingsbury asks whether the main emphasis should be seen in the great value

of the treasure/pearl, in the sacrifice or the total investment, in the hiddenness, or in the searching and finding. He rejects emphasis on the hiddenness because he identifies the kingdom of heaven with the treasure and the pearl and he thinks the kingdom is already manifest. He rightly rejects stress on searching and finding as far as the hidden treasure is concerned, since the treasure is found accidentally. In the case of the pearl, searching and finding is an element in the story. Kingsbury thinks Matthew wishes to emphasize both value and total commitment. He concludes that in the two parables 'Jesus kyrios calls the members of a church that was suffering from the turmoil of internal and external conflict to be disciples who are unremittingly dedicated to the doing of God's will', and that they reveal the secret 'that the response of the disciple to God's kingly rule is to be one of radical obedience to the will of God. The corollary to this "secret" is that the kingdom of heaven in these pericopes is viewed as a present reality' (pp. 116–117).

Once again, parables addressed to disciples in the narrative are read as immediate reflections of the life of the Matthaean church. It may be as well, however, to examine them in their narrative contexts. The parable of the treasure follows immediately upon the vision of God's eschatological kingdom, with the righteous shining like the sun. Could the treasure hidden then revealed refer back to this parable with its focus on the Final Judgment? If so, it encourages disciples to lose everything now (sell all they have) in order to gain that kingdom (the treasure). Such encouragement is not only appropriate at this point, it fits in with Matthaean instruction to the disciples both before (10.24–39) and after (16.24–27) this section. The disciples can look forward to a life of suffering in this world, but to a life of glory after the Parousia of the Son of man (chapters 24–25). Similar encouragement to dedication is found in the parable of the pearl (13.45–46) with additional advice about seeking and finding like that in 6.33 and 7.7–8.

13.47–50 The Parable of the Net

The vocabulary of this parable echoes that of the interpretation of the wheat and the weeds, which may suggest that it is a Matthaean composition. Kingsbury understands the introduction in the usual way, 'It is the case with the kingdom of heaven as with the drag-net'. He interprets the gathering of fish of every kind: 'In the present age, Jesus kyrios calls men of all nations into God's kingly rule through the medium of his earthly ambassadors' (p. 120). 'Fish of every kind' could refer to 'men of all nations' but not necessarily, since the parable goes on to mention two kinds, 'good' and 'bad'. Moreover, the fishing metaphor applies as much to the historical Jesus and the disciples of the narrative, as it does to the exalted Lord of the church. Fishing is an image of preaching (4.19). Within the narrative, Jesus' ministry attracts both good and bad. The most obvious example of 'the bad' is Judas Iscariot, but even Peter denies Jesus, while the rest of the disciples abandon him. Kingsbury interprets the sorting of the fish uncontentiously as the Final Judgment (p. 121). Since the parable is addressed to the disciples, he assumes that it is about Matthew's church and asks what kind of people Matthew has in mind when he speaks of 'evil ones'. He answers the question by listing examples of evil and double-mindedness in the gospel, such as luke-warm commitment, lovelessness, hatred, betrayal, apostasy and false prophecy (pp. 122–123). He rightly notices that the parable does not mention the fate of the good but warns about the future destruction of the bad. The secret which the parable reveals is 'that while it is the resolve of God that the church, the empirical representative of the Kingdom of Heaven on earth, is in the present age a *corpus mixtum*, it is likewise the resolve of God to terminate this state of affairs in the Great Assize at the End of the Age' (p. 125). Because Kingsbury consistently sees the kingdom as a present reality, he tends to identify the kingdom and the church, as in this statement, in spite of his explicit and correct denial of such an identification. His interpretation of the Parable of the Net is the same as his interpretation of the wheat and the weeds.

Looked at without Kingsbury's blinkers, the parable forms a final note of warning within the narrative. It encourages the disciples with the vision of a successful mission, reminds them that the separation of good and bad must await the eschaton, as in the wheat and the weeds, but unlike the interpretation of that parable which highlights the wonderful fate of the righteous, this parable warns of the fate awaiting 'the bad'.

13.51–52 The conclusion

In Matthew's gospel, Jesus' disciples understand his teaching. They are therefore likened to 'every scribe trained for the kingdom of heaven'. In the gospel, 'scribe' seems to refer to a specific group of disciples (23.34); but, in spite of this, Kingsbury proposes that here 'every scribe' means every disciple as a representative of every member of the church. We saw reason to suppose earlier, however, that the disciples addressed by the discourse were being distinguished from the rest of Jesus' followers (e.g. the slaves (disciples) as distinct from the wheat (other followers of Jesus) in the parable of the wheat and the weeds) and it is likely, then, that only these disciples are seen as scribes with special understanding. Kingsbury interprets 'the householder who brings out of his treasure what is new and what is old': 'so the disciple, in that he knows and does God's will, draws from his heart the revelation God has imparted to him through Jesus' (p. 128). Thus Kingsbury, like Matthew, echoes the teaching of the Sermon on the Mount (6.19–21).

● Assessment of redaction criticism in the light of Kingsbury's study

Kingsbury's book has been taken as an example of redaction criticism because, unlike many others, it is explicit and self-conscious about the method used. It therefore illustrates both the strengths and the weaknesses of the method.

Its strength lies in its recognition that Matthew's use of tradition is a creative endeavour, forging new meanings through the appropriation, ordering and altering of old material and perhaps through juxtaposing it with new material. Inevitably, the study throws into relief the differences between Matthew 13 and its sources, but Kingsbury also treats material which he thinks is derived from Mark or Q as in some sense 'Matthaean' because it has been accepted without alteration when, it is supposed, it could have been rejected or altered. Just how freely redactors could adapt their sources, however, is unknown to us. As we mentioned at the beginning, some redaction critics explain apparent contradictions within a gospel on the supposition that traditions were unalterable, and that redactors could modify them only by adding a 'layer' of contradictory teaching. In this way, the gospels are likened to sedimentary rocks. Geological metaphors seem intrinsically inappropriate for anything as slippery as language, however, and in any case, each synoptic gospel's appropriation of its sources (insofar as these can be defined) has involved some adaptation, which is why there is a 'synoptic problem'. Nevertheless, source criticism has also demonstrated that the synoptic evangelists were in many respects conservative rather than inventive. Although, in Matt. 13, on stylistic grounds, the interpretation of the parable of the wheat and the weeds (vv. 36–43) and the parable of the net of fish (vv. 47–50) may be Matthaean compositions, most of the material in chapter 13 is basically 'traditional', derived from older sources and repeated with minor variations. This is what distinguishes the synoptic gospels from the fourth and the apocryphal gospels, and from other histories of the period, like those of Josephus. The synoptic evangelists seem not to have felt completely free to place their own speeches on the lips of Jesus, presumably because enough traditional material was available to serve their purposes, and because they were interested in history as well as theology.

The weaknesses of the method are obvious enough. Reliance on the two-source hypothesis carries with it all the difficulties which the hypothesis encounters. Moreover, even when details are identified as non-Markan or non-Q, they are not thereby shown to be 'Matthaean' if 'Matthew' stands for the final redactor. Much work has been done to distinguish words and phrases characteristic of the redactor as distinct from his sources, but once sources other than Mark and Q are also posited, criteria for making distinctions between a pre-Matthaean redaction and a final redaction become problematic. Because of this interpreters have moved increasingly towards holistic readings of the final text of each gospel.

A second weakness is the practice, found not only in Kingsbury's work, of reading off the situation of the community directly from its gospel's text. Inevitably, this leads to exaggerated claims for the significance of details. It is not that texts are completely unrelated to the social contexts of their composition but that the relationships which exist are multifaceted. Without independent evidence about each community, it is hazardous to infer the social context from the text alone. Moreover, the urge to relate text and community encourages redaction critics to ignore the narrative level of meaning, as Kingsbury repeatedly does. Any narrative takes on a momentum of its own, which means that it may not reflect immediate social concerns. To cite an example briefly. Even references in the narrative to the inevitable persecution of Jesus' disciples could occur in a text produced in social conditions of different kinds. The teaching could be addressed to a community suffering persecution in order to encourage it to see its life as a reflection of Jesus' and his disciples' and to look beyond it to a hope of resurrection. Alternatively, the same teaching could be addressed to a community living a secure life free from persecution in order to awaken it to a realization that it is not living up to the examples Jesus and

221

his disciples offer. Again, the text could reflect the historical circumstances of Jesus and his first disciples which are described for the community in order to evoke not imitation but sympathy.

It was mentioned earlier that Kingsbury, together with many other interpreters of the First Gospel, supposes that the Matthaean community was concerned about its relations with a neighbouring Jewish synagogue from which it had experienced persecution. The gospel occasionally mentions that the disciples should expect such persecution (e.g. 10.17). Should we, therefore, identify the disciples of the gospel with the Matthaean community? The identification is possible but not necessary. The Acts of the Apostles (e.g. 8.1–3; 9.1–2; 14.45; 17.5–9) and Paul's letters (e.g. Gal. 1.13; II Cor. 11.25) mention that the disciples suffered persecution by Jews. Matthew could be referring to these historical facts without implying that the Matthaean community lived near a Jewish synagogue or suffered a similar fate. Once again, just how far the gospel is recounting past history, and how far it is reflecting its own experiences, are matters about which certainty is impossible.

If redaction criticism is to fulfil its aim of discovering the church situations which explain the redactors' concerns and interests, therefore, it must reckon seriously with a whole range of possible relations between text and context. To do so will yield only tentative conclusions, unless evidence from other writings happens to bear directly on the issue, but tentative conclusions are better than misleading ones.

A third weakness redaction criticism shares with perhaps all other methods of reading texts. It fails to prevent the reader from construing texts in the light of presuppositions which blind to other possibilities. Kingsbury's presupposition that the kingdom of heaven is understood by Matthew to be a present reality 'in the person of Jesus and his church' determines his interpretation of the parables. If, however, most methods of reading fail to prevent blindness, we should see this as a weakness of the reader rather than the method. We have tried to suggest alternative interpretations without abandoning redaction criticism, but readers will be only too aware of the myopia our suggestions exhibit.

Finally, redaction criticism assumes that the meaning of a text is given by the author's intention, as the many references to what Matthew wishes or intends or has in mind in Kingsbury's study testify. We have also adopted this style of presentation in citing Kingsbury's work. Had we independent information about the author's intention in writing the Gospel of Matthew, had we letters, for example, explaining why he wrote as he did, the approach could shed light on the gospel, but we have no such evidence. In any case, trying to look through a text to discover what was going on in the author's mind, in distinction from the words used in the text, is an odd endeavour. It assumes that 'thought' is something different from its expression in the words of the text. We tend to make this glib assumption because we are the heirs of John Locke, whose philosophy proposes a dualistic anthropology separating mind and body. In terms of this anthropology, a text has meaning because a transcendent self, a thinking ego, stands behind the text and gives it meaning. But the meaning of words is not private to individuals but public and cultural. If it were not so, communication would be impossible. Moreover, we cannot think without words.

Naturally, we have all experienced the frustration of our inability to express clearly what we want to say, but this is not because we can think independently of language, but because we are still muddled and have not yet thought precisely enough. We can feel without words, but we cannot think without words.

There is little point, then, in trying to reach behind the text to discover a meaning in the individual author's intention. Literary critics have labelled this attempt 'the intentional fallacy' because it treats all texts as if they were a covert form of autobiography. That the existence of a text implies an author or authors is true, but without independent information, it is possible to consider only the 'implied author' not the actual author. The case of the Pauline epistles is somewhat different. The New Testament contains genuine letters written by Paul, in the first person, at different times and to different churches, which refer to episodes and experiences in his life, as well as plans for the future. There are also other letters, probably written by his followers, and an account of his ministry in the Acts of the Apostles. It is possible to discover something of Paul's biography from a critical examination of these sources, and the biography in turn can be used to throw light on matters discussed in particular sections of his letters. We are not in such a happy position with regard to the redactors of the gospels. That the text of the Gospel of Matthew, written in Hellenistic Greek and influenced by the Scripture which it has taken over from Judaism and made its own, implies a Christian author in the Roman Empire of the first century CE, is something that we learn from the text itself, but that text cannot tell us who the actual author was, far less what he or she 'had in mind' if that was different from what was written. To interpret the gospel, we need simply to pay attention to the meaning of the words in the context of the text and its cultural milieu. This is what we shall attempt to do in the chapter on the Genre of Matthew.

Nevertheless, redaction criticism has performed a useful service in drawing our attention to details which contribute to the overall purpose of each of the gospels, read as a whole. It has made us aware of the fact that one gospel presents a slightly different theology in telling the story of Jesus from another, and it recognizes the historical significance of these differences. It has also paved the way for a variety of holistic readings which will occupy our attention in the following chapters, and which are helpful in understanding what redaction critics sought, namely, the theology of the individual evangelists. As we noted at the beginning of this chapter, our own effort to understand each gospel as a whole will be given under 'Genre'.

Further Reading

N. Perrin, *What is Redaction Criticism?*, Philadelphia and London 1970
G. Stanton (ed.), *The Interpretation of Matthew*, Issues in Religion and Theology 3, London and Philadelphia 1983

15   Structuralism and De-Construction

The search for the author's intention was abandoned by those literary critics who regarded it as fallacious. They rejected the view that the successors of John Locke had proposed, namely, that the meaning of a text can be discerned only by discovering what the author intended. They also rejected an alternative account of meaning, that which advocated a picture theory of language. This proposed that words have meaning because there is a one-to-one relationship between a word and the object in the world to which it refers. In the end, definition of words is achieved by pointing to appropriate objects. The theory seemed to work best for scientific language, however, and some critics who accepted it distinguished this kind of language from that of novels and poetry, which they called 'emotive'.[1] A moment's reflection will show, however, that even in simple, uncomplicated non-literary communication, a picture theory of language proves unhelpful. Should we point to a table in the expectation that you would provide an appropriate word to complete the sense of our statement to you, you would be faced with a number of possibilities, depending on the subject of our conversation. If we had been talking about various items of household funiture, your suggestion 'table' might be appropriate, but if we had been talking about the properties of different kinds of wood, your suggestion 'oak' could be more to the point. Were we to be describing the particular hue of a tan jumper bought in a sale, however, neither of these proposals would be of much help, whereas 'bronze' would be more acceptable. Because of these difficulties, this explanation of meaning, too, was rejected by literary critics, and some of them abandoned all attempts to provide an adequate account of language as reference to the world in favour of a sceptical alternative.

Since language does not correspond to reality in the way the picture theory of language supposed, structuralists assert that language does not refer to the world in any understandable way at all. Rather language is autonomous. Meaning is conveyed, not through reference to the world, not by a transcendental self intending a meaning, but through a system of relations and oppositions internal to language itself. Language has no 'essential' meaning, only a 'relational' one. The most important of these relations is binary opposition. A verbal item, for example, is related both to its contrary (black/white) and to its contradictory (black/not black), and longer items of text are grouped in similar fashion, through parallelism, opposition, inversion or equivalence.

Structuralism, as practised in literary criticism, gained inspiration from the linguistics of Ferdinand de Saussure's *Course in General Linguistics*, 1978, the English translation of lectures given between 1907 and 1911, which proposed that a distinction be made between *langue* (the underlying structure of the language) and *parole* (instances of its use). So structuralism seeks the underlying structure of the text in terms of binary oppositions of a quite general nature, like inversion, which has nothing to do with the content of the text (the particular instance of the use of this structure). The following short extract from Terry Eagleton's *Literary Theory* well illustrates the kind of structure seen to underlie texts:

Suppose we are analysing a story in which a boy leaves home after quarrelling with his father, sets out on a walk through the forest in the heat of the day and falls down a deep pit. The father comes out in search of his son, peers down the pit, but is unable to see him because of the darkness. At that moment the sun has risen to a point directly overhead, illuminates the pit's depths with its rays and allows the father to rescue his child. After a joyous reconciliation, they return home together.

This may not be a particularly gripping narrative, but it has the advantage of simplicity. Clearly it could be interpreted in all sorts of ways. A psychoanalytical critic might detect definite hints of the Oedipus complex in it, and show how the child's fall into the pit is a punishment he unconciously wishes upon himself for the rift with his father, perhaps a form of symbolic castration or a symbolic recourse to his mother's womb. A humanist critic might read it as a poignant dramatization of the difficulties implicit in human relationships. Another kind of critic might see it as an extended, rather pointless word-play on 'son/sun'. What a structuralist critic would do would be to schematize the story in diagramatic form. The first unit of signification, 'boy quarrels with father', might be rewritten as 'low rebels against high'. The boy's walk through the forest is a movement along a horizontal axis, in contrast to the vertical axis 'low/high', and could be indexed as 'middle'. The fall into the pit, a place below ground, signifies 'low' again, and the zenith of the sun 'high'. By shining into the pit, the sun has in a sense stooped 'low', thus inverting the narrative's first signifying unit, where 'low' struck against 'high'. The reconciliation between father and son restores an equilibrium between 'low' and 'high', and the walk back home together, signifying 'middle', marks this achievement of a suitably intermediate state. Flushed with triumph, the structuralist rearranges his rulers and reaches for the next story.

What is notable about this kind of analysis is that, like Formalism, it brackets off the actual *content* of the story and concentrates entirely on the form. You could replace father and son, pit and sun, with entirely different elements – mother and daughter, bird and mole – and still have the *same story*. As long as the structure of *relations* between the units is preserved, it does not matter which item you select.[2]

Moreover, since questions of reference are abandoned, the method takes no interest in history, whether that of the author, the text, its publication, or the social and economic conditions of its readers. The approach is synchronic not diachronic, that is, it treats the text as a unified whole existing at one unspecified time and does not probe it to discover earlier sections or later accretions, as redaction criticism does. The method seems to free the interpreter from the relativism of historical study, while providing a 'scientific' analysis of texts which excludes 'subjective' considerations. 'Binary opposition' seemed scientific to a generation learning to use computers.

An Example: G. Vuillod, 'Exercises on some short stories', *The New Testament and Structuralism*[3]

The essay discovers the underlying structure in the miracle story of the healing of two blind men (Matt. 9.27–31) and this structure, with variations, is then discerned in other biblical narratives of miracle, parable and prophetic proclamation. It is the particular structure of binary opposition which gives the story its meaning as a contract.

Vuillod describes the structure of the healing of the two blind men at two levels, the first less abstract, and the second more abstract. At the first level, the analysis is as follows. D1 and D2 indicate the binary opposites of the story's structure, Jesus on the one hand, and the two blind men on the other.

I	Conjunction		
	– Situation (time-space)	D1	And as Jesus passed on from there
	– Entrance on stage	D2	two blind men followed him;
II	Contract		
	– Request	D2	crying and saying: 'Have pity on us, Son of David.'
	– Conditional Response	D1	And when he arrived at the house, the blind men approached him and Jesus said to them: 'Do you believe that I can do this?'
	– Acceptance	D2	They said to him: 'Yes, Lord.'
	– Consequences: Establishment of the contract	D1 D2	
III	Realization		
	– Implementation of the means: + gesture + speech	D1	Then he touched their eyes, saying, 'Let it be done to you according to your faith.'
	– Result (realization of the contract by D1)		and their eyes were opened

IV	Retribution or Recompense		
	– Warning	D1	And Jesus sternly ordered them saying: 'Do not tell anyone.'
	– Glorification	D2	But they (having departed) told it to all the countryside there.
V	Disjunction		(having departed).

(ET p.48–49)

The oddest part of this analysis is the description of section IV as Retribution or Recompense since it consists of Jesus' warning (D1) and the revelation or glorification of Jesus by the two men after the healing (D2), which is actually their violation of Jesus' prohibition; that is, it could be more aptly described as a second contract which was broken. Nevertheless, Vuillod describes the two men's response as 'the realization of the contract by D2' and he comments, 'As we see it, it is the regularity of this function (i.e. retribution or recompense) which forces us to do this. The first function is a denial of the retribution (i.e. D1, warning); the second is an affirmation' (p. 50). The reader may feel at this point that a structure is being imposed on the text, but Vuillod subsequently explains the difficulty by noticing that the story has two separate functions (see below).

The second level of analysis is called 'the narrative grammar' (pp. 50ff.). At this level, Vuillod omits the introductory and concluding sections from level one, i.e. I Conjunction and V Disjunction, because these sequences are found in all sorts of discourse and are therefore not significant for this particular story. Since structuralism takes its cue from structural linguistics, a story is dissected as a sentence would be, and transformations of the story structure are seen in terms of transformations in the grammar of a sentence. The narrative grammar is expressed as A (the contract with its two functions, demand and acceptance as in Section II above) + F (the confrontation or struggle with two functions, confrontation and success as in Section III above) + C (the consequence as in Section IV above). In the narrative of the healing of the two blind men, there is A, the contract with its demand or request for healing and the acceptance of the request by Jesus. This part of the story contains a complication in the structure, however, because the healing is conditional on the faith of those healed, as the exchanges between Jesus and the men make clear. This condition, suggests Vuillod, dramatizes the contract.

Vuillod next notices that in this story the confrontation, F, is actually replaced by manipulation, Jesus touching the men's eyes and giving the command which issues in the result, the healing. Finally C, the consequence, is pictured as the elimination of the lack (of sight), and also, unusually, as the glorification or revelation of the hero. This doubling is due to the fact that the story functions both on its own (the elimination of the lack) and as part of a larger structure, the whole gospel text, in which the hero (the subject, Jesus) transfers an object (the message of his Messiahship) to the receiver (his followers).

The logic of the contract (II above) is then more fully explored by Vuillod. The contract may involve either a demand or a prohibition. It may be expressed from the perspective of the sender who gives an order or forbids the receiver to act. If he gives an order, the possibilities are again two-fold, expressed diagramatically as follows (p. 53):

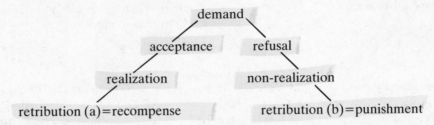

If the sender forbids the receiver to act, again the possibilities are two-fold (p. 55):

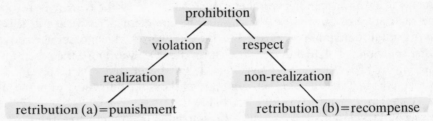

These four possibilities can be expressed as follows:

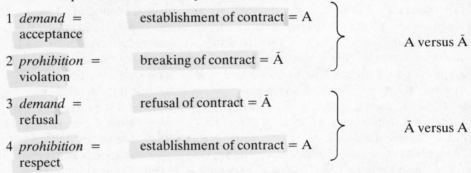

1 *demand* = acceptance   establishment of contract = A

2 *prohibition* = violation   breaking of contract = Ā

A versus Ā

3 *demand* = refusal   refusal of contract = Ā

4 *prohibition* = respect   establishment of contract = A

Ā versus A

2 and 3 are equivalent because in each case the will of the receiver is substituted for that of the sender. 1 and 4 are equivalent because in each the will of the sender is accepted. Vuillod concludes:

> the regularity of the system appears in this completely mechanical exposition. Freedom is only an illusion in these contracts. It is a game within an inexorable structure. All that the sender commands is realized; everything which is transgressed is punished. Retribution always has the last word (p. 60).

Finally, Vuillod discusses possible transformations in the grammar, which can be effected by the suppression and addition of elements, the permutation or movement of elements, and the arrangement of sequences, as in the grammar of sentences. For example, in Matthew 21.28–31, Jesus tells the parable of two sons, one who agrees to carry out his father's command but does not, while the other refuses but does. The story 'suppresses' F, the confrontation, and complicates A, the contrast, by introducing a new dimension of being and appearing. Diagrammatically, it therefore appears as follows (p. 64):

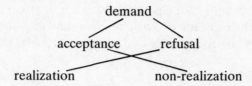

The permutation of elements is illustrated by the story of the Angel Gabriel's announcement of Mary's pregnancy and the birth of her first son in Luke 1.26–38, 46–55, and 2.1–7. In this story, the Disjunction ('And the angel left her') comes before the Realization (the pregnancy and birth) and the Retribution or Recompense (Mary's praise and Joseph's acceptance).

• Application of Vuillod's analysis

The simple basic structure which Vuillod discovers in his exploration of the contract can be seen in many other stories in the Gospel of Matthew. For example, the miracle of cleansing the leper in 8.1–4 exhibits the same structure as that of the healing of the two blind men, this time without the complication of the condition about faith or the final glorification.

I	Conjunction		
	– Situation (time-space)	D1	When he (Jesus) came down from the mountain, great crowds followed him,
	– Entrance on stage	D2	and behold, a leper came to him and knelt before him
II	Contract		
	– Request	D2	saying, 'Lord, if you will, you can make me clean'.
	– Consequence Establishment of the contract	D1 D2	
III	Realization		
	– Implementation of the means: + gesture + speech	D1	And he stretched out his hand and touched him, saying, 'I will; be clean'.
	– Result (realization of the contract by D1)		And immediately his leprosy was cleansed.
IV	Retribution or Recompense		
	– Warning and Command	D1	And Jesus said to him, 'See that you say nothing to any one; but go, show yourself to the priest, and offer the gift that Moses commanded, for a proof to the people'.

229

V   Disjunction

(The story assumes, but does not relate, both the man's departure, and his fulfilment of Jesus' warning and command.)

In the story of the healing of the paralytic, 9.1–8, this structure is both modified and complicated by the inclusion of a dispute between Jesus and the scribes. There are, then, two binary polarities, Jesus and the paralytic with his friends, and Jesus and the scribes.

I   Conjunction
– Situation (time-space)   D1   And getting into a boat, he (Jesus) crossed over and came to his own city.

– Entrance on stage   D2   And behold, they brought to him a paralytic lying on his bed.

II   Contract
– Request   D2   (This is assumed but not stated)
– Initial response   D1   And when Jesus saw their faith, he said to the paralytic, 'Take heart, my son; your sins are forgiven'.

– Dispute   D3   And behold, some of the scribes said to themselves, 'This man is blaspheming'.

– Challenge   D1   But Jesus, knowing their thoughts said, 'Why do you think evil in your hearts? For which is easier, to say "Your sins are forgiven", or to say, "Rise and walk"? But that you may know that the Son of man has authority on earth to forgive sins' –

Consequences:
Establishment of the contract   D1   D2   D3

III Realization
– Implementation of the means + speech (no gesture)   D1   he then said to the paralytic – 'Rise, take up your bed and go home'. And he rose and went home.
– Result (realization of the contract by D1)

IV   Retribution or Recompense (no warning)
– Glorification   D2   When the crowds saw it, they were afraid, and they glorified God, who had given such authority to men.

The two functions, which Vuillod distinguishes in his discussion of the conclusion to the healing of the blind men, and which are also present at the end of the healing of the

230

paralytic, namely, that of the story itself (the elimination of the lack of sight/ movement), and that of the whole gospel (the subject, Jesus, transfers an object, the message of his Messiahship, to the receivers, his followers) may, perhaps, be illustrated again in the stories of exorcisms. For example, the exorcism of the two demoniacs in 8.28–9.1 involves the healing of the demoniacs (the elimination of the lack of sanity) by Jesus, who exorcizes the demons (by Jesus, the Son of God, who destroys God's opponents and thereby conveys the message of his Messiahship to his followers).

I	Conjunction		
	– Situation (time-space)	D1	And when he (Jesus) came to the other side, to the country of the Gadarenes,
	– Entrance on stage	D2	two demoniacs met him, coming out of the tombs, so fierce that no one could pass that way.
II	Contract		
	– Challenge	D3	And behold, they cried out, 'What have you to do with us, Son of God? Have you come to torment us before the time?'
	– Complication	D4	Now a herd of many swine was feeding at some distance from them.
	– Request	D3	And the demons begged him, 'If you cast us out, send us away into the herd of swine'.
	Consequence Establishment of the contract	D1 D3	
III	Realization		
	– Implementation of the means + speech (no gesture)	D1	And he said to them, 'Go'. So they came out and went into the swine;
	– Result (realization of the contract by D1)		
IV	Retribution or Recompense	D3 D4	and behold, the whole herd rushed down the steep bank into the sea, and perished in the waters.
	– Complication	D5	And the herdsmen fled, and going into the city they told everything, and what had happened to the demoniacs.
V	Disjunction (preceded by a second Conjunction)	D5 D6	And behold, all the city came out to meet Jesus; and when they saw him, they begged him to leave their neighbourhood.
		D1	And getting into a boat, he crossed over.

231

The demoniacs themselves, D2, play no part in the story after the initial conjunction, except that they are referred to in the report of the herdsmen. Their healing is assumed, not described. The story centres instead on the battle between Jesus and the demons, who recognize him as Son of God. It therefore functions in the same way as the glorification in other healing miracles as far as the disciples (or readers) are concerned, but not for the herdsmen and citizens who respond negatively. The fourth part of the structure, Retribution, is highlighted in the destruction of the demons with the swine they had entered. Again, the Disjunction is unusual, in that Jesus is the one to leave, not the healed men.

The same structure, with variations, can be discerned in stories other than healings, for example in the two narratives of Jesus calling disciples in Matthew 4.18–22.

First story (vv. 18–20)

I	Conjunction		
	– Situation (time-space)	D1	As he (Jesus) walked by the Sea of Galilee, he saw
	– Entrance on stage	D2	two brothers, Simon who is called Peter, and Andrew his brother, casting a net into the sea; for they were fishermen.
II	Contract		
	– Request	D1	And he said to them, 'Follow me, and I will make you fishers of men'.
	– Acceptance	D2	Immediately, they left their nets and followed him.
	Consequences: Establishment of the contract	D1 D2	
III	Realization		(This is depicted throughout the rest of the gospel. The contract is realized in the disciples' mission (10.5–42), it is broken in Andrew's desertion (26.56) and in Peter's denial (26.69–75), but is re-instated in 28.16–20.)
IV	Retribution or Recompense		(There is no retribution for the disciples' failure to realize the contract. On the contrary, it is re-instated.)
V	Disjunction		(This element can play no part in a story which involves a contract to follow Jesus.)

232   The narrative is an example of the contract: demand-acceptance-realization-

recompense, with a complication in the realization (failure then acceptance). In contrast to the previous stories, in which people request Jesus' help, in this story it is Jesus who makes the request (D1). Also, in this story the final element, Disjunction, is lacking. The second call story (vv. 21–22) has the same structure as the first, and differs only in supplying less detail by omitting the words by which Jesus called the disciples.

Some parables, too, are structured in the same way. Besides the example of the two sons discussed by Vuillod, we may cite a more elaborate example from 25.14–30, the parable of the talents. This narrative is developed in two respects, firstly by describing separate contracts between the man and each of his three servants, and, secondly, by introducing a Disjunction after the contract is made, then a subsequent Conjunction, at which accounts are settled in three different ways, and a final Disjunction, after each servant had received his own Recompense.

Another parable, the ungrateful servant in Matthew 18.23–35, varies the structure in quite a new manner. First of all, the non-fulfilment of the contract by the servant meets with no Retribution, but, when the servant fails to repeat this pattern in relation to his own debtors, the lord finally carries out the full retribution previously withheld.

• Assessment of Vuillod's analysis

Vuillod has discovered a basic structure which is exhibited in many of the stories in Matthew's gospel, and elsewhere in other biblical passages, and the application of the structure helps to bring to light the slight variations from one example to another. There is no doubt that this kind of analysis is very satisfying. It reduces a mass of incoherent detail into variations of a simple structure of binary opposition, it replaces chaos with clarity, it overcomes muddled humanism with scientific precision. But the satisfaction is gained at a high price. Reduction becomes reductionism. To return to Vuillod's main example, 9.27–31, the text 'Two blind men followed him, crying aloud, Have mercy on us Son of David. When he entered the house, the blind men came to him; and Jesus said to them, Do you believe that I am able to do this? They said to him, Yes, Lord . . . He said, . . . according to your faith . . .' becomes 'The Contract' (with the slight complication of the condition). Then F, the confrontation, is actually no confrontation at all but a manipulation by touch and speech. This detail distinguishes the healing of the two blind men from a number of other healing miracles which are structured as confrontations between Jesus and demons. Finally, the text 'And Jesus sternly charged them, See that no one knows it. But they went away and spread his fame through all that district' is misdescribed as 'Retribution or Recompense' when, more appropriately, it could have been reckoned a second demand which was violated. This would mean, however, that Vuillod's generalization, 'Retribution always has the last word' is contradicted, since Jesus' demand for silence is disobeyed by the two men without their blindness returning.

It is only the level of abstraction, in other words, that makes the Matthaean stories look alike. At this level of abstraction, all texts are *made* to look similar. Moreover, the abstract level which gives 'the meaning' seems so remote from the details which

233

create the appeal of the particular story that it is difficult to be interested in structuralism's meaning at all. Most readers of the healing story in Matthew 9 would like answers to such questions as: What is a miracle? What were miracles thought to be in the first century Hellenistic world? Why is the term 'Son of David' used? Why two blind men instead of one? What is the relationship between sight and insight in the narrative? These questions, of course, concern references, both historical and philosophical, which have been abandoned by structuralism, but the reader can hardly help feeling the enforced impoverishment.

Nevertheless, structuralism has brought two major gains to literary criticism. It has shown that what at first seems 'natural' in literature is actually 'cultural'. Stories do not tell everything that could be told about a situation or event. They select and order particular elements, they foreground some matters and leave others unnoticed. More generally, stories, just because they have a beginning, a middle and an end, make life into destiny and duration into meaningful time. The synoptic gospels not only present Jesus' life as the completion of a comprehensible mission, but they thereby give meaning to the whole of human history as part of God's creation and recreation. We shall return to this insight when defining the genres of the gospels.

Secondly, structuralism's articulation of literary relations is a useful device which helps the reader to notice both what is present and what could have been present but is absent from a text, as was demonstrated by the variations of Vuillod's structure in the examples discussed.

Second Example: G. Genette, *Narrative Discourse*[4]

It was stated at the beginning that structuralism finds no 'essential' but only 'relational' meaning in texts. We have illustrated one aspect of this endeavour by examining the contract structure which Vuillod discerns. Genette's study of time and focus in Proust explores other aspects, namely, the binary relations which exist between 'the story' on the one hand and 'the narrative' in which it is told on the other. His careful elucidation of possible relations between any narrative and any story, in terms of time and focus, allows us, once again, to see what kinds of selections the gospel narratives are making. He provides a grid which can be placed over them so that we can see both what is present and what is absent. His study has been used to shed light on the narrative techniques of the Fourth Gospel by R. A. Culpepper.[5]

No attempt can be made here to present Genette's study in all its subtlety. What follows will be a brief sketch of those points relevant to literary relations within the synoptic gospels. His account of time is divided into three sections, order, duration and frequency.

'**Order**' concerns the possible relations between the temporal order of events in the story and the pseudo-temporal order of their arrangement in the narrative. These two orders may coincide, as they very often do in the synoptic gospels, although the progress of time is marked vaguely with 'and', 'after this', 'again'. On the other hand, they may not. For example, Mark relates the meeting of Jesus with a spirit-possessed man in 5.2 and then gives an account of the man's life before the meeting took place, in 5.4–5. Similarly, John the Baptist's death is assumed to be an accomplished fact (Mark 6.14), and later, the way in which he came to die is described (6.17–29). In these instances, the order of the story and that of the narrative are discordant. Sometimes, the temporal relation between one event and another is left open. For example, it is not clear exactly when Judas committed suicide or the chief priests bought the field with the money he returned, in relation to the time of Jesus' trial before Pilate, in Matt. 27.3–10 and 11–26. Occasionally, one event in the story is described as happening at the same time as another. For example, Peter denies Jesus three times (Matt. 26.69–75) while Jesus is being tried before the Sanhedrin (Matt. 26.57–68), or Luke relates that the Pharisees were 'lying in wait for him (Jesus), to catch at something he might say. *In the meantime*, when so many thousands of the multitude were gathered together . . . he began to say . . .' (11.54–12.1). Sometimes the narrative recalls an event already described. For example, in remarking the disciples' slowness to recognize who Jesus is, the narrator explains 'for they did not understand about the loaves, but their hearts were hardened' (Mark 6.52), recalling the story of the feeding of the five thousand in 6.37–44.

A complete temporal **ellipsis** occurs between the birth narratives (Matt. 1–2) and the account of John the Baptist's ministry during which Jesus is reintroduced as an adult, without the slightest hint of what had happened in between. The child Jesus arrives at Nazareth in 2.23 and is next mentioned after John's preaching in 3.13, 'Then Jesus came from Galilee to the Jordan to John'. Between these two verses, years have elapsed but the reader is left to recognize this without help. Luke fills in the gap and adds details. Luke 2.41–51 describes Jesus' visit to Jerusalem at the age of twelve, and concludes the section 'And Jesus increased in wisdom and stature and in favour with God and man' (2.52), a generalization which spans the period until he is reintroduced in 3.21 at his baptism, immediately after which, another statement registers the passing of time, 'Jesus when he began his ministry was about thirty years old' (3.23).

Another kind of chronological discordance is created by **anticipation**, when the narrative hints at or describes events which are yet to take place in the story. In the synoptics, the best examples are prophecies placed on the lips of Jesus, as in the predictions of his own death and resurrection (e.g. Mark 8.31 and parr.) or of Judas' betrayal (Mark 14.18 and parr.) or of the desertion of the disciples (Mark 14.27// Matt. 26.31). Only in the case of Judas' betrayal is it the narrator who anticipates the later occurrence by calling him 'the betrayer' when he is first introduced (Mark 3.19 and parr.). The fulfilment of these predictions later in the story both gives it a unity and creates confidence in Jesus' trustworthiness which may then be extended to predictions made by him that are unfulfilled in the story (e.g. Mark 13.1–37 and parr.). To modern sensibility, these anticipations may appear to mar the story by destroying the sense of surprise at what transpires, but another kind of suspense, that of not knowing *when* the inevitable will happen, is actually created by the device.

'**Duration**' concerns the 'speed' of the narrative, that is the relation between the duration of events in the story and the length of the text in telling them. All narratives vary the speed. For example, almost the whole of Jesus' ministry is related in Mark

235

1.14–13.37, while two complete chapters are devoted to the last few days of his life (14.1–15.47). In general, the recounting of direct speech slows down the narrative, while summaries like Mark 1.32–34, Matt. 19.1–2 or Luke 19.47–48 increase the speed. The five long discourses in Matthew (5–7; 10; 13; 18; 24–25) slow the narrative at those points. Luke presents only three shorter discourses (6.20–49; 8.4–15; 21) and, instead, places much of Jesus' teaching during his long journey from Galilee to Jerusalem (9.51–19.27). Mark provides two discourses (4.2–34; 13). Otherwise, the synoptics intersperse dialogue and action to create a tempo which is somewhere between the speed of the summary and that of the long monologue. What is almost completely lacking in these narratives, however, is the 'descriptive pause' which sets the scene of an event in an extended account of the environment. On the contrary, such settings are indicated with the utmost brevity – 'on the mountain' (Matt. 5.1), 'at home' (Mark 2.1), 'in the Temple' (Luke 20.1). Also, next to nothing is said about the physical appearance of characters within the story. Naturally, these omissions increase the general tempo by allowing a greater proportion of the narrative to be taken up with action.

'**Frequency**' concerns various types of repetition. The possibilities may be set out as follows:

> What happens once in the story is related once.
> What happens more than once in the story is related the same number of times.
> What happens once in the story is related more than once.
> What happens more than once in the story is related once.

The synoptic gospels usually restrict themselves to the first two possibilities. Nevertheless, in Acts, there are three accounts of the single incident of Paul's vision on the Damascus road (Acts 9.1–9; 22.3–11; 26.12–18), one by the narrator and two in Paul's speeches. Also, Luke indicates that Jesus customarily attended the synagogue (4.16), suggesting that what is narrated once happened many times.

Genette's study of *focus* has two aspects, mood and voice. '**Mood**' explicates the point of view of the narrative or its **focalization**, as well as measuring the greater or lesser distance it keeps from what it tells. For example, greater distance is created by the reporting of speech indirectly than directly, since direct speech is dramatic and mimetic. Indirect speech 'says less and in a more mediated way' (p. 163). The synoptics eschew distance by using direct speech, but do not attempt to develop a distinctive style for each character. Luke–Acts tries to conform speeches in Galilee and Jerusalem to the Septuagint style while speeches outside of Palestine are more Hellenistic, but these are distinctions of place not character. Similarly, events can be described more or less 'realistically'. The inclusion of a superfluous detail creates the illusion of immediacy and mimesis, as in the case of Mark's 'to sit down in companies upon the green grass' (6.39). But such details are infrequent in the synoptics. Moreover, distance is retained by the third-person, rather than first-person, narration.

Genette asserts that three different **focalizations** are possible in narrative, that in which the narrator is omniscient, that in which the narrator is one of the characters in the story whose point of view is therefore restricted, and that in which the narrator tells less than the characters know, to create mystery or adventure. The synoptic gospels are of the first type, the narrator is omniscient, although his presence is unobtrusive. For example, the narrator of Mark knows who Jesus truly is (1.1), when divine prophecies are fulfilled (1.2–4), what the heavenly voice said to Jesus alone (1.11), when the Holy Spirit is active (1.12), what Satan, the demons and angels are doing (1.13, 24), and how people feel (1.22, 27, 41; 2.6). The Matthaean and Lukan narrators are similarly aware of everything, from the inner experiences of people (Matt. 2.3; 12.1; Luke 2.19, 50; 4.32; 9.33; 23.8) to the divine purpose (Matt. 8.17; 12.17–21; Luke 7.30; 8.1; 9.43).

The focus of a narrative is also effected by '**voice**', a subject which Genette approaches from three different angles, the time of narrating, the narrative level, and the person, all of which express relations between the narrator and the story told. In Greek (as in English) the story cannot be related without using the present, past or future tenses of verbs, and thereby indicating the relative temporal positions of narrator and story. The synoptic gospels tell their story in the past tense without clarifying how much time has passed between that of the story and that of the narration. Not even in the case of Luke–Acts, which provides a first-person preface (Luke 1.1–4; Acts 1.1), is the interval of time specified. The preface refers to the present dedication of the work to Theophilus and looks back to earlier attempts at recounting the story before actually beginning its own version in Luke 1.5. At the end of the Acts of the Apostles, however, the story finishes before any connexion can be made between it and the time of narrating.

Genette defines the 'narrative level' by saying that any event recounted is at a level immediately 'above' that at which the narrating act producing this narrative is placed. In Luke–Acts, the first person narrator who dedicates the work is at a 'lower' level than the narrative itself and the characters within the story. In Acts, there is a complication of narrative levels, since characters within the story also relate in the summary form of speeches things described in the first book. Compared to the complications of levels in modern fiction, however, the synoptic gospels maintain only the simplest distinctions.

Finally, '**person**' refers to the differences between first-person and third-person narration. Luke–Acts includes first-person narration in the preface and the 'we-sections' of the travelogue in Acts, but the presence of the narrator is felt throughout all three synoptics, in spite of the fact that the narrator is not one of the characters in the story. He is there to explain what is puzzling. He translates foreign terms (e.g. Mark 5.41; Matt. 27.46), or customs (e.g. Mark 7.3–4; Luke 1.8–9), draws out implications (e.g. Mark 7.19; Matt. 7.49; 13.58), makes connexions (e.g. Mark 6.52; Matt. 2.23; Luke 20.27), and alerts the reader (e.g. Mark 13.14; 8.32). His presence is generally unobtrusive, however, because the gospels use their main protagonist, Jesus, to present the narrator's point of view, so that one reinforces the other.

What Genette achieves in his study is a clarification of rhetorical techniques, and his insights could greatly advance and refine New Testament rhetorical criticism, to which we shall turn later. But this 'appreciation' of structuralism would be regarded as suspect by structuralists themselves. Christopher Norris warns, 'The *concept* of structure is easily kidnapped by a tame methodology which treats it as a handy organising theme and ignores its unsettling implications.'[6]

De-construction

The 'unsettling implications' stem from the philosophical position which structuralism espouses, namely, that texts have only a relational not an essential meaning. These implications have been developed further in the work of the French philosopher, Jacques Derrida, who claims to find a latent idealism even in structuralism. Our language is so imbued with the belief in a transcendent rational self that it is impossible to escape from it except by inventing new forms of expression. This is why his writings are peppered with words crossed out, and why he was forced to invent a new French word, *différance*, to capture the elusive quality of language. *Différance* picks up the insights of structuralism, that language has a 'relational' not an 'essential' meaning, in that binary opposition points to differences, but in French the word also carries the nuance 'defer'. All meaning is open ended and deferred. Any text conveys its meaning through the oppositions expressed, but no text completely explores the possibilities inherent in language. In this sense, all texts provide partial views, and it is important for the reader to notice what is *not* expressed in the text, what is absent, what the very shape of the text excludes from discussion. Once this is recognized, the structure begins to collapse, and the text is de-constructed. For example, the synoptic gospels shape their worlds in theological terms, and, in so doing, they virtually exclude the psychological dimension. They show little interest in the development of character or the self-consciousness of protagonists. Nevertheless, occasional references to human motives undermine the neatness of the structure.

Furthermore, Derrida seeks to de-centre the 'self' of Western metaphysics, including the foundation which it implicitly provides as the ground for the structure of structuralism. There is no 'self' transparently present in discourse, since it is discourse which defines who the 'self' is. This scepticism may seem to offer little to New Testament critics, yet it serves as a useful reminder that even theology is a construct which often envisages God as a 'self' who 'grounds' the discourse. In so doing, the structure also excludes as much as it includes, emphasizing the transcendent to the exclusion of the immanent. In particular, theological writing tries to efface its own nature as text. Moreover, Derrida's rejection of traditional questions of reference has led him to explore an alternative. Although for him texts do not refer immediately to the world, they do refer to other texts. The interrelatedness of texts, their 'intertextuality', raises important issues for interpreters of the synoptic gospels, some of which have already been treated under source criticism, and others will be explored later in the discussion of genre. Derrida, however, would not restrict discussion of the interplay of texts to questions of source and genre, since completely different genres, like those exemplified by psychological and theological writings, also throw light upon one another.

For the moment, we shall turn to an alternative interest of post-structuralist literary criticism, popular in Western Germany and North America, which focuses neither on the author nor on the text, but on the reader.

Further Reading

A. M. Johnson Jr (ed.), *The New Testament and Structuralism*, Pittsburg Theological Monograph Series 11, Pittsburg 1976

D. Patte (ed.), *Semiology and Parables*, Pittsburg Theological Monograph Series 9, Pittsburg 1976

Semeia, volumes from 1974–1978

R. Detweiler (ed.), *Derrida and Biblical Studies*, Missoula 1982

16   Rhetorical Criticism and the 'Implied Reader'

Reading 'is a kaleidoscope of perspectives, pre-intentions, recollections. Every sentence contains a preview of the next and forms a kind of viewfinder for what is to come; and this in turn changes the "preview" and so becomes a viewfinder for what has been read'.[1]

Many of us are inclined to see reading as a process in which one object, the reader, is affected by another object, the literary text. Each of the objects is conceived as a self-contained entity, bearing no obvious relation to the other. Reader-response critics like Wolfgang Iser are seeking to make us aware of the social dimensions of reading as a creative and cultural enterprise. They draw to our attention the fact that in reading, the reader tries to *make* sense of what is read, filling in gaps to *make* clear what is left vague. The reader forms the work into a coherent whole, making the potentially unlimited and unmanageable into the limited and manageable. The reader is not a passive object but an agent engaged in creating meaning. Nevertheless, the individual is not isolated in this creative endeavour, but is a member of a linguistic and cultural community that provides the competence for the success of the enterprise.

Moreover, reading is a temporal rather than a spatial experience. It takes time to read each sentence and in doing so we gain expectations of what will come in the next sentence. When our expectations are thwarted, we begin to perceive that the first sentence did not mean what we took it to mean and revise our understanding accordingly. When a text remains ambiguous, however, it forces the reader to pause and reflect.

Reader-response criticism explores the dialectic of text and reader. On the one hand, the text controls the reader's response through its own strategies and conventions, selecting and arranging from contingencies those matters and patterns which it requires the reader to notice. On the other hand, the reader must actualize the world of the text in such a way as to be moved and enlightened by it. Some reader-response critics pay more attention to the strategies of the text and some to the psychology of the reader. Rhetorical criticism focuses attention on the former.

Just *how* the text contrives to control the reader's response is its subject. It is a close examination of the techniques which guide the reader in construing the meanings of a text. This kind of criticism, then, does not undertake an historical quest to discover the actual readers of a text at any particular period and how they understood that text, but is concerned with the 'implied reader' defined by the strategies employed.

An Example: Robert M. Fowler, *Loaves and Fishes: The Function of the Feeding Stories in the Gospel of Mark*[2]

The dissertation makes a detailed study of the two feeding miracles in Mark 6.30–44 and 8.1–10. It begins by using the method of redaction criticism and demonstrates that the paucity of Markan characteristics in the story of the feeding of the four thousand, 8.1–10, indicates the use of a pre-Markan tradition with a redactional introduction and conclusion. On the other hand, the ubiquitous instances of Markan style in the feeding of the five thousand in 6.30–44 suggest that it is a Markan composition, and the integral part the pericope plays in the Markan narrative of chapters 6–8 confirms the suggestion. This means that the disciples' question in 8.4, 'How can one feed these men with bread here in the desert?', takes on a new and ironical significance. It is 'ironical' (a word which should be distinguished from 'sarcastic'), because the reader is in a position to recognize a significance which the characters within the story fail to notice. In this case, the ignorance and denseness of the disciples is highlighted because they had already witnessed a feeding miracle in the desert. Their stupidity is culpable, and the reader is led to evaluate them accordingly. The message is then reinforced by 8.17–21. Jesus is pictured exasperated by them:

> Having eyes do you not see, and having ears do you not hear? And do you not remember? When I broke the five loaves for the five thousand, how many baskets full of broken pieces did you take up? They said to him, Twelve. And the seven for the four thousand, how many baskets full of broken pieces did you take up? And they said to him, Seven. And he said to them, Do you not yet understand?

The recognition of the interplay of the two episodes in the Markan story leads Fowler to express dissatisfaction with a redaction criticism which defines the work of the redactor only in relation to the seams, summaries and insertions into traditional material. He does not belittle the usefulness of the distinction between redaction and tradition, but he affirms that the tradition has become an integral part of the final redaction, making a holistic reading essential. Having noticed the ironical significance of Mark 8.4, he turns to the work of literary critics like Wayne Booth to help with an elucidation of the phenomenon in Mark. Booth made a short study of the Markan passion narrative, in which he shows that the reader understands the ironical significance of the mockery of Jesus as Messiah and Son of God, since, like the centurion, the reader knows that Jesus is truly the Son of God (Mark 1.1).[3] Booth speculates that the effect of irony, rather than plain statement, is to create a larger community of understanding readers because it draws them into sympathetic communion with the narrator and his protagonist, Jesus. Fowler remarks, 'Irony is an especially seductive ploy since it tends to create a comfortable, secure, self-congratulatory community of readers who have successfully deciphered the author's ironies' (p. 96). Perhaps the adjectives 'comfortable, secure, self-congratulatory' are less than appropriate in this case, since the Markan account of discipleship emphasizes its uncomfortable, insecure and self-denying aspects, as Fowler's study makes clear, but certainly, irony involves the reader in the act of deciphering.

Doublets. The importance of reading one feeding miracle in the light of another prompts Fowler to consider other doublets in the Markan narrative. He explores the doublet of the sea stories in Mark 4.35–41 and 6.45–52, and the doublet of the healing stories in Mark 7.31–37 and 8.22–26. He notices resemblances among these doublets and that of the feeding miracles, like the fact that there is a dual element in three of them: a calming of both wind *and* sea (4.35–41), a banquet of bread *and* fish (6.30–44) and a healing of a man who is deaf *and* mute (7.31–37). In the other three stories, a single element dominates: Jesus' walking on the sea (6.45–52), the emphasis on bread (8.1–10) and the healing of blindness (8.22–26). Also, in the first sea story and the first feeding miracle, the miracles meet the disciples' expressed need, whereas in the second of each, it is Jesus who takes the initiative. Moreover, both sea stories and both feeding miracles display the disciples' blindness. They fail to understand Jesus and to perceive the scope of his mission, and 6.51f. makes the connexion, 'They were utterly astounded (at Jesus' walking on the water), for they did not understand about the loaves, but their hearts were hardened'.

A link is made between the two sea stories by the mention of the wind in each. The first draws attention to the obtuseness of the disciples who fail to recognize that Jesus is the Son of God even when faced with his control of wind and sea. Their final question, 'Who then is this that even wind and sea obey him?' therefore operates on two levels. It records the blindness of the disciples, but also reminds the reader of what had already been declared in the opening verses of the gospel, that Jesus is the Messiah, Mark 1.1. Recognizing that this first sea-story forms a backdrop to the second then helps to explain an otherwise peculiar statement in 6.48, that Jesus 'meant to pass by them'. Jesus' intention was not, then, to rescue disciples threatened by the wind, but to reveal his identity. Only the stupidity of the disciples, their inability to recognize him, forces him to abandon his plan. Again, Jesus is revealed to the reader, but the disciples remain ignorant.

The two healing miracles also take on added significance in this context. Much of the phraseology in the two accounts is identical (pp. 105f.). The dissimilarities are determined by the different ailments to be cured. In neither, however, do the disciples play any part. Rather, the relationship of these stories to the disciples is one of contrast, sharpening the focus on their inability to hear, speak and see by showing that Jesus brings hearing, speech and sight to others. Noting the interrelationships among all these stories then helps to elucidate another puzzle in the Markan presentation, 8.14–21, which can now be recognized as a passage which brings all six together: the setting in the boat, the lack of bread, Jesus' characterization of the disciples' failure to perceive, their blindness and deafness, and his attempt to penetrate their dullness by reminding them of the feeding miracles and asking how many baskets of fragments they had taken up after each. When they answer correctly, Jesus replies with a final rhetorical question, 'Do you not yet understand?' The passage prompts the readers, as Jesus' question prompts the disciples, to supply the answer that Jesus is the Messiah (1.1).

Next, Fowler examines other stories in the context of Mark 6–8 to discover their relationship to the six. Mark 6.6b–13 and 30 depict the mission of the disciples, which ends in their failure to discern who Jesus is. Again, bread is at issue. Jesus commands them to take none, and their production of five loaves in the desert shows that they have disobeyed. They also produce bread for the second feeding, and then their concern about having none forces the reader to recognize their denseness.

What part, then, does Mark 6.14–29, Herod's inquiry about Jesus and his order to execute John the Baptist, play in this sequence? Why is it placed where it is, between the beginning and end of the disciples' mission? Fowler suggests that the introduction of four major characters at this point, Herod, John the Baptist, Elijah and a prophet, invites the comparison of Jesus' role with theirs. So Herod's banquet expresses his kingship as Jesus' expresses his, and each sends out men to undertake his commission. It could be, although Fowler does not mention this, that the story of Herod is juxtaposed with the disciples' mission because the disciples understand Jesus' kingship to be like Herod's. Comparison of Jesus with a prophet, on the other hand, has already been made by Jesus himself in 6.4, and the feeding miracles may allude to those of Elijah and Elisha, although Fowler admits this is uncertain (p. 128). Finally, the mention of the Baptist's death casts a shadow over Jesus, since the two are associated throughout the gospel, with John playing the role of Elijah. Pilate's treatment of Jesus will come to mirror Herod's of John.

The presence of the banquets in these chapters leads Fowler to raise general questions about the functions of meals in Mark's gospel (p. 132). He notes both the frequency of metaphorical references to meals (7.27, 8.15, 10.38) and the metaphorical interpretations of meals (2.15–17, 18–20, 14.22–25). Since the disciples fail to understand Jesus, he is the one who has to defend their behaviour when it comes under criticism from his opponents, 'Can the wedding guests fast while the bridegroom is with them?' (2.18–20, see also 7.1–23). Further, because commentators have often suggested that the two feeding miracles are in some sense 'eucharistic', Fowler examines the connexion with the eucharistic narrative in Mark 14.17–25. Fowler's concern, however, is to read Mark 14 against the backdrop of the earlier stories and not vice-versa (pp. 135 and 145). He emphasizes that on the first reading of the gospel, it is the feeding miracles that give readers clues about how to understand the final meal, although he admits that a second reading could also reverse the process. But he does not consider the social situation of the first reading. If it was the case that the community actually celebrated the eucharist, their experience would inform their first reading as well as their second. The advantage of Fowler's procedure can be seen in the way he makes sense of what otherwise would appear odd in the account of chapter 14. He draws attention to the recurrence of the dominant theme of the disciples' failure which he discovered in the earlier stories. In chapter 14, one of the disciples, Judas Iscariot, is plotting to have Jesus killed (14.1–2, 10–11), and the first words of Jesus at the meal declare that he is to be 'delivered up' by one of the Twelve (14.18, 20). Moreover, all the disciples will be offended and scattered (14.27–31) and Peter will deny Jesus. The eucharistic words of Jesus, therefore, are deliberately sandwiched between these two prophecies of betrayal.

The reliable narrator and irony. It becomes clear as Fowler's study develops that an adequate consideration of any individual story in the Gospel of Mark must reckon seriously with its context and function within the whole gospel, as redaction criticism had already demonstrated. More than this, however, the recognition that individual statements can operate on more than one level, both within the story and for the reader, raises the general problem of how a text can make its ironical significance known to the reader. This is the subject of Fowler's final chapter (iv), where he takes an exploratory excursion along the path towards the rhetorical criticism of the whole gospel by providing a list of ways in which the text communicates a perspective to the reader from which to understand the significance of the events described, or as he explains: 'We will note the ways in which the author furnishes a stable, reliable store of knowledge for the reader, just the kind of knowledge over against which an author may construct stable, covert ironies' (p. 154).

Author, implied author and narrator. Fowler could usefully have made a distinction between 'actual author' about whom information is required apart from the text itself, 'implied author' who is the author implied by the particular text, and the 'narrator' who relates the narrative. To take a modern example from fiction, the author of *The Kingdom of the Wicked* is Anthony Burgess,[4] a man born in Manchester in 1917 and currently living in Monaco. A great deal is known about Burgess and about his other literary and musical works. By contrast, the author of the Gospel according to Mark is unknown. Nor are we sure when or where the work was produced because no reliable external information is available. On the other hand, the text itself tells us who the 'implied author' is. *The Kingdom of the Wicked* implies an author who writes in English but knows or has inherited some Greek, Latin, Aramaic and Hebrew expressions. He has an interest both in the origins of Christianity, seen from a Roman Catholic tradition, and in the everyday life of the inhabitants of the Roman Empire in the first century CE. The 'implied author' of Mark is a first-century CE writer of popular Hellenistic Greek who knows or has inherited some Hebrew and Aramaic expressions (e.g. Mark 15.34; 5.41) and is familiar with Scriptures. The 'narrator' of *The Kingdom of the Wicked* is Sadoc, an ex-shipping clerk, suffering from the infirmities that old age brings after a dissolute life, who is spending his final days completing his father's chronicle about Jesus the Carpenter. In other words, this narrator is also a character with his own limited point of view. In the case of Mark, however, the narrator never addresses the implied reader in the first person to give information about himself. He serves merely as the spokesman of the 'implied author'. It is the narrator who provides the point of view from which to understand the narrative, but he may be a reliable or unreliable guide. Fowler might also have distinguished the 'implied reader' from any actual readers of the text. The 'implied reader' is the reader encoded by the rhetorical strategies, that is, the reader who appropriately apprehends those strategies. In this instance, the 'implied reader' is the reader who appreciates irony.

Reliable information. Fowler claims that the Gospel of Mark provides 'reliable' information in a number of different ways. Firstly, the social, ethical and religious norms in the work are consistently adhered to and there are no contradictory tendencies that leave the reader confused. Moreover, the omniscient narrator, who can see into the minds and emotions of his characters, is shown to be a reliable commentator by the use of a particular kind of repetition, that in which the narrator tells the implied reader what will happen and then depicts it as happening (e.g. Mark 3.19; 14.17–21; 14.43). A special instance of this, says Fowler, is the description of Jesus' prophecies which are later fulfilled (e.g. Mark 8.31; 14.43; 16.8). But the voice of the narrator and that of Jesus, the main character in the story, cannot simply be identified, as Fowler admits later in his discussion of characters.

Fowler lists seven ways in which reliable knowledge is communicated to the implied reader, but not all of his categories are equally pertinent. We shall discuss those points which are convincing, and afterwards explain why the others are less helpful. The numbers are Fowler's.

I *The narrator's direct comments*

First of all, a kind of collusive contact is made with the implied reader by the narrator's direct comments. There are few of these in Mark, but they serve their purpose. The prime example is 13.14 'Let the reader understand'. Unfortunately, just what the first readers were meant to understand is unclear to modern readers. What was 'the desolating sacrilege set up where it ought not to be'? Echoes of Daniel 9.27 have suggested to commentators that the reference is to the Emperor Caligula's attempt to have his statue set up in the Temple (40 CE), or to the destruction of the Temple in 70 CE, or to the Antichrist. What is clear to Fowler, however, is that the 'you' of Jesus' discourse in chapter 13 has a double meaning. Within the story it is addressed to four disciples, Peter, James, John and Andrew, who privately question Jesus (13.3), but the narrative is also addressed to readers, since 13.37 states, 'And what I say to you, I say to all; Watch', and the 'all' must include the implied readers of 13.14.

A second instance of direct address is contained in the title and epigraph to the gospel. A title is a major clue to the reader about what to expect in the text, whether it is 'Pride and Prejudice' or 'The Big Sleep'. Mark 1.1 entitles the narrative 'The beginning of the gospel of Jesus Christ, (the Son of God)'. The meanings of 'gospel', 'Christ' and 'Son of God' are gradually unfolded in the story, but there is no uncertainty about Jesus' Messiahship for the implied reader of the gospel. The implied reader is immediately in possession of knowledge which the disciples lack and never quite gain, and this knowledge allows him or her to judge the disciples as slow and obtuse. Hence the ironical effects of so many of their conversations. Moreover, the implied reader recognizes the confessions of the demons as true, and speculations of Jesus' kinsmen about his identity as niggardly (6.14–16, 8.28). In addition, Mark 1.2–3 places the gospel under what Fowler calls the shadow of 'Jewish

Scriptures'. More appropriately, they should be called Markan Scriptures, since, although they have been taken over from Judaism, they are assumed to be authoritative for Christians too. This, says Fowler, alerts the reader to the possibility of scriptural allusions, in spite of the absence of introductory formulae (e.g. 4.12, 11.9, 13.26, 14.62, 15.34). Not only this, however, but Fowler might have noticed that in citing an 'authority' outside the text, almost certainly accepted by the original readers, the argument of the gospel is greatly strengthened.

II *Linking statements*

Some of the direct comments to the implied reader Fowler calls 'linking statements'. For example, at the end of the account of Jesus' walking on the water, a link is made with the preceding feeding miracle by the narrator's explanation, 'For they did not understand about the loaves, but their hearts were hardened' (6.52). In this way, the narrator tells the implied reader to consider the two stories together.

III *Explanations*

Many direct remarks of narrator to implied reader are found in parenthical constructions which explain a fact or detail. For example, they explain customs, which, we have to assume, were foreign to some of the gospel's implied readers. After stating that the Pharisees and scribes noticed that the disciples ate with hands defiled, two explanations are appended. Firstly, 'defiled' is interpreted 'that is, unwashed' (7.2) and secondly, Pharisaic and Jewish custom is briefly outlined, 'For the Pharisees, and all the Jews, do not eat unless they wash their hands, observing the tradition of the elders, and when they come from the market place, they do not eat unless they purify themselves, and there are many other traditions which they observe, the washing of cups and pots and vessels of bronze' (7.3–4).

Also foreign to some of the gospel's implied readers were Aramaic and Hebrew words. These are translated in 3.17 'Boanerges, that is, sons of thunder', 5.41 'Talitha cumi, which means, little girl, I say to you, arise', 7.11 'Corban, that is, given to God', 7.34 'Ephphatha, that is, be opened', 10.46 'Bartimaeus . . . the son of Timaeus', 14.36 'Abba, Father', 15.22 'Golgotha, which means the place of the skull', 15.34 'Eloi, Eloi, lama sabachthani, which means, my God, my God why have you forsaken me?'. For the most part, these are incidental details and the foreign words could have been omitted. Perhaps they are retained in two miracle stories for awesome effect, but only in 15.34 are the words required by the context, to explain why bystanders thought Jesus was summoning Elijah.

Fowler calls some of the parenthetical constructions 'winks at the reader' because they do not interrupt the flow of the narrative. Of the examples mentioned, three are convincing. 3.30 'For they had said, he has an unclean spirit' reminds the implied reader of the introduction to the Beelzebul controversy and therefore of the point of Jesus' statement. 8.32a remarks, immediately after the first prediction of the passion, 'And he said this plainly' to fix the implied reader's attention on a crucially important saying which is to be construed in its clear and obvious, if alarming sense. 11.32 explains the dilemma of the chief priests, scribes and elders caught in a trap by Jesus'

246

question about the baptism of John, 'they were afraid of the people, for all held that John was really a prophet'.

There are many other explanatory clauses in Mark, introduced by *gar* (for), and Fowler selects some which occur, as he puts it, 'after the main moment' in the story. For example, 1.16 explains that Simon and Andrew were casting nets into the sea 'for they were fishermen', 1.22 explains the astonishment of Jesus' audience 'for he taught them as one who had authority, and not as the scribes'. Indeed the whole gospel ends with just such a construction. After receiving a message for the disciples from the young man at the empty tomb, the women flee and say nothing 'for they were afraid' (16.8). These explanations provide the implied reader with matters of fact which throw essential light on the behaviour of characters within the story, and therefore help to create confidence in the narrator as a reliable informant.

Another group of examples, Fowler takes from J. R. Donahue's *Are you the Christ?*.[5] Donahue calls them 'Markan insertions' and suggests that they provide reliable commentary for the reader. Fowler admits, however, that their function varies from instance to instance. For example, in 6.35 the narrator anticipates a statement made by characters, '*And when it grew late*, his disciples came to him and said, This is a lonely place and the hour is now late'. This seems to prove the reliability of the disciples, however, although it also assumes the reliability of the narrator. Similarly, in 8.12, the narrator's statement confirms Jesus' trustworthiness, 'In those days, when again a great crowd had gathered, and *they had nothing to eat*, he called his disciples to him, and said to them, I have compassion on the crowd because they have been with me now three days and have nothing to eat.' This group is therefore less to Fowler's purpose than the preceding examples.

IV *The omniscient narrator*

Since the narrative provides information about the inner emotions, desires, thoughts, intentions and perceptions of characters, the narrator is omniscient. He does not have to rely on action to judge motivation, for example, but knows precisely why people do things. He gives this information about Jesus, his disciples and followers, and his opponents (e.g. 2.6–7, 8f.; 5.25–34; 9.33–37). The perspective of the omniscient narrator is an important feature of the focus of Mark, which it shares with most other biblical narratives, and we ought to pause to consider its significance. The gospel, like its biblical forerunners, claims to be history, to give an account of what happened in the past, but it exhibits nothing of the reticence a modern historian would self-consciously display about the limitations which a human viewpoint inevitably imposes. The narrator in a modern history would cite sources, but could claim to know with certainty neither the secrets of people's hearts, nor the divine purpose. The narrators of biblical history, however, like those of many other ancient civilizations, wrote as if they knew both. In Western culture, the omniscient narrator is not unfamiliar, but his or her role is confined to fiction, which is why biblical narratives seem somewhat like nineteenth-century novels to us.

VI *Reliable characters*

Fowler's sixth group of examples is called 'reliable characters'. Since the narrator's point of view coincides with Jesus' (e.g. 2.5, 8) or with God's (1.11; 9.7), the reliability of each is reinforced. Of more doubtful worth is the support of demons (e.g. 1.24; 3.11), but as supernatural beings, even they have access to true information about Jesus' identity. In addition, the centurion's confession (15.39) may coincide with the gospel's title, and the young man's message of Jesus' resurrection at the empty tomb confirms Jesus' predictions (16.5–7). The relationship of the narrator to each of his characters is an important element in the focus of the gospel, and a full exploration is necessary. Naturally, Fowler was unable to undertake such a task in the final chapter of his dissertion.

• Preliminary assessment of Fowler's categories

Fowler began his chapter by asking how the author of the Gospel of Mark furnishes the reader with a stable, reliable store of knowledge over against which irony can be recognized. He has mentioned the following rhetorical devices: (1) the general coherence of the presentation of norms, (2) the statements directly addressed to the reader which are elucidated in the gospel, (3) the remarks which link different incidents, (4) the explanations of strange customs, terminology and other facts important for understanding, (5) the statements which draw attention to momentous issues, (6) the omniscience of the narrator and (7) the introduction of reliable characters to reinforce the message.

All these details tend in one direction, they establish the trustworthiness of the narrator. Fowler's original statement of his purpose is therefore misleading. He had promised (p. 154): 'We will note the ways in which the author furnishes a stable, reliable store of knowledge for the reader, just the kind of knowledge over against which an author may construct stable, covert ironies'. The gospel does furnish the implied reader with a stable, reliable store of knowledge for the recognition of irony, but it does so, first of all, by establishing the reliability of the narrator. Once this is achieved, everything that the narrator tells the implied reader can be accepted as true and its significance appreciated. By phrasing the statement as he does, Fowler confuses two topics: first, the establishment of the narrator's veracity, and second, on the basis of this, the ways in which the narrator gives information to the reader. Fowler's two sub-categories, Intercalations and Doublets (pp. 165f.), and other categories, V and VII, including the examples from chapters 6 to 8 discussed in his third chapter, are instances of the second not of the first, and can be seen to provide genuine knowledge only after the implied reader's confidence in the narrator has been gained. They should therefore be treated separately. For example, Fowler's category V, rhetorical questions left unanswered in the narrative, certainly structures the implied reader's perceptions and provokes the search for appropriate answers, but, although this is obviously a clever rhetorical device, it does not itself provide the implied reader with reliable knowledge from which to grasp the ironical significance of statements in the story, nor does it prove the narrator's trustworthiness. Rather, it encourages the implied reader to fill in the gaps in the narrative with the information provided by the title.

Similarly, Fowler's seventh category introduces matters which should be considered only after the preliminary question of the narrator's veracity has been settled. It lists prospective passages in the light of which subsequent incidents take on an ironical import. It is here that he places the pericopes discussed in his third chapter from Mark 6–8, but he also includes sections of the gospel which serve to introduce important themes without any ironical twist. For example, Mark 3.1–19 introduces, amongst many others, the following motifs: saving life and killing (3.14), hardness of heart (3.5), the cooperation of Herodians and Pharisees in a plot against Jesus (3.6), and the scope of Jesus' work, extending even to Tyre and Sidon (3.8) (see Fowler, p. 172). These arrangements are essential to the rhetorical impact of the gospel, but they do not, in themselves, prove the narrator's reliability.

• Assessment of Fowler's study

Fowler's sketch of how it is that irony can be perceived by implied readers of the Gospel of Mark, though not clear on all points, is a useful beginning and demonstrates the potential of rhetorical criticism. The work of other literary critics, especially those influenced by structuralism, like G. Genette, discussed in the previous chapter, would have helped to bring clarity to his analysis, as well as making him aware of other rhetorical considerations, like the narrative's structuring of time, its order and duration. In other words, there is still much to be done in Markan rhetorical studies.

Rhetorical criticism is one of those areas of New Testament studies which can benefit from the expertise of other literary critics, not only in English but in Classics, since rhetorical devices change at different periods in history and New Testament texts were written in the first two centuries of the Common Era. Moreover, Markan rhetoric is probably influenced by that of scriptural narratives which seem to lie behind some of the gospel's stories. We shall take up these matters in our discussion of genre.

The implied reader. Since Fowler's reading is restricted to the rhetoric of the gospel, it does not go on explicitly to define the implied reader, the reader inscribed by the strategies of the text, as reader-response critics do. Nevertheless, on the basis Fowler provides, it is possible to do so. As we mentioned above, the implied reader is a person who can appreciate irony. He or she should be able to stand back from the disciples and discern what they do not quite grasp, namely that Jesus is the Messiah. The strategy does not alienate the implied reader from the disciples, however, because the message that a man who was crucified by the Romans is actually God's Messiah is not at all obvious, and even when accepted, it carries the unpalatable implications that followers of Jesus should also take up their cross. The effort demanded of the implied reader, to supply the understanding which the disciples lack, allows him or her to experience these difficulties, and therefore to sympathize with the disciples. This is the great advantage which narrative like the Gospel of Mark has over a credal statement. In requiring the active participation of readers to

249

make sense of the narrative, it draws them into experiencing the world which the text creates. The dialectical relationship between text and readers, in which the text prompts the readers to make concrete and actual a meaning which is only potential, is a dynamic which both affects the readers and is affected by them. And this happens, whether the actual reader fulfils the role of the implied reader inscribed in the text, or not. So, the implied reader of Mark should perceive irony, but the actual reader who does not pick up the hints given by the text, or fill in the gaps to create coherence, may still achieve some understanding.

Reader-response criticism has sometimes been criticized for trying to have the best of two contradictory views. In emphasizing the mere potential of the narrative, and noticing its indeterminacies and gaps, it asserts the openness of the text to a whole variety of interpretations, none of which can claim to represent *the* meaning, but only one possible meaning. On the other hand, in describing the strategies which call for a particular response in a reader, it suggests that some readers are more competent than others, since some respond appropriately and some do not. Hence, some reader-response critics define the 'ideal' reader of a particular work.

Critics and commentators have often accused one another of reading too much into a text, or of failing to discern its subtleties, or, even more seriously, of completely misreading it. In doing so, they imply that some readings are better than others, but if all readings are the creative work of the reader, there is no norm for deciding which is 'better'. All that can be said is that some readings are 'more interesting to us'. No doubt there is much to be said for this openness, but Meir Sternberg proposes another thesis in elucidating Old Testament narratives which may equally well apply to Mark.[6] He argues that these texts can both be under-read, as Mark's would be if the reader did not appreciate irony, and over-read, as some allegorists have done in interpreting Mark, but not counter-read, that is, not completely misunderstood. He suggests that the narratives, in combining history, ideology (or theology), and aesthetics, set up tensions, which the reader must resolve, because history cannot be falsified in the interests of ideology, nor can the reticence of the historian interfere with the function of aesthetics to move and involve the reader. But he also suggests that, since these texts serve the purpose of creating a sense of identity for Israel (or for Mark and the Markan community), they have to provide enough guidance to make sense to most people on a general level, even if subtleties are missed by many readers. This guidance Sternberg labels 'full-proof composition', in which the omniscient narrator creates a consistent story-line, world order and value system. Fowler, too, noted the consistency of norms expressed in Mark, and the reliability of the omniscient narrator.

Some attempts have been made recently to test hypotheses about implied readers by statistical analyses of actual readers' interpretations. This kind of empirical study is fraught with uncertainties, however, because much depends on questions asked, social conditions and the experience of participants. Nevertheless, it would be interesting to compare interpretations of Mark in different historical periods and places. We are all aware of the perceptions and blind spots of commentators, whose readings, like our own, are affected by their particular social and sectarian biases.

Indeed, even our present interest in reader-response may not be entirely unconnected with our participation in a consumer society.

Rhetorical criticism or Reader-Response is one form of holistic reading concerned exclusively with *how* a text achieves its effects on the 'implied reader'. Within its limited sphere, it provides essential insights. It does not deny, of course, that a text can perform other functions, like, for example, giving historical information, but it helps to refine our appreciation of the nature of the text. The recent popularity of holistic readings of the synoptic gospels, however, has brought to the fore a question which scholars have been toying with for many years, namely the question of the genre of each of the gospels, and to this we turn next.

Further Reading

Wolfgang Iser, *The Act of Reading*, A Theory of Aesthetic Response, ET, Baltimore 1978

J. P. Tomkins (ed.), *Reader-Response Criticism*, Baltimore and London 1980

A. Alter and F. Kermode (eds), *The Literary Guide to the Bible*, London 1987

17 The Genre of the First Gospel[1]

It will have become clear that neither structuralism nor reader-response criticism concerns itself with historical questions. Structuralism explicitly eschews historical reference, and reader-response criticism focuses attention on the 'ideal' reader rather than on a particular reader, limited to a specific time and place. One of the valuable perspectives of form and redaction criticism, namely, their interest in the history of tradition, has therefore been by-passed. But the interpretation of texts can be greatly enhanced by a recognition of the cultural and historical conditions in which they were written. It is true that we do not know exactly when or where each of the gospels was produced, but we do know that they were written in the second half of the first century CE in the Graeco–Roman world. In the next three chapters, therefore, we shall attempt to define the genre of each of the gospels by placing them within this cultural milieu.

'Imitation is the sincerest form of flattery' as the old adage goes. Although scholars sometimes suggest that the genre 'gospel' was something new, they also admit that literature always draws on what went before, combining, transforming, dividing motifs and genres already familiar to listeners, readers and writers. Otherwise literature would fail to communicate. Sense must be shared, and to share the sense, listeners and readers must be wooed by familiarity, at least to the extent that they are not completely baffled from beginning to end of a text.

Imitation happens in a variety of ways, however. Vocabulary, phraseology, motifs and story-line can be imitated from texts of a genre different from the imitation – a parody may use the same vocabulary, phraseology, motifs and story-line as a tragedy. Genre defines the whole, the organizing principle which gives individual elements their total significance. Nevertheless, genre cannot be discovered without careful attention to all the details, and rival definitions may be tested by examining which makes sense of most of the parts comprising the whole. Perhaps definition begins with an intuitive guess, but the guess must be informed by a knowledge of as much as possible of the literature available at the time and place of the text's production. From the evidence collected in F. G. Kenyon's *Books and Readers in Ancient Greece and Rome*, 1932, we know that Greek poets, dramatists, philosophers and historians were widely read, especially the works of Homer, Euripides,

Aristotle, Plato and Thucydides, and that commentaries and lexica were also in use. It is doubtful, however, that any of these served as models for the Gospel of Matthew.

• The Gospel of Matthew and Hellenistic Greek literature

1. General considerations.

The Gospel according to Matthew is written in Hellenistic Greek. It is therefore not surprising that scholars have discovered similarities to Greek literature roughly contemporary with the gospel, especially to biographies of religious leaders. G. A. Kennedy, for example, argues that Matthew uses rhetorical devices common in religious rather than philosophical or legal Greek rhetoric.[2] In philosophy, arguments are provided for the probability of premises so that formally valid inferences may be drawn from them. In Matthew and in other Greek religious rhetoric, however, persuasion is not by reason but by authoritative proclamation. Assertions are absolute, and whatever does not fit with them is not refuted but treated as outrageous. In Matthew, as in its Scripture and as in the other synoptics, theological beliefs are simply assumed: God is the creator and giver of life, the world is God's creation, and people are God's creatures, made in his image and likeness but without sharing his transcendent nature. God brings about his salvific purposes by influencing Israel and individual Israelites. This picture is neither analysed nor argued for. Its assumption means that Scriptural quotations can be used as authoritative statements which support the gospel's contentions. The gospel would therefore be recognized by those familiar with Hellenistic Greek literature as a form of religious rhetoric, albeit an odd form to pagan sensibilities since these Matthaean presuppositions would have been shared by no one outside of Jewish and Christian communities in the first century CE.

To suggest, however, that the First Gospel is like a **Hellenistic biography** seems reasonable enough. Like its pagan counterparts, it depicts the public life of the subject, either in chronological order, or thematically through a series of anecdotes (Matthew combines the two), in the third person but giving to characters within the story some direct speech. In form, Hellenistic biographies may be pedagogic (like Matthew), dramatic or entertaining, while in content they may be apologetic, exemplary, laudatory, philosophical or legitimizing, all features to some extent present in Matthew. Indeed, even the individual motifs of some biographies from the period are found in Matthew too, as Downing demonstrates[3] – motifs like family background (viewed in Matthew both positively and negatively), concern for ancestral tradition, travels, deliberate risking of life, omens, prodigies, miracles, divine guidance, quality of thought, concern for law, for justice, for community, death and burial, influence after death. Downing rightly argues that common motifs do not define a common genre, but he goes on to suggest that, nevertheless, the synoptic gospels would have been comprehensible to audiences familiar with pagan biographies. This is true, however, only up to a point. Most pagan biographies depict the lives of military and political figures, and these have few motifs in common with

253

Matthew, but even biographies of religious leaders exhibit differences. These differences will become clear as we compare Matthew with some Hellenistic biographies from roughly the same period.

2. Hellenistic biographies

(*a*) The work of this genre which seems closest to Matthew is Philostratus' *Life of Apollonius of Tyana*, but it is unlike Matthew in a number of obvious respects. Philostratus published the biography in Greek around 217 CE, but it purports to be based on the memoirs of Damis, Apollonius' companion and disciple. Apollonius is said to have lived during the first century CE under emperors from Nero to Nerva. The book can be read in a critical Greek edition with an English translation in Loeb Classical Library. Philostratus' work is partly a travelogue describing the exotic in India and Egypt as Apollonius visits fellow ascetics to improve his techniques of foretelling the future and performing wonders, partly a depiction of a reformer of the cult, and partly the portrait of an adviser to world rulers. The presuppositions of the text are Pythagorean, so that Apollonius is said to be divine in the sense that Pythagoreans believed all true ascetics to be divine. At the end of the story, Apollonius does not die but disappears from mundane sight into the eternal world of the immortals. Although, therefore, motifs appear to be shared by the two texts, especially if they are described in general terms, the different theological and anthropological assumptions determine the range and kind of motifs as well as their significance.

For example, neither Jesus nor Apollonius is married, and the Matthaean Jesus advocates celibacy for the sake of the kingdom of heaven (19.12), but because of belief in the imminent end of the world (16.28) and not from a desire to break free from physical fetters (contrast Apollonius 8.7.7; 8.7.9). Hence, Jesus is neither a vegetarian nor a teetotaller whereas Apollonius is both (1.8).

Again, both Jesus and Apollonius foretell the future. Jesus predicts his own passion (16.21f.; 17.22f.; 20.18f.; 26.2) and the role his disciples will play (26.20–25, 30–35), and he predicts God's imminent final judgment and the transformation of the world (13.36–43; 19.28; 24–25). Apollonius predicts the length of his stay with the king (Book 1.22), pestilence at Ephesus (4.4), who will initiate him into the Asclepian cult (4.18), Nero's attempt to cut a canal through an isthmus (4.24), an earthquake producing new land (4.34), a thunderbolt hitting Nero's cup (4.43), Nero's downfall (5.10–11), the fate of the three emperors who follow (5.13), shipwreck (5.18), the burning of a temple to Zeus (5.30), the manner of Titus' death (6.23), the site of treasure to pay dowries (6.39), Domitian's death (8.23 and 26), his own disappearance and the death of Nerva (8.27f.). Jesus' predictions serve to show that his own execution and his disciples' desertion were part of God's purpose which would be fully realized only at the Final Judgment. Apollonius' predictions prove that his ascetic practices have subordinated his senses to the divine ether in which the gods live (8.7.9).

Moreover, both Jesus and Apollonius perform wonders. Jesus cleanses lepers, heals paralysis, lunacy, fever, blindness, dumbness, haemorrhage, exorcizes demons, raises the dead (e.g. 4.24; 8–9), miraculously feeds the hungry (14.15–21, 15.32–39), stills a storm (8.23–27), walks on the sea (14.22–33), instructs Peter to catch a fish containing a coin to pay the Temple tax (17.24–27), and destroys the fig tree with a curse (21.18–22). Apollonius rids Ephesus of pestilence by persuading the population to stone a demon disguised as a beggar (4.10), is master of the tempest (4.13), exorcizes a demon from a raucous youth (4.20; this example shares two features with the exorcism of the two demoniacs in Matthew 8.28–34: the demons are rebuked and their exit is proved by the effect on something in the vicinity), saves his young pupil from being devoured by his vampire bride (4.25), raises a young girl from the dead by touch and secret spell (4.45), saves a village from the torments of a satyr's ghost by putting it to sleep on wine (6.27), and tames a mad dog who had bitten a boy to effect the boy's cure with the lick of the dog (6.43). In addition, Apollonius displays a miraculous knowledge of languages he has never learned (1.19 but contrast 1.32). Nevertheless, Jesus' miracles are demonstrations of God's forgiveness of sin (9.2–8) or God's creative activity (14.22–33), whereas Apollonius' display the divinity which Pythagorean asceticism releases from its corporeal fetters.

(b) Another work sometimes compared to the gospels in Lucian's *Alexander the False Prophet* (Loeb Classical Library), written in Greek about 180 CE against Alexander, a priest of Asclepius in the second century CE who gained a large following and whose cult flourished for about a century afterwards. It depicts Alexander as a charlatan who claimed to be a divine teacher. Again, in so far as the story portrays Alexander as a healer, the biography has something in common with the Gospel according to Matthew but neither Alexander's frenzied behaviour (12), nor his medical remedies given in writing and based especially on diet and the use of bear's grease (19) have parallels in Matthew. Lucian's work is polemical, seeking to exemplify the sanity of Epicurean philosophy to a fellow Epicurean in contrast to the chicanery of Alexander. Both the cult and Lucian's philosophy held beliefs very different from those in the First Gospel, and these have led to a work whose contrasts are greater than its similarities to the gospel. Contrary to the claim of Morton Smith in *Jesus the Magician*, Jesus' miracles do not function in the gospels as a proof of his divinity, since Jesus shares this activity not only with his disciples (10.8) but also with the disciples of the Pharisees (12.27), and in the First Gospel, human beings do not attain divinity through ascetic or healing practices since human creatures do not share divine transcendence.

(c) Again, H. C. Kee's suggestion that literature which develops the beliefs of the Isis cult may throw light on the miracle stories of the synoptic gospels is useful only in relation to motifs.[4] Indeed, Apuleius' *The Golden Ass* (Loeb Classical Library), written in Latin about 180 CE, which transforms a traditional story about the adventures of a young man too curious about magic for his own good – compare Lucian's shorter Greek version, *Metamorphoses*, written about the same time – into an apology for the Isis cult, since the hero is saved from the consequences of his stupidity by the goddess Isis and enabled by her to live a life of serenity, honour and usefulness, is quite unlike the Gospel of Matthew both because it depicts the religious quest of a disciple and because it is a Platonic allegorization advocating Platonic beliefs which are not shared by Matthew.

(*d*) Nor is Kee's further suggestion, that material found only in Matthew is akin to contemporary histories by Suetonius, Tacitus and Josephus, with their interest in portents, omens and oracles, any more helpful in defining the genre of Matthew. Kee's argument appears more plausible than it is because he treats this Matthaean material out of context and so can give to the individual motifs a significance they do not have in the context in which they are placed. If Matthaean dependence on Scripture is recognized, earthquakes in Matthew are seen to echo the language of its Scriptural theophanies (Ex. 19.18; I Kings 19.11–12; Ps. 114.7), just as dreams giving divine guidance, especially to Joseph, are reminiscent of those given to the Scriptural patriarch Joseph.

(*e*) Further, some motifs in the Matthaean text are never found in Hellenistic literature. Matthew looks beyond its subject's death in ways foreign to Hellenistic conceptions since it announces Jesus' resurrection and expects an imminent final judgment. The eschatological perspective of the First Gospel places it in a genre distinct from that of Hellenistic Greek biography, since it not only creates new motifs but gives to common motifs a different significance (see The Gospel of Matthew and its Scripture, below).

3. Jewish biographies in Greek.

Even contemporary Jewish Hellenistic biographies do not share this eschatological perspective with Matthew.

(*a*) The portraits of Scriptural characters in Josephus' *Jewish Antiquities*, published under Domitian, are 'biblically based but hellenistically conceived',[5] by which Attridge means that they are unified by themes like *pronoia* (foresight) borrowed from Greek philosophy, and that they are made more dramatic by focusing explicitly on psychology (unlike Matthew), by heightening the emotional impact of important scenes (like Luke but unlike Matthew) and by developing the erotic possibilities of some episodes (unlike the gospels) (pp. 212f.). Moreover, Josephus seems to interpret Messianic prophecies to refer to the Flavian house (*War* 3.399–408) and underplays Jewish eschatological beliefs, partly by explaining them away in Greek terms, but mostly by ignoring them. Only in the descriptions of Pharisaic belief is a notion of resurrection rather than the survival of the soul countenanced (*War* 2.163, and *Antiquities* 18.14) and nothing is said in these passages about a connexion with the Final Judgment or the end of the world. From the whole of the Josephus corpus, only two statements refer to the 'revolution of the ages' (*peritropē aiōnōn*), and even these could be construed as Stoic rather than Jewish. One is in the *Jewish War* (3.374) in Josephus' argument against committing suicide to avoid Roman captivity:

> Know you not that they who depart this life in accordance with the law of nature and repay the loan which they received from God, when he who lent is pleased to reclaim it, win eternal renown; that their houses and families are secure; that their souls remaining spotless and obedient, are allotted the most holy place in heaven, whence, *in the revolution of the ages*, they return to find in chaste bodies a new habitation.

– and one in *Against Apion* (2.218) in discussing rewards for obeying the Jewish law:

> Each individual, relying on the witness of his own conscience and the lawgiver's prophecy, confirmed by the sure testimony of God, is firmly persuaded that to those who observe the laws and, if they must needs die for them, willingly meet death, God has granted a renewed existence and in the revolution (*peritropē* without *aiōnōn*) the gift of a better life.

That Josephus himself shared Jewish eschatological expectations is suggested by his reference to Daniel in *Antiquities* 10.210, but he refuses to provide details for his readers. These are merely incidental references, however, which play no part in structuring the texts. On the contrary, the works conform to Hellenistic models of history and apology.

(*b*) Philo's *Life of Moses*, Book I (Loeb Classical Library), has more in common with Matthew since Matthew presents Jesus in some sense as a Second Moses (see below), but Philo's portrait is influenced by Platonism. Philo was trained in Greek as well as Jewish learning in the Alexandria of the first half of the first century CE. Moses is therefore presented as an ideal philosopher-king displaying the virtues of justice, courage and temperence. The text exhibits a theological framework which sometimes equates God and fortune, and sometimes, conforming the vocabulary more closely to that of the Pentateuch, sees God as the saviour of those who suffer. But true to his Platonic beliefs, Philo, unlike the Pentateuch, portrays the Hebrews as free men of high lineage, virtuous and pious, deserving God's graciousness. Philo's anthropology exhibits a Platonic dualism of immortal mind and corrupting body. So the Hebrews are said to have discovered that their souls are sprung from divine seeds and that their stock is akin to God, and Moses at the end of his life is said to leave his mortal life for immortality, summoned by a God who transformed his two-fold nature into a single unity, his whole being into pure mind.

One of the themes of Philo's *Life of Moses* and of his *On Rewards and Punishments* (Loeb Classical Library) is the blessings of a virtuous life and the curses of a vicious life. The rewards are those we would expect a Jewish Platonist to desire, a serene life of virtue in contemplation of God leading to a life of prosperity and health. Beyond death lies immortality for the good man or perpetual grief for the bad man (*On Rewards and Punishments*, 69–70 and 100). Although *On Rewards and Punishments* looks forward to the future triumph of the virtuous with an accompanying transformation of political and natural existence in this world, it does not envisage a final escatological judgment or resurrection into a new creation. Philo's writings do not, then, share Matthew's eschatological perspective.

4. Conclusion.

To those readers acquainted with Hellenistic biographies of religious leaders, therefore, the Gospel according to Matthew would seem familiar enough to be comprehensible, but would also exhibit presuppositions, motifs and details that were jarring and unexpected. For example, pagan readers would be surprised and puzzled by the depiction of Jesus' bodily resurrection and would be inclined to understand

Matthaean eschatology in terms of Stoic expectations about the conflagration which brings the cosmos to a close before everything begins again. These readers would have been unable to play the role of the 'ideal readers' defined by rhetorical and reader-response criticism. Jewish readers, on the other hand, would have been in a much better position to understand Matthaean theology, anthropology and eschatology, together with the motifs, forms and vocabulary these generate, but the gospel would have offended them for other reasons. Matthew's portrait of Jews and Jewish leadership is partial and unsympathetic. It is the kind of caricature, exemplified in the epithet 'hypocrite', which would have alienated first-century Jews as much as it has dismayed their modern counterparts, although first-century Jews had not yet faced Christians as their persecutors who would taunt them with quotations from the Gospel of Matthew.

As we remarked at the end of the chapter on rhetorical criticism, more research needs to be done into the responses of actual readers of the synoptic gospels, but it is reasonable to suppose that pagans and Jews who knew some of the literature discussed in this section would have found the Gospel of Matthew comprehensible enough to continue reading or listening.

• The Gospel of Matthew and its Scripture

We shall now show that an extremely large percentage of the individual motifs and formulations of Matthew are paralleled in its Scripture. Some of these, to be sure, may have been taken over from Mark, but nevertheless they count as Matthaean. In discussing redaction criticism we noted the question of whether or not to count the material copied from Mark as part of what is characteristic of Matthew. That remains a question in redaction criticism, but in a truly holistic reading the answer is clear. What Matthew copied from Mark has become part of Matthew, and it is to be taken fully into account in assessing the overall character and genre of the First Gospel. The same remarks apply to material which is in Matthew because it reflects the lifetime of Jesus. Scriptural motifs could appear in Matthew because Jesus himself modelled his ministry, at least in some respects, on the biblical prophets. Nevertheless, these motifs became part of the Gospel of Matthew. Matthew, for example, may have written that Jesus went up on a mountain because he actually did so; yet once he was on the mountain he became, in Matthew, a kind of second Moses.

In itemizing Matthaean motifs shared with Scripture, we must bear in mind that, numerous though these are, motifs do not necessarily decide genre. Genre is what structures and frames the whole, and we have already seen that Matthew's eschatological world view plays that role to no small degree. Matthew's version of eschatology is not precisely that of any part of its Scripture. The question will be then, whether or not Matthew's scriptural motifs, when understood as part of a post-scriptural world view, allow us to define a 'genre' which explains Matthew better than do those presently on offer. The first task is to see to what degree Matthew is dominated by scriptural motifs and vocabulary.

But what was its Scripture? In the first century CE, no canon of Scripture had been defined by Jewish or Christian communities, but the Torah or Pentateuch (Genesis,

Exodus, Leviticus, Numbers and Deuteronomy) and most of the prophets were regarded as authoritative, hence Matthew's reference to 'the law and the prophets' (e.g. 7.12). In addition, there existed a collection of Psalms (e.g. Matt. 22.44, 47; 27.46). Daniel, which finally found a place among the 'writings' in Jewish Scriptures, but among the 'prophets' in the Christian canon, is quoted at crucial points in the First Gospel (e.g. 13.32; 24.21, 30; 25.46; 26.34). Just which version or versions of Scripture were available is uncertain, since some quotations in Matthew conform to those which survive in the Septuagint text, some to those which survive in the Hebrew text, some are mixtures, and many are combinations of passages from different books, with necessary adaptations. Moreover, evidence suggests that quotations have been integrated into their context in the gospel (e.g. Matt. 2.6).[6] In any case, checking the exact wording of a quotation from a scroll written in continuous script, without divisions between chapters, paragraphs, sentences or words, and almost completely lacking in punctuation, would have been a task irksome enough to have been neglected, when memory could be assumed to supply what was needed.

How far, then, has Matthaean Scripture determined the vocabulary, motifs and genre of the First Gospel? We should recall something mentioned earlier, in the chapters on structuralism and rhetorical criticism, namely that, like their scriptural narratives, all three synoptic gospels present their messages through a narrator who shares God's omniscience. In addition to this general perspective, there is a wealth of particular parallels to Matthew's motifs, vocabulary and arrangement.

1. *The genealogy*. As an introductory summary of religious history, the genealogy in Matt. 1.1–17 imitates parts of that in I Chronicles 1–3. Matthew's genealogy depicts Jesus as son of David, as the Christ, albeit fulfilling only some of the possible Messianic expectations of its Scripture (2.1–12; 21.5–11; 27.11, 17, 29, 37, 42). The prediction of the Davidic king's vengeance against enemies in II Samuel 7.9–11 or Psalm 18.46–50, for example, is unfulfilled in Jesus' life-time, since, on the contrary, Jesus is killed by the Romans, a matter which may explain the text's dissatisfaction with the title in Jesus' reply to Peter's confession (16.13–28) and in his public teaching in the Temple (22.41–46). Vengeance against enemies is deferred by the text till God's judgment. Nevertheless, Jesus is depicted as the Christ, anointed with God's spirit through the actions of a prophet, John the Baptist (Matt. 3.13–17; I Sam. 16.12f.).

The genealogy also declares Jesus to be son of Abraham, engaged in a mission to the Gentiles or nations in fulfilment of Abraham's call, 'By you all the families of the earth shall be blessed' (Gen. 12.3). Jesus begins to bring this about since Gentiles are the first to acknowledge his Messiahship (2.1–12) and he heals four Gentiles during his ministry (8.5–13, 28–34; 15.21–28), but it is the disciples who are to complete the work (28.16–20).

2. *Other motifs from Scripture also appear in the birth narrative.* Joseph, Jesus' legal father, is like the patriarch Joseph, a dreamer who goes down to Egypt and who behaves justly towards a woman whom he supposes has acted badly (Gen. 37–48,

259

especially 39.9; Matt. 1–2). Jesus, like Israel, God's son, is called out of Egypt (Hos. 11.1; Ex. 4.22; Matt. 2.15). This motif is repeated in what follows. As Israel goes through the water of the Red Sea to set out on a journey towards the promised land, so Jesus goes through the water of the Jordan to set out on a journey towards the kingdom of heaven (Ex. 14–15; Matt. 3.13–17). Also, like and unlike Israel, God's disobedient son, Jesus, God's obedient son, is tested in the wilderness (Ex. 14–17, 32–34, Num. 11; Matt. 4.1–11 with its references to Deuteronomy).

3. *The prophets.* Perhaps the most important motifs employed by Matthew come from stories about the prophets. The greatest of the prophets was Moses, and it is surprising that the First Gospel, unlike the Fourth (John 6), does not unambiguously allude to the promise, given to Israel in Deuteronomy 18.18, that in the future God would give Israel a prophet like Moses: 'I (God) will raise up for them a prophet like you (Moses) from among their brethren; and I will put my words in his mouth, and he shall speak to them all that I command him.' Nevertheless, Matthew's Jesus is modelled on Moses. Like Moses, Jesus escapes the wrath of a ruler while his contemporaries are killed (Ex. 1.22–2.10; Matt. 2.13–18). Jesus fasts for forty days in the wilderness, as Moses did (Matt. 4.2; Ex. 34.28). Jesus' sermon on the mount (Matt. 5–7) alludes to Moses' declaration of the law from mount Sinai (Ex. 20–23) and explicitly quotes from it (e.g. Matt. 5.21, 27, 31), and the collection together of ten miracle stories in Matt. 8–9 is reminiscent of the ten wonders Moses performed in Egypt (Ex. 7–12), although only the number affords the connexion, not the actual details of the incidents. Two of Jesus' miracles, however, do parallel those of Moses – the feedings of the people in the wilderness (Matt. 14.13–20; 15.32–38; Ex. 16; Num. 11).

The transfiguration of Jesus' appearance on the mountain also recalls that of Moses, but once again none of the vocabulary of the two stories is identical (Matt. 17.3–5; Ex. 34.29–35). In the Matthaean account, however, Jesus is explicitly associated with both Moses and Elijah. The context in which the passage is placed, immediately after Jesus' first prediction of his future suffering and death (Matt. 16.21), suggests a reason for this: Moses and Elijah were rejected by their own people (Ex. 14.10–12; 17.1–2; I Kings 19.1–4).

One role assigned to Moses in Exodus and Numbers is that of military leader, ensuring, through God's help, the defeat of Israel's enemies. No obvious allusion to this can be found in Matthew, unless the reduction in scale, from Moses with the twelve tribes, to Jesus with the twelve disciples, allows us to see Jesus' victories over enemies in disputes as a transformation of the motif. If so, Moses' military encounters have become wars of words (Ex. 17.8–13; Num. 16; 21.21–30; 31; Matt. 12.1–14; 15.1–20; 19.3–9; 21.23–22.46).

The paradigmatic description of God's mercy to Israel, the Passover and Exodus from Egypt (Ex. 12), is central to the Moses story. It is not surprising to discover, therefore, that the Gospel of Matthew associates the climax of Jesus' ministry with the Passover through the dating of his last meal with his disciples, using the setting to indicate something of the significance of Jesus' death as evidence of God's mercy in forgiving sinners (Matt. 26.2, 17, 28). At the same time, the words of Jesus over the wine, 'This is my blood of the covenant' (Matt. 26.28) interpret 'the blood of the covenant' mentioned in the account of the ratification of a covenant between God and Israel through Moses on Mount Sinai (Ex. 24.5–8).

For its portrait of Jesus, the First Gospel also draws on motifs from narratives about other prophets. Jesus is endowed with the Spirit of God when he begins his public ministry (Matt. 3.16) as the prophets were (e.g. I Sam. 10.6, 10–13; II Kings 2.9–14; Isa. 61; Ezek. 2.2). The specific reference to Elijah with Jesus at the transfiguration has already been mentioned, and some of the Elijah and Elisha miracle stories are more like those of Jesus than Moses' wonders. For example, both Elijah and Elisha raise the dead and feed the hungry (I Kings 17.8–24; II Kings 4.18–37; 4.42–44; Matt. 9.18–26; 14.13–21; 15.32–39), and Elisha cures a leper (II Kings 5.1–18; Matt. 8.1–4). Further, Jesus calls disciples to follow him as Elijah called Elisha (Matt. 4.18–22; 8.18–22; 9.9; 28.16–20; I Kings 19.19f.). In the gospel, however, a more explicit link is made between John the Baptist and Elijah, through quotation (Matt. 11.10), allusion (Matt. 3.4 and II Kings 1.8), and statement (Matt. 17.12). What John and Elijah have in common is that each suffered persecution by a ruler for proclaiming God's oracles (Matt. 14.1–12; I Kings 19.1–3), but Matthew supposes that all prophets and their disciples will face the same fate (e.g. Matt. 5.12; 16.13–26; 23.29f.). Traditions about the martyrdom of the prophets seem to have arisen from the Jewish experience of persecution under Antiochus Epiphanes, 167–164 BCE. *The Martyrdom of Isaiah*, a Jewish work now incorporated in the Christian *Ascension of Isaiah*, depicts Isaiah's death under Manasseh, when he was sawn in two. II Kings 21.16 records that Manasseh shed innocent blood, and the legend assumes that Isaiah was one of the victims (cf. Matt. 23.29–36). The vision of Jesus as a persecuted prophet leads naturally to the use of other motifs from Scripture about the innocent who suffer injustice. Two psalms, 22 and 69, which recount such experiences, are often alluded to or quoted in the Passion narrative.[7]

4. *Other motifs.* These parallels with the prophets are striking and important, but Matthew adds other motifs from its Scripture. The assertion that Jesus is endowed with the Spirit of God may help to explain the curious incident of Jesus' walking on the water (Matt. 14.22–33). The way in which the story is related – Jesus moving across the waters in the darkness – may recall the Genesis account of the Spirit moving across the waters in the darkness as the prelude to creation (Gen. 1.2). If so, this implies that Jesus' ministry is the prelude to God's new creation (Matt. 19.28). Then Jesus' death at the hands of his enemies can be viewed in terms of Amos' prophecy of doom, 'On that day, says the Lord God, I will make the sun go down at noon, and darken the earth in broad daylight' (Amos 8.9; Matt. 27.45). Similarly the suicide of the betrayer, Judas, (Matt. 27.3–10) is recounted with details reminiscent of Zechariah's action to symbolize the breaking of God's covenant (Zech. 11.12–13) and Jeremiah's parable about the potter (God) breaking the spoiled pot (Israel) (Jer. 18.2–3). Finally, the awesome scenes of the resurrec-

ted Jesus' meeting with his followers (Matt. 28.9–10, 16–20) adopt the form of Scriptural theophanies (e.g. Gen. 18; Ex. 3; Judg. 6), as Alsup has demonstrated.[8]

5. *Sentences, phrases and words.* Not only has the gospel made use of Scriptural motifs, however, but individual sentences, phrases and words have the same source. From the prophets come the form of indicative parables, like those of Nathan and Isaiah (II Sam. 12; Isa. 5; Matt. 13.1–52; 21.33–22.14), the woes (Isa. 5.8–12; 33.1; Jer. 13.27; Matt. 23.13–36), the solemn declaration *amen* (Jer. 28.6; Matt. 6.5, 16; and cf. Matt. 16.14), and the term 'Son of man' from Ezekiel (e.g. 2.1, 8; 3.1; Matt. 8.20; 9.6). Blessings come from the Torah and from liturgical and wisdom texts (Deut. 33.29; Ps. 1.1; 2.12; Ecclus. 28.14; 48.11; Tobit 13.14; Matt. 5.3–10, 11–12). There are also collections of wisdom saying (Prov.; Eccles.; Matt. 6.19–7.20) but it is difficult to gauge the significance of wisdom parallels because proverbial forms are common to all cultural traditions. On the other hand, Matthaean use of the Greek words *dikaios* (just), *dikaiosunē* (righteousness, justice) and *eleēmosunē* (mercy, alms) is much closer to the Septuagint than, for example, to Plato (Matt. 1.19; 5.17–20; 6.2–4; Gen. 6.9; Ezek. 18.5; II Sam. 8.15; Deut. 6.25; Isa. 1.27).

6. *Arrangement of material.* Moreover the juxtaposition of short sections of narrative and miracle with discourses and dialogues in Matthew is similar to that in the stories of the prophets Moses in Exodus and Numbers, and Elijah and Elisha in I and II Kings. Nevertheless, a dominant element in most of these stories is almost missing from Matthew, where God rarely speaks directly as he does to Moses, the Israelites or Elijah. In Matthew, instructions from God are conveyed by angels (Matt. 28), sometimes through dreams (Matt. 1–2), and only on two occasions does a voice from heaven testify to by-standers that Jesus is the Son of God (Matt. 3.17; 17.5). The form of the divine declaration is unlike both the usual prophetic 'thus says the Lord' and the stories of prophetic callings in Exodus 3–4, Isaiah 6, Jeremiah 1 or Ezekiel 1–3. It is slightly more like the proof that Elijah is the servant of God when on Mount Carmel he calls down fire on the sacrifice and God answers with fire, or like God's confirmation of Moses' leadership with thunderclaps from Mount Sinai in Exodus 19–20. The form seems to have been developed in the first century CE, since Vermes is able to cite parallels from rabbinic stories about the first century charismatic healer, Hanina ben Dosa.[9]

7. *Preliminary conclusion.* Motifs, sentences, phrases and vocabulary as well as arrangement, then, are shared by Matthew with its Scripture, but sharing these details does not indicate a common genre. Although in Matthew we discern a refocusing of the destiny of Israel and its king through the prism of stories about the prophets, some elements in the portrait of Jesus remain unexplained.

8. *God and Satan.* Firstly, we should note that the theology of much of its Scripture is modified in Matthew by a temporary dualism in which, although the world is God's creation, it has fallen foul of Satan's evil power. Matthew does occasionally make God man's tempter, like its Scripture (Matt. 6.13; 4.1; Gen. 22.1; Ex. 16.4; Amos 3.6), but what seems to have happened is that Scriptural references to beings

in God's court or to angelic messengers have opened the way to reinterpretations (e.g. Ps. 78.25, 49; 138.1; Gen. 16.7–14; 19.1–29; Ex. 3.2; 4.24; 14.19; I Kings 19.5). Job's vision of the adversary Satan or the Devil is used by Matthew in the temptation narrative (Job 1.6–12, Matt. 4.1–11), but elsewhere in the gospel, this picture of Satan is combined with a Scriptural reference to a power opposed to God and represented by an idol, Baalzebub, the god of Ekron (II Kings 1.2, 6). The Hebrew means 'Lord of the flies'. The corruption, *Beelzebul*, which could mean either 'Lord of the lofty place' or 'Lord of filth', may have been deliberate. Elsewhere, in Scripture, idol worship is called sacrificing to demons (Deut. 32.17; Isa. 65.11), and unclean spirits are associated with idol worship in Zech. 13.2. In Matthew, Satan and Beelzebul are identified as 'the prince of demons' (9.34; 10.25; 12.24–32), who tempts people to sin against God and possesses individuals causing illness or madness (e.g. 8.16, 28–34; 9.32–34). In exhortatory sections of the Pentateuch, sin, especially the sin of idolatry, is frequently seen to lead to various kinds of catastrophe – famine, war or illness (e.g. Ex. 23.23–33; Lev. 26.3–33; Deut. 28.1–68), and a woman's sin is said to have caused her son's death in I Kings 17.18 (cf. Ex. 20.5; Matt. 9.1–8). Matthew also links sin and illness through the notion of demon-possession (8.28–34). The connexion was understood to raise questions about God's justice when innocent people seemed to suffer as much illness as blatant sinners (Job, Tobit), but Matthew neutralizes the difficulty by depicting Jesus' healings and exorcisms as instances of God's mercy (9.1–8). The kinds of miracles which Matthew attributes to Jesus, therefore, not only mirror some of those performed by prophets, but also include exorcisms.

In the Septuagint, only the book of Tobit, usually dated around 200 BCE, exhibits a belief in angels and demons like that of Matthew. According to Tobit, the angel Raphael both accompanies Tobias on a journey, as the angel had accompanied the Israelites through the wilderness, and exorcizes Sarah's demon and cures Tobit's blindness. Raphael therefore has something in common with the Matthaean Jesus, who also cures blindness by touch, though without the aid of an ointment made from a fish's gall, and exorcizes demons, though without the aid of smoke from a fish's heart or liver (Tobit 11.5–15; Matt. 9.27–31; 20.29–34; Tobit 8.3; Matt. 8.28–34; 9.32–34). Matthew and Tobit, then, share a belief in angels and demons, but one of the roles given to Raphael in Tobit is given to Jesus in Matthew.

The extra-canonical book of Jubilees, usually dated in the second century BCE, however, has most in common with the Matthaean mythological structure, in spite of the fact that its interests, in dating festivals according to the solar calendar and in justifying its new version of Genesis and Exodus as a revelation, are far from those of Matthew. Jubilees sees Satan as the prince of demons, whose minions take possession of people, corrupt them and make them ill (10.3). In addition, and more optimistically, Jubilees, like Matthew, gives to individuals the protection of guardian angels (Matt. 18.10; Jub. 35.17; cf. Ps. 91.11). It is the Matthaean belief in demon-possession, shared by Jews, Christians and pagans in the first century CE, that determines its exorcisms, with motifs common not only to Jewish literature but also to contemporary pagan biographies.

9. *Eschatology*. Another theological perspective in Matthew is shared with only parts of its Scripture. Statements about the future kingdom, the new world, the parousia of the Son of man, the resurrection and the final eschatological judgment are adapted particularly from the visions of Daniel 7 and 12. Nevertheless, Matthew is not an apocalypse in the form of Daniel 7–12 or of those collected in the extra-canonical book, I Enoch. It is not a revelation of a transcendent reality symbolically represented and interpreted by an angel, whether through a dream or a heavenly journey. Even the so-called 'Matthaean apocalypse' in chapters 24 and 25 is neither an account of a journey to heaven nor a dream, in spite of its clear allusions to Daniel 7 and 12 in the parousia of the Son of man and the final judgment scene. The Matthaean form is different, more like a prophetic prediction, although its content is shared by much apocalyptic literature. Moreover, the angels who appear in Matt. 1 and 2, where they do communicate in a dream, give their divine message to endangered individuals and are not concerned with the Final Judgment. Only in chapter 28 does the angel who announces Jesus' resurrection play the apocalyptic role of interpreter of an eschatological reality. If, then, parts of Matthew pick up apocalyptic motifs but the whole is different, how is it different?

The Matthaean Jesus is not taken on a heavenly journey, nor does he receive revelations in a dream, but he is inspired by the Spirit of God (Matt. 3.16; 4.1; cf. I Enoch 91–104) and reveals God in his earthly life and teaching. Not only are visions of the future and of a transcendent world related to people on earth in chapters 24–25 and 28, but Jesus' earthly life, enlivened by God's Spirit, is understood to provide knowledge of God; while his resurrection, a beginning of the new world (19.28; 27.53), offers proof of the efficacy of his predictions about the imminent Final Judgment and the transformation of creation. The revelation is focused in Jesus and the story of his life, death and resurrection is not just a biography of an individual but a microcosm of God's macrocosmic judgment. Hence the story of the Messiah and prophetic martyr has become a theodicy, a vindication of God's justice and mercy. The Gospel of Matthew retains tragic elements in that Jesus suffers martyrdom, but within the compass of a divine plan which ends with his resurrection and the hope of the future establishment of the kingdom of heaven.

• Summary

More of the individual forms of sayings, the motifs and the arrangements of material are shared by Matthew and its Scripture than by Matthew and pagan Hellenistic biographies. In many respects, the Matthaean Jesus is like a prophet, especially Moses. Moreover, the Scriptural world-view is presupposed by the First Gospel, albeit with a dualistic colouring and an eschatological dimension. What is completely new, and what necessitates a development of the apocalyptic genre, is the belief that Jesus' earthly life exemplifies God's activity, and that his corpse disappeared because God raised him from the dead. Expectations about God's final vindication of the righteous are therefore justified by the story of Jesus' life, death and resurrection.

The presentation of this complex message is surprisingly simple. Anecdotes, dialogues and occasional discourses serve to concentrate the attention of audience or reader on particular theological themes. Superfluous description of individuals, groups or locations is eschewed and no attempt is made to distinguish the speech patterns of one character from another. Earnestness rather than literary sparkle characterizes the style. It is this simplicity which creates the general appeal and guarantees its usefulness for generations of Christians.

From among the terms used by literary critics to define genres, some scholars, like Northrop Frye in *The Great Code*, have selected the traditional designation 'Divine comedy' to encompass the whole biblical story, which begins in paradise, traces the fall of humanity, and recounts God's response in calling Israel and sending the Messiah to restore people to a paradisal life in the new Jerusalem. The term 'comedy', however, seems more appropriate to parts of the Old Testament, like the patriarchal narrative, than to the gospels. Abrams' *Glossary of Literary Terms* defines 'comedy' as: 'a work in which the materials are selected and managed primarily in order to interest and amuse us: the characters and their discomfitures engage our delighted attention rather than our profound concern, we feel confident that no great disaster will occur and usually the action turns out happily for the chief characters.' The Gospel of Matthew, however, is intended to elicit our profound concern for characters whose fidelity to God will involve them in unjust suffering. At the very least, then, the terminology would have to be modified to 'Divine tragi-comedy'. Even so, it fails to give readers a clear impression of what to expect in the synoptic gospels. This is why we have avoided a short designation in favour of a longer description.

The most satisfactory definition of the genre is 'a theodicy about creation and re-creation' (see *palingenesia*, 'new world', 19.28) which is centred in the life, death and resurrection of Jesus. This has several advantages. It adequately expresses the gospel's over-arching view point: the God of Scripture will save not only Israel but also the Gentiles; he has sent for this purpose his Son; salvation will involve a new world order. Re-*creation* points towards the advance of Matthew's eschatological world view beyond the world view of most of its Scripture.[10] The term 'theodicy', while strictly speaking not a biblical term, is appropriate both for parts of biblical history and for Matthew. The story of Elijah is in part a 'theodicy' – a justification of God – since YHWH, who appeared to have been overcome, by the Baal cult, eventually won. The theodicy in Matthew culminates in the death and resurrection of Jesus. This means, however, that Matthew's theodicy differs from that of most prophetic books in looking forward to an eschatological instead of an historical and political resolution.

For Further Reading see p. 298.

265

18   The Genre of the Second Gospel

Most of the material found in the Second Gospel is shared with the First, so that the two texts have much in common, but since some of the contents of Matthew, particularly the discourses, are not found in Mark, each creates a distinctive impression, Mark's being more dramatic and fast-moving, requiring more effort from its implied readers to make connexions which are hinted at but not explained in the text. Do the similarities and differences indicate the same or an alternative genre?

As in the case of the First Gospel, we do not know when, where or by whom the Gospel of Mark was written. Some scholars think that the patristic evidence associating Mark with Peter in Rome is confirmed by internal evidence, and suggest that the gospel was written after Peter's death in the Neronian persecution of 64 CE, i.e. around 68 CE. According to this theory, Mark 13 reflects not only the stereotyped expectations of apocalyptic, but also the troubles in Rome which followed Nero's death.[1] Other scholars think that the gospel was written in a rural not an urban setting, in Galilee or Southern Syria, and that Mark 13 reflects the destruction of the Jerusalem Temple by the Romans in 70 CE. The gospel is then understood as a response to that catastrophe, an attempt to reorganize the Christian community whose centre had been Jerusalem.[2] The paucity of reliable, external evidence means that the text itself has to define its implied author, but it does so in such an ambiguous way that quite different portraits are plausibly reconstructed. Nevertheless, we can be sure that the gospel was written in the second half of the first century CE.

• The Gospel of Mark and Hellenistic Greek literature

Like the Gospel according to Matthew, Mark is written in Greek, but no one would want to claim that it evinces literary pretensions. The limited vocabulary, repetition of phraseology, all-too-frequent use of *kai* (and), of participles, of the historic present, the Aramaisms, the Hebraisms and the Latinisms combine to show that this is a 'popular' not a 'literary' work. But the gospel would have been recognized by Greek readers as a form of religious rhetoric, although, like Matthew's, with peculiar presuppositions. It assumes the theological beliefs of its Scripture: that God is the Creator of the world and that people are creatures made in God's image and likeness.

Hence, scriptural passages are used as an external authority to support the argument of the gospel.

The form of the Second Gospel is, however, even less like a **Hellenistic biography** than that of Matthew. It does not begin with birth stories, and, if 16.8 is the original ending, it is quite without parallel. This is not to deny that it shares features common to Matthew and to Hellenistic biographies in presenting an account of Jesus' public ministry in and around Palestine at the time of Herod Antipas and Pilate, dramatically conceived, with an apologetic, exemplary, laudatory and legitimizing purpose. Of the motifs listed by Downing (above, p. 253), Mark exhibits a negative attitude to family background and ancestral tradition but mentions travels, risking of life, prodigies, miracles, divine guidance, quality of thought, concern for community, death and burial.

Nevertheless, it has been argued, notably by J. M. Hull,[3] that the Markan account of Jesus' miracles conforms more closely to that of magic in the **Hellenistic Magical Papyri** than does Matthew's. Hull suggests that the healing of the deaf mute in Mark 7.32–37 is the best example, since the details which mention that Jesus takes him aside, puts his fingers into his ears, spits and touches his tongue, looks up to heaven and groans, using a command in a foreign language ('Ephphatha'), can be found in accounts from pagan sources about healing miracles, especially in the magical papyri (Hull, pp. 76 and 82f., but note that the unusual term, *mogilalos*, is used in 7.32 and in LXX Isaiah 35.6, suggesting a connexion with the prophetic tradition). A second example is the gradual healing of the blind man in 8.22–26, in which Jesus leads the blind man by the hand out of the village, spits on his eyes, lays his hands upon him and asks whether he can see. When the man replies, 'I see men but they are like trees walking', the ritual is repeated and the cure is complete. Privacy, spittle and laying on of hands are features of the rituals found in the magical papyri. Again, in Mark's account of the raising of Jairus' daughter, an Aramaic command is included, 'Taking her by the hand, he (Jesus) said to her, Talitha cumi, which means, Little girl, I say to you arise' (5.41). Also, like Matthew, with some differences of detail, which again highlight technique, Mark recounts the story of Jesus' exorcism of a demon in Gentile territory, 5.1–20; and the narrative shares with the exorcism in Philostratus' *Apollonius of Tyana*, 4.20, the rebuke of the demon, and the proof of the exorcism in the flight of the swine.

This Markan interest in healing ritual, however, does not serve to show Jesus' divinity as Apollonius' techniques display his. Whatever the merits of a suggestion that behind the present text of Mark lies a source picturing Jesus as a *theios aner* (divine man), the gospel in its present form is better understood as anti-docetic. Jesus is indeed God's Christ and son (e.g. 1.1, 34; 8.29; 9.41; 12.35; 14.61; 15.32; 1.11; 3.11; 5.7; 9.7; 15.39) but this means no more than that he is a human being, obedient to the creator God, whose miracles display God's recreative purpose in defeating Satan and his demons to renew people's lives. The word 'power' (*dunamis*) in the remark in 6.14: 'Some said (about Jesus), John the Baptist has been raised from the dead; that is why these powers are at work in him', or in the account of the healing of the woman with a haemorrhage, 5.30: 'And Jesus, perceiving in himself that power had gone forth from him', refers to the power of God (12.24 and 14.62), so that Jesus' miracles are reasons for praising God (2.12), evidence of the work of the Holy Spirit not of Beelzebul (3.28–30). But does the fact that Mark sanctions exorcisms performed in Jesus' name (9.38–41) suggest, on the contrary, that Jesus' divine power rather than God's is the focus of attention, and that, besides, this power can be manipulated by outsiders? The context of the teaching, sandwiched between an instructionn to receive a child 'in my name' (9.37) and an assurance of reward to those who help anyone bearing the name of Christ (9.41) indicates that 'in the name of Jesus/Christ' points beyond the man Jesus to the God whose mission he performs: 'Whoever receives me, receives not me but him who sent me' (9.37). Hull's study, then, is certainly successful in showing that motifs from Hellenistic descriptions of magic are found in the Gospel of Mark, but their use in another theological context gives them a different significance.

More recently, V. K. Robbins has argued that the rhetoric of Mark's gospel has been deeply influenced by the form exemplified in Xenophon's *Memorabilia*.[4] Robbins thinks Mark combines Jewish and Hellenistic features. Chapter 3 of the study begins by concentrating on the rhetoric of the prophets Elijah, Elisha and Jeremiah, who introduce their prophecies with 'Thus says the Lord', but not only is this formula absent from Mark, it is absent because

> Yahweh functions in the narrative (of Mark) in a manner similar to the functions of a god in Xenophon's *Memorabilia*. The wisdom of both Socrates and Jesus and the necessity of accepting death as a result of a verdict by the established representatives of the people have their ultimate source in the will of the deity. Yet no scenes depict the deity giving specific instructions . . . rather, in contrast to the biblical prophets, both Socrates and Jesus manifest an autonomy of their own that exhibits itself in the unity between speech and action in their lives' (p. 200).

Like Jesus in Mark, suggests Robbins, Socrates is an embodiment of virtue exhibited in his deeds, and of wisdom exhibited in his teaching, and the story, like Mark's, exposes the indictment of the hero as unjust (p. 63).

In spite of these similarities, however, Robbins shows that even a major component in the presentation of the two teachers is handled quite differently. One of the points highlighted by Robbins' comparison is that both Socrates and Jesus attract disciples, but in Mark's gospel, the disciples fail to understand Jesus, whereas in Xenophon's *Memorabilia*, many of Socrates' disciples do understand him and follow in his footsteps. Moreover, there are other striking differences which Robbins fails to take sufficiently into account. Xenophon's style could hardly be less like Mark's, and the literary techniques, especially the intrusive guiding role played by the narrator, are not matched in Mark, as Robbins admits (p. 63). The long dialogues of Socrates, so unlike Jesus' teaching in Mark, are not simply an alternative form of teaching, but that which best exemplifies the virtues Socrates advocates. The teasing questions and answers, the cajoling, the explanations, the topical progression, all express the articulate rationality of Socratic philosophy. Jesus' scriptural quotations, prophecies, parables, woes and wisdom sayings evidence a completely different literary world. Robbins asserts that Mark, like Xenophon's *Memorabilia*, and unlike the Old Testament prophetic books, has no room for threats of judgment and punishment, but he completely overlooks the reference to Gehenna in Mark 9.43–48, the cursing of the fig tree (Mark 11.13f. and 20–21), the Temple incident (Mark 11.15–19) and the cosmic dimensions of the judgment depicted in Mark 13.24–27 (p. 200). In other words, although on a very general level similarities between Mark and *Memorabilia* can be recognized, the different religious and philosophical concerns of each have generated different genres.

Nevertheless, Robbins' argument in chapter 4, although confused, includes some important observations. Beginning once more with biblical traditions, the role of Jesus as teacher in Mark is compared to that of Yahweh and the prophets in Scripture. The patriarchs and prophets are summoned by Yahweh to perform specific tasks and are given detailed instructions. Jesus, in Mark, is summoned by God (1.9–13) but he is not given specific instructions, so that Jesus acts without receipt of a divine command. In this, says Robbins, he is much more like Socrates, who also takes the initiative in attracting students to follow him. But Robbins does not mention Jesus' endowment with the Spirit, like the prophets, which organizes the Markan account.

The vocabulary of summons (*deurō*, 'come') and following (*akolouthein*) is found both in the account of Yahweh's calls in the Septuagint and in accounts of Socrates' life. The vocabulary of teacher (*didaskalos*) and disciple (*mathētēs*), however, is almost entirely absent from the Septuagint, except in variant readings of Codex Alexandrinus (Jer. 13.31; 20.11; 46.9) and in later books which reflect the Hellenistic practice of kings accompanied by teachers (Esther 6.1, II Macc. 1.10). Unfortunately, Robbins fails to take note of the wisdom tradition in the Septuagint, because it uses the term 'son' (*huios*) instead of 'disciple' (e.g. Prov. 1.8, 15; 2.1; 3.1). Rather Robbins' argument moves to the rabbinic tradition, with the remark 'It is customary to presuppose that the teacher/disciple relation in Mark derives from the rabbi/disciple relation in first century CE Judaism', citing the use of the term 'rabbi' in Mark 9.5; 10.51; 11.21; 14.45, and noting the biblical and rabbinic parallels to *akolouthein opisō* and *erchesthai opisō* ('to follow or come after') (p. 101). Nevertheless, the rabbinic tradition does not tell stories about Rabbis who summon disciples, but, on the contrary, about disciples who seek out Rabbis. Nor were the Rabbis itinerant preachers as Jesus was, but teachers settled in particular places. This, of course, was also true of Socrates in Athens, and so Robbins has to look for parallels to Jesus' travelling life-style in Hellenistic literature within the Cynic tradition (p. 88). Even Robbins' recourse to Philostratus' *Apollonius of Tyana*, who was a traveller and a preacher, does not help him here, because Apollonius did not summon disciples, but disciples sought him out, and, although they followed him on a journey, a different verb is used (pp. 105f.). Robbins fails to notice, too, that the purpose of Apollonius' journeys was to learn the arts of the sages in India and Egypt, another major difference from Mark's Jesus. But he does cite Josephus' account of Elijah's call of Elisha, which, he suggests, combines the Hebrew story of the prophet/servant with the Sophist tradition of the teacher/disciple (*Antiq.* 8.354), concluding that Josephus is close to Mark (pp. 99f.). Robbins has performed a useful service in drawing attention to these variations.

Nevertheless, because his study is a socio-rhetorical exercise, two separate questions are muddled in the discussion. The first concerns literary forms, and the second, social realities reflected in the literature. Mark represents Jesus as a teacher who calls disciples to follow him. Does the text impose the literary conventions of Xenophon's *Memorabilia* on the tradition of Jesus, or does the text reflect the historical reality of Jesus' actual mission? The evidence from the rest of the New Testament, particularly from Paul's epistles, indicates that the historical Jesus attracted disciples who played a significant part in the life of the early church. So much Mark presumably inherited from the tradition about Jesus. The historical Jesus may well have owed something to the practice of the Cynic itinerant preachers, since first-century Palestine had long been part of the Hellenistic world, but this practice was mediated by Jewish traditions of messianic heralds.

At the next stage, however, was Mark influenced by the genre, *Memorabilia*, in taking up and presenting traditions about Jesus? The evidence that Robbins presents shows similarities at some points, but he both omits much from Mark in concentrating on Jesus' teaching role, and underemphasizes the differences which are obvious even in the matters inviting comparison, so that his case fails. Near the end of his study, Robbins is forced to admit that

> the role of the teacher to prepare the community for future vindication, the mighty works to validate Jesus' authority, and the title 'Son of man' to link the authoritative earthly ministry of Jesus with the authoritative action within the heavenly realm reveal direct influence from prophetic-apocalyptic traditions nurtured within first century Judaism (p. 186f.).

In Mark, as in Matthew, therefore, motifs are to be found which do not occur in Hellenistic literature, especially those associated with eschatological expectations of resurrection and last judgment (e.g. 1.15; 8.31–9.1; 9.31; 10.33f.; ch. 13; 16.1–8).

• The Gospel of Mark and its Scripture

If, therefore, the genre of the Gospel of Mark cannot be defined purely in terms of the literature of the non-Jewish or non-Christian Hellenistic world, how far does the Scripture it accepts underlie and inform its vocabulary, motifs or genre?

1. *Quotations and allusions.* The Gospel according to Mark quotes Scripture less frequently than the First Gospel, and usually scriptural references are found in Jesus' teaching not in the narrator's voice. In 1.2f., however, John the Baptizer's ministry is prefaced by a quotation formally introduced: 'As it is written in Isaiah the prophet, Behold, I send my messenger before your face, who shall prepare your way; the voice of one crying in the wilderness: Prepare the way of the Lord, make his paths straight'. Jesus very often quotes Scripture in support of his argument (e.g. 7.10; 8.18; 10.6, 27; 11.17; 12.10–11, 26, 29–31, 36; 13.8, 12, 14, 19, 22, 24f., 26, 27; 14.27, 62).

Moreover, the heavenly voice at Jesus' baptism and transfiguration (1.11; 9.7) echoes Ps. 2.7, Gen. 22.2 or Isa. 42.1. The narrator of the Second Gospel, however, seems content more often to allude to Scripture than to quote it, e.g. John the Baptizer is dressed like Elijah (if the longer reading is correct, Mark 1.6; II Kings 1.8), the Son of man coming on the clouds in Mark 13.26 alludes to Daniel 7.13, and there are allusions to Psalms 22 and 69 in the description of Jesus' crucifixion: Mark 15.24 and Psalm 22.18, Mark 15.29 and Psalm 22.7, Mark 15.36 and Psalm 69.21. A. Suhl's argument that the pattern of prophecy and fulfilment is absent from Mark[5] is refuted by this evidence and especially by Mark 14.27.[6]

Mark generally refers to Scripture by *hē graphē* ('Scripture') or *gegraptai* ('it stands written') (11.17; 12.10f.; 14.27), and twice specifically to Isaiah (Mark 1.2 and 7.6f.). God's commandment is quoted as 'Moses said' in 7.10 (and cf. 1.44; 10.4–9; 12.19), and Psalm 110 is introduced by 'David said in the Holy Spirit' in 12.36. Quotations or allusions seem to come mostly from the Septuagint, and particularly from the Pentateuch, the prophets (especially Isaiah but also Malachi, Zechariah, Ezekiel, Jeremiah, Amos, and Joel, with Daniel to the fore in Mark 13 and elsewhere, and a few references to Samuel and Kings) and from the Psalms. There may also be allusions to Job (10.29) and Esther (6.23).

2. *Jesus' titles.* Mark introduces Jesus as the Christ, the Son of God (1.11), if 'Son of God', omitted in some ancient manuscripts, is the correct reading. The opening statement 'The beginning of the *gospel* of Jesus Christ' does not imply that the genre of the text is a narrative gospel, in spite of the fact that later generations seem to have read it in that sense. The word *euangelion* in Mark retains its old meaning of 'good news', and essentially 'good news' about the imminence of the kingdom of God: 'The time is fulfilled, the kingdom of God is at hand. Repent, and believe in the good news' (1.15; cf. 8.35; 10.29; 14.9). In Mark, Jesus is the **Messiah**, the **Son of David**, understood to be predicted in Scriptural passages like Ps. 118.25f. (Mark 11.9f. and 10.47f.), although the title seems to have been reckoned defective in the discussion in Mark 12.35–37. In the Passion narrative, 'the king of the Jews' (Mark 15.2, 9, 12, 18, 26; cf. 15.32) is, nevertheless, a key term in the trial before Pilate and the crucifixion. Generations of scholars have drawn attention to the so-called 'Messianic Secret' in Mark. Although Mark clearly introduces Jesus as 'the Christ' (1.1 and 8.29 etc.), Jesus is represented forbidding disciples from making his identity known (e.g. 8.30). Indeed, even when Jesus explains the nature of his mission (8.31–33), the disciples fail to understand its implications, and their lack of understanding becomes a theme in the rest of the book, culminating in their betrayal, denial and desertion in Jerusalem. Why did Mark organize his work in this way? The most obvious reason for Jesus' prohibition in chapter 8 is because the disciples, like the implied readers, cannot grasp the significance of Jesus' identity until his mission is completed in crucifixion and resurrection, but are there other reasons for the Markan structure? The obtuseness of the disciples may function as a useful rhetorical device to allow repetition, and thereby the clarification of one of the gospel's central themes. We saw earlier that, since the implied reader is let into the secret in the first verse, an ironical

perspective is developed for the reader's appreciation. It could be, however, that the implied reader is meant to sympathize with the disciples in their incredulity, because the acceptance of a suffering Messiah whose disciple is supposed to 'take up his cross and follow him' is as abhorrent to the implied reader as to the disciple. Some commentators have seen the failure of the disciples as Markan polemic against the original leaders of the church centred in Jerusalem (e.g. Kelber), but this hypothesis meets with the difficulty that it overlooks Mark 14.28, prophesying a meeting between Jesus and the disciples after his death and their desertion.[7]

The title '**Son of God**' occurs less frequently in Mark than in Matthew, but at key points. The divine voice at the baptism and transfiguration nominates Jesus as God's Son (1.11 and 9.7); the demons or unclean spirits recognize him (3.11 and 5.7); Jesus answers 'I am' to the High Priest's question, 'Are you the Christ, the Son of the Blessed?' (14.61, contra Matthew); and the centurion acknowledges Jesus' sonship at his death (15.39). Jesus, then, is God's son as Israel was God's son (Ex. 4.22; Hos. 11.1), initiated for his mission through water (1.9–11; Ex. 14–15), travelling along a way determined by God (8.27; Ex. 13.18, 21; and cf. Mark 1.3; Isa. 40.3), and tempted in the wilderness for forty days (Mark 1.12f., Ex. 15.22f.; Israel was in the wilderness for forty years, Ex. 16.35, Deut. 2.7). The reference to wild beasts and ministering angels in the wilderness may reflect Ps. 91.11–13. Moreover Jesus represents Israel as God's servant (1.11 and Isa. 42.1). According to other Scriptural passages, Israel's sonship was focused in the king, and so the same reference in Mark 1.11 also reflects the royal Ps. 2.7 (cf. II Sam. 7.14).

Some scholars have been tempted to interpret the application of *kyrios* (**lord**) to Jesus in both Matthew and Mark as a confession of his divinity, and have inferred from this that 'Son of God' implies Jesus' divinity too. *Kyrios* is used in Mark to refer to God (e.g. 1.3; 5.19; 12.29f.), but it is also used of human beings with responsibility (12.9; 13.35). Its application to Jesus, therefore, recognizes no more than his human dignity (7.28; 10.51). Certainly, the gospels assert Jesus' crucial significance in making God's mercy known to humanity, and the phrase 'Son of God' indicates his importance, but by picturing him as a truly obedient Israelite, not as the Second Person of the Trinity. The synoptic gospels did not formulate questions about Jesus' nature in the terms which exercised later generations of Christians, and hence had no need to use 'Son' in the sense found in the Creeds.

3. *The prophets*. Jesus' ministry is heralded by John the Baptizer, who is identified as Elijah (1.6?; 9.13) in his role as messenger of the eschatological events (Mal. 3.1; Mark 1.2), but Jesus himself is not unlike Elijah in some respects. He too calls disciples as Elijah called Elisha (Mark 1.16–20; 2.14; I Kings 19.19f.), he performs miracles (the healing of the Syro-Phoenician's daughter, Mark 7.24–30, cf. I Kings 17.8–24) and he suffers unjustly (Mark 8.28–33; 9.2–8; I Kings 19.1–3, and cf. the fate of John the Baptist, Mark 6.14–29). The disciples can look forward to suffering likewise (Mark 8.34–38; 13.9–13). In the story of the transfiguration Jesus is also associated with Moses presumably here in his role as persecuted prophet (although Mark 9.2–8 does not echo the vocabulary of Moses' transfiguration in Ex. 34.29–35).

A Moses typology is less developed in Mark than in Matthew; but, like Moses, Jesus is instrumental in feeding the five thousand and the four thousand in the wilderness (Mark 6.34–44; 8.1–10; Ex. 16; Num. 11), leads his twelve disciples to victory in their disputes with opponents (Mark 2.1–3.6; 3.22–30; 7.1–23; 8.11–12; 10.2–9; 11.27–12.40; Ex. 17.8; Num. 16; 21.11, 31.) and is present at a Passover meal (Mark 14.12; Ex. 12–13). Perhaps Jesus' acceptance of the strange exorcist who healed in his name (Mark 9.37f.) was meant to reflect Moses' acceptance of prophets in Num. 11.26–30. Perhaps, too, the failure of the disciples mirrors the failure of the Israelites on their way through the wilderness, so that, in the end, Jesus has to forfeit his life as Moses did. But Jesus is like other prophetic figures as well. He often retires to pray, like Samuel or Elisha (Mark 1.35; 6.46; 14.32–42; I Sam. 7.5; 8.6; II Kings 4.33; 6.17; and see Jer. 7.16) and he is like Elisha in other ways. He is called the Holy One of God (1.24; II Kings 4.9), he performs feeding miracles (Mark 6.34–44; 8.1–10; and II Kings 4.42–44) and he brings the dead back to life by touch (Mark 5.22–34; II Kings 4.18–31; 13.20–21). The Markan Jesus, like the Matthaean, also resembles some of the prophets in telling indicative parables (Mark 4.1–34; 12.1–11; II Sam. 12 and Isa. 5). Finally, Jesus, like the prophet Ezekiel, refers to himself as Son of man, at two key places using the designation to interpret 'Christ, Son of God' (Mark 8.31 and 14.62, cf. Dan. 7.14; Ezek. 2.1, 8; 3.1).

4. *Other motifs.* As in Matthew, the story about Jesus' walking on the water, though without the Matthaean reference to Peter, seems to evoke the Genesis account of the Spirit moving across the waters to begin creation (Mark 6.45–52; Gen. 1.2). To the Markan comment that Jesus meant to pass them by, there are parallels in the stories of theophanies in Ex. 33.18–23 and I Kings 19.11–14, where the same verb is used in the Septuagint, *parerchomai*. The connection between this image of recreation and that of the feeding miracle in the desert is brought out by the Markan condemnation of the disciples, 'And they were utterly astounded, for they did not understand about the loaves, but their hearts were hardened' (6.51f.).

The climax of the Markan story of Jesus is reached in the Passion narrative, in which many themes and motifs from Scripture are called into play. A motif of punishment and destruction is emphasized in the cursing of the fig tree (11.13, 20–21; Jer. 8.13). Jesus' suffering and death is the fate of the innocent man persecuted by vicious enemies, as in Psalms 22 and 69 (e.g. 15.24, 31, 34, 36). The darkness which follows Jesus' death is a fulfilment of Amos' prophecy about God's judgment (Mark 15.33; Amos 8.9). The significance of Jesus' death had already been explained by Jesus' words over the bread and wine at the last supper, seen as a Passover (14.2). The broken bread/body points to innocent martyrdom, and the wine/blood is the blood of the covenant (Ex. 24.6–8) which establishes a covenant between God and 'many'. The Matthaean account includes a reference to forgiveness of sins (26.28), not found in Mark.

5. *Sentences, phrases and words.* Similarity of themes and motifs is matched by similar sentence forms, phrases and vocabulary, although the amount of teaching

273

material as well as the range of parallels is not as great as it is in Matthew. For example, there are no blessings in Mark, and *dikaios* (righteous) is used only in Mark 2.17, 6.20, while *dikaiosunē* (righteousness) appears not at all. Nevertheless, *amēn* is used in solemn declarations (Mark 3.28; 10.15, 29; 11.23; 13.43; 13.30; 14.9, 25, 30) and there are woe-sayings (Mark 13.17 and 14.21) and wisdom sayings (Mark 2.17, 19, 21ff.; 3.24, 28, 34; 4.11f., 24f.; 9.37, 40–50; 10.14f.; 11.23–26), while Jesus' teaching is described as 'wisdom' in 6.2.

Moreover, Mark's story of Jesus, like Matthew's, resembles the stories of prophets in Exodus, Numbers, I and II Kings, with their episodic narratives punctuated by dialogue and miracle. The same proviso must be entered in the case of Mark as of Matthew, however. Although Mark pictures Jesus praying, he includes no divine speech, except in the stories of Jesus' baptism and transfiguration, and these accounts are more like rabbinic than scriptural counterparts.

One of the features of the Markan text to which commentators draw attention is the insertion of one story in the middle of another so that the two are read in juxtaposition. The story of Jesus healing the woman with a haemorrhage (5.22–34) is inserted into that of the raising of Jairus' daughter (5.22–24 and 35–43), the details of John the Baptizer's death (6.14–29) are inserted between the Twelve's missionary charge and their return (6.5–13 and 30), the Temple incident (11.15–19) is inserted into the account of the fruitless fig tree (11.12–14 and 20–21), and Jesus' trial before the Sanhedrin at night (14.55–65) is inserted into the narrative of Peter's denial (14.53–4 and 66–72). This kind of insertion is also a feature of parts of Mark's Scripture. For example, the stories of Judah's marriage, the birth of his children, the fate of Onan and Tamar (Gen. 38) are inserted between the sale of Joseph to Potiphar in Egypt (Gen. 37.36) and Joseph's success in Egypt (39.1–6). The insertions provide interludes which add to the tension of the first story, and sometimes point a contrast (Peter and Jesus, Joseph and Judah).

6. *Satan.* Although the Matthaean and Markan stories differ in many details, then, it is true of both that they imitate vocabulary, phrases, sentence-style, motifs, themes, structures and focus from their Scripture. Mark's portrait of Jesus closely resembles Scriptural portraits of prophets (Mark 6.4 and 14.65). Nevertheless, just those modifications of most of its Scripture already noticed as features of Matthaean theology which have affected its literary form are present in Mark too. Like its Scripture, Mark attributes unbelief at some points to God's hardening of people's hearts (e.g. Mark 6.52; cf. Ex. 7.22; 8.32); but, like Matthew, Mark's theology envisages a power in opposition to God, called Satan or Beelzebul, the prince of demons, whose minions are demons or unclean spirits (1.23–28, 34) which have to be exorcized. There are, however, dissimilarities in detail between Mark and Matthew. Mark differs from Matthew in not calling Satan 'the tempter' (cf. Matt. 4.1–11), although it pictures Satan tempting Jesus, using the same verb. Nor does Mark use *ho diabolos* (the devil) as Matthew does, not only in 4.1–11, but also in 13.39 and 25.41. Mark more than Matthew shares with the book of Tobit an interest in the rituals accompanying exorcism, although the details are different. It also shares with Tobit a

belief in angels, but they play a smaller part in Mark than in Matthew (Mark 1.13; 8.38; 13.27, 32; the young man in the white robe at the empty tomb may also be an angel, 16.5). Again like Matthew, Mark has most in common with Jubilees' teachings about Satan but Mark does not join Matthew and Jubilees in their belief in guardian angels.

7. *Eschatology.* The eschatological perspective which dominates Matthew, and which reflects that of Daniel but not most of Scripture, exercises a commanding influence in Mark too. Again like Matthew, Markan instruction is given without the usual apocalyptic literary conventions of visions, heavenly journeys or symbolic figures. Jesus, the prophetic martyr, is raised from the dead, and is expected to return in judgment (16.1–8; 13.26f.) as part of a cosmic transformation. The life, death and resurrection of Jesus, therefore, have human and cosmic significance as evidence of the creator God's judgment and mercy. Jesus, the prophet of the eschaton, inspired by God's spirit (1.10, 12; 3.29), reveals God's plan to establish his kingdom in power (9.1 and 13.24–27), and himself leads the way through death to resurrection. This story is not a tragedy of innocent martyrdom, but a theodicy of creation, fall and recreation through suffering and death. In spite of differences in detail and scope, therefore, it seems fair to conclude that the genre of Mark is the same as that of Matthew.

For Further Reading see p. 298.

19   The Genre of the Third Gospel

• The Gospel of Luke and Hellenistic Greek Literature

   1. *Historiography*. After one reads the gospels according to Matthew and Mark, the opening preface to Luke creates surprise. The formal address to Theophilus, the reference to earlier attempts at writing the narrative, the elaborate 'literary' style, not quite consonant with the rigorous standards of Atticism, but superior to anything in the other gospels, the self-conscious purpose, immediately take the reader into the world of Hellenistic literature. The preface conforms to a well-established convention with many verbal parallels, of which Josephus, in the two-volume *Against Apion* written about 95 CE, provides the closest:

> In my history of our Antiquities, most excellent Epaphroditus, I have, I think, made sufficiently clear to any who peruse that work the extreme antiquity of our Jewish race . . . Since, however, I observe that a considerable number of persons, influenced by the malicious calumnies of certain individuals, discredit the statements in my history concerning our antiquity, and adduce as proof of the comparative modernity of our race the fact that it has not been thought worthy of mention by the best known Greek historians, I consider it my duty to devote a brief treatise to all these points; in order at once to convict our detractors of malignity and deliberate falsehood, to correct the ignorance of others, and to instruct all who desire to know the truth concerning the antiquity of our race. As witnesses to my statements I purpose to call the writers who . . . (*Against Apion* I.1–5; Loeb Classical Library)

> In the first volume of this work, my most esteemed Epaphroditus, I demonstrated the antiquity of our race. . . . (*Against Apion* II.1; cf. Acts 1.1–2)

The Lukan preface claims a similar purpose, to establish the truth (*asphaleia*), but in a less polemical context, since it is left unclear whether previous attempts at telling the story are approved or disapproved. Moreover, since the matter to be related in Luke and the Acts of the Apostles has happened only recently, appeal can be made to eyewitness accounts. Like that of Josephus, however, the Lukan preface introduces two volumes and the terms used are appropriate to the whole work rather than its parts. That the two volumes are described as a kind of history, therefore, does not preclude the possibility that the first volume is a biography of Jesus.

Other details in Luke–Acts seem to confirm the work as a contribution to Graeco–Roman history-writing. 1.5 begins 'In the days of Herod, King of Judaea' and chapter 2 links the events to be described to those of Roman history: 'In those days a decree went out from Caesar Augustus that all the world should be enrolled. This was the first enrolment, when Quirinius was governor of Syria. And all went to be enrolled, each to his own city'. It is a pity that these two statements are historically irreconcilable. Herod died in 4 BCE and was succeeded by his three sons. Only when his son Archelaus was exiled in CE 6 did Judaea become subject to the legate of Syria, who, at that time, was Quirinius. He conducted a local census of property in CE 6–7. In other words, the gospel dates the events both before 4 BCE and in CE 6. In addition, a census of all the (presumably Roman) world is mentioned by no other historian of the period, and there is no evidence that Rome required people to go to their ancestral cities for a census, a rule which would have caused chaos to no purpose. This shows, however, no more than that an historian is only as good as his sources, judicious good sense and skill in presentation. Perhaps we may presume that correct information would have been given had it been available.

Again, chapter 3, probably the original beginning of the gospel before the birth narratives were finally added, dates the public ministries of John and Jesus 'in the fifteenth year of the reign of Tiberius Caesar, Pontius Pilate being governor of Judaea, and Herod being tetrarch of Galilee, and his brother Philip tetrarch of the region of Ituraea and Trachonitis, and Lysanius tetrarch of Abilene; in the high priesthood of Annas and Caiaphas.' The Herod mentioned is Herod Antipas, who appears later in the gospel at 3.19; 8.3; 9.7, 9; 13.31; 23.7–15. 'The high priesthood of Annas and Caiaphas' (see also Acts 4.6) causes some historical difficulty because Annas became high priest in CE 6 but was deposed in CE 15, whereas Caiaphas was high priest from CE 18–36. The best that can be made of this is to suppose that Annas retained some authority even after his deposition since Jews regarded the high priesthood as an office for life, although Annas was not the only deposed high priest who was still alive. Curiously, neither of the names Annas or Caiaphas is mentioned elsewhere in the gospel, not even in the Lukan passion narrative when Jesus is held in the high priest's house before being questioned by Pilate and Herod Antipas (22.54). Pilate is mentioned again in 13.1. The other rulers are named only here because the action of the gospel narrative takes place in the territories of Antipas and Pilate.

The picture in the Acts of the Apostles is much the same, with occasional references to rulers and Roman officials, some of which are hard to square with other contemporary historical evidence.[1] These references, then, confirm the preface's suggestion that the whole work is meant to be historical.

Nevertheless, to return to the preface for a moment, the purpose expressed in 1.4, 'that you may know the truth concerning the things of which you have been informed', may imply something more than the recounting of mundane events as they happened. It could be a claim to give assurance about the eternal significance of Jesus' life, and only the contents of the gospel and Acts can determine what is meant.

Other details in Luke also betray Hellenistic literary conventions. Although Luke retains some of the Hebrew words transliterated in its sources – amen, Beelzebul, Gehenna, mammon, Pascha, Sabbath, Satan – it sometimes omits or translates other foreign words used in Mark, eliminating the barbarity of the source: talitha cumi – Mark 5.41/Luke 8.54; Simon the Canaanaean – Mark 6.18, becomes Simon the zealous one – Luke 6.15; Hosanna Mark 11.9/Luke 19.38; Golgotha – Mark 15.22/ Luke 23.33; Corban – Mark 7.11; ephphatha – Mark 7.34; Eloi, Eloi, lama sabachtani – Mark 15.34, although the last three occur in passages the whole of which Luke omits. Luke also prefers to call Jesus 'Lord' or 'Master' instead of 'Rabbi' (Mark 9.5/Luke 9.33; Mark 10.51/Luke 18.41;), and sometimes replaces 'scribe' by 'lawyer' (Mark 12.28/Luke 10.25; Matt. 23.13/Luke 11.52). Assimilation of cultural details to a Hellenistic environment may also have happened. Vocabulary about house construction is different from the source. Mark 2.4 mentions the removal of a clay roof in a Palestinian house, through which to lower a paralytic to Jesus, but Luke 5.19 refers to tiles, commonly used outside of Palestine. Again in the parable about houses built on rock or sand, Luke refers to 'digging foundations' (6.48; cf. Matt. 7.24), a practice which may have been unusual in Palestine but common in the rest of the Hellenistic world. Similarly, references to days seem to reckon the beginning of the day from dawn according to the Graeco–Roman custom rather than from evening according to the scriptural (Mark 14.1, 12/Luke 22.1, 7; contrast Matt. 26.2, 17; and Luke 22.34 contrast Mark 14.30).

Moral and theological subjects may also reflect Hellenistic motifs. Luke repeats common Greek philosophical teaching about wealth, characterizing opponents as lovers of money (Luke 16.14 of Pharisees) and friends as those who hold all things in common (like the apostles in Acts 4.32–37), although Luke adds to the Greek notion 'the company were of one *psyche*' ('soul', 'life'), the Septuagint expression 'and of one heart'. Some of Luke's soteriological vocabulary also seems to pick up terms from Hellenistic sources. Luke calls Jesus 'saviour' (Luke 2.11), a title given to rulers and great men like Ptolemy Epiphanius (the Rosetta Stone) or Julius Caesar,[2] who, like Jesus, were thought to bring men 'salvation', another key Lukan term (1.69, 71, 77; 2.30; 3.6; 19.9). Here the force is polemical with the claim that 'there is salvation in no one else (but Jesus), for there is no other name under heaven given among men by which we must be saved' (Acts 4.12). This salvation is once characterized as 'peace' (2.14; cf. Acts 9.31) to counter the contention that the Emperor Augustus (27 BCE–CE 14) brought peace to the world.

2. The magical papyri. Given this obvious contact with Hellenistic literary practice, Luke might be expected to borrow elements from such sources in its portrayal of Jesus as a healer. J. M. Hull claims that more than elements have been borrowed when he entitles his chapter on Luke 'the tradition penetrated by magic'.[3] His study covers three subjects, angels, demons and power, of which the last is the most important. Luke–Acts is particularly interested in angels, but since its motifs are derived entirely from its Scripture, the subject will be treated in the next section. Luke–Acts is also interested in demons and is aware of magicians who rival

Christians in their ministries. Hence Acts records stories in which Peter confounds Simon Magus (Acts 8.9–24) and Paul Elymas (Acts 13.6–12). Nevertheless, Luke omits from Mark the two miracle stories which show the closest parallels with Hellenistic magical ritual (7.32–35 and 8.22–25); but since these stories form parts of Luke's 'great omission' from Mark (Mark 6.45–8.26) too much significance cannot be attached to the fact, especially as Luke includes the story of the exorcism of the Gerasene demoniac (Luke 8.26–33/Mark 5.1–20).

Hull's thesis is that 'both Mark and Luke recognize the classes and characteristics of demons and that Luke sometimes adds a detail or class' (p. 105). Thus Luke describes 'a clear, detailed and literal demoniac world' (p. 100). That Luke's writing is vivid and concrete no one would like to deny, but that its treatment of demons is therefore 'literal' or that it provides evidence of 'the tradition penetrated by magic' is another matter.

Much of Hull's evidence comes from a comparison of Lukan versions of stories with their Markan or Matthaean counterparts, but many of his assertions are not justified by the texts. His best example of Lukan interest in specific kinds of demons is the story of the slave girl 'with a spirit of divination' (*pneuma puthōna*) who followed Paul around, pronouncing an oracle about his mission until he exorcized the spirit (Acts 16.16–18). Hull correctly defines 'the spirit of divination' as a Pythonic spirit specializing in oracles (p. 102). Thus Hellenistic belief in the divine inspiration of women who gave oracles is countered in the story by depicting the spirit conquered by 'the name of Jesus'.

Hull is also correct in drawing attention to the fact that Luke transforms the healing of Simon's mother-in-law in Mark 1.29–31 into an exorcism by adding 'he rebuked the fever' (Luke 4.39), but the reason for this seems to be Luke's interest less in distinguishing different demons than in pairing male and female stories, since 'rebuke' repeats the word in the previous account of the man with 'a spirit of an unclean demon' (4.35), and the same 'rebuke' is used in the summary which follows the dual miracles (4.41).

Hull's examples of 'desert loving demons' (p. 104) are even less compelling. He cites Luke 8.29, where the demons 'legion' drive the man into the desert (contrast Mark 5.3, 5, which describes the man living among tombs and in mountains, but note that Luke 8.27 also mentions that the man lives among tombs), and Acts 1.20, which interprets Judas' death as a fulfilment of the Scripture 'Let his habitation become desolate' (Psalm 69.25), remarking that 'the death of Judas left Satan in a congenial place' (p. 104). Hull had already noted that Jesus confronted Satan in the desert, according to the temptation story (p. 97 and Luke 4.1–13), assuming an identification of 'Satan' with 'the devil' or 'the tempter' which rather tells against his thesis that Luke makes distinctions. But the Lukan use of the Psalm in reference to Judas has a meaning other than that attributed to it by Hull. Judas died in a field, not in the desert, Satan is not mentioned in the story, which is seen to fulfil Scripture not Satan's desire, and the quotation of the Psalm is made not as a prediction of the manner of Judas' death but of the fact of his death, in order to justify filling the apostolic position left vacant ('desolate'). Further, Hull's conclusion (p. 104) 'that these are not fluctuating whims of the devils concerned but are part of their constitution, part of that which they reveal under compulsion as being their nature' is not justified by these examples, since Satan's activity in the Gospel of Luke and Acts is not confined to the desert. On his way to Jerusalem, in a synagogue, Jesus heals a woman bound by Satan for eighteen years (13.16), and Satan's actions in Jerusalem are mentioned three times (Luke 22.3, 31; Acts 5.3). In one place too, Luke, with no synoptic parallels, mentions Satan's fall from heaven when Jesus replies to the Seventy (-two)'s* account of their success, 'Lord, even the demons are subject to us in your name', with the statement 'I saw Satan fall like lightning from heaven. Behold I have given you authority to tread upon serpents and scorpions, and over all the power of the enemy' (10.17–19). This makes use of the imagery of Isa. 14.12, to which allusion had been made a few verses earlier (10.14), 'How you are fallen from heaven, O day star, son of Dawn'. The mythological potential of the passage was developed in apocalyptic and other literature (e.g. Rev. 20.1–3; Test. Levi 18.12; Test. Judah 25.3; Test. Asher 7.3). Jesus' promise presumably explains why the odd story about the viper biting Paul's hand without harming him is recounted in Acts 28.3–6.

The case of the dumb demon is hardly more convincing. In comparing Luke 11.14 ('Now he was casting out a demon that was dumb; when the demon had gone out, the dumb man spoke') with Matt. 9.32–33 ('Behold a dumb demoniac was brought to him. And when the demon had been cast out, the dumb man spoke'), Hull comments, 'In Matthew it is the man who is dumb. But in Luke the demon causes dumbness because it is a dumb demon' (p. 104). Actually, both Luke and Matthew refer to the man as a 'dumb man' and the difference between the first part of each sentence may be merely stylistic, Luke generally avoiding the participle of the verb *daimonizomai* ('demoniac') and preferring the less cumbersome 'demon' (except 8.36; compare Mark 5.1–13 with Luke 8.26–33).

Hull's treatment of the Lukan version of the Gerasene exorcism (Luke 8.26–33) also fails to justify his claims. He draws attention to the Lukan 'and they begged him not to command them to depart into the abyss' (Luke 8.31) for the Markan 'and he begged him eagerly not to send them out of the country' (Mark 5.10), citing examples from the Testament of Solomon to show that water is believed to be a demon-destroying force in Hellenistic literature, a matter which Luke is assumed to be acknowledging (p. 100). But Luke follows the Markan ending of the story, in which the swine fall into the sea, and simply integrates this feature into the earlier discussion with the demons to give the story more coherence and force. The 'abyss' is the watery deep of scriptural imagery, the chaos which contrasts with creation (e.g. Gen. 1.1–2), and the Lukan Jesus brings about just what the demons seek to avoid, their exclusion from creation.

Elsewhere in the study, Hull uses the same story to illustrate Lukan belief in combinations of demons, here 'Legion' (8.30 as in Mark 5.1–13). In two other places, seven demons are mentioned: in connexion with Mary Magdalene, 'from whom

*'Seventy' is the most commonly accepted reading, but some important early manuscripts read 'seventy-two'.

seven demons were cast out' (Luke 8.2 no parallels) and in the saying in 11.26 (cf.
Matt. 12.45) which describes an unclean spirit bringing seven other spirits more evil
than himself. A comparison of this last Lukan passage with its Matthaean parallel is
said to show that in contrast to Matthew, where it functions as an allegory about the
generation that rejects Jesus, Luke provides 'an actual description of behaviour and
reactions under certain conditions of varieties of evil spirits' (p. 102). In fact, the
Lukan context interprets the saying as a warning against opposing Jesus' mission
(11.23) and against failing to hear and do the word of God (11.28), and as a
condemnation of those who accuse Jesus of casting out demons by Beelzebul (11.15).
So Lukan use is no less allegorical than Matthaean, and leads in the same way to the
condemnation of 'this generation' (11.29).

What do these arguments amount to? That Acts polemicizes against magicians and
oracles has already been noted, but that in doing so, Luke–Acts depicts Jesus'
healings and exorcisms as evidence that he is inspired by the creator God's spirit (e.g.
Luke 4.18; Acts 2.22), and his followers perform similar wonders 'in Jesus' name', an
expression derived from Mark 9.38/Luke 9.49–50 (cf. Acts 3.6; 16.18). In the gospel,
Luke adopts essentially the same position as its sources, Mark and Matthew or Q,
picturing Satan or the Devil or the Tempter or Beelzebul as the prince of demons,
whose minions tempt people to sin and possess them, sometimes associating these
demons with places away from civilization, like a desert or a graveyard, but showing
them active everywhere. Mark, no less than Luke, recognizes distinctions of
demons, as Hull admits (Mark 9.29, 'This *kind* cannot be driven out by anything but
prayer'), and Matthew or Q mentions an association of seven demons (12.45), so that
even the Lukan transformation of the story of the healing of Simon's mother-in-law
into an exorcism (Luke 4.39), or the mention of the seven demons expelled from
Mary Magdalene (Luke 8.2) hardly introduces entirely new elements into the
tradition. Moreover, the Lukan expression, to cast out demons 'by the finger of God'
(11.20) is an allusion to another of Luke's sources, the Septuagint of Ex. 8.19.

But if Hull's detailed comparison of Lukan passages with Mark and Matthew fails
to justify the title of his chapter on Luke, the third part of his study seems to make a
more substantial claim. Under the heading 'magical power', Hull argues,

> In the thought of Luke, the most remarkable feature is the concentration upon
> *dunamis* not as miracle itself but as miracle-working power. It is regarded by
> Luke as a substance, a *mana*-like charge of divine potency, spiritual insofar as it
> emanates from the world of spirits, but as actual, as vital as the beings who
> possess it. Luke does not stress that Jesus possessed the impressive authority of
> prophets, nor that he had moral power, nor does he use the expression in the
> sense that Jesus had great power (as we say) to perform feats, as if it were an
> ability of skill. 'Power' is not a metaphor but is that reality which carries the actual
> potency of the spirit world into our world (p. 105).

When Hull goes on to ask about the origin of these presuppositions, he replies
(pp. 108f.)

Certainly not from the Old Testament. There is hardly a trace in the Septuagint of the particular meaning given to the word in Mark and Luke. 'Power' is not used to describe miracle-working power in any noticeable way at all, nor for miracle itself, for God's power was just as truly manifest in the great winds and thunder (Psalm 29) as in what we would call supernatural events. The New Testament use we are examining does not spring from the Hebrew conception of nature and history, but from the ancient universal idea of the magical miracle, which in turn rests upon a primitive conception of *mana*.

Some of these generalizations need qualification. Luke does, in fact, use *dunamis* in two senses found in the Septuagint, in the sense of a miracle itself (Luke 10.13; 19.37; Acts 2.22; 8.13; 19.11; Ps. 77.14; 145.4; Bar. 2.11) and in the sense of 'the hosts of heaven' (Luke 21.26/ Mark 13.25; Isa. 34.4 especially the readings in ms B). Moreover, Luke associates *dunamis* with God, 'the Son of man shall be seated at the right hand of the *power* of God' (Luke 22.69; 5.17; cf. Ps. 21.13; 54.1 and especially Ps. 140.7 in the Septuagint version, 'Lord, Lord, power of my salvation'), and with the Holy Spirit, 'And Jesus returned in the *power* of the Spirit into Galilee . . . and he taught in their synagogues being glorified by all' (Luke 4.14; cf. 1.17, 35; 24.49; Acts 1.8; 10.38; Ps. 33.6; and cf. Isa. 61.1–2, a quotation programmatic for Luke, 4.18–19, which associates the Spirit with both miracles and preaching, although the word *dunamis* is not used until the observation in 4.36). This counts against Hull, p. 106, where he treats in isolation the alterations to Mark 1.27 ('What is this? A new teaching. With authority he commands even the unclean spirits and they obey him') in Luke 4.36 ('What is this word? For with authority *and power* he commands the unclean spirits and they come out'). Elsewhere, Luke, like Mark, connects 'power' with the Son of man's future return: 21.27, 'The Son of man coming in a cloud with power and great glory' (Mark 13.26; cf. Dan. 7.13–14, which uses *exousia* 'authority' not *dunamis* 'power', but Luke often associates the two, as in 4.36).

This means that of the 25 instances of *dunamis* in Luke–Acts, 15 seem straightforwardly to reflect Septuagint usage. Moreover, in doing so, twice a link is made between miracles and the mission of a prophet. John the Baptist will come 'in the spirit and power of Elijah' (1.17) and Jesus is the prophet predicted in Isa. 61.1–2 (4.18–19).

It may be helpful to list the remaining instances to discover whether Hull's description elucidates them:

4.36 With authority and power he (Jesus) commands the unclean spirits (cf. Mark 1.27).

5.17 And the power of the Lord was with him to heal/was present to heal them (contrast Matt. 9.1/Mark 2.1).

6.19 For power came forth from him and healed them all (contrast Matt. 4.24–25; Mark 3.10–11).

8.46 For I (Jesus) perceive that power has gone forth from me (parallel Mark 5.30).

9.1   And he (Jesus) gave them (the Twelve) power and authority over all demons.
      (See Mark 6.7, which uses 'authority' but not 'power'.)
(10.19 Behold I (Jesus) have given you authority . . . over all the power of the
      enemy.)
(Acts 3.12 As though by our own power of piety we (Peter and John) had made
      him walk.)
Acts 4.7   By what power or by what name did you (Peter) do this?
Acts 6.8   Stephen, full of grace and power, did great wonders and signs among
      the people.
(Acts 8.10 This man (Simon Magus) is that power of God which is called great.)

We should consider whether, in the context of the whole of Luke–Acts, these statements attribute to 'power' the meaning '*mana*-like charge of divine potency'. Hull demonstrates that taken out of context they can be read in that sense. Within the framework of the Lukan belief in a creator God whose acts of creation and recreation express his power, however, Hull's suggested meaning appears inappropriate. It is just because this power is not a *mana*-like substance that it cannot be sold (Acts 8.18). The notion that, as Hull says on p. 107, 'power' is 'a property which can be conveyed either with the will of the donor, as in Luke 9.1, or without it, as in 8.46' misses the point of who the ultimate donor is, God, although, in view of Acts 3.12, on p. 108 this point has to be conceded. Even in Luke 6.19 and 8.46, 'power' is no *mana*-like substance behaving like electricity. 6.19 occurs in a summary of Jesus' preaching and healing – the crowds 'came to hear him and to be healed' (6.17), and the story in which 8.46 plays a part ends with the climax 'Daughter, your faith has made you well', referring to the woman's faith in God whose agent Jesus is.

In footnote 40, p. 164, Hull remarks that 'in II Maccabees 3.38 great care is advised in the selection of ambassadors to Jerusalem "because there is some peculiar power of God about the place" . . . This is the only case in which *dunamis* is used in the Lukan sense in Old Testament or Apocryphal writings.' By 'the Lukan sense' Hull means 'a *mana*-like substance'. II Maccabees 3.38 forms the end of a story about Heliodorus who tried to gain access to the Temple treasury but was prevented because 'the Ruler of spirits and of all power produced a mighty apparition, so that all . . . were stricken with terror at the power of God' (3.24). Heliodorus then 'bore witness to everyone of the miracles of the supreme God' (3.36). The whole section in II Maccabees does have much in common with Luke, but because each text sees miracles as the expression of the creator God's power, not because each sees power as a *mana*-like substance.

Hence, Luke–Acts does not represent 'the tradition penetrated by magic', but the eschatological tradition of Mark and Matthew or Q extended and clarified through additional examples.

3. *Symmetrical patterns*. A completely different argument in favour of Lukan dependence on Hellenistic literature is advanced by C. H. Talbert.[4] The first part of the book details the patterns structuring Luke–Acts that provide evidence of duality

and balance like that displayed in architecture and art throughout the Mediterranean world, including Palestine, although the whole study gives much more weight to the important place such considerations played in Graeco–Roman literature and education.

> The Greek loved symmetry, pattern and balance. From at least the time of Isocrates, the form of what was said was regarded as more important than what was said. The Greek not only liked his creations to be symmetrical or patterned, he also believed that the universe at large must be so ordered . . . Therefore, Greeks tended to impose pattern where it was not in fact to be found . . . At the beginning of the Christian era, moreover, the Roman educational process tended to reinforce and cultivate the classical perspective just as Greek education had done prior to this time. This was true both of what was read and of how it was read. In what was the equivalent of our secondary schools Vergil . . . was the foundation of the Latin course. Next to him, Horace was most read. Homer's works, of course, were the basis of the Greek course. It is precisely in these works that the architectonic skills of the classical world are greatest. (pp. 69–70)

Chapters 2, 3 and 4 of Talbert's study give details of a similar architectonic design in Luke–Acts. Not all of Talbert's examples are convincing, as J. A. Fitzmyer remarks in his commentary,[5] but the following seem to evidence deliberate patterning. Five features in the first part of the gospel and of Acts correspond: a preface dedicating the book to Theophilus (Luke 1.1–4; Acts 1.1–5); Jesus/the disciples praying before receiving the Spirit (Luke 3.21; Acts 1.14, 24); the Spirit descending with physical manifestation (Luke 3.22; Acts 2.1–13); the ministry opening with a sermon which gives the theme for what follows, fulfilment of prophecy and rejection of Jesus (Luke 4.16–30; Acts 2.14–40); fulfilment exemplified in teaching and healing, rejection in conflicts/persecution (Luke 4.31–8.56; Acts 2.41–12.17). Again, both the gospel and Acts picture their chief protagonists, Jesus and Paul, making a journey to Jerusalem, and some of the events which happen in Jerusalem are similar. Both have a positive attitude in visiting the Temple (Luke 19.45–48; Acts 21.26), the Sadducees do not believe their teaching of the resurrection but the scribes/Pharisees support Jesus/Paul (Luke 20.27–39; Acts 23.6–9), both undergo trials (Luke 22.26; 23.1; 8, 13; Acts 23–26), in which some of the details also correspond: each is declared innocent three times (Luke 24.4, 14, 22; Acts 23.9; 25.25; 26.31), both are questioned by one of the Herods (Luke 23.6–12; Acts 25.13–26.32) and by a Roman official (Luke 23.1; Acts 24.1; 25.1), the Jews cry 'Away with this man/him' (Luke 23.18; Acts 21.36), a centurion favours Jesus/Paul (Luke 23.47; Acts 27.3, 43).

Acts 1–12 and 13–28 also display a symmetrical pattern. Each begins with a manifestation of the Spirit (Acts 2.1–4; 13.1–3) which results in preaching (Acts 2.14–40; 13.16–40) and a miracle healing a man lame from birth (Acts 3.1–10; 14.8–13). After speeches, both Stephen and Paul are stoned by Jews but the result is that the preaching nevertheless spreads into new territory (Acts 6.8–8.4; 14.19–23). Both Peter and Paul are forced by divine guidance into a mission to the Gentiles, which each has to justify in Jerusalem (Acts 10–11; 13–21). Both suffer imprisonment, but chapters 12 and 28 end with a statement about the success of the word of God (Acts 12.24; 28.31).

Other passages draw out parallels between Peter and the other Apostles in the early chapters and Paul in the later chapters. Both Peter and Paul confront magicians (Acts 8.9–24; 13.6–12), both raise a Christian from the dead (9.36–43; 20.9–12), both restrain Gentiles from offering them worship (10.25–26; 14.13–15), both are miraculously delivered from prison (12.6–11; 16.24–26), the Spirit is given by their laying on hands (8.14–17; 19.1–6), they are defended by a Pharisee(s) before the Sanhedrin (5.34–39; 23.9), each is designated a witness by the risen Lord (1.8; 23.11; 26.16).

Sometimes it is difficult to decide whether the patterns Talbert discerns are part of a design or simply occasioned by the limited repertoire of the text. Alternations of healings, explanatory speeches, opposition or imprisonment, miraculous escape, could occur more by accident than plan. Most of the examples listed by Talbert in chapters 2 and 3 are of this kind. Repetition is, of course, an aide-memoire as well as an aesthetic delight, as Talbert admits. But the parallels between the birth stories of John the Baptist and Jesus in Luke 1 and 2 are acknowledged by all commentators. J. A. Fitzmyer (p. 313f.) recognizes a step-parallelism in which Jesus is shown always to be superior. The announcement of each birth follows a similar pattern: the parents, who expect no child, are introduced (1.5–10; 1.26–27), an angel appears (1.11; 1.28), Zechariah/ Mary is troubled (1.12; 1.29), the angel tells each not to fear (1.13; 1.30), the birth of a son and his name, John/Jesus, is predicted (1.13; 1.31), John is to be great before the Lord and Jesus is to be great (1.15; 1.32); Zechariah/ Mary asks how this will happen (1.18; 1.34), a sign is given (1.20; 1.36), and finally there is a contrast between Zechariah's forced silence and Mary's answer (1.23; 1.38). The similarity continues in the accounts of each child's birth (1.57–58; 2.1–20, Jesus' with angelic choir accompaniment), circumcision and naming, with canticles praising God for sending his agent (1.59–80; 2.21–40).

4. *Diogenes Laertius' Lives of Eminent Philosophers*. In chapter 6, Talbert begins to draw out the implications of his findings for the definition of genre. He claims that Luke–Acts is influenced by popular literature depicting philosophers, suggesting that these texts contain the following typical elements:

1. The philosopher is pictured as a wandering preacher whose journeys are sometimes the result of a divine command.
2. The philosophy expounds a way of living rather than an explanation of life.
3. The philosophy is learned by imitation of life-style as well as by remembering precepts.
4. Lists of successors (*diadochoi*) designate where the 'living voice' of the philosophy can be found.

In general, Luke–Acts seems to share these features. Jesus and the apostles are itinerant preachers, the preaching is a way of living in imitation of the founder, and a succession is traced from Jesus to the Twelve apostles, to Paul and to the elders, although Acts is not a succession list, but a narrative in which the term *diadochos* is not applied to Jesus' followers. It is, however, used of Festus (Acts 24.27), showing that the word was familiar but not applied to the apostles.

In chapter 8, Talbert develops his thesis by comparing Luke–Acts with *Lives of Eminent Philosophers* by Diogenes Laertius (text and translation in Loeb Classical Library), a work probably written at the beginning of the third century CE, but conforming to a long-established genre. The inclusion of pithy sayings, anecdotes and personal descriptions in books 6 and 7, however, may reflect the tastes of the third century, according to the Loeb translator, R. D. Hicks. Two philosophical successions are described, the Ionic in the east (book 2) and the Italian in the west (book 8).

Talbert notes the following contents of the work. Philosophers are depicted as sons of God. For example, Laertius' epitaph to Plato reads: 'If Phoebus did not cause Plato to be born in Greece, how came it that he healed the minds of men by letters? As the god's son Asclepius is a healer of the body so is Plato of the immortal soul' (3.45). Followers of these philosophers, therefore, comprise a cultic community (8.68; 10.18) imitating their god (e.g. 4.19). Accounts of each school are often concluded by summaries of their teaching (e.g. 2.86–104; 3.47–109; 7.38–160; 8.48–50; 10.29–154). In form, each biography is topical rather than chronological and therefore exhibits no development of character. The summaries of doctrine are arranged either topically or by quoting letters and maxims. Lists of writings by the founder or disciples are divided into genuine and sham. The purpose of the work, it seems, is to provide accurate accounts of various ways of life exemplified in the founders and imitated by true followers, and sometimes to justify them against false accusation (e.g. 10.29).

Luke–Acts, claims Talbert, follows the structure of Laertius' *Lives* in giving a life of the founder of the religion, and a narrative of successors. Moreover, as the *Lives* recognizes differences and developments between the doctrine of the founder and his followers, the lack of identity between the teaching of Jesus in the gospel and that of the disciples in Acts causes no problem. In purpose, both the *Lives* and Luke–Acts seek to present an authentic understanding of a particular way of life.

Nevertheless, Talbert does notice differences between the two works. Luke–Acts gives an account of only one way of life, whereas the *Lives* indicates several. Accounts of single philosophical schools seem to have existed, however, and Talbert surmises that collections like the *Lives* were literary productions intended for public reading, whereas accounts of single philosophies were cult legends intended for use by the school, as Luke–Acts was. Another difference is that Luke–Acts does not include a summary of docrine as a final section but intersperses teaching throughout both volumes. A third difference lies in the extent and content of Acts, which is not a list of successors nor, as sometimes in the *Lives*, a list supplemented by a few anecdotes, maxims and writings, but a fully-fledged book, with dedication, speeches, miracle stories, letters and a travel narrative. These features bring Acts closer to Hellenistic history and romance. Talbert, however, argues that much of Acts is actually a biographical genre, admittedly with motifs from the romance.

In addition there are many differences in content. There is nothing in the *Lives* like Acts' emphasis on the gift and guidance of the Holy Spirit in bearing witness and preaching the word. Such differences are, however, brushed aside by Talbert with the disclaimer that content does not determine genre. Actually, that depends on the kind of content. Eschatological beliefs about the Holy Spirit and the resurrection, presupposed by Luke–Acts, generate stories like the angelic visitations, Jesus' baptism, and his resurrection appearances in the gospel; and Pentecost, the appearance to Paul, the visions and visitations in Acts. These elements are justified by discourses expressing a belief in an imminent divine judgment (Luke 21.25–33; Acts 3.21; 10.42; 17.31) which constitutes the future perspective of the narrative. And it is this belief that generates the form of Acts. Acts is not a biography of Paul, nor a series of biographies of the apostles. Nothing is related about their families or upbringing and only the deaths of Stephen and James are mentioned. The book ends with Paul in prison in Rome, a most unsatisfactory conclusion to a biography. No, Acts is an account of the fulfilment of God's promises, given through Scripture and Jesus. The astonishing success of God's plan for people's salvation, undeterred by opposition and difficulties, is plotted through the world, from the centre of Israel, Jerusalem, to the centre of the Empire, Rome. The breath-taking expansion, which brooks no hindrance, even converting an arch-enemy into an articulate advocate, defines a mission to all peoples as the natural outcome of God's actions and promptings. At the end of Acts, the church in Rome is poised to accomplish that mission before the Final Judgment.

This is not to deny, however, that the existence of a literary genre like that of Laertius' *Lives* may have been one among many influences which led to what seems to be a Lukan innovation. It is clear that Luke–Acts reflects the influence of Hellenistic literature. The biographical series, especially in the form it took to depict philosophical schools, may have helped to make possible the conception of a work in two volumes, the gospel and the Acts of the Apostles.

5. *A biography of Jesus?* Nothing has yet been said about Talbert's interpretation of the Gospel of Luke as a biography of Jesus. As Barr and Wentling have shown, there is good reason for reading it as Hellenistic biography.[6] It contains not only a birth narrative but an anecdote about Jesus in the Temple at the age of twelve which expresses the purpose of Jesus' life in terms of his presence in his Father's house. The form is pedagogic and dramatic, and it serves explanatory, apologetic and legitimizing purposes, through a roughly chronological and geographical arrangement leading from Galilee to Jerusalem and his Father's house. The third person narration includes first person speeches from the characters. In general, characters are vividly portrayed and the Lukan Jesus is much more sympathetic than the Matthaean or Markan. Gone is the emotional violence attributed to him (e.g. Mark 1.41/Luke 5.13; Mark 3.5/Luke 6.8), which could evince an accusation of madness (Mark 3.21). Also missing are the negative remarks about Jesus' family (Mark 6.4/

Luke 4.24; Mark 3.21, 31–35/Luke 8.19–21; note Luke's positive descriptions in Luke 1–2; Acts 12.2, 17), and Jesus' vitriolic confrontations with scribes and Pharisees (Matt. 15.1–20/Mark 7.1–23; Matt. 19.1–9/Mark 10.1–12). Luke does include criticisms of Pharisees and scribes (e.g. 11.39–52), but he does not attribute the accusation that Jesus performed miracles by Beelzebul to either group (11.14–23, contrast Matthew and Mark), and refers three times to Jesus' acceptance of invitations to meals from Pharisees (7.36; 11.37; 14.1), while mentioning in Acts 15.5 that some Pharisees had become Christians. The character of Jesus in Luke, viewed positively, is noble, viewed negatively, verges on the sentimental. He is the friendly teacher who accepts invitations to dinner parties, even from Pharisees, and whose table talk forms much of his discourse (e.g. 7.36–50; 14.1–24; 22.24–38). This feature may be borrowed from novelistic writings like Petronius' *Satyricon*. Descriptions of Jesus' emotions in Mark are replaced in Luke by dramatic scenes which hint at the intensity of his presence (Luke 19.5; 23.61). He is generous to sinners (Luke 19.1–10), and his generosity leads him to continue his preaching even on the way to the cross (Luke 23.27–31) and on the cross itself (Luke 23.34, 39–43). His courage never fails him, and he dies not in the agony of isolation, as in Mark (Mark 15.34), but with full confidence in his Father (Luke 23.46). This Jesus, then, exemplifies the Greek virtues of goodness, justice and courage.

Nevertheless, Barr and Wentling note that in the Gospel of Luke, there is a lack of focus on the hero. Not only does the story not begin with Jesus, but with John, it also reaches back far behind John to the history of Israel, and of all humanity. It is not a biography of Jesus but a story of God bringing salvation to his people. The narrative discerns a pattern in history as the outworking of God's purpose, which Jesus' life substantiates, but which does not come to an end with his death. It is God who is the dominant force in the story, and John, Jesus, Peter, Judas, the Pharisees and the other characters are agents bringing about or opponents trying to thwart his purpose. Luke is therefore closer to Hellenistic history than biography, but it is a history viewed from the perspective of a creator God whose design will bring history to an end in resurrection and judgment. The patterning of balance and duplication demonstrates the unity of the divine plan and human response. Jewish leaders repeatedly reject God's agents, the prophets, John the Baptist, Jesus and the apostles, but their blindness becomes the occasion for the expansion of the mission to include all nations. Luke, more than other New Testament texts, uses *dei* 'it is necessary' to express God's purpose in the development of the plot, e.g. Luke 4.43; 9.22; Acts 5.29; 27.24.

6. *History which idealizes the past*. Talbert, however, makes a separate and more interesting suggestion on pp. 99f. He notices that Luke, like much Graeco–Roman writing about the past, idealizes the earliest period of the church's history. The introductory remarks of Livy's history typify the attitude:

> My subject involves infinite labour, seeing that it must be traced back about seven hundred years, and that proceeding from slender beginnings it has so increased as

now to be burdened by its own magnitude; and at the same time I doubt not that to most readers the earliest origins and the period immediately succeeding them will give little pleasure; for they will be in haste to reach these modern times, in which the might of a people which has long been very powerful is working its own undoing. I myself, on the contrary, shall seek in this an additional reward for my toil, that I may avert my gaze from the troubles which our age has been witnessing for so many years, so long at least as I am absorbed in the recollection of the brave days of old, free from every care which, even if it could not divert the historian's mind from the truth, might nevertheless cause it anxiety. (Loeb Classical Library, preface 4–5)

Livy wrote under Augustus and lived from 59 BCE to CE 17. Josephus' portrait of Moses and the Israelites in *Antiquities* shows a similar tendency to present an utopian past. To suppose that Luke–Acts shares this tendency explains otherwise puzzling features of the narrative. For example, according to Acts 15, problems relating to the Gentile mission are settled by the church in Jerusalem, which expresses a single, coherent policy agreed by all participants and put into effect without Christian opposition. It is Peter, not Paul, who is the first to admit Gentiles without their accepting circumcision and the Levitical food laws (Acts 10), and he is forced to do so by the God who enlightens him in a vision and who gives the Holy Spirit before baptism, just as, later in Acts, Paul is forced to go to the Gentiles by a vision of a man from Macedonia (Acts 16.9) and by the obduracy of the Jews (e.g. Acts 13.44–52 and 28.23–28). Nothing of the acrimony between James, Peter, Barnabas and Paul, which Galatians 2 describes, is allowed to intrude into the idyllic picture. Nor does Acts recognize any awkwardness in discovering just when the Holy Spirit is guiding the church. 'Speaking in tongues and extolling God' (Acts 10.46) is sufficient evidence of the Spirit's presence. The simplicity of the presentation would appear naïve were it not suspected that simplicity is the aim. Similarly, the ingenuous singleness of Jesus' life and the message of God's forgiveness to sinners in the gospel may be explained as the result of the same inclination.

All this contrasts markedly with dominant accounts of the remote past in Luke's Scripture, in which God brings about his purpose in spite of the repeated failings of even his most devoted servants. Israel in the wilderness is a mob of discontented ne'er-do-wells, always dissatisfied with God's provisions, ready to return to hard labour or escape into idolatry at any provocation. Aaron leads them into idolatry (Ex. 32) and even Moses shares the fate of all those who left Egypt, never to enter the promised land (Num. 14.20–23). Nor do the patriarchs fare better. Abraham, Isaac and Jacob know nothing of the virtues of prudence or courage, nor are they paragons of moral behaviour. They lie and cheat their ways through life. On the whole, this scriptural assessment of human frailty and divine forbearance is more reassuring than Graeco–Roman and Lukan utopian idealism, but it is less encouraging of moral endeavour. The characters of Luke–Acts, unlike those of Genesis and Exodus, can serve as suitable models for imitation. Only in two of the Lukan parables does the text dare to draw lessons from the behaviour of immoral individuals (the friend at

289

midnight, 11.5–13; the unjust steward, 16.1–9). Even Peter's failure in denying Jesus (Luke 22.54–64) is toned down by omitting Peter's curse upon himself (Mark 14.71), by intensifying Peter's remorse ('and he wept bitterly'), by perhaps including him among the acquaintances who witnessed the crucifixion (Luke 23.49, 'all his acquaintances'), by specifying Jesus' command 'And when you have turned again, strengthen your brethren' (22.32), and by rehabilitating him as a witness of the resurrection (24.34). Perhaps, too, this is why Peter, at the beginning of his association with Jesus, is portrayed as a penitent sinner (5.8), and why Luke fails to record the Markan rebuke of Peter as Satan after his confession (9.20f.; Mark 8.33).

This characteristic idealism of Luke–Acts, above all, demonstrates its indebtedness to Graeco–Roman literature, although whether the troubles of the church at the time of its writing and circulation prompted such nostalgia, as in Livy's preface, it is impossible to decide.

It seems fair to conclude, therefore, that the Gospel of Luke is closer to the genre of Hellenistic history writing than that of Matthew or of Mark. All the same, it is still true to say of Luke that some motifs are foreign to Hellenistic literature, especially those occasioned by the gospel's eschatological beliefs.

• The Gospel of Luke and its Scripture

Although the Acts of the Apostles can have Paul justify his arguments to Athenians on the basis of a quotation from Aratus' *Phaenomena* 5, 'For we are indeed his offspring' (Acts 17.28), statements, when they are given support, usually cite passages from Luke's scripture, even in Acts (e.g. 13.40f.; 15.15f.) and always in the gospel (e.g. Luke 4.4, 8, 10f.; 6.3f.). Further, Lukan theological presuppositions fundamentally conform to those of its Scripture with its belief in a creator God, in whose image and likeness people are made (3.38). Once more, therefore, it is necessary to discover how far Scripture has determined the vocabulary, motifs and genre of the work.

1. *Quotations, allusions and Septuagintisms.* Scriptural quotations or allusions are found in both Luke and Acts to every book in the Pentateuch, to the former prophets (Judges, I and II Samuel, I Kings and I Chronicles), to the prophets Isaiah (most frequently), Jeremiah, Ezekiel, Daniel, Hosea and Amos, and very often to the Psalms. In addition, Luke seems to refer to II Kings, II Chronicles, Ruth, Micah, Zechariah, Malachi and Proverbs, while Acts to Joshua, Joel, Nahum, Ecclesiastes, Wisdom of Solomon and I Maccabees. More than this, however, parts of Luke–Acts seem to be conscious imitations of the style of the Septuagint. J. A. Fitzmyer provides a list of 'Septuagintisms', that is, Lukan expressions derived from the Septuagint, on pages 114–125 of volume I of his commentary. Fitzmyer's judgment is that all the so-called Hebraisms of Luke–Acts are in fact Septuagintisms. The gospel and Acts 1–12 are particularly noted for Septuagintisms, and, of the gospel, the first two chapters are most obviously imitative of the style and ethos of Lukan Scripture, especially the story of the birth of Samuel in I Samuel 1–3. Apart from the obvious parallels in subject-matter (God giving a son who would become a prophet) and

setting (the Temple), Mary's canticle in Luke 1.46–55 echoes Hannah's in I Sam. 2.1–10, and the description of the boy Jesus in 2.52 is like that of Samuel in I Sam. 2.26. But there are also many other allusions to Scripture in these chapters. The angel Gabriel is derived from Dan. 8.16, and other verses seem to draw on Daniel – Luke 1.12–13 on Dan. 10.7, 12; Luke 1.19 on Dan. 9.20–22; Luke 1.26–29 on Dan. 9.21–24; Luke 1.64–65 on Dan. 10.16–17. The story of Elizabeth and Zechariah, an elderly childless couple, is also reminiscent of Abraham and Sarah's (Gen. 16). Elizabeth's blessing of Mary (Luke 1.41) alludes to Deborah's of Jael (Judg. 5.24), the leaping of the baby in Elizabeth's womb (Luke 1.44) to the leaping of the twins in Rebecca's womb (Gen. 25.22) and the wrapping of Jesus in bands (Luke 2.7) to Solomon's (Wisd. 7.4–5). It is not surprising to discover, therefore, that the lives of John, Jesus and the apostles are seen as the fulfilment of prophetic expectations, and the Gospel of Luke, like Mark's and Matthew's, provides formal quotations which are said to be fulfilled in the events described, like Luke 3.4–6 (Isaiah) in John's ministry, and Luke 4.18–21 (Isaiah) in Jesus' (cf. Acts 2.16–21 (Joel) in the apostles').

2. *Sentences, phrases and words.* Apart from the Septuagintisms listed by Fitzmyer, other individual sentences, phrases and words seem to imitate Scripture: blessings (Luke 6.20–22; Deut. 33.29; Eccles. 10.17), woes (Luke 6.24–26: 10.13; 11.42–44; 17.1; 21.23; 22.22; Isa. 5.8–12; 33.1; Jer. 13.27), *amēn* as a solemn declaration (e.g. Luke 4.24; 12.37; Jer. 28.6) and wisdom sayings (Luke 6.32–38).[7]

3. *The prophets.* Lukan imitation also makes use of scriptural motifs. That the Gospel of Luke portrays Jesus as a prophet is clear from the quotation of Isa. 61 (Luke 4.18–21). He is anointed by the Spirit of the Lord at his baptism (3.22) to preach good news to the poor (6.20). Presumably Luke interpreted 'release to the captives' (4.18) metaphorically as release from sin, which is a major theme of the gospel (5.20, 30–32; 7.34, 47; 15.1–7; 18.9–14; 19.1–10; 24.47). 'Sight to the blind' is given by Jesus in 18.35–43 and referred to in Jesus' reply to John the Baptist's question (7.22). 'Liberty to those who are oppressed' is effected by Jesus' many exorcisms, already detailed. Jesus himself calls his mission prophetic: 'I must go on my way today, and tomorrow and the day following; for it cannot be that a prophet should perish away from Jerusalem' (13.33 and 4.24), and his enemies taunt him with the designation (22.64), while those who witness the raising of the widow of Nain's son acknowledge him 'a great prophet' (7.16). This story is, of course, reminiscent of Elijah's raising of the widow's son (I Kings 17.17–24; cf. Luke 9.8, 19). The disciples on their way to Emmaus also describe Jesus as 'a prophet' (24.19). The echo of Deut. 18.15, 'Listen to him', in Luke's account of the transfiguration (Luke 9.28–36) and the conversation about Jesus' 'exodus' (9.31) suggest that Luke links Jesus not only with Elijah but especially with 'the prophet like Moses' and this is confirmed by Acts 3.22–23 and 7.37, where Moses' rejection by the people is stressed. Like the other synoptics, too, Luke records the feeding of the five thousand (9.11–17), a possible allusion to Moses' feeding miracles (Ex. 16; Num. 11). Also Moses' successful

291

leadership of the twelve tribes in victories over their enemies (Ex. 17.8; Num. 16; 21.21; 31) may be mirrored in Jesus' successful leadership of the twelve apostles in verbal victories over disputants (Luke 4.23–30; 5.17–32; 6.1–11; 10.23–37; 11.14–28, 37–53; 14.1–6; 15.1–32; 16.14f.; 20.1f.). Luke's presentation of disputes, however, accords more space than do the other synoptics to parables, taking up the form of Nathan's parable to David (II Sam. 12.1–7). With Mark, Luke recounts Jesus' acceptance of the unauthorized exorcist (9.49f./Mark 9.38–40), which perhaps echoes Moses' acceptance of unauthorized prophets (Num. 11.26). Luke alone depicts a mission of the Seventy(-two) (Luke 10.1–20). If the original reading is Seventy, it would offer another link with Moses and his appointment of the seventy elders. (Ex. 24.1; Num. 11.16, 24), but it is more likely that reference is being made to the table of the nations of the world in Gen. 10.2–31, where the Hebrew text includes Seventy and the Septuagint Seventy- two.

Connexions seem to be indicated between Jesus and other prophets as well. Jesus calls disciples to follow him as Elijah called Elisha (Luke 5.1–11, 27; I Kings 19.19f., but contrast Luke 9.62 and I Kings 19.20), and, like Ezekiel, Jesus refers to himself as 'Son of man' (Luke 5.24; 6.5, 22; 7.34f.; Ezek. 2.1, 8; 3.1). Apologetically, it is important for Luke, as for Matthew and Mark, to picture the suffering of Jesus (13.33; 6.23; 11.47–48) and his disciples (9.23) in the light of the fate of prophets in the past (13.33; Acts 7.35, 39, 52), but the understanding of prophecy as endowment with God's spirit is also important, as in the case of Elisha, 'the holy one' dedicated to God's service (II Kings 4.9; Luke 1.35; 4.34; 4.27, 30). Nevertheless, Jesus' refusal to call down fire on the Samaritan village seems to be a direct anti-type of the Elijah story (Luke 9.52–56; II Kings 1).

4. *Titles of Jesus*. According to Luke, Jesus is anointed with God's Spirit not only because he is a prophet but also because he is the **Christ**, fulfilling some of the expectations of a future David. Born in Bethlehem (2.4) and descended from David (2.4; 3.31), the child announced by the angel will be 'a Saviour who is Christ the Lord' (2.11 cf. 2.26; Acts 13.22). In 4.41, 'Christ' is identified with 'the Son of God' confessed by the demons. In the Passion narrative, 'Christ' is interpreted as 'king of the Jews', taking up the confession of Jesus' followers as he rode towards Jerusalem (19.38, different from Mark and Matthew), and weaving it into the narrative as a major theme (22.67; 23.2, 3, 23, 35–39; cf. Acts 17.7). Nevertheless, some of the political overtones of the title are not developed in the gospel, which, on the contrary, predicts not political success but personal disaster (9.22; Acts 3.18; 17.3; 26.23). Also Luke, following the other synoptics, raises the question about Jesus' Davidic sonship in one of Jesus' disputes in the Temple (20.41–44). Nevertheless, the title 'Christ' is used very frequently in Acts (e.g. 2.31, 36, 38; 3.6, 18, 20), and members of the new sect are named 'Christians' (Acts 11.26; 26.28). Some other features of Acts' references to 'the Christ' are difficult to co-ordinate with the gospel usage. In Acts 2.36, Peter states, 'God has made him both Lord and Christ, this Jesus whom you crucified' as if Jesus became Christ only at his resurrection, and Acts 3.20 may envisage Jesus becoming Christ at his Parousia –

'that he (the Lord) may send the Christ appointed for you, Jesus, whom heaven must receive until the time for establishing all that God spoke by the mouth of his holy prophets of old'. It seems, therefore, that some aspects of Lukan usage are inconsistent, but that the main emphasis rests on the Scriptures which predict that the Christ must suffer. In this way, the fates of the prophet and the Christ are identified.

Jesus is referred to as *kyrios* in the Gospel of Luke not only by characters within the story (e.g. Luke 5.8, 12) but also by the narrator (e.g. 7.13, 19). The title draws attention to Jesus' dignity but does not attribute divinity to him. Elsewhere in the gospel, *kyrios* refers either to human beings with authority (e.g. 12.37, 47; 13.25) or to God, following the Septuagint (e.g. 2.23, 26; 3.4; 4.8, 12, 18, 19). God is also called *Despotēs* 'Lord' (Luke 2.22; Acts 4.24), a title used both in the Septuagint and in Graeco–Roman literature.

Again, like Matthew and Mark, Luke presents Jesus as the '**Son of God**', giving him the same metaphorical relationship to God which Scripture gives to Adam (3.28), to Israel and to Davidic kings (Ex. 4.22; Hos. 11.1; Ps. 2.7 quoted in Acts 13.33). Like Israel, Jesus, the Son of God, goes through water to begin his journey along the way (3.21–22; Ex. 14–15), but in the wilderness, Jesus proves himself to be God's obedient son unlike Israel (Luke 4.1–13; Ex. 14–17; 32–34; Num. 11). The story functions to define the nature of Jesus' sonship, already announced by the angel (1.35) and the heavenly voice at the baptism (3.22) and later at the transfiguration (9.35, see also Acts 9.20), in terms of obedience to God's will. The title is used to make a claim about Jesus' knowledge (10.22), although the disciples who follow Jesus also become sons by learning from him or by becoming like angels at the resurrection (20.36 cf. Ps. 29.1). 'Son of God' is sometimes replaced by 'Son of the Most High' (1.32; 8.28; cf. Dan. 7.18, 22, 25, 27) and disciples are called 'sons of the Most High' (6.35 cf. Ps. 82.6).

5. *Other motifs are adopted from Luke's Scripture*. Jesus' genealogy is traced back through David and Abraham to Adam, God's son (3.38), utilizing material from scriptural genealogies (Gen. 5.3–32; 11.10–26; Ruth 4.18–22; I Chron. 1.1–4, 24–28; 2.1–15) to give Jesus' life a universal significance. Abraham is also given special prominence as the one to whom promises had been made which would be fulfilled in Jesus (Luke 1.55, 73; 13.16; 16.22–31; 19.9; 20.37; Acts 3.13, 25; 7.2, 16, 17, 32; 13.26).

Luke's account of the Last Supper, albeit with many differences from the Matthaean and Markan versions, especially if the shorter text is accepted as original,[8] retains the connexion with Passover (22.15), and the Passion narrative depicts Jesus' death as the martyrdom of an innocent man, alluding to Psalms 22 and 69 (Luke 23.34–35/Ps. 22.18, 7; Luke 23.36/Ps. 69.21). In addition, Luke's reference to Jesus' acquaintances may allude to Psalms 88.8 and 38.11. The darkness at Jesus' death, recorded in Luke 23.44, seems to make a connexion with the judgment of Amos 8.9. Moreover, Luke's resurrection appearances take their form from scriptural theophanies (e.g. Gen. 18; Judg. 6.11; I Sam. 3; Tobit 5.12). But the resurrection appearance to Cleopas and a second disciple on the road to Emmaus

(Luke 24.13–32) has often been compared to that section of Philostratus' *Apollonius of Tyana* in which Apollonius disappears from his trial before the Emperor Domitian and reappears before his disciples Damis and Demetrius (7.41). Like Jesus' disciples, Damis and Demetrius are concerned about the events affecting Apollonius, when Apollonius is suddenly present with them in corporeal form to relate the happenings that interest them on their journey back to the city. But, although these similarities have prompted the comparison, essential differences should also be noticed. Luke's Jesus was crucified and buried before his appearance on the road to Emmaus, whereas Apollonius simply disappeared from the courtroom, miraculously travelling a vast distance in a short time, like Philip (Acts 8.39–40). Also, the assurance that Apollonius gives his disciples is that he has escaped the machinations of a wicked Emperor, and that he is, in any case, not human but divine (8.13). Hence the story does not conclude with Apollonius' disappearance, but with his retiring to sleep. In spite of these differences, however, could Luke's story be an adaptation of Philostratus'? Apollonius of Tyana, like Jesus, is supposed to have lived in the first century CE, but Philostratus' account was written in the third century, after the Lukan gospel. Unless we are to suppose that the individual story was well-known before it became part of Philostratus' work, any literary dependence is likely to have operated the other way round.

To return to the list of motifs shared by Luke with its Scripture, the ascension stories (Luke 24.51; Acts 1.9–11) make use of the imagery of the ascension of both Enoch (Gen. 5.24; Ecclus. 44.16) and Elijah (II Kings 2.11; I Macc. 2.58), as well as alluding to Daniel's vision of one like a Son of man with the clouds of heaven (Dan. 7.13 cf. Acts 1.11). Finally, the story of Judas' death (Acts 1.18–19, contrast Matt. 27.3–10) seems to express the typical fate of an evil-doer (II Macc. 9.8; Wisd. 4.19; Acts 12.23).

Although it has been granted that Luke–Acts is influenced by Hellenistic history-writing, still, the form of the narrative, interspersing miracle, parable, discourse and dialogue, is most reminiscent of those sections of Scripture which describe the lives of prophets (Exodus, Numbers, I and II Kings), but without giving God such a vocal role. This means that, as in the case of Matthew and Mark, Luke shares motifs, sentences, phrases, vocabulary, style, arrangement, and focus with its Scripture, but it also differs from much of its Scripture in espousing an eschatology which generates new motifs.

6. *Satan and angels*. Lukan demonology has been discussed earlier, as well as Luke's indebtedness to Daniel for its angelology in the birth narratives, although Gabriel's announcements in Luke refer to extraordinary historical events not to visionary intimations of the Last Judgment. The content and form of these announcements, therefore, have more in common with scriptural theophanies like Gen. 18 (see also Acts 8.26; 10.3; 27.22). In Acts, the role of angels in rescuing apostles from prison (Acts 5.19; 12.7) is more like Raphael's in the book of Tobit. 'The multitude of the heavenly host' in Luke 2.13 refers to God's warriors in Scripture (e.g. II Kings 22.19; Neh. 9.6). The appearance of the 'two men . . . in

dazzling apparel' (Luke 24.4), presumably angels, in the empty tomb announcing the resurrection makes less use of apocalyptic conventions than Matthew's story (28.2). Finally, Luke shares the belief in guardian angels of individuals (Acts 12.15; cf. Matt. 18.10; Jub. 35.17).

7. *Eschatology*. This brings us to the most contentious issue in defining the Lukan genre in relation to that of Matthew and Mark, namely the extent to which the Gospel according to Luke has modified the eschatological perspective of the other synoptics. It has often been suggested that the very existence of a second volume, tracing the early history of the church, expresses a shift from the expectation of an imminent final judgment to a history of salvation, in which 'the kingdom of God' has become a present reality – 'the kingdom of God is not coming with signs to be observed; nor will they say, "Lo, here it is!" or "There!" for behold the kingdom of God is in the midst of you' (17.20–21; cf. 11.20).[9] Such a shift, the argument runs, has led to a modification of Jesus' apocalyptic discourse (Mark 13/Luke 21), in the Lukan version of which Jesus clearly predicts the destruction of Jerusalem by the Roman armies as an event within history (21.20–24). Moreover, a statement like Acts 1.6–8, 'They asked him [the risen Jesus], "Lord, will you at this time restore the kingdom to Israel?" He said to them, "It is not for you to know times or seasons which the Father has fixed by his own authority. But you shall receive power when the Holy Spirit has come upon you"', has been read to mean that Luke–Acts replaces the expectation of the imminent Parousia by the fulfilment of eschatological expectations in this world through the advent of the Holy Spirit (Acts 2.17, the fulfilment of the Joel prophecy, cf. Luke 19.11).

Against this interpretation, Eric Franklin contends that although Luke–Acts envisages a postponement of the Final Judgment (e.g. Luke 19.11–27), looking back over a period of delay, it does not look forward to an indefinite future.[10] In spite of the changes to the Markan apocalypse, including the reduction of its awesome impact by making the teaching public not private, and the separation of persecution from eschatological woes by seeing the end of suffering in death (21.19), the discourse does in fact retain teaching about the expectation of an imminent end of the world, even claiming that 'this generation will not pass away till all has taken place' (21.32 cf. 9.27). 21.25–28 predicts

> There will be signs in sun and moon and stars . . . men fainting with fear . . . for the powers of the heavens will be shaken. And then they will see the Son of man coming in a cloud with power and great glory. Now when these things begin to take place, look up and raise your heads, because your redemption is drawing near' (cf. 17.24; 18.1–8; Acts 3.20f.; 10.42; 17.3).

Then what is the relationship between the present kingdom of God and the future kingdom 'in power' expected at the Parousia of the Son of man (21.31, 'So when you see these things taking place, you know that the kingdom of God is near', cf. 10.9; 11.2; 22.18)? Franklin suggests that Luke understands the kingdom to be present as a transcendent reality to which earthly events bear witness. The defeat of Satan – 'I saw

Satan fall like lightning from heaven' (10.18) – is Jesus' interpretation of the success of the Seventy(-two)'s subjugation of demons. Yet Satan is still active on earth (e.g. 22.3, 31–32, 53; Acts 26.18; 14.22). To this transcendent kingdom Jesus ascends, after the resurrection had reversed the injustice of the cross (Luke 24.51; Acts 1.9–11), to send the Holy Spirit to his chosen apostles. The fulfilment of eschatological expectations in the gift of the Spirit, nevertheless, is not a replacement of an imminent Parousia but a guarantee of its imminence. Meanwhile, those believers who die can look forward to entering the transcendent kingdom to join Jesus immediately – 'Today you will be with me in Paradise', the reversal of Gen. 2–3 (Luke 23.42; Acts 7.59). The future advent of the kingdom of God at the Parousia of the Son of man will bring the transcendent realm to earth with the final defeat of Satan there.

Certainly, Franklin's suggestion makes sense of most of the Lukan references to the kingdom. But 17.20f. still remains slightly puzzling. If the present kingdom is a transcendent reality, why does Jesus answer the Pharisees' request, 'The kingdom of God is not coming with signs to be observed; nor will they say, Lo, here it is, or, There, for the kingdom of God is in the midst of you'? Presumably, the first part of Jesus' reply is to be understood as a denial that the kingdom will come with signs during his ministry, not that there will never be signs, since these are predicted in 21.25. But how can it be that a transcendent kingdom can be said to be in the midst of the Pharisees, immanent in the world? If H. J. Cadbury's proposal, on the basis of papyrus evidence, that *entos hymōn* can mean 'within your reach or grasp' were accepted, this would solve the problem, but his suggestion has been challenged, for example, in Fitzmyer's commentary (Vol. II pp. 1161–62). Although, then, Franklin is correct in emphasizing the transcendence of the present kingdom and seeing exorcisms merely as intimations on earth of the heavenly defeat of Satan, nevertheless, it seems to have been possible for Luke to express this idea loosely as the actual presence of the kingdom on earth, 'But if it is by the finger of God that I cast out demons, then the kingdom of God has come upon you' (11.20). In any case, Luke has retained the synoptic perspective of the complete transformation of the world at the Final Judgment of the Son of man in the near future.

This means that the life of Jesus is understood to give knowledge of a transcendent kingdom of God, while the gift of the Holy Spirit to the apostles, as a result of Jesus' resurrection and ascension, is understood as assurance of the final and imminent defeat of Satan on earth and the establishment in the near future of God's kingdom in power. Jesus' life, therefore, has a double significance. It offers those who believe in him a life after death in a transcendent realm should death intervene before the Parousia, or, if not, it promises participation in the final victory of God over Satan and his minions, and life beyond history in the kingdom of God on a transformed earth.

• Summary

This seems to mean that Luke is of the same genre as Matthew and Mark. Nevertheless, that genre has been modified in the light of the conventions of

Graeco–Roman history writing. It is fair to say that Luke–Acts could not have existed in its present form without knowledge of such Graeco–Roman texts. Perhaps H. J. Cadbury is correct in supposing that the sources Luke used were too incorrigible to allow a complete transmutation into Graeco–Roman history at the first attempt. But, to return to the preface, the truth for which the work offers Theophilus assurance is not just the accurate reporting of past events, nor the discernment of patterns in history, nor the exact depiction of a holy community worthy of imitation or admiration, but the story of the creator God who repeatedly offers people salvation, through the prophets, through Jesus and through his apostles, and whose sovereignty is about to be finally established by replacing the kingdom of Satan on earth with that of God. Historical motifs are swallowed up by eschatological, and history is understood from the perspective of creation and recreation.

Implications of the definition of genre

What does it matter how the genre of the synoptics is defined? Would we seriously misinterpret them if we took them to be lives of a prophet? In any case, definition of genre cannot restrict the questions that may be directed appropriately at a text. The main interest of a particular poem may be love, but this does not mean that we cannot find answers to questions about food or fashion, matters which may be peripheral to the purpose of the poem but which may be touched upon nevertheless. Of course, defining the genre of a text provides the emotional and intellectual satisfaction of putting things in perspective. It dispels the sense of vertigo experienced, for example, at a party when you are uncertain whether your hostess is trying to convince you that she is *au fait* with modern jazz or with computer programming.

To call the Gospel according to Matthew, for example, 'a theodicy' about creation and recreation, attempts to give to its parts a satisfying coherence, but it does not imply that questions concerning the historical Jesus cannot be asked of it. Indeed, it invites such questions. Even though a lot of it echoes its Scripture, we noted that the relationship between these scriptural allusions and the historical Jesus may be reciprocal: events in the life of Jesus may have brought scriptural passages to mind; and the latter, once noted, may have influenced the way the story was told. The reciprocal relationship with Scripture, however, does mean that answers about history cannot be gained in the way they would be if they were asked of a text like Robert Gittings' *Young Thomas Hardy*.[11] The tradition about Jesus had another source of 'information' than the remembered words and deeds of Jesus. It also had the Scripture, which he was believed to have fulfilled, and which therefore could be called on to give significance to the account of his life.

Moreover, the synoptics, although they do not themselves examine their theological presuppositions, invite questions about God as Gittings does not. Gittings' treatment is confined to history, while those of the synoptics are both historical and theological.

All three synoptic gospels refer to Jesus of Nazareth as a man who lived in

Palestine during the first century CE, when Herod Antipas ruled Galilee, and who was crucified by the Romans when Pilate ruled Judaea. Each, however, presents a different account of Jesus' life, death and resurrection. Then are any of their historical claims true? What can be known about Jesus of Nazareth?

Further Reading

C. H. Talbert, *What is a Gospel?*, London 1978, and the review by M. Pamment in *New Blackfriars*, April 1980, pp. 197–8

D. E. Aune, 'The Problem of the Genre of the Gospels' in *Gospel Perspectives* II, ed. R. T. France and D. Wenham, Sheffield 1981

P. Shuler, *A Genre for the Gospels*, Philadelphia 1982

E. Best, *Mark – The Gospel as Story*, Edinburgh 1983

M. Hooker, *The Message of Mark*, London 1983

W. Telford (ed.), *The Interpretation of Mark*, Issues in Religion and Theology 7, London and Philadelphia 1985

G. W. E. Nickelsburg, 'The Genre and Function of the Markan Passion Narrative', *Harvard Theological Review* 73, 1980, pp. 153–184

D. L. Barr and J. L. Wentling, 'The Conventions of Classical Biography and the Genre of Luke–Acts', in C. H. Talbert (ed.), *Luke–Acts*, SBL Seminar Papers, New York 1984

Part Five

Research into the Life and Teaching of Jesus

20 The Quest and its Methods : 1

• On seeking the historical Jesus

Most people who read the synoptics do so in order to find out about Jesus, though there are other very good reasons for reading them. We have seen that the study of the first three gospels is difficult and complex, and after all this analysis the reader may well fear that asking the crucial question – what about the Jesus of history? – will lead straight into a quagmire. It turns out, however, that finding out about Jesus is easier than solving the synoptic problem and about as difficult as discovering Mark's distinctive theology; that is, harder than finding Luke's, but by no means impossible.

There will be things which will prove to be impossible to find out, but basic knowledge about Jesus can be uncovered. The gospels present impressionistic portraits of Jesus. We can learn from these impressions, but we can also discover quite objective information. We shall see that, although intimate inner knowledge will elude us, we can obtain excellent information of a broader and more general kind. How is it done?

The basic means of establishing evidence is cross-examination. The gospels must be treated as 'hostile witnesses' in the court room. It is, of course, not the gospels which are hostile, but rather the inquisitor who asks for information about 'mere facts' or 'pure history'. The gospels want the reader to believe that Jesus is the son of God and that faith in him saves. The material in them is shaped – more or less completely – to this end. In attempting to persuade the reader, however, the evangelists used material, and that material as a whole has some relationship to the historical man Jesus. The patient investigator can persuade the gospels to yield up their data.

When people recognize that seeking historically sound material in the gospels goes a bit against their grain, by no means all respond, 'Let us press on and drag it out of them'. There are three common responses to the conflict between the thrust of the gospels and the historian's curiosity which we think to be incorrect but which require consideration.

1. Some will argue that, since the gospels intertwine kerygma ('proclamation') and history, we cannot examine them in search only of the latter. All that the modern can

301

do is either simply to quote them, pointing out their biases, or to apply to them his or her own biases. Impartiality, especially when dealing with strongly propagandistic evidence, is impossible.

This argument sounds plausible, but it is actually only sophistry, which will be rejected by anyone who has ever engaged in an investigation of any sort. The police, judges and juries face this situation all the time, but they nevertheless persevere in trying to establish objective truth; and most of us will grant that they are often able to do so. The historian faces precisely the same situation. All the witnesses may be biased in one way or another, but that does not mean that cross-examination will uncover nothing but deeper levels of bias. It is not infrequently possible to distinguish what a gospel uses from what use the gospel made of it – the material from the propaganda.

It would be extremely helpful, however, if we had sources which were biased against a favourable view of Jesus, sources which regarded him as a charlatan, fraud or deluded visionary. With regard to Socrates, for example, antiquity offers us three portraits – by Plato, Xenophon and Aristophanes. From these sources, two sharply different characterizations emerge. The Socrates of the Platonic dialogues is a wise, kindly seeker of truth who cares for nothing else. We know, however, that many Athenians regarded him as a corruptor of the young and an 'atheist', and that he was forced to commit suicide on these charges. Further, Aristophanes' play *Clouds* presents him as an irritating and ridiculous figure. The historian who has two portraits biased in opposite directions has a good chance of being able to construct at least aspects of a rounded and full portrayal.

At first it seems that all the evidence is biased towards Jesus. It is, however, extremely important to note that, while we have for Jesus no equivalent to Aristophanes on Socrates, we can discern in the gospels that he offended many and that he was executed on a serious charge. That is, the gospels, though biased in his favour, give us a glimpse of views held by those who were biased against him.

Once we can discern both favourable and unfavourable portraits of Jesus, we can ask what is common to both portraits, and we may have considerable confidence that what is common is historically sound. The discovery that sources are biased should not lead to the view that they are useless, but rather to patient and careful analysis and examination to ferret out the hard historical data which they have employed for their own purposes.

2. Some will argue that one *ought* not to ask questions which documents do not 'want' to answer. James M. Robinson, for example, argued that it is theologically 'illegitimate' to seek the answers to ordinary historical questions, since faith should not seek that kind of external support.[1] Others may think that, out of respect for ancient documents, one should allow them to say what they 'want' to say, and not press them to tell us other things.

These two views seem to us to be off-target for slightly different reasons. While it is true that Christianity cannot be verified by historical evidence, it could conceivably be falsified. That is, learning matters of fact about what Jesus said and did cannot possibly prove the Christian claim that in him God acted to save the world. Learning that he never lived, however, would destroy Christianity; learning that he was a fraud and a cheat would seriously damage most people's trust in the Christian message. For this reason theology cannot refuse fearless investigation; on the contrary, it must foster and support it. Otherwise it becomes ostrich-like, fearing to look up and face the world.

Nor is it correct that intellectual honesty and respect for sources should deny historical investigation. We must, among other things, be true to ourselves, and our own integrity requires us to learn whatever we can about matters which are important to us. We should respect ancient sources, but not in a way which requires us to deny the validity of our own questions. The modern historian in a room full of tombstones from a first-century cemetery would be asked by them to pray for the dead person, to hold a feast in his or her memory, to reflect on the meaning of life and death – and so on. The historian, however, might ask instead, 'What percentage of the population was Jewish?' The tombstones may not 'like' the question, but it is a legitimate one for the modern to ask; and, to some degree, the tombstones can be compelled to answer it.

3. Some will say that the material in the gospels is privileged: not only do the gospels intertwine kerygma and history, the two really were intertwined, and therefore in this special body of material they may not be distinguished. The gospels ask the reader to believe that Jesus was raised from the dead and that he had already been declared Son of God (Mark), or had been born such (Matthew and Luke). This is either true or not. If not, the material may all be discarded, since it has lied. If the claim is true, however, the gospel material is exempt from the normal tests for historicity, since it does not deal with a normal person.

The historian, again on grounds of personal integrity and honesty towards his or her calling, will not be persuaded to abandon the critical search for ordinary history. The theologian should reject this view even more emphatically, though some, alas! do not. Official Christianity was officially saved from docetism – the denial that Jesus was a real human being – by the doctrine of the incarnation (the word really did become flesh, and did not just appear to do so) and by the affirmation of two natures in Christ, one being 'very man of very man'. The doctrine which officially 'saved' the church from docetism has not, however, managed to save all believers from the theological error of denying that Jesus was a real man and, in consequence, lived a real history. We think that a full affirmation of 'truly human' must be made and must not be compromised by supposing that Jesus is not a fit subject of historical enquiry.

In a similar way, some may claim special privilege for the gospel material on the ground that it is revealed. The believer *knows* that Jesus was raised, that his miracles were truly supernatural, and so on. This special revelation means that the ordinary canons of critical investigation cannot be applied. Perhaps the erroneous nature of this insidious form of obscurantism (*we* know secrets which you cannot know) may best be shown by pointing to its logical consequence. The person who argues this way when it comes to knowledge about Jesus may apply the same argument to any number of issues. The Bible says that the world was created in six days. Does this then give the believer access to cosmological information which should supplant the evidence of astronomy, geology, archaeology, chemistry and physics? A few will argue that it does. This chapter is clearly not for them: they are at a level of fundamentalism which is beyond reasonable argumentation. Many others, however, will grant to science free rein in its own domain, but will want a protective wall built around their portrait of Jesus, which they will see as based on revelation. A sufficiently detailed exploration would show that what is revealed to one person is not to another: that the appeal to 'revelation' about Jesus as a historical figure usually masks entirely human biases, individual preferences and wishful thinking. The academic historian may have biases and presuppositions, but they can be exposed by people using the same critical tools, and thus progress can be made towards sound historical knowledge. The appeal to revelation as the ground of historical information essentially denies the possibility of learning, and that is an extremely unfortunate denial. Those who are tempted to look for a protective wall are urged not to do so, but to be genuinely open to investigation which leads to historical knowledge and insight.

The historian, in any case, whatever her or his theological beliefs, has no choice but to soldier on. Academic study has its own rules, and one of them is that nothing is exempt from scrutiny and verification.

What, then, do we do if we wish to ask, against the grain of the material, resolutely historical questions? We begin by asking them against the grain. Returning to the point with which we began, we cross-examine the witnesses.

The result will be that some aspects of Jesus' teaching and career are firmly established, some things attributed to him are disproved, and most of the material is placed somewhere in between. Here we drop the courtroom analogy and suppose neither that the material is 'innocent until proved guilty' nor 'guilty until proved innocent'. That is, we do not put the burden of proof entirely on the side of either the assertion of authenticity or its denial.[2] Rather, we weigh and assess the evidence and assign to it various degrees of probability. It is to be emphasized that even the words 'proof' and 'disproof' refer to degrees of probability. They are a convenient shorthand for the fuller phrases 'beyond reasonable doubt' and 'so improbable as to be unworthy of further consideration'. In historical research there is no means of establishing absolutely what is 'true' and 'false', and we deal instead with probabilities. In broad terms we seek 'proof', but we shall have to be content with 'beyond reasonable doubt', which shades over into 'highly probable' and then to 'probable', 'possible', and so forth.

We shall here be able to consider only a few representative passages in order to illustrate how historical information is sought and confirmed. In each instance we begin with a basic point which is 'beyond reasonable doubt', and then show how points which interrelate with it are assessed and assigned various degrees of probability.

Test 1: *Strongly against the grain; too much with the grain*

We began with the basic means of verification and falsification: cross-examination. A passage or a theme is shown to be historically reliable if it is directly against what the evangelists wished to be so. Conversely, it is historically unlikely if it agrees too closely with what they wished and corresponds to Christian doctrine.

Thus stated, this criterion will turn out to be too crude, and we shall see below that the evangelists, and the churches which they represented, built their own faith and practice on traditions about Jesus which can be historically verified by some other means. We shall demonstrate below that some material which is 'with the grain' is also historically reliable. But, nevertheless, to get started, 'with the grain' and 'against the grain' are useful criteria and we begin with points which illustrate their applicability.

One last prefatory remark is required: the use of this test assumes that the evangelists did not rewrite their material entirely, so as to make it all harmonious with their own views (see above, 'Redaction Criticism', p. 202). Luckily, this assumption will prove to be true. The assumption may surprise the reader, whose intuition may be that an author of strong views would recast all the material to agree with them. There are two points to be observed: (1) Imposing a completely consistent view on diverse sources is in fact quite hard. Modern academic work will provide a lot of examples. Those of us who read doctoral theses spend a fair part of our time checking for consistency from one part to another, but perfect consistency is nevertheless often not obtained. The problem of consistency is of course less acute in a short work than in a long one, and the gospels are short. Despite this, not one of them is perfectly consistent.[3] This leads us to the second point. (2) Ancient writers not infrequently incorporated their sources whole, or only slightly edited, with the result that the final work contains glaring inconsistencies and even contradictions. The ancients seem to have been less troubled by inconsistency than moderns are, and what strikes us as a blatant internal disagreement may have been viewed in some other light by the original author and readers.

Since, then, the gospels are not perfectly consistent internally, we are able to ask what they contain that is 'against the grain'. As we have seen, we can establish the main lines of the theology of the gospels, and this allows us to find material that does not perfectly cohere with those views.

We take now the first complex of interrelated material.

1a. *Jesus, Gentiles and the people of Israel.* The principal point about the historical Jesus, which can be proved beyond reasonable doubt, is that he limited his own mission to the people of Israel. The evangelists all believed in the Gentile mission and in the universal scope of the church, embracing both Jew and non-Jew. Matthew is most explicit: The gospel concludes with the command of the risen Lord to 'go to all the Gentiles' (usually translated 'all the nations') and to make disciples of them (Matt. 28.19). In the genealogy which begins the gospel four women are mentioned, all Gentile or with Gentile connections: Tamar (Matt. 1.3; Gen. 38.6; from the context probably a Canaanite), Rahab (Matt. 1.5; Josh. 2.2, a Canaanite), Ruth (Matt. 1.5; Ruth 1.4, a Moabite), Bathsheba (Matt. 1.6, 'the wife of Uriah'; II Sam. 11.3, married to a Hittite). Near the middle of his gospel Matthew puts a quotation from Isaiah which states that the 'Servant of the Lord' will 'proclaim justice to the Gentiles' (12.18). Luke's pro-Gentile view is most strongly expressed in the second volume of the work, Acts, where great emphasis is laid on the conversion of Gentiles (e.g. 11.18; 13.48; 15.3).

Mark tried almost desperately to produce positive contact between Jesus and Gentiles. After a passage which depicts Jesus as nullifying the Jewish food law (discussed immediately below), Mark puts a rapid trip to 'the region of Tyre and Sidon' in Syria. A pagan Syrophoenician woman[4] met him and persuaded him to exorcize her daughter, despite Jesus' reluctance and his attempt to dismiss the request by saying, 'It is not right to take the children's bread and throw it to the dogs' (7.24–30). After this one incident Mark then states that Jesus returned from the region of Tyre, travelling through Sidon and the Decapolis on the way back to Galilee (7.31). In the area of the Decapolis Jesus healed a man who was deaf (7.32). The geographical summary in 7.31 seems to be confused, since Sidon is north of Tyre, and one would not go through it in order to travel from Tyre southeast to Galilee. The verse, in fact, depicts Jesus as touring a lot of Gentile territory. After reaching the region of Tyre, where the meeting with the woman took place, he travelled approximately twenty miles north to Sidon, back south to Tyre, east approximately forty miles to the area of the Decapolis, and then at least thirty miles southwest to the region of the sea of Galilee (if the last leg followed the shortest route). This trip of at least a hundred and ten miles is more than double the direct route from Tyre to Galilee. Fairly steady walking will cover approximately fifteen miles a day, and thus Mark depicts a trip of eight days or so, even without stops to heal or teach. Mark, we have just seen, places two healings in this trip. Most scholars, making the form-critical observation that within the text of the second healing there is no reference to time or place, take it to be an isolated story which Mark has placed in the Decapolis in order to flesh out the account.

In all probability we owe the long tour to Mark's desire to maximize Jesus' contact with Gentiles, even though he had only one solid story of the healing of a Gentile, a story which indicates a very negative attitude towards Gentiles, though the cure was performed. It is noteworthy that, during the trip into Gentile lands, Jesus is not described as preaching or teaching. Mark depicts him as seeking isolation (7.24), not converts.

If Mark invented or elaborated the long tour, he is not likely to have invented the saying, which is extremely derogatory towards Gentiles: 'Let the children first be fed, for it is not right to take the children's bread and throw it to the dogs' (7.27). The word 'first' probably is what permitted the saying to be used in a gospel written for Gentiles: now it was their turn. The tour seems designed to give a harsh saying a setting which softens it.

Mark places one other story in Gentile territory: the healing of the demoniac in Gerasa, one of the cities of the Decapolis (Mark 5.1–20). The healed man, according to Mark and Luke (not Matthew) remained behind to preach, but Jesus immediately recrossed the lake to Galilee.

We must evaluate this scanty material about Jesus' direct contact with Gentiles in the light of Mark's own Gentile setting. It was necessary to explain to the readers, for example, that 'all the Jews' wash their hands before eating, as well as cups, pots and the like (7.3–4). The word 'all' is probably not entirely accurate, but whether an accurate description of Jews in general or not, the explanation was clearly written for a Gentile audience. The evangelist, that is, wrote for a church which was dominated by Gentiles, and it follows from this that he accepted the Gentile mission. Despite this, he had little that was favourable to Gentiles to recount when it came to Jesus' activity.

It is not surprising that Matthew and Luke add a further passage about the healing of a Gentile, or at least the servant of a centurion who was a Gentile. The gospels place this healing in Capernaum (Matt. 8.5–13//Luke 7.1–10). Most readers, including many professional commentators, take the centurion to have been a Roman. But in Galilee a centurion would not have been an officer in the Roman legion, since Roman troops were not quartered in the villages of Galilee in Jesus' day. The government was in the hands of Herod Antipas, who, though ultimately answerable to the Roman overlords, had his own troops. He used them at least once, in a small war with the Arab king Aretas, following Antipas' dismissal of his first wife, Aretas' daughter. The king took affront, invaded Galilee, and soundly defeated Antipas' army. The Romans were not engaged in this military action (*Antiq.* 18.113–115).

The gospels do not say that the centurion was a Roman, but they do indicate that he was Gentile: according to both, Jesus said that he had not found such faith 'even in Israel' (Matt. 8.10; Luke 7.9), and Luke has the elders of the Jews say to Jesus that the centurion 'loves our nation, and he built us our synagogue'. Luke seems to be assimilating this centurion to the one of Acts 10.2 and, indeed, to the whole class of 'God-fearers'.

Nothing in this story is incredible, but 'not incredible' is not the same as 'beyond doubt'. The story is not incredible simply because Antipas could have had Gentile centurions. Gentiles lived in his domain, and, besides, he may have used mercenaries. One does suspect, however, that the evangelists, especially Luke, have at least enhanced the story. The good centurion, who loves the Jewish people, and who comes to faith in Jesus, is a bit too much like the centurion in Acts 10 and many other Gentiles in Acts to be true. Luke's story is 'too much with the grain'. This judgment, however, may be limited to Luke's special touches, which are not in Matthew. Matthew certainly 'milks' the story, and he follows it up with a promise that 'many would come from east and west . . ., while the sons of the kingdom will be thrown into the outer darkness' (8.11–12). That is, the Gentile centurion prefigures the change which Matthew saw – though he saw it after Jesus' lifetime: few Jews accepted Jesus, while many more Gentiles did. But the fact that Matthew gets mileage out of the story of the centurion's servant does not prove that he thought it up. We recall that we must try to distinguish the material which is used from the use of the material. The story may well have been traditional to Matthew. He and Luke both may have thought of the centurion as a Roman, having given as little thought to the question of where Roman troops were stationed as have many

307

modern scholars, who sometimes write about 'the Roman occupation' of 'the land of Israel'.[5]

Let us leave this story open for a bit and consider the material on the Gentiles more generally. Thus far we have a wandering trip through Gentile territory, where only two events take place, one of which is a clear story of the healing of a Gentile, along with a contemptuous remark about them; a second trip to Gentile territory, where there was a healing, which was followed by Jesus' immediate return to Jewish territory; a slightly dubious story about a centurion in Capernaum. It is quite possible that the only solid bit of information about Gentiles is the saying about feeding the children before the dogs (Mark 7.27). Mark may have started with this saying, designed a tour of Gentile territory to give it a more favourable setting, and then placed a further healing story in the same trip. We should recall that sayings are more resistant to change than are settings.

The paucity of material on Gentiles in all three synoptics shows that there were limits on invention even in a good cause. To say that Jesus' restriction of his own ministry to Israel is 'against the grain' does not in this case mean that it is 'against the testimony of the material in the gospels'. Its testimony is 'little contact, no sustained mission'. This is against the grain of *the evangelists*, and presumably of their churches. They all would have liked more contact between Jesus and Gentiles, and they attempted to amplify what little they had; thus we say that having no more positive stories about Jesus and Gentiles was 'against the grain', and that Jesus' limitation of his own work to Israel is confirmed. This is in agreement with the general evidence of the gospels, evidence which the evangelists tried to modify. Mark expands on the length of Jesus' trip to Gentile territory; Matthew and Luke have a healing story not in Mark; Matthew thinks of Jesus as proclaiming 'justice to the Gentiles', though he has no story to back it up; Luke elaborates on the centurion as a God-fearer, one of the class which is absolutely crucial to his theory of how the Christian movement later spread in Asia Minor and Greece (in Acts). These efforts highlight the basic fact by contrast.

We gain here *very sound evidence of a general kind*. Jesus went to his own people. He may have run into Gentiles on the way; he may have healed one or more; if so one or more may have trusted in him. But these events are incidental: the main fact is the focus of his energy on Israel.

When we ask about details, our knowledge becomes slightly less certain. The saying to the Syrophoenician woman, which uses 'dogs' as a metaphor for 'Gentiles', is against the grain of the gospels and must be accorded the status 'highly probable'. The saying presumably originated during some contact between Jesus and a Gentile, and the saying draws the healing story into the 'probable' category. We are suspicious about the other stories for different reasons, only some of which were mentioned above. There is nothing intrinsically improbable about Jesus healing a centurion's servant, though we are suspicious about this one and his presence in Capernaum, especially in Luke's version, which implies that he was stationed there. Shall we accord this story the status, 'generally probable, dubious in detail'? The Gerasene demoniac is one of the most curious stories in the gospels, which makes it hard to evaluate; and the data which help evaluate it lie outside the issue of 'mission to Gentiles, mission to Israel'.[6] Thus we leave it aside. The other healing story, Mark 7.32, is extremely vague and may simply be added to other stories which show that Jesus was known as a healer.

1b. *Jesus' predictions which refer to Gentiles.* If we stay with passages about the Gentiles, we shall see an issue which is more complex. This is the question of whether or not Jesus predicted that in the last days Gentiles would join Israel in the worship of God. Such an expectation would fit perfectly in general Jewish hopes for the future, and it would also coincide with what in fact happened. Needless to say, it would have agreed entirely with the biases of our gospels. The principal passages are these:

> Mark 13.10: the gospel must be preached to all nations; Matt. 24.14 adds 'throughout the whole world' and 'then the end will come'.

> Matt. 10.18: when punished the disciples will bear testimony before the Gentiles.

> Matt. 8.11–12: many will come from east and west, but the sons of the kingdom will be cast out; Luke 13.28–29 has Jesus address the prediction of expulsion to the Jews in the second person.

The specific sayings of Mark 13.10//Matt. 24.14 and Matt. 10.18 correspond so perfectly with what happened following the death of Jesus, and they are so well exemplified by Paul's mission (the Gentile mission about which we know the most), that they must be regarded as 'predictions' after the fact. That is, the sayings are too much with the grain and so are to be judged to be inauthentic. It is conceivable that Jesus predicted what happened, and some would wish to argue that he actually said anything attributed to him if it is not totally impossible. The evenhanded assessment of evidence, however, which assumes neither 'authentic until proven inauthentic', nor 'inauthentic until proven authentic', leads us to consider such sayings as these 'highly improbable'.

Many scholars, however, maintain the substantial authenticity of Matt. 8.11–12. The image of coming from east and west, and of a banquet with Abraham and the other patriarchs, corresponds to a large body of figurative speech in which Jesus compared the kingdom to a banquet. Further, the expectation that Gentiles would join Israel in the last days was so widespread that it is easily possible that Jesus also shared it. Nevertheless, the prediction that the 'sons' would be cast out of the kingdom is best seen as 'retaliation' on the part of the subsequent church. The Jews in general (though certainly not all) rejected Jesus and his movement, and subsequently Christians responded by having Jesus predict their destruction.

We indicated above that the word 'disproof' would be too blunt, and we may see the point here. In historical reality the early Christians took a little while before deciding on a world-wide mission. By the last stage of his career, Paul clearly had the vision of preaching the gospel in the whole world so that the end could come (Rom. 15.23–24; 11.25–27), and his behaviour before he wrote Romans indicates that this conception of his mission was earlier. Further, numerous other Christians travelled in order to preach the gospel. Yet the issues of going to the Gentiles and the terms of their admission were extremely vexed, and by no means all Christians agreed. The party which supported the Gentile mission won, and it is *that party's* mandate which has been retrojected and attributed to Jesus in the verses which we are considering.

Yet judging these *verses* to be inauthentic does not prove that *Jesus himself* did not think that Gentiles too could enter the kingdom. He may very well have thought that they could and would; and, in light of the common view that Gentiles would one day convert, it would have been strange had he not expected that to happen.

Thus far we rule out the particular sayings attributed to Jesus in Mark 13.10; Matt. 10.18; Matt. 8.11–12, but grant that we have not 'disproved' that Jesus actually held such views. This apparently paradoxical position rests on a distinction between **good evidence** and **exhaustive evidence**. The passages which have Jesus say that Gentiles would enter the kingdom are not good evidence; ruling out evidence for one view, however, does not establish the opposite view as true. Another way of saying this is that negatives are very hard to prove. Our positive evidence that Jesus included the Gentiles in his vision of the future is too weak to be relied on, but this weakness cannot be converted into strong proof of a negative, that he had no such expectation.

But is there evidence that Jesus held a negative view of a Gentile mission? Can it be shown, on the basis of positive evidence, that Jesus did not expect Gentiles to enter the kingdom? Here we turn to Matt. 10.23: 'Truly, I say to you, you will not have gone through all the towns of Israel, before the Son of man comes.' This verse allows insufficient time before the final cataclysm for there to be a Gentile mission, much less one which embraced the whole world. Is this view with or against the bias of Matthew and his community?

The basic answer is simple: it is against the grain. Thus the saying is 'proved'. Now we come to still greater complexity. The saying is against the grain of the Gospel of Matthew as we have it, but it may not have been against the grain of all the communities which contributed to that tradition. There may well have been a hard-line group of Jewish converts which had a heightened eschatology and which opposed the Gentile mission entirely. This saying could have been invented by them and attributed to Jesus.

We have now encountered two extremely harsh statements: (1) that the 'sons of the kingdom', the Jews, would in the end be cast into the outer darkness (Matt. 8.12); (2) that the end would come even before the disciples would finish the circuit of the cities of Israel (Matt. 10.23), which implies that most Gentiles would have no chance of heeding Jesus' message. In terms of the rigid assessment of evidence, the first statement is to be rejected and the second confirmed. Most Jews were in fact 'cast out' as far as the Christian church was concerned; the end did not come before the disciples could go to all the cities of Israel. The prediction which came true (the sons of the kingdom will be cast out) is historically dubious, that which did not (the Son of man will come before the completion of the mission in Palestine) is more likely the one which was made. This judgment rests on the rule that what is against the grain is more likely to be authentic. The complication, we have seen, is that the gospels contain traditions from different times and places, and the second prediction may have been made after Jesus' death, but before the mission had time to progress very much. That is, the limitation of the disciples' mission to Israel may have been made in a community for which it was not against the grain.

In assessing these extreme statements as evidence for what Jesus himself thought, we would do well to back off and enlarge the categories. Did not Jesus believe that God's mercy was all-embracing and that he was endlessly compassionate, seeking to save the lost and to rescue the sinner? The answer will be unanimous that he believed precisely that (see **Test 3** below). Would he, then, have predicted the loss of either the Jews or the Gentiles *en masse*? Neither seems likely.

It is our judgment that the prediction of Matt. 10.23 (the Son of man will come before you go to all the cities of Israel) represents neither Jesus nor the evangelist Matthew, but an intermediate Christian prophet in the earliest days of the church. We also doubt that Matt. 8.12 (the sons of the kingdom will be cast out) goes back to Jesus. Matt. 8.11 (many will come from east and west) by no means implies 8.12 as its conclusion. This phrase and similar ones are fairly frequent in Jewish literature, where they refer not to Gentiles but to the dispersion of Jews (cf. Isa. 49.12; 43.5; Ps. 107.1–3; Baruch 5.5; Ps. Sol. 11.3–7; Zech. 8.7).[7] It is possible that a saying by Jesus on the reassembly of Israel has been reversed into a prediction of their rejection. This cannot, however, be more than 'possible'. Suggestions about revision or re-setting of pericopes may illuminate an issue, but without corroborating information we cannot say any more than that they are possible (cf. above, p. 134).

The evangelists, or at least Matthew and Luke, faced with not very helpful material on the Gentiles, made sense of it by dividing history into two periods. Jesus *during his own lifetime* did not go to Gentiles, though he himself favoured a Gentile mission. The distinction between Jesus' lifetime and subsequently makes its first appearance in Mark 7.27, 'let the children *first* be fed'. The full theory, however, is clearest in Matthew. There a saying of Jesus explicitly confines his own activity to Israel (Matt. 15.24). The charge to 'go nowhere among the Gentiles, and enter no town of the Samaritans' (10.5), Matthew himself probably understood as being valid only during Jesus' own ministry, and he assigns the commandment to convert Gentiles to the risen Lord (Matt. 28.19). Luke attributes the insight that Gentiles should be won to Peter, after the death and resurrection of Jesus (Acts 10.45–48). The few passages about the healing of Gentiles function in their gospels only as precursors of things to come. The evangelists made historical fact into a theological virtue, and thus were not compelled to attribute many favourable statements about Gentiles to Jesus himself, though the predictions of a future mission to the Gentiles (Mark 13.10; Matt. 10.18) probably are inventions of the church. The evangelists probably also understood the parable of the banquet as pointing to the Gentile mission (Matt. 22.1–10; Luke 14.16–24).

We might reconstruct Matthew's thinking as he faced the saying in 10.23 like this: I have this saying, which states that the Son of man will come before there is a Gentile mission; yet there has been a Gentile mission; it must be, then, that when Jesus spoke the saying he had in mind his own resurrection, not the coming of the Son of man which marks the end of this age. Possibly, he meant only that during his lifetime there should be no Gentile mission. Thus I am not compelled to cut it out.

311

As predicted, we have drifted from relatively clear judgments to less clear ones. We might stratify the evidence as follows:

1. It is **virtually certain** that Jesus himself conducted no substantial mission to Gentiles, but rather restricted himself to preaching in Israel.
2. It is **highly probable** that he put feeding the 'children' above feeding the 'dogs'.
3. It is **probable** that the preceding statement was made when he healed a Gentile.
4. It is **probable** that he foresaw a time when God would act to save Gentiles as well as Jews. This rests on the general probability that a Jew who looked to the future would expect the eventual conversion or entry of Gentiles, and on the strong evidence (which we have not discussed here) that Jesus believed that God would seek the lost.
5. It is also **probable** that some early Christians opposed the Gentile mission. This accounts for Matt. 10.23.
6. It is **probable** that the flat predictions that the gospel would be preached to Gentiles throughout the world (Mark 13.10//Matt. 24.14), and that Christian missionaries would be hauled into Gentile courts (Matt. 10.18), are later inventions which reflect the Gentile mission, which by then was well established.
7. It is **probable** that Matthew and Luke understood Jesus to have restricted his mission to Israel, while only hinting that Gentiles who accepted him would be saved. This means that when Matthew included 10.5 (go only to Israel) and 15.24 (I am sent only to Israel) he took these statements as being valid only for Jesus' lifetime.
8. It is **possible** that Jesus said that 'many would come from east and west', referring to the dispersion of Israel, and that this was converted into a prediction that the Jews would be cast out (Matt. 8.11–12).

2. *John the Baptist.* For our second complex of material we turn to the traditions about John the Baptist. We shall now consider passages in much less detail than in the previous section.

There are basically four types of material which involve John the Baptist:

1. Jesus was baptized by John (Mark 1.9 and parr.).
2. Subsequently Jesus praised John but also contrasted his own mission with that of John (Matt. 11.7–18//Luke 7.24–35).
3. John recognized in advance who Jesus was (Matt. 3.14; Fourth Gospel).
4. While in prison John sent disciples to Jesus to ask who he was (Matt. 11.2–6//Luke 7.18–23).

It appears that the early Christians had a problem in defining themselves over against the followers of John the Baptist. On the one hand they wanted to accept and even profit from a positive relationship between Jesus and John; on the other hand they wanted Jesus to be John's superior. Underlying this dilemma was, apparently, John's popularity. From the evidence available, it appears that John probably attracted more attention than did Jesus.[8] Further, he retained many followers even after his death, and these may have offered appreciable competition to the Christian movement (Acts 18.25).

The difficulty which the Christians had with regard to the Baptist's popularity and authority is indicated in Matt. 3.14, which has John say to Jesus, 'I need to be baptized by you, and do you come to me?' This acknowledges that Jesus was baptized by John (thus becoming his follower), while claiming that John recognized Jesus' superiority at their first meeting.

Here we shall make one of our rare excursions to consider the Fourth Gospel. There we find remarkable emphasis on John's acknowledgment of Jesus' superiority: *'This is he of whom I said*, "After me comes a man who ranks before me, for he was before me"' (John 1.30; contrast Mark 1.7; see also John 1.21,26–27,29–34,35–36). On the other hand Jesus is made even more dependent on John than he is in the synoptics. According to the Fourth Gospel Jesus drew his first disciples from among the Baptist's followers (John 1.40). We have here, with emphasis, the two themes which seem to have governed the Christian view of John: Jesus began his public career by being baptized by John; John knew all along that Jesus was his superior. The church could present Jesus as John's ally as long as it could also attribute to John an acknowledgment of Jesus.

If these were the considerations that dominated, how can we use them to assess the material about the Baptist? We should assume that Jesus really did approve of John's work and really did begin as his follower. Had the church been freely inventing here, it probably would have reduced the appearance of Jesus' discipleship under John and portrayed Jesus as being more independent. Free invention might have led it to depict John as testifying to Jesus' importance without any indication that Jesus began his public career by being baptized by John. We should doubt the material in which the Baptist proclaims Jesus, especially in advance, and accept the passage in which he asks who Jesus was as well as the tradition that Jesus was baptized by John. We shall lay out the probabilities as before:

1. It is **virtually certain** that Jesus was baptized by John.
2. It is **almost certain** that Jesus praised John, calling him the greatest 'among those born of women' (Matt. 11.11//Luke 7.28), and that he appealed to John's authority as a prophet when attempting to assert his own (Mark 11.27–33 and parr.).
3. It is **very probable** that when in prison John sent disciples to ask Jesus who he was (Matt. 11.2 and par.).
4. It is **probable** that Jesus contrasted his own ministry with John's: John came 'neither eating nor drinking . . .; the Son of man came eating and drinking' (Matt. 11.18–19 and par.).
5. It is **most unlikely** that John recognized Jesus as his superior at the time of the baptism (Matt. 3.14; John 1).

We shall even more briefly consider a few further passages.

3. *Jesus and the sinners*. In the synoptics Jesus is depicted as the 'friend of tax collectors and sinners' (Matt. 11.19 and par.), and one of his followers was a tax collector (Mark 2.14 and parr.; cf. 2.15–17 and parr.). In Matthew, however, there are two slighting references to tax collectors: 'Do not even tax collectors do the same?' (Matt. 5.46); 'let him be to you as a Gentile and a tax collector' (Matt. 18.17). The early church in Jerusalem was extremely upright according to the law (see e.g. Gal. 2.11–13). While it is possible to reconcile the pro-tax collector material with that which denigrates them, by taking the negative statements to refer to tax collectors who did not follow Jesus, it is quite likely that Jesus actually sought tax collectors, while the early church in Jerusalem excluded them.

4. *Food laws*. The most obvious meaning of Mark 7.15 ('there is nothing outside a person which by going in can defile; but the things which come out are what defile') is that 'all foods are clean', as the author comments (7.19). We have seen that the gospels are all in favour of the Gentile mission, and it follows that those parts of the Jewish law which separated Jew from Gentile were not favoured by them. The saying is very much 'with the grain' of the Gentile mission. In a way it may also be said to be disproved by the lack of multiple attestation (multiple attestation is considered below). Paul would have found it very useful to be able to quote Jesus on his side in his dispute with Peter over eating with Gentiles (Gal. 2.11–14). Acts 10 represents the rejection of Jewish food laws as being revealed to Peter in a series of visions after Jesus' death and resurrection. It is unlikely that Jesus was known to have said that 'what goes in' does not make one unclean.

The saying can be 'saved' as authentic if its meaning is understood to be, 'What matters morally is what comes out' or 'What comes out is much more important'. The 'not . . . but' contrast can mean 'not this only, but much more that', as two examples will make clear. When Moses told the Israelites that their murmurings were *not* against Aaron and himself, *but* against the Lord, the Israelites had just been complaining to him (Ex. 16.2–8). The sentence means, 'Your murmurings directed against us are in reality against the Lord, since we do his will'. Similarly Mark 9.37, 'Whoever receives me, receives *not* me *but* the one who sent me', means 'receiving me is tantamount to receiving God'.[9] '*Not* what goes in *but* what comes out' in Mark 7.15, then, could well mean, 'What comes out is what really matters'. This interpretation of the saying, however, grants the point that as it is intended in Mark 7 it is inauthentic.

5. *The twelve*. According to Matt. 19.28 the twelve disciples would judge the twelve tribes of Israel. Luke 22.30 says only that the disciples would judge the twelve tribes. The Matthaean form gives Judas a role in the coming kingdom and is thus more likely to be authentic.

6. *Jesus' family*. There is a lot of anti-family material in the gospels: e.g. Matt. 10.34–39//Luke 12.49–53, 'a man's foes will be those of his own household'. Cf. Mark 3.21 (his family tried to seize Jesus); 3.31–35 ('who are my mother and my

brothers?'); Mark 10.29–30 and parr. (those who leave their families for Jesus' sake). According to Matt. 15.4–6 and Mark 10.19 and parr. Jesus supported the commandment to honour father and mother. Possibly, again, these passages can be reconciled, but if one has to choose one should choose the former. In the early church James the brother of Jesus was a leading member (Gal. 1.19; 2.9,12; Acts 15.13–21), and Mary was venerated (the birth narrative of Matthew and Luke; cf. Acts 1.14). Thus the church probably would not have created sayings by Jesus which were anti-family.

7. *The threat to the temple.* All three synoptics accept that Jesus *predicted* that the temple would be destroyed (Mark 13.1–2 and parr.). They wish the reader to think that he did not *threaten* its destruction. According to Mark 14.58 witnesses at his trial testified that he had said, '"I will destroy this temple that is made with hands, and in three days I will build another, not made with hands"'. According to Matt. 26.60–61 two people testified to this statement (Matthew does not include 'made with hands', 'not made with hands'), but they testified falsely. These two gospels also depict scoffers at Jesus' crucifixion taunting him by saying, 'You who would destroy the temple and build it in three days, save yourself . . .' (Mark 15.29–30; Matt. 27.40). Presumably the reader is intended to remember that this was a false charge. Luke, it is noteworthy, lacks both passages.

The evangelists seem not to have wanted Jesus to appear as a disturber of the public order or a threatener of major institutions. This makes it likely that they watered down the charge which was in fact levelled against him: that he threatened the destruction of the temple. If, of course, he said 'I will destroy', he meant himself as God's agent. He did not have the machinery, the manpower or the engineering expertise to allow him actually to hurt the temple. Even the Roman legions found it difficult to conquer.

We may take it as 'virtually certain' that Jesus said something about the destruction of the temple, and 'highly probable' that what he said was easily construed as a threat rather than a simple prediction.

In these last examples, more detailed discussion would lead to better nuance, but we think that these short summaries will help illustrate the method of cross-examination. Now we move on to a different test.

21   The Quest and its Methods: 2

Test 2: *Uniqueness*

The test of uniqueness is closely related to 'cross-examination'. It is sometimes called 'the criterion of dissimilarity' though 'the criterion of double dissimilarity' would be more accurate. According to this criterion, material can be safely attributed to Jesus if it agrees neither with the early church nor with the Judaism contemporary with Jesus. Setting this sort of double test has seemed to many to be especially rigorous and scientific. Numerous scholars, however, have objected that the criterion by definition attributes to Jesus only what is unique and thus unnecessarily cuts him off from his contemporary culture and from the movement which followed him. We think that this objection is sound, as is another: we do not in fact know enough about either Judaism or early Christianity to decide what is unique and what is not. These objections, however, do not altogether dispose of the criterion, since it may be argued that it would be useful to find out what about Jesus was unique as far as our knowledge goes, without supposing that he was altogether unique.

It is our own view that one should be very hesitant in talking about 'early Christianity' and what is 'dissimilar' to it, partly because it is not fully known by us, but partly because what is known points to great diversity. In discussing 'cross-examining' the witnesses, we saw that some material might agree neither with the evangelist nor with Jesus, but with someone in between (with regard to Matt. 10.23). That is, each case must be studied, and one must do one's best to find likely and unlikely sources, but it will never be possible simply to say that a given theme is 'dissimilar' to all forms of early Christianity.

Approximately the same is the case when we look at the other side: what about Jesus was 'dissimilar' to Judaism? As usually conducted in the academic literature these discussions are not infrequently ignorant about and biased against Judaism. Even when not, there are two difficulties which we can do little more than mention here: (1) Like early Christianity, Judaism was very diverse, and consequently it is seldom possible to be completely confident that something attributed to Jesus was 'dissimilar' to all of Judaism. When we take up the prohibition of divorce (under *Multiple attestation*), we shall glimpse one point which illustrates Jewish diversity.

Unfortunately we have to leave the topic with this caution and one illustration. (2) Forced arguments are often resorted to in order to emphasize Jesus' superiority to the rest of Judaism. Bias against Judaism has deeply coloured New Testament scholarship, and the work of some major scholars has even included wilful misrepresentation of Judaism, so as to make Jesus artificially better. We shall neither exemplify nor comment further on this sad fact here.[1] We shall, however, when we discuss a theme which is probably authentic – love of enemies – see an example of forced argument even when there is no intention to impugn Jewish moral or spiritual values.

1. *Let the dead bury the dead.* This saying is the conclusion of the principal passage which can be firmly established by the test of uniqueness. A would-be disciple asks that, before following Jesus, he be allowed first to bury his dead father, and Jesus commands him, 'Follow me, and leave the dead to bury their own dead' (Matt. 8.21–22//Luke 9.59–60). The passage has been extensively discussed by Martin Hengel in *The Charismatic Leader and his Followers* and more briefly in Sanders' *Jesus and Judaism*, pp. 252–255. Basically three points emerge, which we shall state only in summary:

1. The use of 'dead' for the man's father is probably not metaphorical: the father has really died. The saying, 'let the dead . . .' is not comprehensible without the request to be given time for the pious duty, and this is one instance in which the saying should not be separated from its immediate context.

2. The saying is so objectionable, if meant literally, that it would be unlikely to have been coined as a metaphor. Ancient Greek and Hebrew society alike placed great emphasis on the burial of the dead, and burying one's parents was an extremely strong obligation, as recalling Sophocles' *Antigone* will show. Jewish society of Jesus' day probably considered the burial of dead parents to be included in the commandment to honour father and mother, and Jesus here, in effect, is saying that following him is a higher duty. We saw above that 'anti-family' passages are probably, on the whole, authentic, and we shall subsequently see that the anti-law aspect of this saying is compatible with the prohibition of divorce, though the latter passage does not actually require transgression of the law. In any case the saying is strongly dissimilar to anything found in Greek or other Jewish literature.

3. The early church, as far as we know, made nothing of the saying: the Jewish law would be challenged, but neglecting to bury the dead is never mentioned. The saying not only comes from nowhere (if not from Jesus), but also it goes nowhere.

Thus it is best to accept the passage as authentic on the grounds of its uniqueness, with only the caution that we can never be totally sure of the category 'unique'.

2. *'Love God; love the neighbour; love enemies; pray for persecutors.*
We may illustrate the difficulty of applying the category 'uniqueness' if we focus on material about love, especially of enemies and persecutors. This material cannot be said to be truly unique, since much of it also appears in Paul, and considering it will allow us to explore only the claim that it is unique vis à vis Judaism. Jesus' distinction

317

from other Jewish prophets and teachers is, however, of first importance, and the temptation to resort to forced arguments in order to demonstrate his moral superiority to 'Judaism' is very great. Thus claims for uniqueness must be very carefully assessed. We should emphasize that we do not doubt the substantial authenticity of the sayings, and the grounds for this will be given below.

We shall first give summaries of some of the key passages in the gospels and Paul's letters:

Jesus: You have heard that it was said, 'You shall love your neighbour and hate your enemy', but I say, Love your enemies and pray for those who persecute you (Matt. 5.43–44//Luke 6.27–28).

The two greatest commandments are 'Love God with all your heart . . .' (Deut. 6.4–5) and 'Love your neighbour as yourself' (Lev. 19.18) (Mark 12.28–34 and parr.).

Paul: When reviled, we bless; when persecuted, we endure; when slandered, we try to conciliate . . . (I Cor. 4.11–13).

Bless those who persecute you (Rom. 12.14).

'If your enemy is hungry feed him; if he is thirsty, give him drink; for by so doing you will heap burning coals upon his head'. Do not be overcome by evil, but overcome evil with good (Rom. 12.19–21, quoting Prov. 25.21–22).

'Love your neighbour as yourself' (Lev. 19.18) sums up the law (Gal. 5.14; Rom. 13.9).

New Testament scholars say very diverse things about these passages and their significance, and we shall not attempt a summary of views, but rather focus only on the question of whether or not these passages, or some of them, are 'unique'. The first passage, which begins 'You have heard that it was said', seems to attribute to the Bible, or to Judaism, the view that one should hate one's enemies, and thus it implies that loving one's enemy is peculiar to Christianity. Many readers accept this implication and deny the ideal of loving one's enemy to Judaism. Beare, for example, wrote that Lev. 19.18 (love the neighbour) means only 'love fellow Jews' and that 'hate enemies' is 'a summary statement of the manner in which [Lev. 19.18] was generally taken by Jewish interpreters'.[2] Some regard 'love' itself as characteristic of Christianity rather than of Judaism.[3] Others more accurately focus on 'bless those who persecute you' as being the point at which Christianity goes beyond Judaism.[4]

Careful scholars will admit that statements similar to most of the above passages are found in Jewish literature but may still claim that on these points the gospels and Paul's letters surpass Judaism. Thus, for example, Schrage grudgingly grants that in Jewish literature there is 'some similarity in content to Jesus' command to love enemies', but sees it as telling that 'there is no direct positive admonition to love one's enemy'. Later he contrasts 'the double commandment of love' (of God and neighbour) with 'the casuistry and trivialization of God's will in Jewish ethics' – a conclusion which is not supported by any of his detailed comments.[5]

The truth is that all the statements above are paralleled in Jewish literature *except* the commandment to pray for one's persecutors. Without attempting to exhaust the evidence, we may note the following points:

1. The command 'Love your enemies' (Matt. 5.44), in just those words, is not attested elsewhere. The Jewish Scripture, and consequently most of its interpreters, fixed on specific points in the treatment of enemies. These are the two principal biblical passages:

> If you meet your enemy's ox or his ass going astray, you shall bring it back to him. If you see the ass of one who hates you lying under its burden, you shall refrain from leaving him with it, you shall help him to lift it up. (Ex. 23.4–5)
> If your enemy is hungry, give him bread to eat; and if he is thirsty, give him water to drink; for you will heap coals of fire on his head, and the Lord will reward you. (Prov. 25.21–22)

Josephus, summarizing and slightly expanding Jewish law, wrote that enemies should be given a decent burial (*Antiq.* 4.265; cf. Deut. 21.22, which refers to condemned criminals). He also noted that Jews are required to give the necessities (shelter, food and fire) to all who ask and to 'show consideration even to declared enemies'. In his legislation Moses

> does not allow us to burn up their [the enemies'] country, or to cut down their fruit trees, and forbids even the spoiling of fallen combatants; he has taken measures to prevent outrage to prisoners of war, especially women. . . . [He] bade us even in an enemy's country to spare and not to kill the beasts employed in labour. (*Against Apion* 2.211–212)

For the most part, this passage simply summarizes the commandments of Exodus and Proverbs, as well as Deut. 20.19 and 21.10–14, but Josephus has attributed further regulations to Moses: not to despoil corpses nor to kill the enemies' beasts of labour, and to offer one's needy enemy fire as well as bread and water.

Constructively, these commandments can be summarized as 'love your enemy', and one can claim no more than that the wording attributed to Jesus is unique. 'Love' in biblical usage, both in the New Testament and the Old, refers not so much to an interior emotion as to outward actions. One 'loves' someone by treating her or him in the right way. Leviticus 19.18, 'love your neighbour as yourself', is a summary of commandments in 19.9–17, which require leaving food in the field for the poor, not stealing, not oppressing one's neighbour or cheating one's servant, and so on. The person who acts in these ways 'loves' the neighbour. As far as we know, no Jew other than the Jesus of the Sermon on the Mount applied the summary word 'love' to the commandments and other traditions requiring that enemies be well treated, and thus one can say that the wording is 'unique'. This is true even when Paul is taken into account, since his passage on enemies (Rom. 12.19–21) relies not on Matt. 5.43f., but directly on Proverbs, which does not contain the word 'love'.

2. With regard to the two-fold summary of the law, 'Love God . . . Love your neighbour', one finds an even weaker claim to uniqueness. 'Love God with all your heart . . .' is presented in Deut. 6.4–9 as a summary, and the passage requires remembering and teaching 'all the words which I command you this day', including especially the Ten Commandments of Deut. 5. First-century Jews in general

recognized that the *Shema'*, as the passage is called in Hebrew, is a summary or, better, epitome of the law which they were to recall every day. (*Shema'* means 'hear': the passage begins, 'Hear O Israel: The Lord our God is one Lord; and you shall love . . .'). Many followed the practice required by Deut. 6.8f. of binding the commandments on their hands and placing them on their doorposts, and for these purposes they used epitomes or summaries, often including Deut. 6.4–9 and related passages.[6]

As we saw just above, Lev. 19.18, 'Love your neighbour' is presented in that chapter as a summary of commandments to treat neighbours with justice and charity. Beare took this to exhaust Jewish views about love: love only the neighbour, that is, fellow Jews. But Lev. 19 proceeds to give commandments about the treatment of 'strangers' – resident aliens –, and these are summarized in 19.34: 'The stranger who sojourns with you shall be to you as the native among you, and you shall love him as yourself.'

Leviticus 19.18 was commonly recognized as a summary of the law, and it was often cited as such. Sometimes it was turned into an aphorism, such as 'what is hateful to you, do not to your neighbour' (e.g. Babylonian Talmud Shabbath 31a; Tobit 4.15). A similar aphorism, 'the Golden Rule', is attributed to Jesus: 'Whatever you wish that people would do to you, do so to them; for this is the law and the prophets' (Matt. 7.12). The conclusion shows that the statement is intended as an epitome. Paul's use of Lev. 19.18 as a summary of the law (Gal. 5.14; Rom. 13.9) seems not to have been based on Jesus-tradition, but on Jewish usage generally. He did not put the two love commandments together, and in his use of Lev. 19.18 he reflects knowledge of the 'negative' form of the aphorism: 'Love does *no wrong* to a neighbour; therefore love is the fulfilling of the law' (Rom. 13.10).

Thus when Jesus singled out Deut. 6.4–5 and Lev. 19.18 as the two greatest commandments, he simply chose the two which many Jews would have said give the essence of the law, and which are presented in the Bible as summaries. Further, Jewish thinkers were well aware that these two commandments summarize the two aspects of the law, sometimes called the 'two tables': laws which govern relations between people and God; laws which govern relations among people: love God, love your neighbour. According to Philo the two main heads of the law are duty to God and duty to one's fellows (*Special Laws* 2.63; *Decalogue* 106–112; *Who is the Heir?* 168–173). In a longer presentation of the law he rewords these two commandments and places each at the beginning of a longer discussion: 'God asks nothing . . . difficult, but only . . . just to love Him'; the law 'stands pre-eminent in enjoining fellowship and humanity' (*Special Laws* 1.299f., 324). The word translated 'humanity' is *philanthrōpia*, which here as elsewhere in Philo and Josephus means 'love of all humanity', not just love of other Jews.[7]

The claim of 'uniqueness' for Jesus' combination of these two commandments, then, can be only that he explicitly quoted them together one after the other. Other Jews quoted one or the other as a summary or epitome of the law, or re-worded them and combined them, or used them as heads under which the laws were discussed.

3. On one point, however, it can be said that the material attributed to Jesus truly is 'unique' as far as present knowledge goes. That is the admonition to pray for one's persecutors. This may be echoed in I Cor. 4.12, but more clearly in Rom. 12.14: 'Bless those who persecute you'.

Endurance of persecution and even giving thanks for sufferings can be richly paralleled from Jewish sources. These themes arise, of course, principally during persecution, times when obeying God led directly to suffering. The two major periods in which this situation occurred were the persecutions at the time of Antiochus Epiphanes IV (175–164 BCE) and Hadrian (*c.* CE 130–138). Daniel, written during the first period, depicts Daniel and his friends as not only enduring persecution but flourishing during it (Dan. 1; 3.19–30). IV Maccabees, written at an uncertain date but looking back on this period, eulogizes endurance under persecution. From the time of the Hadrianic persecution one finds Rabbinic statements which praise suffering as bringing atonement and which state, in effect, 'Happy are those who suffer'.[8] We do not, however, find prayers for the persecutors. The attitude, rather, is one of defiance: we will be true to God's law despite the worst you can do, and he will save us:

> O children of Abraham, you must die nobly for piety's sake. And you, guards of the tyrant, why leave off your work [of torture]? (IV Macc. 6.22–23)

> You know, O God, that though I could have saved myself I am dying in these fiery torments for the sake of the Law. Be merciful to your people and let our punishment be a satisfaction on their behalf. Make my blood their purification and take my life as a ransom for theirs (6.27–29).[9]

Joseph Fitzmyer has proposed a Jewish parallel even to the idea of prayer for persecutors.[10] The Genesis Apocryphon from Qumran depicts Abraham as praying for Pharaoh after the latter had restored Abraham's wife to him (1 QapGen 20.28). This seems not to be a good parallel, since at the time of the prayer Pharaoh could not be said to be 'persecuting' Abraham.

Neither doing good to enemies nor enduring persecution gladly nor finding value in suffering is foreign to Judaism. The distinctive point is *prayer for the persecutor*, which is not only recommended by both Jesus and Paul, but also attributed directly to Jesus on the cross by some manuscripts of Luke 23.34 and to Stephen when at the point of death (Acts 7.60).

Some scholars who wish to depict Jesus as uniquely superior to 'Judaism' on all these points will cite less charitable passages than we have quoted, and then claim that the worse statements 'neutralize' the better, leaving Jesus' noble statements in effect unparalleled.[11] This is manifestly unfair. Idealist should be compared with idealist, not one idealist with the generality of a whole nation. That Jesus' ethics were higher than average will not be doubted. One should compare the ethics of Jesus with those of Philo, not with those of Jews who feared or despised Gentiles, some of whom certainly existed. It would be unworthy of a Jewish scholar to accuse 'Christianity' on the basis of John Chrysostom's virulent anti-Jewish polemics, and Christian scholars should behave no less worthily.

This study serves not only to demonstrate the need to study Jewish literature carefully before claiming that gospel material is 'unique', it also reveals two pitfalls in arguing for uniqueness. Once one begins an argument for uniqueness, it is easy to expand it so as to deny to Judaism values and attitudes which are well-attested. Trying to prove that Jesus was different from his contemporaries and predecessors easily turns into arguing that he was better, and this argument in turn often deteriorates into overlooking or denying Jewish values. Thus Schrage, though he recognized that Jewish material on enemies is substantially the same as 'love your enemies', nevertheless tried to find an unique value in Jesus' statement of the commandment, and he claimed that the dual commandment of love is to be set in contrast to Jewish 'trivialization' and 'casuistry' – though again the substance of the dual commandment is well-attested in Jewish literature.[12]

The second pitfall is that, when one finds a point which is unique, there is the supposition that it must come from Jesus, and there is a tendency not to explore other possibilities. We have found an unique point (as far as our knowledge goes): bless persecutors. Prayer for persecutors is most likely to arise in a time of persecution. During his Galilean ministry did Jesus feel persecuted? Perhaps he did, but we should be open to another possibility: conceivably these traditions arose during the period of the persecution of the early church – a persecution which we know to have taken place. It could have been members of the Christian movement who first added to the general admonition to treat one's enemies well the more specific charge to pray for one's persecutors. It is noteworthy that the theme is bigger in Luke–Acts than elsewhere. This need not show that it was a late development, but it does at least show that, once started, it could be amplified. Paul had a good deal to say about suffering, and in passages not quoted he elaborated the theme of persecution (e.g. II Cor. 11.22–29; Rom. 8.35–39). These elaborations arose from his own experience, and he could comfort himself by quoting Scripture (Rom. 8.36 quotes Ps. 44.22). Would he or anyone else ever have pressed on to say, 'Pray for your persecutors' simply because they were being persecuted and also believed in loving one's enemies, if Jesus had not said it first? We do not know the answer to the question, but perhaps posing it shows what is involved in the discussion of 'uniqueness' and how fine the point is – once one grants moral and spiritual stature to others besides Jesus.

The 'uniqueness' of the admonition to pray for one's persecutors does not, then, completely prove that Jesus said it. Some early Christian could have arrived at it by applying the rule 'love your enemies' to the particular circumstances of persecution. We do not wish to argue that Jesus did *not* say it; he could have, and if in the Galilean ministry he felt persecuted he probably did.

The saying 'love your enemies', while substantially not unique to Jesus, is nevertheless probably authentic. 'Non-unique' does not prove 'inauthentic': on the contrary, we should suppose that Jesus held the higher ideals of the Judaism which nurtured him. If one adds together the biblical injunctions to do good to enemies, their expansion in Josephus' idealized depiction of Judaism, Paul's statements on the topic and the attribution of the saying to Jesus, one comes up with the general probability that he said it. Here continuity with the biblical tradition at its best, rather than 'dissimilarity', establishes the statement as 'highly probable'.

Test 3: *Multiple attestation*

The techniques considered under the headings 'cross-examination' and 'uniqueness' contain a natural bias towards negative conclusions. If we doubt materials in the gospels which are 'with the grain' we obviously must doubt quite a lot of the material: the evangelists must often have agreed with what they wrote. Seeking what is 'dissimilar' or 'unique' has the same result: it may not be entirely true that 'there is nothing new under the sun' (Eccles. 1.9), but not very many thoughts or deeds can be called 'unique'. We now turn, however, to a technique which is biased towards positive results: multiple attestation. The rule is this: A passage is more likely to go back to Jesus if it has been preserved in two or more sources which are independent of each other.

There are potentially several ways of defining 'multiple': one could mean material which occurs (1) in more than one gospel, (2) in more than one source, (3) in more than one form-critical genre (e.g. parables and wisdom sayings), or (4) both within the gospels and in other Christian literature. Applying this test within the gospels obviously depends on one's view of sources. Those who firmly maintain the independent existence of Q can find a few such passages, such as Collusion with Satan (Mark 3.20–30 and parr.). Those who accept Goulder's hypothesis find no such passages, except for the doublets in Mark (for example the two feeding stories).

For the present purposes we shall use only the strongest group of passages under this head: those which are found both in one or more gospel accounts and in Paul's letters. Paul shows remarkably little interest (at least in the letters which survive) in the teaching of the historical Jesus. He quite often appeals to Scripture as proof of his points, and not infrequently to Christian experience, whether his own or that of his converts. Only three times in the surviving correspondence does he explicitly quote 'the Lord' and then attribute to him a saying which is also in the gospels.[13] Thus we cannot think that he freely invented sayings by 'the Lord' (see above, ch. 9, Creativity).

His knowledge of the teaching of Jesus also seems to have been independent. Either the collections of sayings material which surfaced in the gospels had not yet been made, or he was ignorant of them. For a lot of his arguments, sayings by Jesus would have been useful. 'The Son of man is Lord of the sabbath' (Mark 2.28) could have stood him in good stead in debating whether or not keeping 'days' was required (Gal. 4.10; Rom. 14.5–6). His failure to cite it helps establish his susbstantial independence of the sayings material as we now have it. The gospels, we have seen, were composed, at least in their present forms, between the late 60s and the 80s, while the last of Paul's letters was written in the 50s. It is also unlikely that the authors of the gospels used Paul's letters. They were written earlier than the gospels, but they seem to have been collected, edited and published in the 90s. Thus when Paul cites a saying by the Lord, he provides the greatest possible independent attestation of it.

Besides the three explicit quotations, there are a large number of agreements between the teaching of Paul and that attributed to Jesus, and in some of these cases one may think that Paul had been influenced by what he had heard about Jesus. In the previous section, on love of enemies and prayer for persecutors, we saw some parallels, some of which may have been the result of dependence on a common source – the Bible. Some parallels cannot be explained in this way, however, and a full list of parallels between the synoptics and Paul provides a useful number of sayings of Jesus which may have circulated in Paul's day. Those who wish to study parallels between Paul and Jesus may consult lists compiled by W. D. Davies and Michael Goulder.[14]

We wish to highlight the three passages in which Paul quotes 'the Lord' and for which there is a close parallel in the synoptics. These belong to the passages which are 'authentic beyond reasonable doubt'. This does not mean, however, that there are no difficulties which require study; on the contrary, there are.

1. *The prohibition of divorce.* This passage stands head and shoulders above others in terms of the degree of confidence which we may have in its authenticity. Its relative importance in the lifetime of Jesus is harder to assess, but in terms of our knowledge of what he said it is preeminent. It is, for one thing, triply attested, appearing in Paul and in two different forms in the synoptics. Secondly, it counts as 'against the grain'. We shall see that both Paul and Matthew had a bit of trouble with the prohibition. The evidence is this:

In I Cor. 7 Paul discusses marriage and celibacy, favouring celibacy (7.1,6–7,8,32–34,37–38,40) but permitting marriage as a concession to human desire and need (e.g. 7.6,9). On the topic of remaining single he admits that he has 'no command of the Lord' (7.25). This presumably means that he had not heard of the discussion which is attributed to Jesus and the disciples in Matt. 19.12. On the issue of divorce, his concern is with marriages in which one partner is a Christian but not the other. He favours staying together, on the ground that the believing partner may make the other 'holy' (7.14), but he is prepared to grant divorce: 'If the unbelieving partner desires to separate, let it be so; in such a case the brother or sister is not bound' (7.15). It is clear that, left to his own devices, he would not have come up with a prohibition of divorce. But, as an honest man, he knew that he should give the command of the Lord:

> To the married I give charge, not I but the Lord, that the wife should not separate from her husband (but if she does, let her remain single or else be reconciled to her husband) – and that the husband should not divorce his wife (I Cor. 7.10–11).

In this form of the saying divorce is not entirely forbidden, but remarriage to another person apparently is. This is the point on which Paul in fact fixes, and in 7.12–16 he discusses divorce as a live possibility for the Christians in Corinth. He could have written his chapter without the saying of the Lord; he did not make it up.

In the gospels the saying about divorce appears twice in Matthew, once in Mark and once in Luke. In terms of the two-source hypothesis, the saying is in both Mark and Q, and so is doubly attested even apart from Paul's use of it. Whatever one's explanation of the synoptic problem, one immediately sees that there are two forms of the tradition: a long form and a short form. We may look at them in parallel columns:

Matt. 19.3–12	**Mark 10.2–12**
[3]And Pharisees came up to him and tested him by asking, 'Is it lawful to divorce one's wife for any cause?' [4]He answered,	[2]And Pharisees came up and in order to test him asked, 'Is it lawful for a man to divorce his wife?' [3]He answered them, 'What did Moses command you?' [4]They said, 'Moses allowed a man to write a certificate of divorce, and to put her away.' [5]But Jesus said to them, 'For your hardness of heart he wrote you this commandment. [6]But from the beginning of creation, "God made them male and female."
cp.v.7,8	
'Have you not read that he who made them from the beginning made them male and female, [5]and said, "For this reason a man shall leave his father and mother and be joined to his wife, and the two shall become one flesh." [6]So they are no longer two but one flesh. What therefore God has joined together, let not man put asunder.' [7]They said to him, 'Why then did Moses command one to give a certificate of divorce, and to put her away?' [8]He said to them, 'For your hardness of heart Moses allowed you to divorce your wives, but from the beginning it was not so.	[7]"For this reason a man shall leave his father and mother and be joined to his wife, [8]and the two shall become one flesh." So they are no longer two but one flesh. [9]What therefore God has joined together, let not man put asunder.'
	cp.v.3–5
[9]And I say to you: whoever divorces his wife, except for unchastity, and marries another, commits adultery.'	[10]And in the house the disciples asked him again about this matter. [11]And he said to them, 'Whoever divorces his wife and marries another, commits adultery against her; [12]and if she divorces her husband and marries another, she commits adultery.'

[10]The disciples said to him, 'If such is the case of a man with his wife, it is not expedient to marry.' [11]But he said to them, 'Not all men can receive this saying, but only those to whom it is given. [12]For there are eunuchs who have been so from birth, and there are eunuchs who have been made eunuchs by men, and there are eunuchs who have made themselves eunuchs for the sake of the kingdom of heaven. He who is able to receive this, let him receive it.'

Matt. 5.31–32	Luke 16.18
³¹'It was also said, "Whoever divorces his wife, let him give her a certificate of divorce." ³²But I say to you that everyone who divorces his wife, except on the ground of unchastity, makes her an adulteress; and whoever marries a divorced woman commits adultery.'	¹⁸'Every one who divorces his wife and marries another commits adultery, and he who marries a woman divorced from her husband commits adultery.'

With regard to the short form, we may note the following:

1. It basically agrees with Paul: the fault of divorce is not in itself, but in its consequences: remarriage, which, according to this passage, is adultery. Luke applies this to both man and woman. In the short form Matthew applies it only to the woman who remarries. He saves the statement about the man who remarries for his long version in ch. 19.

2. The wording of the three short forms (Matt., Luke and Paul) is appreciably different. (*a*) Paul begins with the case of a woman who wishes divorce, whereas Matthew and Luke deal only with the man. (See further below on Mark's version of the long form.) (*b*) The sayings in Matthew and Paul state (Matthew) or imply (Paul) that the woman who remarries commits adultery, while Luke mentions only the man. (*c*) Matthew, however, assumes that a divorced woman must remarry (presumably for financial reasons), while Paul thinks that she has a choice. Matthew apparently assumes that the man who divorces his wife need not remarry. (*d*) Paul's version is in the third person imperative (wife/husband should not), while in the gospels the saying is in the third person indicative, a simple statement of fact. (*e*) The statement that remarriage constitutes adultery is applied to men in two different circumstances in Luke. The others do not mention the man who marries a divorced woman (though they may imply it). Matthew postpones this application until his long form.

3. Matthew's exceptive clause (except for (prior) adultery) is the logical consequence of his short version and is virtually tautologous.* A man should not divorce his wife, since that will drive her into remarriage (=adultery) – unless, of course, she is already an adulteress, in which case making her commit it formally, by remarriage, would not aggravate her situation. Scholars almost universally believe that Matthew added the clause in both forms, and that is the simplest explanation of the fact that it appears in both his passages but not in the other three. It does not, however, change the thrust of his short version.

*Matthew reads literally, 'anyone who puts away his wife except for *porneia* makes her commit adultery'. *Porneia* in the New Testament may refer to any form of sexual immorality, but in this context it probably means 'infidelity by having intercourse with another man': i.e., anyone who divorces his wife except for adultery makes her commit adultery.

With regard to the long form:

4. Its conclusion (Matt. 19.7–9//Mark 10.10–12) basically agrees with the short form: the problem with divorce is that it leads to remarriage, which is adultery.

5. There are, again, differences between the two versions of the long form: (*a*) Mark mentions the case of a woman who divorces her husband, while Matthew does not. Mark here supports Paul. We should note that Paul's terminology reflects his own knowledge of Jewish law. He states that a woman should not 'separate from' or 'leave' her husband, while the man should not 'put away' his wife. In Jewish law only the man could initiate a legal divorce, which he did by writing for the woman a bill of divorce and (at least in some traditions) repaying her the dowry which he had received from her father. The woman could 'leave' the man, but not 'put him away'. Mark uses the verb 'leave' for both the husband and the wife, probably being ignorant of this rather fine point of Jewish law. It remains uncertain, however, whether Jesus himself explicitly dealt with the issue of a woman who leaves her husband. (*b*) Mark has the adultery count on both sides, the man's and the woman's. Matthew mentions only the man who divorces and remarries. He had dealt with the woman in the short form. (*c*) Matthew again has an exceptive clause. The effect this time is to *allow* a man to remarry if his divorce was the result of his wife's infidelity. (*d*) In Mark the conclusion to the passage comes 'in the house', away from the Pharisees, while in Matthew the scene does not change. (*e*) This leads to alterations in the sequence: the counter argument, that Moses allowed divorce, comes earlier in Mark than in Matthew.

When we compare the long form and the short, we see the following:

6. In the long form proof texts are given: Gen. 1.27, 'God made them male and female' (Matt. 19.4//Mark 10.6); Gen. 2.24, which ends 'and the two become one flesh'.

7. From the proof texts is derived a hard conclusion: 'What God has joined together let no one put asunder'. This seems to be a complete prohibition of divorce, rather than just an admonition against it followed by the warning that it leads to remarriage, which is the force of the short form.

There can be no reasonable doubt that Jesus really said something about divorce, but what was it? Which of these rewordings catches the nuance of what he said?

'It is better not to divorce, and I counsel you against it, but if you do divorce do not remarry' (so Paul).

'Do not divorce because this leads inevitably to remarriage=adultery *on both sides*' (so the conclusion of Mark's version).

'Do not divorce your wife, since that makes her an adulteress, unless she has already committed adultery; and do not marry a divorced woman' (so Matt.'s short form).

'Do not divorce your wife and remarry, since that is adultery, *unless* your wife previously committed adultery (the conclusion to Matt.'s long form).

'It is against the order of creation to divorce; do not do it' (the proof texts of the long form).

327

As we pointed out above, one cannot study this passage – the most securely attested saying by Jesus – and conclude that he carefully taught his disciples to memorize his sayings and that they did so. On the contrary, the teaching was revised as it was applied to different situations.

The consequence of this revision is that, with regard to *historical authenticity*, we can be sure that Jesus said something about divorce, but we do not know the precise nuance. He was against it. What else?

The simplest way to proceed is to ask what is common. This will lead us to a short hypothetical version: remarriage after divorce constitutes adultery. We cannot know whether this was originally applied to the wife who is divorced by her husband (Matt. 5.32), the man who marries a divorced woman (Matt. 5.32; Luke 16.18), the man who initiates divorce and then remarries (Luke 16.18; Matt. 19.9; Mark 10.10); or the woman who initiates divorce and then remarries (Mark 10.12; implied in Paul). It perhaps does not matter very much, since one case may be held to imply the others. Still, it would have been interesting to know just which one(s) Jesus cited.

The larger question is the authenticity of the long form. In Mark 10 and Matt. 19, Jesus appeals to the order of creation as establishing a norm for life. This norm is prior to and overrides the Mosaic law, which permits divorce. This very argument, using one of the same proof texts, 'Male and female he created them', appears in one of the Dead Sea Scrolls (CD 4.21). Thus the synoptic passage is not entirely 'dissimilar' to everything else in Palestinian Judaism, but rather would be at home in rigorist sectarian Judaism. This does not count against it. The argument that present life should re-create the order of creation implies the dawning of eschatological existence: the new age will be like Eden before the fall. It seems intrinsically likely that Jesus would have argued this particular case by citing Scripture, and the long form has a good deal to be said for it.

The scriptural argument in the long form implies a more radical stance than the short form and the conclusion of the long form: '"the two become one flesh"' and 'let no one put asunder' seem to prohibit divorce entirely, not just remarriage. It is not difficult to believe that the saying started out radical and was revised in the direction of practicability. Paul's discussion shows that simply forbidding divorce was not (in his view) appropriate. He tried to deal with cases in a differentiated way, and he had the prohibition of remarriage only as the bottom line. Up to that point there is more than one possibility. Matthew clearly shows the attempt to make the rule practicable, and the 'except' clause is probably to be explained as an escape clause. Further, he adds a discussion between the disciples and Jesus after the long form in ch. 19. It begins with the disciples saying that, if one cannot divorce and remarry, it is better not to marry the first time (Matt. 19.10). On the view that the prohibition was progressively watered down, we may think that it began as a complete denial of divorce.

On grounds of *what is common* we are inclined to accept the short form in general: remarriage was prohibited. On grounds of *intrinsic probability* the long form looks more likely. We cannot resolve this problem, and so we leave it here. We have gained *good general knowledge* about a saying by Jesus, but we do not have the precise nuance, and we cannot be certain of the grounds for his statement.

2. *The Lord's supper.* We shall continue the practice of reducing the detail of the discussion after the first example, and so we give only the principal points in summary form.

1. The 'words of institution' at the supper (this is my body, etc.) appear in I Cor. 11.23–25; Matt. 26.26–29//Mark 14.22–25//Luke 22.15–20.

2. Altogether there are four versions:[15]

(*a*) Paul's, according to which Jesus said of the bread, 'this is my body', but of the cup, 'this cup *is* the new *covenant* in my blood'. Paul does not have the saying about drinking again in the kingdom, but he concludes with the comment, 'you proclaim the Lord's death until he comes'.

(*b*) Matthew and Mark's, which has, over the bread, 'this is my body', and over the cup 'this *is* my *blood* of the covenant'. This version concludes, 'I shall not drink . . . again until that day when I drink [it] new in the kingdom'.

(*c*) The long form in Luke (supported by many manuscripts). This version puts first the cup and the saying about drinking when the kingdom comes, second the saying over the bread, 'this is my body', and third the saying over the cup, 'this cup is the new covenant in my blood' (agreeing here with Paul).

(*d*) The short form in Luke (supported by some manuscripts), which is like (*c*) above but lacks the second saying over the cup.

3. Again, we do not know precisely what was said, but we may accept what is common: a saying about both the bread and the cup; the statement 'this is my body' about the bread. *Some* statement about the cup, the blood and the new covenant is supported by Paul, Matthew/Mark and the long form of Luke. The prediction about drinking from the fruit of the vine *in the kingdom* (Matthew/Mark and Luke) seems to be supported by Paul's saying that the Lord's death is proclaimed *until he comes*.

Thus we may think that Jesus, foreseeing his own death, spoke of the bread and the wine as symbols of its meaning, which included a 'new covenant', and looked forward to the kingdom.

3. *The return of the Lord, the coming of the Son of man.* Paul stated that he had the following 'word of the Lord':

. . . we who are alive, who are left until the coming of the Lord, shall not precede those who have fallen asleep. For the Lord himself will descend from heaven with a cry of command, with the archangel's call, and with the sound of the trumpet of God. And the dead in Christ will rise first; then we who are alive, who are left, shall be caught up together with them in the clouds to meet the Lord in the air; and so we shall always be with the Lord (I Thess. 4.15–17).

There are closely related sayings in the gospels. Paul's repeated 'who are left', once preceded by 'who are alive', recalls Matt. 16.28//Mark 9.1//Luke 9.27, 'some standing here will not taste of death until' they see 'the Son of man' (Matthew) or 'the kingdom of God' (Mark and Luke) 'coming' (Matthew) or 'having come' (Mark). The preceding saying in Matt. 16.27 and parr. refers to the angels of the Son of man, while Matt. 24.31 predicts that the Son of man will send his angels 'with a loud trumpet'.

It is not difficult to think that Paul changed 'the Son of man' to 'the Lord', accepting the (by then) common Christian view that the 'coming Son of man' sayings referred to the return of Christ, and that he added the 'dead in Christ' in order to meet his present problem, which was that some of his converts had died before the coming of the Lord. If we count these points as Paul's own changes and ignore them, we still have a common core: the appearance of a heavenly being accompanied by angels and the end of the present age. Paul seems to have known one or more sayings very much like that of Matt. 16.27–28 and parr. (including Matt. 24.31).[16]

This saying, more securely than any others, results in our assigning to Jesus an explicit future eschatology: in the lifetime of his hearers a dramatic event would take place. In the synoptic saying the angels separate humanity into the 'elect' and the rest. In Paul's view those in Christ, whether dead or alive, would be taken up into heaven to 'meet the Lord'. In either case life as we know it comes to an end. (On whether or not this means 'the end of the world', see the next chapter.)

These three sayings – divorce, the bread and wine, and the coming end – are as reliable as any in the gospels. Many scholars, to be sure, doubt the third, attributing it to an early Christian prophet rather than to Jesus. That is possibly correct, but it cannot be shown to be so on the basis of the evenhanded assessment of evidence. The argument which proves the pericope on divorce to be basically authentic does the same for the saying on the coming of the Son of man (the return of the Lord).

Test 4: *View common to friend and foe*

At the outset we noted that it would be worthwhile to see Jesus through his opponents' eyes. The gospels are based on 'propaganda', bias (in this case, in a good cause). We would understand more about Jesus and his impact – or lack of it – if we knew what his enemies thought. What friend and foe agreed on is presumably reliable material. Two facets of his career and message stand out as proved on this basis.

1. *Miracles*. In *Jesus the Magician* Morton Smith pointed out that we possess the enemies' view of Jesus as a miracle-worker. He was a magician. He could, they granted, cast out demons, but he did so by invoking Beelzebul, 'the ruler of demons' (Mark 3.32 and parr.). Some aspect of his behaviour – Smith suggests that it was connected with exorcism – led 'those around him' (usually thought to include his family) to want to take hold of him; 'for they said, "He is beside himself"' (Mark 3.21). We noted above that there is anti-family material in the gospels, and here we seem to see the matter through their eyes: they agreed in part with his opponents and wished to suppress him, perhaps to keep him safe.

The authors of the gospels saw Jesus' miracles as signs either of the 'inbreaking' kingdom of God ('if I cast out demons . . . the kingdom of God has come upon you', Matt. 12.28//Luke 11.20) or of his special relationship to God. He said to the paralytic, 'your sins are forgiven', presumably by God (Mark 2.9 and parr.); and after the healing the onlookers 'glorified God' and said, '"We never saw anything like this"' (Mark 2.12). That is, his friends saw the miracles as the work of God, not of Beelzebul.

They agreed that he was a miracle-worker, especially a healer. We may accept this as proved by the test.

It will be recalled from ch. 11 that we do not wish to attempt to reconcile the eighteenth-century view of 'the laws of nature' with the first-century world view, much less to discuss 'science and religion in the present age'. We must stay with the first-century world view: some people could perform what many saw as miracles. Within these parameters, we can say that Jesus' ability to perform miracles is *proved*, since not only his followers, but also his opponents, knew him as a miracle-worker.

2. *The kingdom.* According to all four gospels Jesus was crucified as 'king of the Jews'. Pilate interrogated him about the claim to be king (Matt. 27.11//Mark 15.2// Luke 23.3; John 18.33). The inscription 'king of the Jews' was put on the cross (Matt. 27.37//Mark 15.26//Luke 23.38; John 19.19), and Jesus was mocked by this title (Matt. 27.29//Mark 15.18; John 19.3; Matt. 27.42//Mark 15.32//Luke 23.37). From the point of view of the evangelists, this claimed too little, and it is not likely that they made it all up. We may conclude that his opponents saw him as *falsely* claiming to be 'king' in some sense or other.

Pilate did not think that Jesus and his followers constituted a military threat. The proof is simple: the followers survived. They fled at first but later returned to Jerusalem, where they conducted a mission. They were harrassed by the chief priests but not executed by the Romans. Jesus' claim was laughable to the imperial power. The inscription therefore did not mean 'armed insurgent'. Pilate probably saw Jesus as a possible focal point for discontent and wished to execute him before he stirred up a mob. He had said something which allowed the charge to be made that he claimed to be king.

From the point of view of his followers and friends, the word 'kingdom' served as a summary of Jesus' message. Many of the parables liken 'the kingdom of God' to various human situations. Jesus compared John the Baptist to 'the least in the kingdom' (Matt. 11.11 and par.); he promised the kingdom to the 'poor in spirit' or 'the poor' (Matt. 5.3; Luke 6.20); he discussed entry into the kingdom (e.g. Matt. 5.20; 19.23); his disciples debated 'the greatest in the kingdom' (Matt. 18.1; cf. Matt. 20.24–28 and parr.). According to Mark 10.35–40 James and John asked to sit on each side of him in his 'glory', for which Matthew has 'kingdom' (20.21). It would have been difficult to hear anything about Jesus and not to have heard talk of 'kingdom'.

His followers seem to have thought of the coming kingdom as 'his': thus the passage about James and John. He may actually have spoken only of the kingdom of the coming Son of man, or simply of the kingdom of God (see e.g. Matt. 16.28 and Mark 9.1), but he thought that the kingdom had something to do with himself. His followers would judge the tribes of Israel (Matt. 19.28 and par.), and he stood at their head. In Jerusalem some people besides his followers may have discussed whether or not he was the 'Messiah' or 'Son of David', the expected king (Matt. 21.7–9 and parr.). Whatever others thought, he is said to have ridden into Jerusalem on 'the foal of an ass', as predicted of the coming king in Zechariah 9.9 (Mark 11.7–10 and parr.).

We may be sure, beyond reasonable doubt, that friend and foe alike thought that Jesus made claims which could be summarized by using the word 'king' or 'kingdom'. He very likely did not use the word 'king' (or 'Messiah') of himself; rather, the evidence is that he did not wish to say what he called himself (Mark 8.27–30 and parr.; cf. Matt. 11.2–6, the ambiguous reply to the question of John). According to Matthew and Luke this reserve was maintained when he was on trial, though Mark has him confess to being 'Christ' (Greek for 'Messiah': Mark 14.62 and parr.). Since the authors firmly believed him to be 'king' or 'Messiah', this refusal to say may be taken as 'highly probable'.

Whether he called himself 'king' or not, his followers thought that he was leading them into the kingdom of God.

We do not know just how this kingdom was conceived. There are two depictions. (1) We saw above passages in which the idea essentially is that the present age will end: the Son of man (or 'the Lord') will come with angels, those in Christ will be taken up (so Paul), or the elect will be separated from the rest (Matt. 24.31). (2) The world will continue, but there will be a new order, which will require the creative act of God. The disciples will judge the twelve tribes, which means that they will be reassembled. This is distinct from the idea that angels will separate the elect from the rest. In the kingdom, Jesus' followers will sit at his side. Wine will be drunk. (On whether or not these two depictions are conflicting, see the next chapter.)

Neither of these things happened, and so naturally scholars have sought another meaning of 'kingdom': it was present in the ministry of Jesus, and evidence of its existence was given in Matt. 11.2: 'the blind receive their sight and the lame walk, lepers are cleansed and the deaf hear, and the dead are raised up, and the poor have good news preached to them.'

In the case of 'kingdom' we shall not attempt to use our tests to 'solve' the question of the precise nuance of the theme, since now it is necessary to pause and achieve a larger view. The theme 'kingdom' is beyond doubt. Beyond this, we may simply note that the eschatological end of the present age is attributed to 'the Lord' by Paul and has good claim to authenticity. We also note that the prediction that the end would come in the lifetime of the first followers (both I Thess. 4 and Mark 9.1 and parr.) did not come true. Surely the evangelists did not invent it. The view that the kingdom would involve a social order also has strong support. The request of John and James to sit at Jesus' right and left hands makes them look grasping and probably was not invented later. The prohibition of divorce, especially the long form, points to an ideal new age which will be like Eden before the fall – earthly but perfect. Behind each depiction of the kingdom there is some good evidence. As usual, we see that we gain *good general knowledge* but not precision and nuance. It was reasonable for friend and foe alike to think of Jesus as claiming 'kingship', but in precisely what sense it is hard to say. We may rule out armed rebellion, but the other possibilities still stand.

What is needed is a total view which will help us see what to do with the various bits of evidence which are produced by the kind of piecemeal testing which has just been exemplified. There are other 'tests' that can be run, but the ones we have considered are the best and most widely applicable. Now we must look at the larger picture.

NOTE

Aramaisms and Bad Greek

There is one frequently-cited test of authenticity which appears to us to be useless, but since it is widely known we shall offer a few remarks about it. The supposed test is to search for 'Aramaisms' – signs of Aramaic syntax or grammar in the Greek of the gospels. The thinking is this: Jesus spoke Aramaic, but the gospels are in Greek. If the Greek shows Aramaic influence, the material is closer to what Jesus said than if it does not.

This view is far too simple. Jesus spoke Aramaic, but so too did his disciples and many of the early converts. Christianity also spread to areas where Syriac – a language very close to Aramaic – was spoken. Some Christians who were able to preach in Greek probably had Aramaic as their native tongue. Aramaisms could have entered the tradition at any point in its transmission.

Further, what counts as an Aramaism is by no means certain. Aramaic shares many particulars with Hebrew, and the Scripture influenced the language of early Christians – terminology, grammar and syntax. Luke is full of 'Septuagintisms', imitations of the Hebrew Bible in Greek translation. Many of these cannot be Aramaisms or even first-century Hebraisms, since the Hebrew which is being imitated is that of the classical period (seventh–eighth centuries BCE). An example is 'And it happened . . . and . . .'. This introductory narrative device is common in older Hebrew literature, such as I Samuel, and when it appears in Luke it is probably to be attributed to his reading of the Bible in Greek, since the Hebraism was kept in the Greek translation, even though it results in very bad Greek. If this was the case with one idiom, it could have been the case with others. 'Aramaisms' may be simply 'Semitisms', and Semitisms in turn may be 'Septuagintisms'.

When Aramaic differs from Hebrew it not infrequently agrees with vulgar Greek (known, for example, from the non-literary papyri) and Latin. Much of Mark is 'asyndetic', lacking in conjunctions before main clauses. Greek has a wealth of conjunctions, and sentences ordinarily are linked to what has gone before by using one of them. The simplest are 'and', 'but' and 'for', but there are many others. Aramaic, however, does not often begin a sentence with a conjunction. Since Mark's sentences not infrequently begin without a conjunction, some have seen here Aramaic influence. But Latin begins sentences without a conjunction. Mark is often thought to have been written in Rome, and if so perhaps the scribe was influenced by Latin. Further, in vulgar Greek the rich use of conjunctions declines. Mark's Greek

333

is a bit coarse, and the relative paucity of conjunctions may simply reflect the author's level of Greek in general.

Supposed Aramaisms, then, may not be Aramaisms at all. They might be Septuagintisms, Latinisms or vulgarisms. Even if they are Aramaisms and cannot be anything else, they may come from a speaker of Aramaic other than Jesus. There are so many possibilities that we think Aramaisms not to be a test of authenticity.

The same is true of poor Greek, which is often thought to indicate early material. This supposition has often been used as an argument for the priority of Mark – which is written in 'worse' Greek than is either Matthew or Luke. It is surprising that academics can hold this view, since they have often read student essays which are culled from books and articles, but which are written in much worse English than their sources. Authors wrote then as now at their own level. Mark's Greek is more 'vulgar' than that of Matthew and Luke, but this does not prove it to be earlier.

22   Putting the Material Together

• Extrapolating to hypotheses

There is no end to testing the synoptic material. Whatever tests are employed, however many passages 'pass' the tests, the result is always the same. We end with individual bits of information sorted into lists – 'virtually certain', 'completely unlikely', and everything else in between. We must then make sense of it. 'Making sense of' does not mean 'adding it up'. We cannot say that what tells us most about Jesus is necessarily the theme or themes which occur most often in the most probable passages. These might turn out to be commonplaces, or they might be peripheral. 'Making sense of' means 'developing a hypothesis about'. Hypotheses should reflect the material, but they may go beyond it. The question is whether or not they explain it.

Hypotheses can be formed by extrapolating from small bits of evidence to a larger view. Let us return to the three traditions which are confirmed by Paul: the words of institution, the saying on divorce and the climatic return of the Lord (or the coming of the Son of man). The world view which is presupposed by the long form of the saying on divorce is pretty clear and straightforward: the coming time will be, at least in part, a return to the original order of creation. 'In the beginning' male and female were indissolubly joined; they became 'one flesh'. So it should be now – or so it will be in the future. Whether now or in the future, an ideal is envisaged which is based on the creation. This implies a social order, but an ideal one.

Since we are only seeking hypotheses, let us continue down this line rather than take up the prohibition of remarriage (which in and of itself does not necessarily presuppose an ideal order, but rather a rigorous practice which is followed in ordinary life). Continuing to enquire about an ideal world, we note the prediction in Mark 14.25 and parr.: 'I shall not drink again of the fruit of the vine until that day when I drink it new in the kingdom of God'. This, we noted, may be reflected in Paul's statement that, in partaking of the bread and wine, the believer 'proclaim[s] the Lord's death until he comes' (I Cor. 11.26). 'I will drink wine' may be, of course, only metaphorical; possibly physical wine and a real banquet are not in view. On the other hand, possibly they are. In the latter case Jesus would have been looking forward to the ideal age when there would be peace and joy.

We may term this form of future expectation 'social', since it implies an ideal society. Other passages which fit into this category are the prediction that the twelve tribes would be restored and judged by the disciples (Matt. 19.28) and the disciples' expectation that they would occupy the chief places in the new order (Mark 9.33–37 and parr.; Mark 10.35–45 and parr.). It is possible to contrast with this the 'cosmic' expectation (the sun would be darkened; the Son of man or the Lord would come with angels or an angel; a trumpet would sound; there would be a judgment: Matt. 24 and parr.; I Thess. 4.14–17). These may be antithetical, but they need not be, since the cosmic signs might be only the prelude to a *renewal* of the creation, not to its destruction. It is noteworthy that the 'social' hope includes the expectation of a 'new creation' (Matt. 19.28).

We learn here about extrapolation and its limits. The 'social' expectation might be pushed in the direction of socio-political reform; the 'cosmic' expectation can be thought of as meaning 'the end of the world' in the sense of its annihilation. It is also possible to combine them: there would be a cosmic event which would result in a 'new world' and a new social order. One may prefer, however, to hold back and not take each depiction to its logical limit, bearing in mind the normal exaggerations of pictoral language. In this case, we would take the view that we do not know for certain what Jesus thought. We may grant the authenticity of all the passages here in mind (social: Matt. 19.28; Mark 10.35–40; 14.25; cosmic: I Thess. 4.16f.; Matt. 16.27f.; 24.31) and still hesitate to say that we have penetrated Jesus' thought and know its precise nuance. Extrapolation does not, in and of itself, produce assured results, since we do not know how far to push it. It is, however, enlightening. We learn from it how to pose interpretative options. The effort to move from individual passages to a 'world view' also forces us to wrestle with first-century categories and keeps us from interpreting the material according to our own outlook.

Some scholars, we recall, have found another possibility for what Jesus thought about his mission. Building on the statement that Jesus' exorcisms mean that 'the kingdom of God has come upon you [the Pharisees]' (Matt. 12.28 and par.), and on his reply to the Baptist (Matt. 11.5f.), they extrapolate to the overall view that the kingdom was proleptically or symbolically present in Jesus' ministry. These passages are by no means as firmly supported as are the core passages in the previous paragraph, which are predictions that did not come to pass, or which were otherwise unpalatable in the second generation (James and John were self-seeking). If one starts with Matt. 12.28 and 11.5f., however, one can extrapolate from them to an overall view of 'Jesus and the kingdom' which is compatible with any conception of a future kingdom, since present and future do not compete over the same ground.

The method of extrapolation would, if followed, lead us to see how far we could walk down each possible path and explain the synoptic material. If we went in search of material pointing to a new order on earth, for example, we would find ourselves able to take in numerous other passages, including most of the ethical material in the Sermon on the Mount. It is a useful exercise to turn the pages of the gospels and to ask, 'How reliable is this passage, and what world view does it presuppose?' We leave this, however, in order to pursue an even more necessary task if we wish to make sense of the evidence.

• Finding a context

We need an overall scheme into which to fit the parts. We need a context.

Nothing is known without context. If we have a piece of information but no context, we make one up by assigning to foreign or ancient material our own world view (see above, p.240). This provides a context for it, but it may distort it entirely. A simple example: one of the 'slogans' of Apollo, carved in stone at Delphi, was 'Know thyself'. In the post-Freudian world, this is readily taken to be a call to introspection: search your heart, examine your motives, know what is within. In the ancient Greek world, however, it meant, 'Know your limits, do not transgress them, do not be guilty of presumption, *hybris*'. *Nemesis* punishes *hybris*.[1] Introspection does not come into it.

Above we discussed extrapolation from bits of evidence to world view, and now we may see with greater clarity the significance of recapturing an ancient world view: a world view is a context. Knowing it may explain the original meaning of a saying such as 'Know thyself', but it may only establish a range of possible meanings. We have our own mental horizons, and even to know what ancient material might have meant we have to recover the ancient horizons. Let us return once more to the material about the kingdom. If we put the idea of 'Jesus as king' into our own world view, we would probably be able to imagine only two possibilities: he was a rebel leader who wished to overthrow Roman rule, at least in Palestine; he intended to found a spiritual religion, a kingdom which resides in each individual person who accepts it. Our mental horizons incline us to think of practical politics or spiritual idealism. Above, however, we glimpsed a third possibility, one that would not be an expected meaning of 'king' without study of the ancient world: the ruler of a social order rather like this, but one which exists in a new world created by God. This may strike moderns as unlikely, impossible or even ridiculous, but it was none of those things then. Let us consider the context.

Jews of Jesus' day had read Exodus and Joshua, and so they knew that God could, if he wished, defeat Pharaoh when the Israelites were weaponless, lead them through the desert, provide food and water, defeat Amalek, give his law, and establish a new society. They still believed in that God. After Jesus there would arise other prophets. One looked for the Jordan river to part to allow him and his followers to cross; another expected the walls of Jerusalem to fall at his approach. The former thought of Moses, the latter of Joshua.[2] People followed them, and in each case the Romans took steps to stop the movement. As a reasonable, Bible-believing Jew, Jesus could well have thought that God could recall or re-create the twelve tribes of Israel and appoint him and his followers at their head.

At least one other Jew of Jesus' day expected a kingdom to be created on a renewed and transformed earth: Paul.[3] We have noted that *in theory* a cosmic event, such as the return of the Lord, may be either antithetical or complementary to the hope for a transformed society. In Paul's case, it appears to be complementary. Paul did not think of the return of the Lord as immediately entailing 'the end of the world' in the sense of its annihilation, but rather of its re-creation. Those in Christ would, when the Lord returned, 'meet' him in the air, but probably only to accompany him down to the earth. According to Phil. 3.20f., the Christians' 'commonwealth' is in heaven, and they expect their saviour to come *from* there. He will transform their *bodies* to be like his, not take their souls to heaven. In II Cor. 5 Paul speaks of a house 'eternal in the heavens', and he longs to put on the 'building *from* heaven'; that is, the heavenly building will come down and encompass the mortal body (5.1–2; this is not clear in the translations[4]). The idea of putting on the immortal over the mortal, swallowing it up, appears also in I Cor. 15.54. In Rom. 8 Paul looks forward to the time when 'the creation itself will be set free from its bondage to decay' (8.21). Had Paul been pressed on his future expectation, he might have said of the cosmos what he said of people who would experience the resurrection: it would have a 'spiritual body' or a body of 'glory' (cf. I Cor. 15.43f.; cf. II Cor. 3.18). In this new world, when one no longer sees 'as in a mirror, dimly', but rather face to face, faith and hope, keys to the Christian life in the present age, may still abide, but full understanding and love will mark the human–divine relationship (I Cor. 13.13). Paul, in short, supports the idea of a new or transformed creation in a way that makes his 'cosmic' expectation compatible with the synoptic passages which point to a new creation and a new society. I Cor. 15.23–24 (Christ comes, and then comes the end, when he hands the kingdom over to God) may point towards a final dissolution of the material universe, but even if so Paul maintains the view that Christ comes to earth and is joined there by the resurrected or transformed Christians.

Our terms to distinguish 'social' and 'cosmic' expectations of the kingdom, then, need not be held apart and can be combined in the idea of a new world.

This general conception of the kingdom did not immediately disappear from Christianity.[5] Justin Martyr (*c*. 150) was of the view that Jerusalem would be rebuilt, that Christians would be gathered together there, and that they would rejoice with Christ, the patriarchs, the prophets and others (Dialogue with Trypho 80). Irenaeus (*c*. 180) thought that at the time of the kingdom the creation would be 'restored' to its original state. Animals would willingly obey humans, lions would eat straw, and food would be abundant:

> The days will come, in which vines shall grow, each having ten thousand branches, and in each branch ten thousand twigs, and in each true twig ten thousand clusters, and on every one of the clusters ten thousand grapes, and every grape when pressed will give five and twenty metretes of wine. (Against Heresies 5.30–33, quotation from 5.33.3)

When Jesus said that wine would be drunk in the kingdom, he meant it! (or so Irenaeus).

The evidence that Jesus held this general view of the kingdom is fairly strong, but it also indicates that his expectation was less detailed and precise than Irenaeus'. But whether or not Jesus expected this kind of 'new creation', we cannot even consider its possible significance in his life without recapturing this aspect of ancient thought.

A context may be large or small, general or particular. In the case of Jesus we must be prepared to admit that we never know the immediate context. In discussing the 'authenticity' of individual passages we never referred to the setting given by the evangelists – for the very good reason that the individual settings were subject to change. We accept the basic form-critical principle that the evangelists had individual units (some perhaps already strung together) and that they supplied narrative settings. We may recall that the parable of the Lost Sheep in Matthew is addressed to the disciples, as admonition, but in Luke to the Pharisees, as rebuke. We may also recall that Jeremias rejected Matthew's setting and accepted Luke's as reflecting the original context. There is, however, no more reason to accept one than the other.

Similarly we noted (p. 64) that in Luke the saying 'You will not see me until you say, "Blessed is he who comes in the name of the Lord!"' is fulfilled when Jesus enters Jerusalem (Luke 13.35; 19.38), while in Matthew it comes later and is still unfulfilled at the close of the gospel – thus pointing to the return of the Lord (Matt. 23.39). Even if we know beyond doubt that Jesus said it, we could not know what it meant unless we could reconstruct the context.

The sayings themselves were not transmitted with perfect accuracy, but they were more carefully repeated than were the original settings. The changes that we can see by simply comparing the gospels presumably reflect the way the material was handled throughout.

The loss of immediate context does not mean that no meaning can be obtained, for other contexts can point the way to meaning. It will be useful to consider the potential significance of knowing closer and larger contexts by taking a couple of examples.

1. Politicians, with good reason, frequently complain that they have been quoted out of context and therefore misunderstood. In 1987 two British parties, the Liberals and the Social Democrats, decided to merge. Most members of the two parties joined to make up the Social and Liberal Democratic Party. On a BBC news programme it was reported that the new party, if it came to power, would place VAT (value added tax, a sales tax) on food and childrens' clothes, items previously untaxed. David Steel, the leader of the Liberal Party, was then interviewed, and he pointed out that the document said that new sources of revenue would have to be sought and that the new party, were it to form a government, would have to consider a range of measures, including VAT on food and childrens' clothes. The next night the same news programme reported that the SLD would tax food and childrens' clothes. So much for setting the record straight. It was more newsworthy to lift the two items out of their context in the document. We shall return to the relative significance of the loss of the immediate context after citing the next example.

2. A patriotic song which is universally known in the United States includes these verses:

339

My country, 'tis of thee,
Sweet land of liberty,
Of thee I sing.
Land of the pilgrims' pride,
Land where my fathers died,
From every mountain side
Let freedom ring.

Our fathers' God, to Thee,
Author of liberty,
To Thee we sing.
Long may our land be bright
With freedom's holy light.
Protect us by Thy might,
Great God, our King.

Without context, one knows that the singers affirm their love of country, especially the quality of freedom, and that they regard freedom as God-given. That is, we have some general knowledge. We do not know just what 'freedom' means. The word notoriously changes its meaning with contexts – rather like 'kingdom'. In this case, a further piece of evidence provides us with context and precision of meaning. To comprehend the force of the song, one must know that it is sung to the tune of Britain's national anthem, 'God save the Queen'. One then sees that this is a polemical assertion of a particular freedom: freedom *from Great Britain*. The height of polemic is reached in the last line: the former colonies have God as their King – unlike Britain, which has an earthly monarch.

If one then knows a bit of the historical context one can define 'freedom' more closely. We know enough American history to do so with precision: it means *the* freedom of adult, white males living in the American colonies to elect their own representatives, and *the* freedom not to be taxed by the mother country. Freedom would be progressively redefined in subsequent history, but these are the principal freedoms referred to in the song.

Let us return now to the example about the taxation of food and children's clothes. We have seen that the person who heard only the announcer's description of the SLD document would not know that these two items had been taken from a larger list. Even hearing Mr Steel's clarification helps only a bit, since he did not give the other items. It would be important to know what they were: higher taxes on tobacco, alcohol and fuel? taxes on pay toilets and air pollution control devices? If later history knew only that the SLD would consider taxing two essentials it might condemn the party as neither social nor liberal. If it had a longer list and discovered that taxing children's clothes was preferred to taxing luxuries the suspicion would be confirmed. The context matters.

Let us imagine that the document was lost and that no one knew that there was a further list, let alone what was on it. We would nevertheless know something about the SLD if we knew about the policies of the EEC ('Common Market') and the other two main British parties.

At the time of the SLD statement Britain was facing the possibility of being compelled to tax food and children's clothing in order to conform its practice to that of its European partners. The ruling Conservative party had vowed that it would not agree. The SLD, then, may be seen as taking a more European stance. Within Britain, there was a another debate. The Conservative government had progressively cut taxes but also social benefits (relative to the economy as a whole). The other parties opposed the reduction of benefits, but credible opposition required them to consider higher taxes. The Labour Party favoured only higher income taxes, while the SLD was prepared to consider higher or additional sales taxes. We can now fix them on the spectrum of political thought. Sales taxes are 'regressive' rather than 'progressive', since they fall more heavily on the poor than on the rich. The SLD wanted to increase social benefits but was prepared to consider increasing regressive taxes in order to do it: more liberal than the Conservatives, more conservative than the Labourites.

One more act of imagination. Let us suppose that we had to choose between knowing the immediate context of the statement about sales taxes and the general context of debate over taxes and public expenditure. Which would we rather have? Either would be a loss and reduce our understanding, but losing the immediate context would in many ways be preferable to losing the larger. If we had only the larger context, we would at least know what the issues were. If we had only the longer list of taxes to be considered, we would know more details, but not their overall significance.

The same is true of 'My country, 'tis of thee'. We do not need to know the composer's name or precisely where he lived, or even his precise dates. We understand What the Song is Really About if we know the larger context of the American Colonies' break with Great Britain and the issues which led to it.

The application to Jesus is obvious. We do not have the immediate context of individual sayings, but we know a great deal about aspects of larger contexts. Which context we have matters more in some instances than in others. Fully to understand 'love your enemies' and 'pray for your persecutors' we would need to know the fairly close context: does it mean 'love a foreign army of occupation' as many scholars think (incorrectly supposing Galilee to have been occupied by Romans)? If the enemy is Rome, we would still need to know whether or not the speaker had direct knowledge or counselled love from afar. On the other hand, the saying might mean only 'love the neighbour who gossiped about you'. The modern homiletician can apply the saying to all sorts of situations. To understand its original force, however, requires a first-century context. In this case we do not know the precise context.

More important aspects of the reliable material about Jesus can be better understood on the basis of a large context, and it is this fact which allows us to have confidence that we have good general knowledge about him. Much about his larger context is known. It is possible, for example, to consider him in the context of Jewish hopes for the future or Jewish protest movements, or to view him in relationship to

341

Jewish charismatic prophets and miracle-workers. Studies such as these are enlightening, and we can recommend especially Geza Vermes, *Jesus the Jew*; Martin Hengel, *The Charismatic Leader and His Followers*; Gerd Theissen, *The Shadow of the Galilean*; Ellis Rivkin, *What Crucified Jesus?*; and Richard Horsley, *Jesus and the Spiral of Violence*. We shall only comment here, not argue, that Jesus is better understood in these contexts (future hope, charismatic prophets and wonder-workers) than in the context of study and teaching of the law. He of course knew the law, and sometimes commented on it, but we get him wrong if we think of him primarily as a Rabbi.[6]

We think, however, that it is possible to find a still more informative context: the *movement of which he was a part*.

Sanders' *Jesus and Judaism* argues that it is possible to know the basic facts of Jesus' career, including its prologue and its aftermath, and that this knowledge gives a context for understanding him. Among other things, it sets limits. We have already seen one: Jesus and his followers were not regarded as a military threat, since only he was executed. The present state of the world – like that in many past times – makes it attractive to many to see Jesus as a social reformer, even as a rebel. The non-execution of the disciples belongs to the context of the career of Jesus himself, and it sets a limit on how he is understood. In and of itself it does not deny the possibility that Jesus was a reformer, but it does prohibit thinking of him as an armed insurrectionist.

In temporal terms, the context of Jesus' movement runs from John the Baptist to the early Christian community. John the Baptist was a preacher of repentance in view of the impending judgment, and Jesus began his public career by accepting his baptism. It seems that John expected something dramatic to happen soon. People who came to him were fleeing 'from the wrath to come', and he thought that the axe was 'even now' 'laid to the root of the trees' (Matt. 3.7–10 and parr.).

Our surest knowledge of Jesus' movement after his death comes from the letters of Paul. Paul too looked for the judgment to come and spoke of escaping the wrath of God; and, we have seen, he thought that the Lord would soon return (Rom. 2.5–8; 5.9; I Thess. 1.10; 4.15–17).

As general ideas, 'wrath' and the coming judgment of God are derived from the prophets. But the idea that 'the hour is now', which is common to John the Baptist and Paul, puts Jesus directly in the context of people who saw the final act of ordinary history as imminent. When we then discover that sayings in this vein are attributed directly to Jesus, we find them confirmed by the context. We know more in detail about what Paul expected than about what Jesus expected, but that he saw his own time as the last time of the present age seems certain.

Let us return to the question of Jesus as a reformer. Granted that he did not wish to use force in changing society, did he nevertheless want to change it in preparation for the coming kingdom? What does the context say? Paul was not a social reformer. His advice on social institutions such as marriage and slavery was 'do not change; this world is passing away' (I Cor. 7.26–31). Paul argued with other Christians, including at least some of the leaders in Jerusalem, about such things as the necessity of keeping parts of the Jewish law and the terms on which Gentiles could be brought into the movement. He seems not to have argued with them about whether or not something was about to *happen* for which *they should wait* (except for calling others to faith). That is, they thought so as well. The general attitude of the disciples in Jerusalem seems to have been that they should spread the word that Jesus was Messiah and that faith in him would save, while *waiting for God to do something*: more precisely, while waiting for the return of the Lord. They did not, for example, attack the apparatus of the temple service. If Jesus was a reformer who thought that it must be changed, either he failed to communicate this to his followers, or they were simply afraid. In all probability he thought that God would do whatever had to be done with regard to the temple. His overturning of tables (Mark 11.15 and parr.) was apparently a symbolic gesture which the disciples did not feel compelled to convert into a social programme. They awaited the return of the Lord, as did Paul. Similarly John the Baptist had baptized near the desert, and people came out to hear him. He may have criticized Herod Antipas, but he seems not to have organized a movement against him. Jesus seems to have had no more socio-political ambitions than did his predecessor and his followers. They all seem to have agreed: John, Jesus, his disciples and Paul expected something to happen, and they thought that God would do it.[7]

This is not an argument for social pacifism on the part of contemporary church members, whose situation is different. Research into the life and teaching of Jesus is often hampered by the desire to make him fit our context, and we wish to avoid that particular mistake.

We stay with Jesus' movement for one more sub-point: Paul's argument with other Christians about the terms on which Gentiles were to be brought into the movement (whether or not circumcision, food laws and sabbath observance were mandatory) reflects a general agreement that Gentiles should come in. Jesus himself conducted no substantial mission to Gentiles. His followers, however, saw it as a reasonable or even necessary continuation of his work. They probably had in mind the numerous prophetic passages which predict that, when God establishes the people of Israel, Gentiles will convert and turn to worship the one God (e.g. Isa. 2.2–3; 56.6–8; Zech. 2.11; Tobit 14.6–7).[8] In other words, after his death Jesus' followers expected the establishment of God's kingdom in the way predicted by the prophets: Israel would be restored and Gentiles brought in. This makes it all the more likely that Jesus looked for the restoration of all Israel.

We stop here. We are in possession of most of the ingredients of the *general* knowledge about Jesus which we can have with *virtual certainty*. Drawing both on the context and on the examination of various passages in the synoptics, we may list what we know, to the degree that we have covered it. Other things can be known besides those listed here. We have, for example, good information about Jesus' family, especially his brother James.[9] The list which follows is slanted towards what we can know about his mission and about his view of 'the kingdom'.

1. Jesus expected 'the kingdom of God' either as a dramatic cosmic event, or as a new social order – or both, one leading to the other.

2. He saw his own mission as being the call of Israel to the kingdom.

3. He meant the inclusion of all Israel, both the lost ten tribes (note the symbolism of the twelve disciples) *and* the present 'lost sheep of the house of Israel'.

4. He saw his work as continuing John's, but with a difference. John preached repentance and practised abstinence. Jesus sought sinners, did not dwell on their failings, and was known as one who ate and drank with them.

5. He believed that love of the neighbour included not only love of the outcast, but also love of the enemy.

6. He did not himself call Gentiles, but this was a reasonable continuation of his work.

7. He thought that the new order demanded new ethical standards, and he (for example) forbade or strongly discouraged divorce, possibly looking to the order of creation as the standard of the new age.

We emphasize that this is by no means all that can be known about Jesus, but these points are important for understanding the particularity of his mission, when compared with that of others, and for grasping his importance in history. We know quite a lot about Jesus – and about the synoptic gospels. They repay the work which they require.

Notes

1. *Definitions, Authorship and Dates*

1. Those interested in etymology may wish to know that 'spell' in the meaning 'text, message or form of words' survives in the modern phrase 'cast a spell'. *Euangelion* is eu + angelion. *Eu* as the prefix to a Greek word always means 'good' or 'nice', as in 'euthanasia' (mercy killing) or 'eulogy' (praise: a favourable saying). *Angelion* means 'message', and from it we derive 'angel', messenger.

2. On how ancient books were published, see Bruce M. Metzger, *The Text of the New Testament*, 1964, pp. 14–16 and references there.

3. There is another possibility: that the last event has simply been inserted into the already finished gospel by another hand. That possibility is not likely in the particular cases which affect the dating of the synoptics, though the issue of later insertions does sometimes arise in discussing the gospels.

4. Eusebius, *Ecclesiastical History* III.39.15, trans. Kirsopp Lake, LCL, slightly altered.

5. On the popularity of Matthew, see e.g. H. B. Swete, *The Gospel According to St Mark*, 1905, pp. xxxii, xxxiv–xxxviii.

6. The question of whether early church fathers quoted our gospels or (for example) their sources is of long-standing and probably cannot be decisively settled. The Didache is not infrequently thought to contain pre-synoptic material, which may be true, but the case cited above seem to show reliance on our Matthew.

7. For further passages from Irenaeus, see Swete, *St. Mark*, p. xxxii.

8. John Knox, *Marcion and the New Testament*, 1942; repr. 1980; cf. Knox, 'Marcion's Gospel and the Synoptic Problem' *Jesus, the Gospels, and the Church*, ed. E. P. Sanders, 1987, pp. 25–31.

9. B. H. Streeter, *The Four Gospels*, 1924, p. 562.

10. Swete, *St Mark*, p. xv.

11. Vincent Taylor, *The Gospel According to St Mark*, 1959, pp. 1–8, 26; Martin Hengel, *Studies in the Gospel of Mark*, ET 1985, pp. 2–7.

12. John A. T. Robinson, *Redating the New Testament*, 1976, pp. 19–21, 26f.

13. Josephus was a Jewish priest who lived approximately CE 37–100. He fought in the war against Rome (66–73 or 74), but surrendered and lived to be its historian. The Emperors Vespasian, Titus and Domitian were his patrons, and he had access to Roman records. His work is of prime importance for the understanding of Jewish Palestine in the first century. For the entirety of his work, see the Loeb Classical Library edition, 10 vols, 1926–1965.

14. See James Moffatt, *Introduction to the New Testament*, 3rd ed. 1918, pp. 29–31.

15. Joseph A. Fitzmyer, *The Gospel according to Luke I–IX*, 1981, pp. 53–57.

2. *Genre and Purposes*

1. Albert Schweitzer, *The Quest of the Historical Jesus*, ET 1910, p. 204, discussing H. J.

Notes   Holtzmann, *Die synoptischen Evangelien*, 1863.

2. These are derived from Sanders, *Jesus and Judaism*, 1985, p. 328.

3. George Tyrrell, *Christianity at the Cross-Roads*, 1909, p. 49: 'The Christ that Harnack sees [in *The Essence of Christianity*], looking back through nineteen centuries of Catholic darkness, is only the reflection of a liberal Protestant face, seen at the bottom of a deep well.' Tyrrell's discussion makes it clear that this description would apply to others besides Harnack. We are grateful to Leslie Houlden for this reference.

4. We shall not pursue Luke's Septuagintisms in detail, but rather mention only a few points. Besides the parallels between the songs of Hannah and Mary, one may note also the influence of the healing story of I Kings 17.8–24 on Luke 7.11–17. Luke's syntax not infrequently imitates that of the Septuagint: compare Luke 5.17; 8.1 with I Kngdms 8.1; 9.26; 23.6.

5. See the discussion of Quirinius just below, and of Judas the Galilean and Theudas in ch. 1.

6. Hans Conzelmann, *The Theology of St Luke*, ET 1960, p. 69.

7. See Norman Bentwich, *Josephus*, 1914 pp. 121f. Bentwich took the point from Adolf Schlatter.

8. Martin Hengel, 'Luke the Historian and the Geography of Palestine in the Acts of the Apostles', *Between Jesus and Paul*, ET 1983, pp. 97–128.

9. See the conclusive evidence discussed by Joseph Fitzmyer, *The Gospel According to Luke I–IX*, pp. 399–405.

10. Ramsey MacMullen, *Roman Government's Response to Crisis A.D. 235–337*, 1976, p. 25. Few ancient historians had the sophistication of Thucydides, to whom many of the comments do not apply.

11. Philip Shuler, *A Genre for the Gospels*, 1982.

12. This case has been well argued by Birger Gerhardsson, especially in 'Der Weg der Evangelientradition', *Das Evangelium und die Evangelien*, ed. Peter Stuhlmacher, 1983, pp. 79–102; see also his *The Origins of the Gospel Tradition*, ET 1979. We discuss the issue further below, pp. 132f., 194f.

Part Two
The Synoptic
Problem

3. *The Basic Relationships and the Common Solution*

1. See Thomas R. W. Longstaff, *Evidence of Conflation in Mark?*, 1977.

2. F. Gerald Downing, 'Redaction Criticism: Josephus' Antiquities and the Synoptic Problem I, II', *Journal for the Study of the New Testament* 8, 1980, pp. 46–65; 9, 1980, pp. 29–48; cf. also 'Compositional Conventions and the Synoptic Problem', *Journal of Biblical Literature* 107, 1988, pp. 69–85.

3. The canons of Eusebius are given in *Novum Testamentum Graece*, 26th ed., pp. 74*–78*, and they are carried on the inner margins of the pages of the text.

4. Heinrich Greeven, 'The Gospel synopsis from 1776 to the present day', *J. J. Griesbach: Synoptic and Text-Critical Studies 1776–1976*, ed. B. Orchard and T. R. W. Longstaff, 1978 pp. 22–49.

5. Allan Barr, *A Diagram of Synoptic Relationships*, 1957.

6. The classic statement in English remains that of B. H. Streeter, *The Four Gospels*, originally published in 1924 and often reprinted. See ch. 7, 'The fundamental solution'. There are numerous histories of research. See especially W. R. Farmer, *The Synoptic Problem*, 1964; H.-H. Stoldt, *History and Criticism of the Marcan Hypothesis*, 1983, pp. 3–7 and notes.

The most prolific and formidable recent supporter of the priority of Mark (and the existence of Q, below) is Frans Neirynck, some of whose work will be cited below. Tuckett and many others have argued strongly for this position.

7. See Streeter, *The Four Gospels*, rev. ed., 1930, pp. 159–160.

8. By W. R. Farmer, *The Synoptic Problem*, and others. For a critique, see Tuckett, *Revival*.

9. Proposed by Austin Farrer, 'On Dispensing with Q', *Studies in the Gospels*, ed. D. E. Nineham, 1954; worked out in detail by Michael Goulder, especially in *Midrash and Lection in Matthew*, 1974.

10. B. C. Butler, *The Originality of St Matthew*, 1951.

11. This derivation has occasionally been doubted, but it seems to be the correct one. See H. K. McArthur, 'The Origin of the "Q" Symbol', *Expository Times* 87, 1976–77, pp. 119f.; Frans Neirynck, 'The Symbol Q (=Quelle)' *Ephemerides Theologicae Lovanienses* 54, 1978, pp. 119–125; 'Once More: the Symbol Q', *ETL* 55, 1979, pp. 382–383; both reprinted in Neirynck, *Evangelica*, 1982, pp. 683–690.

4. *Complexities and Difficulties*

1. W. C. Allen, *The Gospel According to St Matthew*, 3rd ed. 1912, p. 87.

2. Streeter, 'St. Mark's Knowledge and Use of Q', *Oxford Studies in the Synoptic Problem*, ed. W. Sanday, 1911, pp. 165–183, here p. 177.

3. Streeter, 'St. Mark's Knowledge . . . of Q', p. 167.

4. *The Four Gospels*, p. 187.

5. *Further Complexities and a Different Solution*

1. See Tuckett, *Revival*, pp. 125–126.

2. Neirynck maintains that The Great Commandment is not a Mark–Q overlap: *Interpreters' Dictionary of the Bible*, suppl. vol., p. 845. See further Tuckett, *Revival*, pp. 125–133.

3. David Dungan, 'Mark – The Abridgement of Matthew and Luke', *Jesus and Man's Hope* I, 1970, pp. 51–97, here p. 63.

4. Tuckett, *Revival*, pp. 16–21.

5. Tuckett, who has a degree in mathematics, applies statistics in discussing Matthew–Luke agreements in order: 'Arguments from Order: Definition and Evaluation', *Synoptic Studies*, ed. Tuckett, 1984, p. 204.

6. Frans Neirynck, *Duality in Mark*, 1972, pp. 41–43.

6. *Further Hypotheses: Simple and Complex*

1. Goulder, *Midrash and Lection in Matthew,* 1974.

2. R. L. Lindsey, 'Introduction' to *A Hebrew Translation of the Gospel of Mark*, with an approving foreward by David Flusser, no date (late 1960s).

3. Rudolph Bultmann, *History of the Synoptic Tradition*, p. 132.

4. For references, see Sanders, *The Tendencies of the Synoptic Tradition*, p. 293.

5. Emil Wendling, *Ur-Markus*, 1905.

6. F. C. Grant, *The Gospels. Their Origin and their Growth*, 1957, pp. 130–131.

7. F. C. Grant, *The Gospels*, p. 51.

8. Robert Funk, *New Gospel Parallels* I, p. 109, emended. We are grateful to Prof. Funk for permission to use the chart and for confirming that our proposed emendations represent the original intention.

9. M.-E. Boismard, *Synopse des quatre évangiles* II, 1972, p. 17, omitting the Gospel of John, which Boismard includes.

10. M.-E. Boismard, 'The Two Source Theory at an Impasse', *New Testament Studies* 26, 1979, pp. 1–17. Parts of the following explanation depend on *Synopse* (previous note).

7. *Conclusion*

1. See B. M. Metzger, *The Text of the New Testament*, pp. 14–16.
2. Streeter, *The Four Gospels*, p. 183.
3. Streeter, 'On the Original Order of Q', *Studies in the Synoptic Problem*, pp. 141–164, here pp. 142f.
4. Streeter, 'Order of Q', p. 143.
5. We are in part indebted for this point to John Fenton.
6. Hans Dieter Betz, *Essays on the Sermon on the Mount*, 1985.
7. David Wenham, *The Rediscovery of Jesus' Eschatological Discourse*, 1984.
8. Kenneth Newport, *The Sources and 'Sitz im Leben' of Matthew 23*, Oxford D. Phil., 1988.
9. On Proto-Mark, see Wendling, *Ur-Markus*. On Q, see Adolf Harnack, *The Sayings of Jesus. The Second Source of St Matthew and St Luke*, ET 1908.
10. See Downing, 'Compositional Conventions and the Synoptic Problem', *Journal of Biblical Literature* 107, 1988, pp. 69–85.
11. G. D. Kilpatrick, *The Origins of the Gospel According to St. Matthew*, 1946, p. 12.

8. *Introduction*

1. William Wrede, *The Messianic Secret*, ET 1971 from German 1901. The significance of Wrede's work for historical Jesus research lies outside the scope of this study. One may see the essays collected by Christopher Tuckett, *The Messianic Secret*, 1983.
2. Karl Ludwig Schmidt, *Der Rahmen der Geschichte Jesu*, ['the framework of the history of Jesus'], 1919.
3. Martin Dibelius, *From Tradition to Gospel*, ET from German 2nd ed. 1933 (1st ed. 1919), p. 39.
4. Rudolf Bultmann, *History of the Synoptic Tradition*, pp. 12–27, 39–54.
5. Rudolf Bultmann, *Jesus and the Word*, ET 1934 from German 1926, pp. 12–14.
6. Vincent Taylor, *The Formation of the Gospel Tradition*, 2nd ed. 1935 (1st ed. 1933).
7. See, for example, Albert B. Lord, 'The Gospels as Oral Traditional Literature', in William O. Walker (ed.), *The Relationships Among the Gospels*, 1978, esp. pp. 42–44, and the subsequent discussion summarized on p. 108 and n. 13.
8. E. P. Sanders, *The Tendencies of the Synoptic Tradition*, 1969.
9. Birger Gerhardsson, *Memory and Manuscript*, 1961; *Tradition and Transmission in Early Christianity*, 1964; *The Origins of the Gospel Traditions*, 1979; *The Gospel Tradition*, 1986.
10. Gerhardsson, *The Gospel Tradition*, pp. 39f.
11. See Willi Marxsen, *Mark the Evangelist*, ET 1969; Erhardt Güttgemanns, *Candid Questions Concerning Form Criticism*, ET 1979, ch. 4.
12. Klaus Berger, *Formgeschichte des Neuen Testaments*, 1984; *Einführung in die Formgeschichte*, 1987.
13. Sanders, *Jesus and Judaism*, 1985, pp. 3–5, 129–139.

9. *Creativity and Oral Tradition*

1. See Plato, Phaedrus 274c–275a and the discussions in Gerhardsson, *Memory and Manuscript*, pp. 124–126; Sanders, *Tendencies*, p. 294.

2. See the evidence of Babata's legal material in Yigael Yadin, *Bar Kokhba*, 1971, p. 241.

3. Eusebius, *Ecclesiastical History*, V.20.5–7, LCL, translation by Kirsopp Lake, slightly emended; Lake has 'their miracles' and 'their teaching'.

4. Eusebius, *Ecclesiastical History* III.39.4, LCL.

5. Ian Henderson, *'Sententiae Jesu': Gnomic Sayings in the Tradition of Jesus*, Oxford DPhil, 1988.

10. *Chreiai*

1. Berger, *Formgeschichte*, pp. 80–93.

2. Ronald F. Hock and Edward N. O'Neil, *The Chreia in Ancient Rhetoric*, vol. 1, *The Progymnasmata*, 1986, e.g. p. 26: a chreia is 'a saying or action that is expressed concisely, attributed to a character, and regarded as useful for living'.

3. Plutarch, *Brutus* II.3–4, ET Bernadotte Perrin, LCL.

4. Quoted from Hock and O'Neill, p. 101.

5. See, for example, W. R. Farmer, 'Notes on a Literary and Form-Critical Analysis of Some of the Synoptic Material Peculiar to Luke', *New Testament Studies* 8, 1962, pp. 301–316, with bibliography on p. 307.

6. Martin Albertz, *Die synoptischen Streitgespräche*, 1921; Taylor, *Formation*; W. L. Knox, *The Sources of the Synoptic Gospels* I, 1953; Arland J. Hultgren, *Jesus and His Adversaries*, 1979; Jarmo Kiilunen, *Die Vollmacht im Widerstreit*, 1985.

7. For the point that the Pharisees did not control Palestine, see for example Morton Smith, 'Palestinian Judaism in the First Century', repr. in H. A. Fischel (ed.), *Essays in Greco-Roman and Related Talmudic Literature*, 1977, pp. 183–197; Jacob Neusner, *From Politics to Piety*, 1973; Sanders, *Jesus and Judaism*, pp. 309–317.

11. *Miracles*

1. On Jesus' relation to Gentiles, and the historicity of the story of the Centurion's servant, see ch. 20.

2. John M. Hull, *Hellenistic Magic and the Synoptic Tradition*, 1974, pp. 134f.

3. Birger Gerhardsson, *The Mighty Acts of Jesus According to Matthew*, 1979, p. 53.

4. Bultmann argued that the construction is pre-Markan (*Synoptic Tradition*, p. 214). Taylor stated that 'the intercalation of narratives is not a feature of Mark's method' (*St Mark*, p. 289). For another intercalation, see Mark 11.12–25 (the fig tree and the cleansing of the temple). This and other examples are discussed below, p. 274.

5. On magicians, see Morton Smith, *Jesus the Magician*, 1978. On would-be prophets, see the discussion of Theudas above.

12. *Parables*

1. Joachim Jeremias, *The Parables of Jesus*, rev. ET 1963.

2. See Sanders, *Jesus and Judaism*, pp. 277–279.

3. Bultmann, *Synoptic Tradition*, p. 169.

4. Günther Bornkamm, *Jesus of Nazareth*, ET 1960, p. 70.

5. John Drury, *The Parables in the Gospels*, 1985, pp. 2–3.

6. Adolf Jülicher, *Die Gleichnisreden Jesu*, 2 vols., 1899; rev. ed. 1910.

7. C. H. Dodd, *The Parables of the Kingdom*, 1935; rev. ed. 1961, pp. 1–2.

8. Jülicher, II, p. 596.

Notes   9. Drury, cited above; Matthew Black, 'The Parables as Allegory', *Bulletin of the John Rylands Library* 42, 1960, pp. 273–287.

     10. Arrian, *Discourses of Epictetus* 3.22.1–4, quoted from David R. Cartlidge and David L. Dungan, *Documents for the Study of the Gospels*, 1980, p. 146.

13. *Conclusion*

     1. Morna Hooker, *Continuity and Discontinuity*, 1986, p. 21. Cf. the discussion of this passage above, p. 155, where we point out that it has probably been added to the Question about Fasting.

Part Four
Holistic Readings

14. *Redaction Criticism*

     1. Hans Conzelmann, *The Theology of Luke*, ET 1960 (from German 1954); Günther Bornkamm, G. Barth and H. J. Held, *Tradition and Interpretation in Matthew*, ET 1963 (from 2nd German ed. 1961; 1st ed. 1960).

     2. Willi Marxsen, *Mark the Evangelist*, ET 1969 (1st German edition 1956).

     3. ET 1968 (1st German ed. 1966).

     4. Jeremias, *Parables*, pp. 82f.

     5. K. Stendahl, *The School of Matthew*, 1968, p. 118.

15. *Structuralism and De-Construction*

     1. E.g. C. K. Ogden and I. A. Richards, *The Meaning of Meaning*, 1930.

     2. Terry Eagleton, *Literary Theory, an Introduction*, 1983, p. 95, and see also the discussion, pp. 103–108.

     3. Ed. A. M. Johnson, 1976, pp. 47–72.

     4. ET 1980. And see his more recent *Narrative Discourse Revisited*, ET 1989.

     5. R. A. Culpepper, *Anatomy of the Fourth Gospel*, 1983, chs. 2 and 3.

     6. Christopher Norris, *Deconstruction, Theory and Practice*, 1982, ch. 1.

16. *Rhetorical Criticism and the 'Implied Reader'*

     1. Wolfgang Iser, *The Implied Reader*, ET 1974, p. 279.

     2. SBL Dissertation Series 54, 1981.

     3. Wayne Booth, *The Rhetoric of Irony*, 1974, pp. 28–29.

     4. Anthony Burgess, *The Kingdom of the Wicked*, 1985.

     5. J. R. Donahue, *Are you the Christ? The Trial Narrative in the Gospel of Mark*, 1973.

     6. Meir Sternberg, *The Poetics of Biblical Narrative*, 1985.

17. *The Genre of the First Gospel*

     1. An earlier and slightly different version of this chapter appeared as Margaret Davies, 'The Genre of the First Gospel', *Language, Meaning and God*, ed. Brian Davies, 1987, pp. 162–175.

     2. G. A. Kennedy, *New Testament Interpretation through Rhetorical Criticism*, 1984.

     3. F. G. Downing, 'Contemporary analogies to the gospels and Acts: "Genres" or "Motifs"?', in C. M. Tuckett, ed., *Synoptic Studies*, 1984.

     4. H. C. Kee, *Miracles in the Early Christian World*, 1983.

5. H. W. Attridge in *Jewish Writings of the Second Temple Period*, ed. M. E. Stone, 1984, p. 225.

6. See R. H. Gundry, *The Use of the Old Testament in Matthew's Gospel*, 1967.

7. See Matthew 26.36f./Psalm 22.20; Matthew 27.34/Psalm 69.21; Matthew 27.35/Psalm 22.18; Matthew 27.39/Psalm 22.7; Matthew 27.42/Psalm 69.9; Matthew 27.45/Psalm 22.1; Matthew 27.48/Psalm 69.21.

8. J. E. Alsup, *The Post-resurrection appearance stories of the Gospel Tradition*, 1976.

9. G. Vermes, *Jesus the Jew*, 1973, p. 260.

10. Scripture does sometimes look beyond the history of Israel, but even so a 'new world' is not expected.

18. *The Genre of the Second Gospel*

1. See M. Hengel, *Studies in the Gospel of Mark*, 1986.

2. See W. H. Kelber, *Mark's Story of Jesus*, 1979.

3. *Hellenistic Magic and the Synoptic Tradition*, 1974.

4. V. K. Robbins, *Jesus the Teacher. A socio-rhetorical interpretation of Mark*, 1984.

5. *Die Funktion der alttestamentlichen Zitate und Anspielungen im Markusevangelium*, 1965.

6. See Rohde, *Rediscovering the Teaching of the Evangelists*, pp. 140f.

7. For a recent discussion and selection of literature on the topic, see C. M. Tuckett, ed., *The Messianic Secret*, 1983.

19. *The Genre of the Third Gospel*

1. See the chronology of Acts in E. Haenchen, *The Acts of the Apostles*, 1971, p. 60.

2. J. H. Moulton and G. Milligan, *The vocabulary of the Greek Testament*, 1930, pp. 287 and 621.

3. Hull, *Hellenistic Magic and the Synoptic Tradition*, ch 6.

4. C. H. Talbert, *Literary Patterns, Theological Themes and the Genre of Luke–Acts*, 1974.

5. J. A. Fitzmyer, *The Gospel according to Luke* I, pp. 95f.

6. D. L. Barr and J. L. Wentling, 'The Conventions of classical biography and the genre of Luke–Acts', in C. H. Talbert, ed., *Luke–Acts*: New Perspectives from the Society of Biblical Literature Seminar, 1984.

7. See H. J. Cadbury, *The Making of Luke–Acts*, 1958, p. 146.

8. See G. D. Kilpatrick, *The Eucharist in Bible and Liturgy*, 1983, pp. 28–42.

9. E.g. H. Conzelmann, *The Theology of Luke*, Part 2, pp. 95–136.

10. Eric Franklin, *Christ the Lord, a study in the Purpose and Theology of Luke–Acts*, 1975

11. Gittings, *The Young Thomas Hardy*, rev. ed. 1978.

20. *The Quest and the Methods:1*

1. James M. Robinson, *The New Quest for the Historical Jesus*, 1959, p. 44.

2. With regard to the settings of individual pericopes, we proposed above (p. 188) that the assumption should be 'inauthentic unless proven otherwise'. This assumption does not apply to the pericopes themselves.

3. The Gospel of John shows that a high degree of internal consistency could be imposed on diverse material, but even so the gospel is not perfectly consistent on some points, which has led some scholars to the view that a later editor inserted passages which contradict the main body of the work on some points, such as eschatology. Compare 14.1–4 with 6.40,54.

4. Mark's designation 'a Greek, a Syrophoenician by nationality' is not entirely clear, but in any case the reader is to understand that the woman was Gentile.

5. Alan Segal, *Rebecca's Children*, 1986, p. 35.

6. See the discussion in ch. 11.

7. References from *Jesus and Judaism*, p. 220, adding Zech. 8.7, which was omitted there.

8. (1) Josephus wrote that John attracted 'the multitude' and that a subsequent defeat of Antipas' army was commonly believed to be punishment for the execution of John (*Antiq.* 18.116–119). We cannot say what role, if any, Jesus played in Josephus' original account, because Christian scribes have rewritten the text. John, however, is certainly portrayed as a preacher who made considerable public impact. (2) John created enough disruption to be executed by Antipas, while Jesus did not. (3) Jesus' question, 'Was the baptism of John from heaven or from men'? (Mark 11.30), which was posed to justify his own authority, implies that John the Baptist was widely regarded as a prophet, as the continuation of the passage makes clear, while Jesus' status was doubted.

9. For these and other examples see A. B. DuToit, 'Hyperbolical Contrasts: A Neglected Aspect of Paul's Style', *A South African Perspective on the New Testament*, ed. J. H. Petzer and P. J. Martin, 1986, pp. 178–186.

21. *The Quest and its Methods: 2*

1. See Sanders, *Jesus and Judaism*, p. 215; 'Jesus and the Kingdom: The Restoration of Israel and the New People of God'; *Jesus, the Gospels, and the Church*, p. 230.

2. Francis Wright Beare, *The Gospel according to Matthew*, 1981, p. 161; cf. p. 443.

3. Raymond F. Collins, 'The Unity of Paul's Paraenesis in I Thess. 4.3–8. 1 Cor. 7.1–7, a Significant Parallel', *New Testament Studies* 29, 1983, pp. 420–429, here p. 422.

4. James D. G. Dunn, *Romans 9–16*, Word Biblical Commentary 38B, 1988, pp. 744ff.

5. Wolfgang Schrage. *The Ethics of the New Testament*, ET 1988, pp. 76f., 87.

6. See Josephus, *Antiquities* 4.212–213. *Mezuzot* and *tefillin*, containing key passages which were bound on the hand or arm, or attached to the doorpost, have been found at Qumran and elsewhere. For details see Sanders, 'The Synoptic Jesus and the Law', section J §2 and notes, in *The Jewish Law from Jesus to the Mishnah*, forthcoming.

7. Josephus, *Against Apion* 2.146, 213, 261; Philo, *Special Laws* 2.63; *Decalogue* 110–111 and often.

8. For passages, see *Paul and Palestinian Judaism*, pp. 168–172 and n. 123.

9. There are further passages on response to persecution in II Macc. 6–7.

10. Fitzmyer, *The Gospel According to Luke I-IX*, p. 638.

11. So Schrage, p. 77.

12. Schrage did not take into account either Philo or Josephus on the points discussed in this section, but even so he found substantial parallels to the gospel passages.

13. Besides the three passages discussed below, compare also Matt. 10.10//Luke 10.7 with I Cor. 9.14 ('the Lord commanded that those who proclaim the gospel should get their living by the gospel'). This shows Paul's knowledge of a saying of Jesus, but it is not a direct quotation.

14. W. D. Davies, *Paul and Rabbinic Judaism*, 4th ed., 1980, pp. 138–41; Goulder, *Midrash and Lection in Matthew*, ch. 8. Goulder argues that Matthew used the letters of Paul.

15. There is a further version in The Didache, ch. 9.

16. Part of the symbolism is biblical: Isa. 27.13 refers to a trumpet and the reassembly of the scattered Israelites, and Zech. 9.14 refers to the Lord's arrow, which 'go[es] forth like lightening', while he sounds the trumpet. The sayings in Matthew and Paul, however, also

have angels (or an angel) and the expectation that some of those then alive will be present at the climatic moment.

22. *Putting the Material Together*

1. Nemesis: the goddess who personifies 'righteous indignation, particularly that of the gods at human presumption' (H. J. Rose in *The Oxford Classical Dictionary*, 2nd ed., p. 726).

2. On Theudas, the Egyptian and others, see Josephus, *War* 2.258–263; *Antiquities* 20.97–98, 167–172. Acts 5.36 refers to Theudas.

3. This paragraph represents a revision of Sanders' view of Paul's expectation (*Jesus and Judaism*, p. 230). It springs from a helpful remark by Benedict Viviano.

4. The Greek is literally 'our dwelling from heaven', but the RSV, NEB and JB all translate 'from heaven' as 'heavenly', implying that one puts on the new dwelling in heaven. This rather fine point of Pauline exegesis is not much discussed. In favour of the view taken here, see Herman Ridderbos, *Paul. An Outline of his Theology*, ET 1975, pp. 533–536: I Thess. 4.14, 'brings with him', means that Christians will be at Christ's side at his appearance. They will neither remain in heaven when they meet the Lord, nor will they return there after his appearance. The kingdom will be on earth.

5. We are indebted for this point to Robert Wilcken.

6. This was argued by Sanders in *Jesus and Judaism*, pp. 237–241; and ch. 9. The synoptic passages on the law have been given short shrift in this chapter. They are all discussed at length in Sanders, *The Jewish Law from Jesus to the Mishnah*, forthcoming.

7. For a forceful but unconvincing argument that Jesus wished to reform Jewish society, especially the temple, and to break down Judaism's barriers against Gentiles, see Marcus Borg, *Conflict, Holiness and Politics in the Teachings of Jesus*, 1984.

8. See the fuller list in *Jesus and Judaism*, p. 214.

9. See Matt. 13.55//Mark 6.3; Acts 12.17; 15.3; 21.18; I Cor. 15.7; Gal. 1.19; 2.9,12; James 1.1; Jude 1; Josephus, *Antiq.* 20.199–202.

Bibliography

Ancient Literature

Aboth de R. Nathan, ed. S. Schechter. Corrected ed., New York 1967 (orig. pub. 1887). ET *The Fathers According to Rabbi Nathan*, trans. Judah Goldin, Yale Judaica Series 10, New Haven 1955.

Apuleius, *The Golden Ass*, ET W. Adlington, rev. S. Gaselee, LCL 1915.

Ascension of Isaiah, in *OTP* II.

I Clement, in *The Apostolic Fathers*, 2 vols., ET Kirsopp Lake, LCL 1912, 1913.

Didache, in *The Apostolic Fathers*, *see* I Clement.

Diogenes Laertius, *Lives of Eminent Philosophers*, 2 vols., ET R. D. Hicks, LCL 1925.

Epictetus, *The Discourses* as reported by Arrian, the Manual, and Fragments, 2 vols, ET W. A. Oldfeather, LCL 1946, 1952.

4 Ezra, = The Fourth Book of Ezra, in *OTP* I.

Eusebius, *The Ecclesiastical History*, 2 vols, ET Kirsopp Lake (vol. 1) and J. E. L. Oulton (vol. 2), LCL 1926, 1932.

I Enoch, in *OTP* I.

Gospel of Thomas, in *The Nag Hammadi Library in English*, ET ed. James M. Robinson, Leiden 1977, or in *The Gnostic Scriptures*, ET ed. Bentley Layton, New York and London 1987.

Ignatius, To the Smyrnaeans, in *the Apostolic Fathers* (see I Clement).

Irenaeus, *Against Heresies*, in *The Ante-Nicene Fathers* I, ET ed. Alexander Roberts and James Donaldson, American ed. A. Cleveland Coxe, orig. publ. Edinburgh 1867, repr. Grand Rapids n.d.

Joseph and Aseneth, in *OTP* II.

Josephus, *Works*, 10 vols. (The Life; Against Apion; The Jewish War; Jewish Antiquities), ET H. StJ. Thackeray, Ralph Marcus, A. Wikren and L. H. Feldman, LCL 1926–1965.

Jubilees, in *OTP* II.

Justin, *Apology* I and *Dialogue with Trypho*, in *The Ante-Nicene Fathers* I (see Irenaeus).

Livy, *History*, ET B. O. Foster, LCL 1919, vol. 1.

Lucian, *Alexander the False Prophet*, ET A. M. Harmon, LCL 1925, vol. 4.

Lucian, *Metamorphoses* or *The Ass*, ET M. D. Macleod, LCL 1967, vol. 8.

IV Maccabees, in *OTP* II.

Mekilta de-Rabbi Ishmael, ed and ET Jacob Z. Lauterbach, Philadelphia 1933–1935.

Numbers Rabbah, in *Midrash Rabbah*, general eds. H. Freedman and Maurice Simon, 10 vols., Soncino ed., London 1939.

Petronius, *Satyricon*, ET M. Heseltine, rev. E. H. Warmington, LCL 1969.

Philo, *Works*, 10 vols (Life of Moses and On Rewards and Punishments), ET F. H. Colson and G. H. Whitaker. LCL 1929–1962.

Philostratus, *Life of Apollonius of Tyana*, 2 vols, ET F. C. Conybeare, LCL 1912.

Plato, *Phaedrus*, ET H. N. Fowler, LCL 1914.

Plutarch, *Works* (*Lives* in 11 vols, ET B. Perrin, LCL 1914–26; *Morals* in 16 vols, ET F. H. Sandbach et al., LCL 1928–69).

Psalms of Solomon, in *OTP* II.

Rabin, Chaim, ed., *The Zadokite Documents*, 2nd ed. Oxford 1958.

Septuagint, LXX, ed. A. Rahlfs, 2 vols, Stuttgart, 1935.

Shabbath, *Babylonian Talmud, Moed* I, ET H. Freedman, Soncino ed. 1938.

Testaments of Levi, Asher and Judah, in Testaments of the Twelve Patriarchs, *OTP* I.

Vermes, Geza, transl., *The Dead Sea Scrolls in English*, 3rd ed. Harmondsworth 1987.

Xenophon, *Memorabilia*, ET E. C. Marchant, LCL 1923.

Modern Authors

Abrams, M. H., *A Glossary of Literary Terms*, 3rd ed. London and New York 1971.

Albertz, Martin, *Die synoptischen Streitgespräche. Ein Beitrag zur Formgeschichte des Urchristentums*, Berlin 1921.

Allen, W. C., *The Gospel According to S. Matthew*, 3rd ed. Edinburgh 1912.

Alsup, J. E., *The Post-resurrection appearance stories of the Gospel Tradition*, London 1976.

Alter, A., and Kermode, F. (eds), *The Literary Guide to the Bible*, London 1987.

Attridge, H. W., 'Josephus and his Works', *Jewish Writings of the Second Temple Period*, ed. M. E. Stone, Assen and Philadelphia 1984, pp. 185–232.

Aune, D. E., The Problem of the genre of the Gospels, in *Gospel Perspectives* II, ed. R. T. France and D. Wenham, Sheffield 1981.

Barr, Allan, *A Diagram of Synoptic Relationships*, Edinburgh 1957.

Barr, D. L. and Wentling, J. L., 'The Conventions of Classical Biography and the Genre of Luke-Acts', in C. H. Talbert (ed.), *Luke-Acts*: New Perspectives from the Society of Biblical Literature Seminar, New York 1984.

Beare, Francis Wright, *The Gospel according to Matthew*, Oxford 1981.

Bellizoni, A. J. with Tyson, J.B. and Walker, W. O. (eds), *The Two-Source Hypothesis. A Critical Appraisal*, Macon 1985.

Bentwich, Norman, *Josephus*, Philadelphia 1914.

Berger, Klaus, *Einführung in die Formgeschichte*, Tübingen 1987.

Berger, Klaus, *Formgeschichte des Neuen Testaments*, Heidelberg 1984.

Best, E., *Mark – the Gospel as Story*, Edinburgh 1983.

Betz, Hans Dieter, *Essays on the Sermon on the Mount*, Philadelphia 1985.

Black, Matthew, 'The Parables as Allegory', *Bulletin of the John Rylands Library* 42, 1960, pp. 273–287.

Bibliography

Boismard, M.-E., *Synopse des quatre évangiles* II, Paris 1972.
— 'The Two Source Theory at an Impasse', *New Testament Studies* 26, 1979, pp. 1–17.
Booth, Wayne, *The Rhetoric of Irony*, Chicago 1974.
Borg, Marcus, *Conflict, Holiness and Politics in the Teachings of Jesus*, New York and Toronto 1984.
Bornkamm, Günther, *Jesus of Nazareth*, ET New York and London 1960 (=3rd German ed. 1959; 1st ed. 1956).
Bornkamm, G., Barth, G. and Held, H.J., *Tradition and Interpretation in Matthew*, ET London and New York 1963 (=2nd German ed. 1961; 1st ed. 1960).
Bultmann, Rudolf, *The History of the Synoptic Tradition*, rev. ET Oxford 1968 (=2nd German ed. 1931; 1st ed. 1921).
— *Jesus and the Word*, ET New York 1934 (=*Jesus*, 1926).
Bultmann, Rudolf and Kundsin, Karl, *Form Criticism. Two Essays on New Testament Research*, New York 1934.
Burgess, Anthony, *The Kingdom of the Wicked*, London 1985.
Butler, B. C., *The Originality of St Matthew*, Cambridge 1951.
Cadbury, H. J., *The Making of Luke-Acts*, London 1958.
Cartlidge, David R. and Dungan, David L., *Documents for the Study of the Gospels*, Cleveland, Ohio 1980.
Collins, Raymond F., 'The Unity of Paul's Paraenesis in 1 Thess. 4.3–8. 1 Cor. 7.1–7, a Significant Parallel', *New Testament Studies* 29, 1983, pp. 420–429, here p. 422.
Conzelmann, Hans, *The Theology of St. Luke*, ET London and New York 1960 (from 2nd German ed. 1957).
Culpepper, R. A., *Anatomy of the Fourth Gospel*, Philadelphia 1983.
Davies, Margaret, 'The Genre of the First Gospel', *Language, Meaning and God*, ed. Brian Davies, London 1987, pp. 162–175.
Davies, W. D., *Paul and Rabbinic Judaism*, 4th ed., London and Philadelphia 1980.
Detweiler, R. (ed.), *Derrida and Biblical Studies*, Missoula 1982.
Dibelius, Martin, *From Tradition to Gospel*, ET New York n.d., Cambridge 1971 (from 2nd German ed., 1933; 1st ed. 1919).
Dodd, C. H., *The Parables of the Kingdom*, rev. ed. London 1961 (1st ed. 1935).
Donahue, J. R., *Are you the Christ?, The Trial Narrative in the Gospel of Mark*, SBL DS 10, Missoula 1973.
Downing, F. Gerald, 'Redaction Criticism: Josephus' Antiquities and the Synoptic Problem I, II, *Journal for the Study of the New Testament* 8, 1980, pp. 46–65; 9, 1980, pp. 29–48.
— 'Compositional Conventions and the Synoptic Problem', *Journal of Biblical Literature* 107, 1988, pp. 69–85.
— 'Contemporary analogies to the gospels and Acts: "Genres" or "Motifs"?', in C. M. Tuckett (ed.), *Synoptic Studies*, pp. 51–65.
Drury, John, *The Parables in the Gospels*, London 1985.
Dungan, David, 'Mark — The Abridgement of Matthew and Luke', *Jesus and Man's Hope* I, 1970, pp. 51–97.

Dunn, James D. G., *Romans 9–16*, Word Biblical Commentary 38B Dallas 1988.

DuToit, A. B., 'Hyperbolical Contrasts: A Neglected Aspect of Paul's Style', *A South African Perspective on the New Testament. Essays by South African New Testament Scholars presented to Bruce Manning Metzger during his Visit to South Africa in 1985*, ed. J. H. Petzer and P. J. Martin, Leiden 1986, pp. 178–186.

Eagleton, Terry, *Literary Theory, an Introduction*, Oxford 1983.

Farmer, W. R., 'Notes on a Literary and Form-Critical Analysis of Some of the Synoptic Material Peculiar to Luke', *New Testament Studies* 8, 1962, pp. 301–316, with bibliography on p. 307.

— *The Synoptic Problem. A critical review of the problem of the Literary relationships between Matthew, Mark and Luke*, New York 1964.

— (ed.), *New Synoptic Studies*, Macon 1983.

Farrer, Austin, 'On Dispensing with Q', *Studies in the Gospels*, ed. D. E. Nineham, Oxford 1955, pp. 55–88.

Fitzmyer, Joseph A., 'The Priority of Mark and the "Q" Source in Luke', *Jesus and Man's Hope*, vol. 1, Pittsburg 1970, pp. 131–170.

— *The Gospel according to Luke I–IX*, Anchor Bible 28, New York 1981.

Fowler, Robert M., *Loaves and Fishes, the function of the feeding stories in the Gospel of Mark*, SBL DS 54, Missoula 1981.

Franklin, Eric, *Christ the Lord, a study in the Purpose and Theology of Luke-Acts*, London 1975.

Frye, Northrop, *The Great Code*, London 1981.

Funk, Robert, *New Gospel Parallels* I, Philadelphia 1985.

Genette, G., *Narrative Discourse*, ET Oxford, 1980 (= *Discours de récit* in *Figures III*, 1972).

— *Narrative Discourse Revisited*, ET Ithaca 1989.

Gerhardsson, Birger, *The Gospel Tradition*, Lund 1986.

— *Memory and Manuscript. Oral Tradition and Written Transmission in Rabbinic Judaism and Early Christianity*, Uppsala, Lund and Copenhagen 1961; repr. 1964.

— *Tradition and Transmission in Early Christianity*, Lund 1964.

— *The Mighty Acts of Jesus According to Matthew*, Lund 1979.

— *The Origins of the Gospel Tradition*, ET London and Philadelphia 1979 (=1st Swedish ed. 1977).

— 'Der Weg der Evangelientradition', *Das Evangelium und die Evangelien*, ed. Peter Stuhlmacher, Tübingen 1983.

Gittings, Robert, *Young Thomas Hardy*, revised ed. Harmondsworth 1978.

Goulder, Michael, *Midrash and Lection in Matthew*, London 1974.

Grant, F. C., *The Gospels. Their Origin and their Growth*, London 1957.

Greeven, Heinrich, 'The Gospel Synopsis from 1776 to the present day', *J. J. Griesbach: Synoptic and Text-Critical Studies 1776-1976*, ed. B. Orchard and T. R. W. Longstaff, SNTSMS 34, Cambridge 1978, pp. 22–49.

Gundry, R. H., *The Use of the Old Testament in Matthew's Gospel*, Leiden 1967.

Güttgemanns, Erhardt, *Candid Questions Concerning Gospel Form Criticism. A Methodological Sketch of the Fundamental Problematics of Form and Redaction Criticism*, Pittsburgh 1979(=2nd German ed. 1971, with author's additions to 1978).

Haenchen, E., *The Acts of the Apostles*, ET Oxford 1971 (=14th German edition, 1965).

Harnack, Adolf, *The Sayings of Jesus. The Second Source of St. Matthew and St. Luke*, ET London 1908 (from German 1907).

Henderson, Ian, '*Sententiae Jesu*': *Gnomic Sayings in the Tradition of Jesus*, Oxford DPhil., 1988.

Hengel, Martin, 'Luke the Historian and the Geography of Palestine in the Acts of the Apostles', *Between Jesus and Paul*, ET London and Philadelphia 1983.

— *The Charismatic Leader and his Followers*, ET Edinburgh 1981 (*Nachfolge und Charisma* 1968).

— *Studies in the Gospel of Mark*, London and Philadelphia 1985.

Hock, Ronald F. and O'Neil, Edward N., *The Chreia in Ancient Rhetoric*, vol. 1, *The Progymnasmata*. Texts and Translations 27, Graeco-Roman Religion Series 9, Atlanta 1986.

Holtzmann, Heinrich Julius, *Die synoptischen Evangelien. Ihr Ursprung und geschichtlicher Charakter*, Leipzig 1863.

Hooker, M. D., *The Message of Mark*, London 1983.

— *Continuity and Discontinuity*, London 1986.

Horsley, Richard, *Jesus and the Spiral of Violence*, San Francisco 1987.

Hull, John M., *Hellenistic Magic and the Synoptic Tradition*, SBT Second Series 28, London 1974.

Hultgren, Arland J., *Jesus and His Adversaries. The Form and Function of the Conflict Stories in the Synoptic Tradition*, Minneapolis 1979.

Interpreter's Dictionary of the Bible, New York and Nashville 1962–76.

Iser, Wolfgang, *The Implied Reader*, ET Baltimore and London 1974 (=*Der Implizite Leser*, Munich 1972).

— *The Act of Reading*, A Theory of Aesthetic Response, ET Baltimore and London 1978 (=*Der Akt des Lesens*, Munich 1976).

Jeremias, Joachim, *The Parables of Jesus*, Rev. ET London 1963 (from 6th German ed. 1962; 1st German ed. 1947).

Johnson Jr, A. M. (ed.), *The New Testament and Structuralism*, Pittsburgh Theological Monograph Series II, Pittsburgh 1976.

Jülicher, Adolf, *Die Gleichnisreden Jesu*, 2 vols, 2nd ed. Tübingen 1910.

Kee, H. C., *Miracles in the Early Christian World*, Yale 1983

Kelber, W. H., *Mark's Story of Jesus*, Philadelphia 1979

Kennedy, G. A., *New Testament Interpretation through Rhetorical Criticism*, North Carolina 1984.

Kenyon, F. G., *Books and Readers in Ancient Greece and Rome*, Oxford 1932.

Kiilunen, Jarmo, *Die Vollmacht im Widerstreit. Untersuchungen zum Werdegang von Mk 2, 1–3, 6*, Annales Academiae Scientiarum Fennicae, Dissertationes

Humanarum Litterarum 40, Helsinki 1985.

Kilpatrick, G. D., *The Origins of the Gospel According to St. Matthew*, Oxford 1946.

— *The Eucharist in Bible and Liturgy*, Cambridge 1983.

Kingsbury, J. D., *The Parables of Jesus in Matthew 13*, London 1969.

Kloppenborg, John S., *The Formation of Q*, Philadelphia 1987.

Knox, John, *Marcion and the New Testament*, Chicago 1942.

— 'Marcion's Gospel and the Synoptic Problem' *Jesus, the Gospels, and the Church*, ed. E. P. Sanders, Macon 1987, pp. 25–31.

Knox, Wilfred L., *The Sources of the Synoptic Gospels*, vol. 1, *St Mark*, Oxford 1953.

Koch, Klaus, *The Growth of the Biblical Tradition. The Form Critical Method*, ET New York 1969 (=*Was ist Formgeschichte?* 1964).

Lindsey, Robert Lisle, 'Introduction' to *A Hebrew Translation of the Gospel of Mark. Greek-Hebrew Diglot with English Introduction*, Jerusalem n.d. (late1960s).

Longstaff, Thomas R. W., *Evidence of Conflation in Mark? A Study in the Synoptic Problem*, SBLDS 28, Missoula 1977.

McArthur, H. K., 'The Origin of the "Q" Symbol', *Expository Times* 87, 1976–77, pp. 119f.

MacMullen, Ramsay, *Roman Government's Response to Crisis A.D.235–337*, New Haven 1976.

Marxsen, Willi, *Mark the Evangelist*, ET Nashville 1969 (originally published in German in 1956, 2nd German ed. 1959).

Metzger, Bruce M., *The Text of the New Testament,* Oxford 1964.

Moffat, James, *Introduction to the New Testament*, 3rd. ed. Edinburgh 1918.

Moulton, J. H. and Milligan, G., *The Vocabulary of the Greek Testament*, London 1930.

Neirynck, Frans, *Duality in Mark*, Leuven 1972.

— with Hansen, T. and Van Segbroeck, F., *The Minor Agreements of Matthew and Luke against Mark with a Cumulative List*, Leuven 1974.

— 'The Symbol Q (= Quelle)' *Ephemerides Theologicae Lovanienses* 54, 1978, pp. 119–125.

— 'Once More: the Symbol Q', ibid., 55, 1979, pp. 382–383. This and the previous article are reprinted in Neirynck, *Evangelica. Gospel Studies – Études d'évangile. Collected Essays*, ed. F. Van Segbroeck. Bibliotheca Ephemeridum Theologicarum Lovaniensium 60, Leuven 1982, pp. 683–690.

Neusner, Jacob, *From Politics to Piety*, New Jersey 1973.

Newport, Kenneth, *The Sources and 'Sitz im Leben' of Matthew 23*, Oxford DPhil., 1988.

Nickelsburg, G. W. E., 'The genre and function of the Markan Passion narrative', *Harvard Theological Review* 73, 1980, pp. 153–184.

Norris, Christopher, *Deconstruction, Theory and Practice*, London and New York 1982.

Ogden, C. K. and Richards, I. A., *The Meaning of Meaning*, London 1930.

Bibliography

Pamment, M., Review of Talbert, *What is a Gospel?* in *New Blackfriars*, April 1980, pp. 197–8.

Patte, D. (ed.), *Semiology and Parables*, Pittsburgh Theological Monograph Series 9, Pittsburgh 1976.

Perrin, N., *What is Redaction Criticism?*, Philadelphia and London 1970.

Ridderbos, Herman, *Paul. An Outline of his Theology*, ET Grand Rapids 1975, London 1976 (= *Paulus: Ontwerp van zijn theologie*, 1966).

Rist, John M., *On the Independence of Matthew and Mark*, SNTSMS 32, Cambridge 1978.

Rivkin, Ellis, *What Crucified Jesus?*, Nashville 1984 and London 1986.

Robbins, V. K., *Jesus the Teacher. A socio-rhetorical interpretation of Mark*, Philadelphia 1984.

Robinson, James M., *The New Quest for the Historical Jesus and other essays*, Philadelphia 1983 (*New Quest* first pub. 1959).

Robinson, John A. T., *Redating the New Testament*, London 1976.

Rohde, Joachim, *Rediscovering the Teaching of the Evangelists*, ET London 1968 (from German 1966, with revisions to 1968).

Rose, H. J., 'Nemesis', *The Oxford Classical Dictionary*, 2nd ed., 1970, pp. 72ff.

Sanders, E. P., *Paul and Palestinian Judaism*, London and Philadelphia 1977.

— *Jesus and Judaism*, rev. ed. London 1987 and Philadelphia 1989.

— *The Tendencies of the Synoptic Tradition*, SNTSMS 9, Cambridge, 1969.

Ferdinand de Saussure, *Course in General Linguistics*, ET London 1978.

Schmidt, Karl Ludwig, *Der Rahmen der Geschichte Jesu. Literarkritische Untersuchungen zur ältesten Jesus überlieferung*, Berlin 1919.

Schrage, Wolfgang, *The Ethics of the New Testament*, ET Philadelphia 1988 (from German 1982).

Schweitzer, Albert, *The Quest of the Historical Jesus*, ET London 1910 (from German 1906).

Segal, Alan, *Rebecca's Children*, Cambridge Mass. 1986.

Semeia, volumes from 1974–1978.

Shuler, Philip, *A Genre for the Gospels. The Bibliographical Character of Matthew*, Philadelphia 1982.

Smith, Morton, *Jesus the Magician*, New York and London 1978.

— 'Palestinian Judaism in the First Century', *Israel, Its Role in Civilization*, ed. Moshe Davis, New York 1956, pp. 67–81; repr. in H. A. Fischel, (ed.), *Essays in Greco–Roman and Related Talmudic Literature*, New York 1977, pp. 183–197.

Stanton, G. (ed.), *The Interpretation of Matthew*, Issues in Religion and Theology 3, London and Philadelphia 1983.

Stein, Robert H., *The Synoptic Problem. An Introduction*, Grand Rapids 1987.

Stendahl, K., *The School of Matthew*, Gleerup 1968.

Sternberg, Meir, *The Poetics of Biblical Narrative*. Ideological Literature and the Drama of Reading, Indiana 1985.

Stoldt, Hans-Herbert, *History and Criticism of the Marcan Hypothesis*, ET Macon 1980 (from German 1977).

Streeter, B. H., *The Four Gospels. A Study of Origins*, rev. ed. London 1930 (1st ed. 1924).

— 'St. Mark's Knowledge and Use of Q', *Oxford Studies in the Synoptic Problem*, ed. W. Sanday, Oxford 1911, pp. 165–183.

— 'On the Original Order of Q', ibid., pp. 141–164.

Styler, G. M., 'The Priority of Mark', in C. F. D Moule, *The Birth of the New Testament*, 3rd ed. London 1981, pp. 285–316.

Suhl, A., *Die Funktion der alttestamentlichen Zitate und Anspielungen im Markusevangelium*, Gütersloh 1965.

Swete, H. B., *The Gospel According to St Mark*, London 1905.

Talbert, C. H., *Literary Patterns, Theological Themes and the Genre of Luke–Acts*, Missoula 1974.

— *What is a Gospel?*, London 1978.

Taylor, Vincent, *The Formation of the Gospel Tradition*, London 1957 (1st edition 1933).

— *The Gospel According to St Mark*, London 1959.

Telford, W. (ed.), *The Interpretation of Mark*, Issues in Religion and Theology 7. London and Philadelphia 1985.

Theissen, Gerd, *The Shadow of the Galilean*, London and Philadelphia 1987 (= *Der Schatten des Galiläers*, 1986).

Tompkins, J. P. (ed.), *Reader-Response Criticism*, Baltimore and London 1980.

Tuckett, Christopher, 'Arguments from order: Definition and Evaluation', in Tuckett, ed., *Synoptic Studies*, pp. 197–219.

— (ed.,), *Synoptic Studies. The Ampleforth Conferences of 1982 and 1983*. JSNTSS 7, Sheffield 1984.

— (ed.), *The Messianic Secret*, Issues in Religion and Theology I, London and Philadelphia 1983.

— *The Revival of the Griesbach Hypothesis*. SNTSMS 44, Cambridge 1983.

Tyrrell, George, *Christianity at the Cross-Roads*, London 1909.

Vermes, G., *Jesus the Jew*, London 1973; 2nd edition London and Philadelphia 1983.

Vuillod, G., 'Exercises on some short stories', ET in *The New Testament and Structuralism*, ed. A. M. Johnson, Pittsburgh Theological Monographs 11, Pickwick Press, Pittsburgh 1976, pp. 47–72.

Walker, W. O. (ed.), *The Relationships among the Gospels. An Interdisciplinary Dialogue*, San Antonio 1978.

Wendling, Emil, *Ur-Markus. Versuch einer Wiederherstellung der ältesten Mitteilungen über das Leben Jesu*, Tübingen 1905.

Wenham, David, *The Rediscovery of Jesus' Eschatological Discourse*. Gospel Perspectives 4, Sheffield 1984.

Wrede, William, *The Messianic Secret*, Cambridge and London 1971 (originally published in German in 1901).

Yadin, Yigael, *Bar Kokhba. The rediscovery of the legendary hero of the Second Jewish Revolt against Rome*, New York 1971.

Index of References

OLD TESTAMENT

NEW TESTAMENT